COMPETITION LAW YEARBOOK 2002

COMPETITION LAW YEARBOOK 2002

Edited by

MICHAEL HUTCHINGS

and

MADS ANDENAS

THE BRITISH INSTITUTE OF INTERNATIONAL AND COMPARATIVE LAW

Published and Distributed by
The British Institute of International and Comparative Law
Charles Clore House, 17 Russell Square, London WC1B 5JP

British Library Cataloguing in Publication Data
A Catalogue record of this book is available from the British Library

ISBN 0-903067-92-7

Typeset by Cambrian Typesetters
Frimley, Surrey
Printed in Great Britain by Biddles Ltd
Guildford and King's Lynn

CONTENTS

CHAPTER ONE

Introduction to the Yearbook

Mads Andenas and Michael Hutchings

The International Competition Law Yearbook brings together many of the papers presented at the major competition law conferences and workshops at the British Institute of International and Comparative Law in 2001/2, together with transcripts of some of the discussions.

At a formal level this is a compendium without any pretension. Contributions are presented as they were at the day or as they appear in the transcripts. At the same time the papers include important statements of policy by competition regulators such as Commissioner Monti, Bill Kolasky and Margaret Bloom, as well as in-depth analysis of current issues by European and north-American academics and practitioners.

The subjects covered include highly topical issues in the fields of mergers, IPR, e-commerce and banking, as well as public policy analysis of procedural and enforcement questions. The choice of papers reflects the Institute's role as a focus for debate in the field of international law, and illustrates the Institute's growing involvement in the development of global antitrust policy. Francis Jacobs, Advocate General of the Court of Justice and chair of the Institute's Advisory Board on European Law, and Michael Hutchings, chair of the Institute's Executive Committee, have been the main initiators of the programme.

There is a need for a centre for the discussion of European competition law and policy in London to complement what is going on elsewhere. There is also a need to create a centre for the transatlantic dialogue in trade and competition law. The Institute has attempted to provide this centre or forum. Our hope is that this *Yearbook* displays some of the ways in which the Institute has fulfilled this need.

In parallel the British Institute has developed its programme in the field of international trade law. WTO law is an interesting field for comparison with EU law. The increasing need for transatlantic dialogue is already mentioned. In 2003 the British Institute will continue its programme of competition and WTO law lectures, conferences and workshops (the programme can be found at www.biicl.org).

The Institute has also established a new centre for European competition and antitrust policy and law—the Competition Law Forum (details at www.competitionlawforum.org). It provides a forum in which the practical application of competition policy will be considered by lawyers, economists, senior business managers, trade unionists, public servants, public affairs professionals, consumer bodies and other specialist practitioners. The Forum identifies areas requiring debate and development, and will contribute to policy initiatives. The Forum produces cutting-edge applied research, analysis and recommendations on the content, methodologies and application of competition policy at all levels of governance—national, European and global. The Competition Law Forum has its secretariat at the British Institute. Its mission is:

To record, analyse and improve the conduct of competition policy practice by:

- establishing a collective voice for those practitioners who recognise the value of constructive dialogue with governments, policy makers and regulators on the conduct of competition policy at all levels—national, European and global;
- providing a wide-ranging series of programmes and courses targeted at practitioners, civil servants and senior managers;
- creating tailor-made courses for both public and private sector organisations which seek to improve their ability to address competition and antitrust matters;
- carrying out research on issues of pressing importance to competition specialists and publishing papers and the results of research work.

The Competition Law Forum consists of persons and organisations with a strategic interest in contributing to the pursuit of the study, development and application of competition policy. Forum members include judges, academics, economists, in-house counsel, public affairs advisers and lawyers in private practice. Regulators and civil servants are, from time to time, invited to participate in Forum meetings. CLF members are leaders in their field and may come from firms, chambers, companies, government departments, regulatory bodies, law faculties, or other individual specialists. Members have a direct influence on the agenda of the Forum and are invited to recommend topics for debate in the group. Members have the opportunity to participate in an independently run Forum that aims to influence competition law policy, which provides an arena for ongoing and constructive debate with regulators and other decision-makers. They can also suggest research or other work to be carried out and have access to research carried out by the Forum Director and other staff. They meet quarterly for the plenary Forum meetings.

We very much hope to see you as a participant at the different competition law activities at the British Institute!

CHAPTER TWO

Introduction to the Second Annual Conference on International and Comparative Competition Law

Mads Andenas*

I would very much like to welcome you to the Second Annual Conference on International and Comparative Competition Law here at the British Institute. We held the first conference last year, and it was a great success. The programme, and your participation, makes this year's conference look an even greater success.

The leading forum for the discussion of European competition law has for many years been the annual conference at Fordham University School of Law. An annual conference at the European University Institute has become the second forum. Today, opening our second annual conference on International and Comparative Competition Law here at the British Institute, we have established a third and complimentary forum for European, international and comparative competition law, and also for the transatlantic dialogue that needs to be developed. The British Institute's two first annual conferences on WTO dispute settlement have located another important international event in London, in a related field. The next challenge is to build research programmes to support these policy discussions and dialogues. We are developing an infrastructure for future research programmes and a number of research projects are well under way. The Competition Law Forum is a new initiative where we have got the support from leading regulators, corporates, law firms, barristers and academics. It will become a forum for policy discussion and for research.

Research institutions for European, International and Comparative law exist in the US and the larger European countries. They are generally better funded than the British Institute. They offer their countries an advantage over the United Kingdom in many different contexts. The development of competition, company and commercial law in Europe is one such context. The discussion about a European constitution is another. International competition law, international trade law, and the

* The Director, British Institute of International and Comparative Law.

development of international organisations are other contexts where the infrastructure for policy discussion and research could strengthen the position of the United Kingdom. There is another problem common to all countries. The well-established legal approaches, limited by narrow definition of disciplines and by national traditions, fall short of the present needs. In comparative law the encyclopaedic collection and organisation of materials is still useful but not sufficient. The traditional teaching and scholarship in public international law, and indeed in the still relatively young disciplines of European law, are equally inadequate. An additional problem here is the focus on one's own national approaches (to public international law and to EU law), which while practically important, needs to be complemented by a broader perspective. Fundamental assumptions about the nation state based on nineteenth century thinking still rule. There is a need for an international and European institutional basis for research and policy discussion. Some of this can be done through cooperation and networks involving existing institutions. The British Institute has a role to play here, and it is in the process of increasing its involvement in this form of cooperation where it has long and important traditions. It is also possible to make a greater and even more distinct contribution if additional funding is obtained to strengthen the research staff and institutional support at the Institute. The international, transatlantic, Commonwealth, and European dialogues in the different areas of law require a forum for policy discussion but also support by research.

Back to us here and today. We have a very hectic week at the British Institute. On Monday we had a seminar on the two new decisions from the European courts—the Court of First Instance judgment and the opinion by General Jacobs—expanding the standing concepts in European community law.

On Tuesday we held a seminar on ITLOS, the International Tribunal of the Law of the Sea, which now has been in function for nearly 6 years, and yesterday we held the large conference on the World Trade Organisation and its dispute resolution system. We had all the members of the Appellate Body who had just retired, the first batch of members of the Appellate Body, and in spite of being about 100 people in this room, we had a remarkably free and interesting exchange of views and of experiences and prospects for development of the dispute resolution system. There's another WTO seminar this afternoon, where we look particularly at the developing countries' perspective in our Library at the British Institute. Also this afternoon and for all of tomorrow, the Society for European Contract Law meets and will discuss recent proposals from the Commission in developing European contract law.

It is not like this every week at the British Institute. This conference is the jewel in the crown if you like, and it is the initiative of Michael Hutchings, who is the Chairman of the Executive Committee of the British Institute, and of Francis Jacob who also chaired the first conference last year, and we are of course enormously grateful to them. We have this year a long list of sponsors, which we hope you have acknowledged, on all the publicity; and in the packs you have received with the different materials; the publishers, who are exhibiting here today, have also been extremely helpful with publicising the event, and I therefore just have to mention that they have exhibits, and that they provide us with a lot of free material of different kinds. You will see that all publications of Sweet & Maxwell, for instance, are free there in the corner—do pick it up! And other publishers will have their periodicals and will also sell their books, most of them at the discounted rate, as we do at the British Institute.

The last thing I would like to mention is of course that the British Institute is a membership organisation—we undertake research and we organise events like this, and we have a rather expanding and active programme. We depend on our members, and I would like to encourage each one of you to join as individual members. In return for membership you get the *ICLQ*, four issues of *National Comparative Law Quarterly* per year. Membership is very inexpensive—we have a desk with two people sitting outside the hall there, and you can sign up and have a word with them. You'd be surprised what you get in return for that conference. Just signing up for this conference at the Members' rate would have paid for more than your full year's membership subscription. There is also the possibility for your company or institution to join as an institutional members, and I hope you do not find that I have oversold this, because it is extremely important for us as an institute, which is a membership organisation of course, to have a large and active membership And there is no better group of people to encourage to join than those of you who have come here for today's discussion. Francis Jacobs is chairing the conference, and of course needs no introduction—Francis.

ADVOCATE GENERAL FRANCIS JACOBS

Thank you, Mads. Well it's my pleasure to open this second annual conference on international and comparative competition law; and in doing so, I'd just like to endorse what the Director of the Institute has just said. This conference is simply one of a number of outstanding events organised by the Institute throughout the year; it has a totally extraordinary programme of conferences, meetings, discussion groups, seminars, research activities and publications, and I would very strongly urge you all, if you are not already members (and I can hardly understand how you couldn't all be members), but if by any chance some of you are not yet members, I would very strongly urge you to join it, which you can do, I understand, just outside the doors. Don't do it just this moment, but do when the first opportunity arrives—make sure that you become members of the Institute.

This conference is the second annual conference—we had a most successful conference a year ago at this time. It is designed to cover international and comparative competition law, reflecting the aims of the British Institute; I think it really is unique in its kind. But as Mads has said, I had the very great pleasure of taking part yesterday in the second annual conference on World Trade law; some of you were also present for that conference, and you will have found it, I'm sure, as I did, and I remained to hear every word spoken yesterday, a quite extraordinary conference. It was masterminded by Professor John Jackson, who is the leading figure in the field; it was an outstanding programme with speakers such as one could not really have imagined a better list. And we've really got the same today and tomorrow; we've got a remarkable programme put together on the really live issues in competition law today.

So it really is, I think, a great tribute to the Institute that they've put together this programme, and it's great pleasure for me to open the conference. It only remains to me to welcome our first speaker, who's going to deliver the keynote address, and that is Mr Kirti Mehta, Director for Competition Policy and Co-ordination, and for International Affairs and relations with Other Institutions, and Competition Director-General of the European Commission. I take pleasure in calling upon him. (Here follows applause).

CHAPTER THREE

Towards Global Competition Law—Papers and Discussion from the First and Second Annual Competition Law Conferences

1. Towards Global Competition Law

Mario Monti*

I think it is a particular privilege to be a speaker on the first occasion when the British Institute of International and Comparative Law, which has such a long-standing reputation in the field of international and comparative law, is launching a new range of activities in the field of European Community law.

This year's topic 'Towards Global Competition Law' I think has been very well chosen; the emergence and consolidation of a global economy raise important questions, as we all know, for the design and application of an effective competition policy. Indeed markets, the core object of competition rules, are in a process of fundamental transformation concerning their functioning and their scope. Of course, globalisation itself is not a new phenomenon; it has been a constant theme for many decades. However, its scope and impact has been markedly changed through a combination of worldwide economic liberalisation, a progressive reduction in trade barriers, and a very dramatic increase in the volume of goods and services being traded across borders. From an anti-trust viewpoint, it has also become clear that an increasingly common response to greater global competition is for firms to enter alliances or joint ventures. Mergers that cross borders and jurisdictions have become almost commonplace. They have highlighted the importance of seeking to ensure a maximum of convergence and co-ordination between the growing number of competition enforcement systems. The competition analysis is further complicated by the fact that one of the main drivers of globalisation is the rapid development of high-tech markets. The cost of global communications has fallen spectacularly; the convergence of the telecommunications software and media sectors promises, and has started to deliver, one should say, the most fundamental economic transformation since the Industrial Revolution.

From a competition perspective, the changes will be largely positive; the new economy will in many instances create new markets, or will increase the efficiency with which resources are used in existing markets. I think the new economy is a fundamental, hugely helpful potential ally of competition. This however does not mean that the competition rules have lost their relevance in the EU economy. The Internet is a wonderfully enabling

* European Commissioner for Competition. Keynote speech opening the proceedings of the First Annual Conference on International and Comparative Conmpetiton Law, BIICL, May 2001.

technology, but it's not immune from competition problems. The key challenge is to keep markets contestable, while allowing firms to innovate and react quickly to the changing market place. This is not a simple matter for a competition authority; case evaluation can be difficult in dynamic markets where the past is often a poor indicator of likely future developments. These and other problems mean that all competition authorities, including of course the European Commission, will have to reassess the effectiveness of some of the tools they have traditionally used when analysing market power. Thus, globalisation today confronts competition authorities with a wider range of situations than in the past; all the way from agreements between small and medium-sized enterprises operating in local markets up to worldwide cartels or mergers of truly multinational companies. In the competition field, therefore, we need to adapt our institutional architecture in order to address all these situations in an efficient manner.

The focus of my remarks this morning will be how EU competition policy is trying to meet these challenges. In short, Mr Chairman, we are following a two-pronged strategy, combining the reform of our internal rules and increased international co-operation. Both elements are aimed at increasing the efficiency and effectiveness of EC anti-trust enforcement, something that was put in place in terms of original architecture when the overall landscape was entirely different. Internationally, there was very little need for coordination, convergence or exchange of views among competition authorities, and within the European Union, when the treaty was signed, when the venerable Regulation 17 was introduced in 1962, the landscape was one of a nice desert in terms of competition, culture and institutions. There were these fundamental newborn articles in the treaty; there was in one of the then six member states of the European Union a well-established, albeit young, institution, the Bundeskartellamt, there was nothing else. Now, the landscape has of course considerably changed; it would be a guilty form of inertia, in my view, to be too emotionally and practically linked to the heritage from the past, which was built on this entirely different landscape of the past.

Let me start with a brief description of the two-pronged strategy we are trying to pursue, with changes to our internal policies. Well, precisely the present EC anti-trust enforcement system was, as you all know, basically created in 1962. Regulation 17 is based on the direct applicability of the prohibition rules of Article 81 and 82; in other words, these prohibitions can be applied by the Commission as well as by national competition authorities and courts. However, the Commission was given the exclusive power to grant exemptions to prohibition of Article 81, to those restrictive agreements that proved beneficial for the economy and the consumer. A system of prior notification of those agreements seeking exemption was also put in place. I think that this highly centralised implementation system was a good choice for that historical phase; today, I think it is a totally inappropriate model.

Markets have been already integrated to a very large extent; national competition laws have been enacted by all member states, reflecting in most cases the content of EC rules, and national competition authorities have been set up in all member states to enforce them. And a competition culture, which is probably the most important aspect of all, is now solidly established across the Union. In this new context, the centralised system of Regulation 17 no longer provides us with the means for efficient enforcement.

First, the notification regime no longer constitutes an effective tool for the protection of competition; it only rarely reveals cases that pose a real threat to competition, but keeps the Commission busy dealing with minor issues. Second, and even more important, the Commission's monopoly on the application of Article 81 Paragraph 3 is a significant obstacle to the effective application of the rules by national competition authorities and courts. In other words, our governance tools in this area are outdated and need to be re-designed. That's why the Commission has launched a reform, precisely with this purpose, the nutshell of which you will know is that the reform is intended to provide, to promote decentralised action by national competition authorities in order to allow them to deal with those cases for which they are better placed than the Commission. At the same time, it will make the Commission more effective in dealing with its own responsibilities, particularly by the strengthening of its investigative powers. All this should be achieved, however, without compromising the common interest; and therefore the reform will also aim at ensuring coherent action by all the enforcers in the new system. In this spirit, last September the Commission adopted a draft regulation to amend Regulation 17, and this proposal, Article 81 (3), is to become directly applicable by all enforcers in the Community. This means that in addition to the Commission, national competition authorities and national courts will be able to apply Articles 81 and 82 in their entirety; their enforcement potential will thus be unblocked, and the application of the competition rules thereby set on a decentralised basis. National courts, in particular, will also be able to apply fully Articles 81 and 82, and of course the European Court of Justice, as until now, will continue to play a central role in assisting the courts, and can I add, all of us, in doing our respective work, by providing us all with the authentic interpretation of community law. All the enforcers in the new system will work together in a network; this will not only allow a flexible allocation of cases among them, but also a much stronger exchange of information and mutual assistance than at present. Under the Commission's reform proposal, finally, all competition situations that have an impact on the wider single market should be dealt with under one set of common rules. That is why the Commission has proposed exclusive application of the EC competition rules to cases that affect trade between member states. National competition laws should be reserved for situations that do not affect trade between member states; in other terms, do not have an impact on the single market.

The Commission's reform proposal is currently being examined by the Council, the European Parliament is being consulted and is preparing a resolution for June this year. Many questions need to be examined in detail with these institutions; generally speaking, the legislative process is well under way, and I must say I was pretty encouraged that by the *Tour de Table* that took place for the first time at ministerial level at the Industry Council last Monday; and we expect that we will be able to implement the new regulation in 2003. So, not to be or look over-optimistic; a lot of the work remains to be done on several important aspects. It would be surprising if it were otherwise, since this is a major, fundamental structural reform; but I think the rate of progress in the discussion and in the convergence of views relative to the publication of the white paper and relative to last September, when the draft regulation was adopted by the Commission, is pretty encouraging. And a reasonable extrapolation of that trend allows us to be fairly optimistic both as to the conclusion of the process and to the time of that conclusion, even though we've always said for such a fundamental reform, quality and shared consensus should be at a price relative to speed at all costs.

International cooperation, Mr President, is the other aspect that I see more and more as in fact institutionally entirely different, but logically inextricably linked with this cooperative subsidiarity, that you are trying to put in place within the European Union. A parallel to that is a much wider and deeper international cooperation; that is, the external policy, the external competition policy of the European Union, let me underline, involving the Commission and all the national competition authorities. More and more cases are likely to fall within the jurisdiction of several competition authorities beyond Europe, with the risk of contradicting decision; increasing international competition is becoming by the day a more and more evident need. One of our main instruments to approach that is bilateral cooperation; bilateral cooperation particularly with the USA anti-trust authorities. Over the past decade, we have satisfied this need by concluding two competition law enforcement cooperation agreements within the United States; a basic cooperation agreement in 1991, and a more developed in 1998, including positive comity obligations. Both agreements, and everybody recognises this from the inside and the outside, have been marked a success; bilateral EU and US cooperation has worked very effectively, particularly so in merger cases, substantially reducing the risk of divergent or incoherent rulings.

Today, it has become normal for Commission staff to be in close and daily contact with their counterparts at the Department of Justice and the Federal Trade Commission. The close daily contact between case teams is conducive to mutual confidence building, accrued knowledge of the substantive and procedural rules in each other's jurisdictions, substantial convergence in competition analysis, and the spread of best practices in both substantive and procedural methods. However, in spite of these undeniable benefits, and needless to say, we continue to attach whatever the scenario concerning different administrations in the United States, well, it's less easy to speak in that respect of different administrations in the European Union; at any rate, whatever the evolution of the ultimate political determinants, we are more and more, not less and less, convinced that the US-EU bilateral co-operation is of great importance in itself, and indeed a building block of whatever we may have to say about international coordination at large.

However, bilateralism, even at its best, has its limitation; limitations that are obvious in cases with significant overlaps that cross multiple jurisdictions. Further more, we cannot realistically expect to build the same intensive cooperative relationship with all of our counterparts around the world; the price, in terms of expenditure of scarce administrative resources, would simply be too high. It is therefore, in our view, time to look beyond co-operation based on bilateral country to country agreements, and to intensify the pulse rate of multilateral and plurilateral solutions. This includes our efforts to do things—simple to say, a bit less simple to achieve. One, to start negotiations on a WTO competition agreement; and two, the creation, the idea about the creation of a global competition forum.

Of course, one hesitates to speak about the WTO after a day in this room that I understand was extremely deep and successful in terms of discussion; but let me just say a word, by stressing that in the European Commission, in the European Union, we are convinced that the first pillar of multilateral cooperation would have to be a WTO framework agreement—probably not a very ambitious one, but ensuring the respect of certain basic competition principles. The European Union has been calling for a WTO agreement on competition for several years now, and that proposal has been well received by an increasing number of WTO members. A WTO agreement on competition would rest on a commitment by member countries to establish and enforce domestic competition laws. We believe that these laws should be based on a few essential core principles—non-discrimination, transparency and due process—and furthermore, WTO members should commit themselves to take all necessary measures to stamp out hard-core cartels.

But I should be clear about one thing: in calling for a WTO agreement, we are definitely not seeking to erode the sovereignty of national authorities. On the contrary, strong national enforcement agencies are indispensable to the success of a framework agreement. Also, we are not proposing a harmonisation of substantive competition laws; nor are we proposing that individual decisions of national competition authorities be subject to dispute settlement under the WTO. I am very hopeful that we can convince our trading partners, not excluding the largest of them all, of the importance of this initiative; and that substantive negotiations can be undertaken as part of the next trade round. I am also very convinced politically, that several apparently disparate and irreconcilable constituencies would gain and be reassured by such a move—consumers around the world, developing countries, NGOs, all of them having irrational and emotional fears about the globalisation process, probably all of them a bit reassured if they were to see that there is the beginning of a co-ordinated public policy response to the integration of markets and companies. But, I believe that business would also have to be keenly interested in having a gentle, gradualistic framework in place, ensuring in due course the avoidance of an explosion of divergences and indeed some convergence in the way in which their transnational operations are treated by the different competition authorities.

The second pillar and the last point of my presentation: the second pillar of multilateral cooperation would be the creation of a broadly based forum for the discussion between those responsible for the development and management of competition policy worldwide. This design, now known as the global competition forum, has been the object of considerable talk, but with reflection associated with the talk, over the past year; and I am an enthusiastic proponent of the idea. There was an interesting occasion to discuss the design and to exchange views on this idea at Ditchley Park some months ago; it was an extremely positive brainstorming. What we retained from the Ditchley meeting is that there was a broad consensus on the timeliness of the initiative, in view of the rapid transformation of the world economy. The main mission of the forum should be in my view to put in place an inclusive venue where those responsible for competition policy worldwide could meet, engage in constructive dialogue and exchange their experiences on enforcement policy and practice; competition authorities and other participants in the forum should try to achieve a maximum of convergence on fundamental issues, such as the substance, the economics of competition policy, the enforcement priorities of competition authorities, and other issues such as those raised by the new economy. Such consensus should result from a common understanding about the best approach to solving the problems; that could then lead to the promulgation of general GATT guidelines or the issuing of non-binding best practice recommendations. And the forum, last but not least, should foster and develop a common worldwide competition culture, and in particular be open to deal with issues of importance to developing economies and economies in transition.

I think, also from an existential and political point of view, the newly-born competition authorities in countries around the world that definitely do not have a markets tradition, let alone a competition policy tradition—those authorities would feel a bit more like authorities and would be more respected in their domestic constituencies if they were perceived over there as belonging to a respected network of competition authorities, including those from countries where there is a long-standing tradition of implementing competition policy. The forum should address enforcement issues related to the role, the priorities and the enforcement procedures of the bodies entrusted with the application of the substantive competition rules, including of course aspects like an effective review of global mergers falling under multiple jurisdictions. The forum should not be a new international institution; it should require a minimum of permanent infrastructure with support primarily provided by its participants. However, it should draw together all interested parties both public and private—business, professional, consumer and academic bodies. And the aspects of the way of involving business, the legal profession and consumer organisations is of course an important and delicate one; I envisage that the forum should have a variable geometry with certain of its activities exclusively reserved to the competition authorities, like peer review exercises, with however many other activities raising also the contribution around the table, in forms to be determined, by the legal profession, by business, for example, when it comes to assessing the merger review procedures and having ideas for greater convergence in that crucial area.

Needless to say, we are not imagining a forum as an antagonist initiative to the trade and competition chapter in the WTO; we are very attached to the multilateral competition law framework at the WTO; but we see the two initiatives as complementary. The work of the forum will, in my view, reinforce an emerging consensus and extend it to other aspects of competition policy. So the two avenues can be followed in parallel and be mutually reinforcing in their pursuit of the same ultimate competition policy objectives. Reform of the architecture of competition policy within Europe, objective of much greater international cooperation bilaterally and multilaterally at the WTO, at the global competition forum: I think this is a moment of lively conceptual imagination on the part of the whole of the competition policy community in Europe and elsewhere. Today marks the beginning of a series that I am sure will prove successful, and we have all noted down the dates for next year; I hope that this series will be able to measure the progress along the axes of these initiatives, and of course to feed them with criticisms and constructive suggestions. Thank you very much.

ADVOCATE GENERAL FRANCIS JACOBS

Thank you very much, Commissioner Monti. I think you have made this event, in a sense, the beginnings of a global competition forum. I think the ideas that you have put forward about the future development of the competition policy and the way in which it is to be implemented, both in the European Union and globally, have raised in the minds of all of us some extremely large questions as to how this is going to operate. On the one hand, within the European Union the decentralised application and enforcement of competition law, which will certainly give rise to substantive problems, problems of procedure, problems of enforcement and problems of jurisdiction; and on the global level, the two aspects that you have mentioned, the idea of a framework competition agreement within the WTO on the one hand, and on the other the global competition forum. These are also matters that will raise some extremely interesting and exciting questions.

So we are all, I'm sure, extremely grateful for your opening statement, and we will proceed with this debate in today's proceedings and, as you have indicated, I think we hope to come back to some of these issues next year. You have kindly agreed to take one or two questions, and so I would invite participants now to put questions on the topics that the Commissioner has addressed. I don't think we need adopt any rigid structure in relation to that, because we have sufficient expertise in the hall to make that unnecessary; but if you have one or two questions that you would like to put on the subject of the address, please indicate. There are some roving microphones that will come round, so please don't speak until the microphone arrives. Who would like to open the proceedings? Yes?

REED BLANDBERG

Reed Blandberg with Bloomberg News. You talked about stamping out hard-core cartels through this international forum through the WTO. I just wonder if you could talk about what hard-core cartels you have in mind—and whether you're talking about OPEC? I just wonder if you could talk about what sort of hard-core cartels you have in mind that this forum should address? Whether you're talking about OPEC, and what sort of reception you expect for this idea when the WTO meets in Qatar later this year?

MARIO MONTI

Well, thank you for the suggestion, first of all. Perhaps there is scope for ambitious and not unrealistically ambitious fight against hard-core cartels. Of course, not to be conducted within the WTO—I would contradict myself if I were to assign an enforcement role to the WTO, that has to stay with the individual competition authorities. But their action would gain strength and co-ordination if on some substantive points there will be a binding agreement within the WTO; and I believe that stamping out hard-core cartels should be one of those substantive points; with the rest we have in mind core principles more than substantive points, like transparency, due process, non-discrimination and the like. Now the issue OPEC would perhaps deserve a conference of its own; I am non-imaginative there, and rather classical. I'm afraid OPEC is not a cartel in the sense that lends itself to be pursued by existing competition law rules; it's not an agreement between undertakings. This does not mean that competition authorities should be uninterested, or are without weapons, concerning the overall developments of what comes with oil prices; and we could mentioned several interventions by several competition authorities in Europe and elsewhere, concerning the oil market more broadly.

MARK CLOUGH

Commissioner, my name is Mark Clough from Ashurst Morris Crisp. I very much enjoyed your presentation, and I'd like to ask you what I'm afraid is a deliberately provocative question. Would the Commissioner accept that if the member states say that they will co-operate with each other, and indeed cooperate with the commission to guarantee the uniform application of EC competition law, they could have no objection to the Commission proposing a single supranational system of enforcement, both at the judicial and at the administrative levels in order to prevent the opening of the door to the disintegration of the, in my view, most successful common policy to date.

MARIO MONTI

Thank you for the 'most accessible'. We try to keep it accessible; we believe that in the new scenario that is opening up in Europe, without an architectural form, this successful and accessible common competition policy would be eroded and would gradually lose enforcement effectiveness. Now we believe that the role of the national competition authorities should be enhanced, both taking them individually and taking them as components of a lively network; and there is much to be said both about horizontal co-operation among the various national competition authorities in Europe, as well as, and I hate to use the adjective 'vertical', but at any rate cooperation between the authorities and the Commission.

You speak of a single supranational system; the inspiration of our form is that community, as opposed to national competition law, should be more and more applied, but for this to be possible, the number of agents applying community competition law must be increased, and those agents must be put into condition to gain the synergies from a network approach. So we do not consider that this reform is a re-nationalisation of competition policy; much to the contrary, we look at it as a greater role for community competition policy, but with a more important enforcement role within that perspective by the national competition authorities and indeed the national courts.

PROFESSOR SIRAGUSA

Commissioner Monti, Professor Siragusa. In order to ensure the homogeneous enforcement and cooperation among the authorities and the central role of the Commission in your system, I think the provisional Article 3 of the new draft regulation proposed by the Commission is essential. This is the provision that says that Community law should apply to the exclusion of national law to cases that have an effect on traders in member states. Now we also know that this very provision is not yet fully accepted by all member states. I think it's a key change in the articles of the Commission; it's an extremely important provision, which I think would be important in achieving the goal of the reform. Will you be willing to oppose any attempt by member states to water down that aspect of the proposal? And do you think that you will be able to keep Article 3 in the final regulation?

MARIO MONTI

Thank you Professor Siragusa, for underlining this point. Indeed Article 3, in a sense, logically, is Article 1 of the reform; it has a key role in it, and it is true, as you say, that a number—I should add a small number—of member states still have difficulties in accepting this article. In the Council Working Group under Swedish presidency, there hasn't yet been an in-depth discussion of this specific point; it will come in the month of June. We will be better able then to see concretely the degree of resistance. In the *Tour de Table* accounts the other day, I must say that several Member States appreciated the coherence that such an article would bring about; and of course we know that the European Parliament is basically in favour of that; we know that business is also. In this there is a good component of a reassurance relative to its original concern about legal insecurity and incoherent application. So, having said all this, I will be determined to achieve—it remains to be seen whether the present drafting of Article 3 or the essence of its objective, we should never of course undergo a council discussion with an excessively rigid attitude, but I share definitely the importance that you attribute to this article.

ADVOCATE GENERAL FRANCIS JACOBS

Thank you very much. I'm sorry that we will have to stop the debate at this point; I think that we could well have carried on for the rest of the morning, but I think that we have to move on to the next panel, on which Commissioner Monti will remain. And I would only like to say now, on behalf of us all, thank you to you, Commissioner, for the ideas with which you've launched this conference and for getting our proceedings off to what I'm sure we all agree is the best possible start. And we look forward to seeing you here again at a future event. Thank you very much.

2. North Atlantic Competition Policy: Converging Toward What?

William J Kolasky*

Good morning. It is delightful to be here today, in one of my favourite cities in the world. I made it a point to visit Berkeley Square last night, hoping to hear the nightingales sing.

This address grows out of the discussions we had with the EU last fall over GE/Honeywell,[1] but is not really about GE/Honeywell. What we discovered as we explored the reasons for our different outcomes in that case was that they reflected some deeper differences between competition policy in the United States and in Europe, especially in the area of abuse of dominance and monopolization.

As I began to investigate about these differences, I happened to read an article in The Economist entitled *'The Need for Shock Treatment'* reporting on concerns in Europe about a 'growth gap' with the United States: in 1991 America's per capita GDP was 42 per cent greater than the EU average; a decade later the gap had widened to 54 per cent.[2] The article attributed this growth gap to the slow pace of market liberalisation in several key sectors of the European economy. Examination of the relationship for OECD member countries between economic growth and an OECD index of market regulation tends to support that thesis. It shows that countries with less regulation tend to have higher growth rates.

The Economist article started me thinking about whether differences in competition policy may be contributing to the slower growth of the European economy. In the United States, we have gone through a complete reform of our competition policy over the last quarter century. While it is always hard to determine cause-and-effect, this fundamental shift in antitrust policy coincided with the fastest period of economic growth the United States has enjoyed since the period immediately after the Second World War.

* Deputy Assistant Attorney General for International Enforcement, Antitrust Division, US Department of Justice. These remarks reflect my personal views and not necessarily those of the Department. I want to thank the many people who contributed importantly to this paper, including Nancy Garrison, Caldwell Harrop, Greg Werden, Robert Nicholson, John Fonte, Michael Klass, Christina Akers, and, of course, my assistant, Gloria Jenkins. I also want to thank Barry Hawk, Eleanor Fox, Douglas Melamed, and Michael Katz who provided useful comments on earlier drafts. Any mistakes found in this speech are, of course, my own.

1 *General Electric/Honeywell*, Case No M 2220, Commission decision of 3 July 2001.

2 *The Need for Shock Treatment—the EU Barcelona Summit*, Economist, 9 Mar 2002, at 52.

We see Europe going through a similar transition today. I think you all would agree that before 1995 European competition law suffered from many of the same problems under which US antitrust law laboured a generation ago. EU competition law relied on wooden, formalistic rules. And, as has sometimes been the case in the United States as well, EU law sometimes placed more emphasis on protecting competitors than consumers, and viewed efficiencies suspiciously.

Under the leadership of Karel Van Miert, Mario Monti, and Alex Schaub the picture has changed dramatically over the last seven years. These three have initiated a series of reforms that will change competition policy in Europe every bit as dramatically as the Chicago School revolution changed it in the United States a generation ago. These include, most notably, the Notice on Vertical Restraints, the Modernization Initiative, the new leniency policy, the Technology Block Exemption Report and, most recently, the Merger Process Reform Green Paper. Alex Schaub, who oversaw the implementation of many of these reforms, will be leaving DG Comp this summer, but he should be very proud of what he has accomplished during his tenure.

As important as these reforms are, none was more significant than Commissioner Monti's firm embrace, at a speech at Merchant Taylor's Hall in London last July, of the consumer welfare approach to competition policy. In that speech Commissioner Monti became the first Competition Commissioner to declare unequivocally that '[T]he goal of competition policy is consumer welfare.'[3] Not 'a' goal, but 'the' goal. We in the United States applaud Commissioner Monti's bold leadership in embracing the consumer welfare model of competition policy.

In the interest of promoting greater convergence, not just in how we talk about competition policy, but in how we practice it, I attempted in a speech I gave in Capetown, South Africa in March to articulate six guiding principles for sound competition policy.[4] I do not propose to cover these in detail today. Instead, I would like to show how these principles might be applied in practice by examining what we see as five areas of historical divergence between US and EU competition policy. The five areas are: efficiencies, fidelity discounts, predatory pricing, essential facilities, and monopoly leveraging.

[3] Mario Monti, *The Future for Competition Policy in the European Union*, Address at Merchant Taylor's Hall, London (9 July 2001).

[4] William J Kolasky, *Comparative Merger control Analysis: Six Guiding Principles for Antitrust Agencies—News and Old*, Address to the International Bar Association Conference on competition Law and Policy in a Global Context, Cape Town, South Africa (18 Mar 2002) (available at http://www.usdoj.gov/atr/public/speeches/10845.htm).

My purpose in shining a light on these areas is not to try to tell you what your policies should be. We have different legal traditions, different institutions, and different economies. Any sound competition policy must take account of these differences. What works for us is not necessarily best for you. My purpose instead is simply to identify the key issues and to propose that we work together to address them.

I. EFFICIENCIES IN MERGER REVIEW

In the United States, our Merger Guidelines have included what some refer to as an 'efficiencies defence' since the Baxter merger guidelines were issued in 1982. In Europe, by contrast, it was widely believed until very recently that the Commission would not treat efficiencies as a defence to a merger that created or strengthened a dominant position, and that it might even view efficiencies as an additional reason for prohibiting a merger on the ground that they would further entrench the merged firm's dominant position.[5]

In his Merchant Taylor's Hall speech, Commissioner Monti took a critical step toward clarifying the Commission's view of efficiencies. He announced that, 'We are not against mergers that create more efficient firms. Such mergers tend to benefit consumers, even if competitors might suffer from increased competition.'[6] The director of the EU Merger Task Force, Goetz Drauz, built on these remarks at the ABA Section of Antitrust Law's Spring Meeting last month. He invited merging parties to tell the MTF about the efficiencies they expect to realize from their transactions, assuring them that efficiencies will not be used as a reason to challenge a merger.

Now that the Commission has clarified that efficiencies should be viewed positively, the question is, as Goetz Drauz put it in Washington, 'not whether, but how.' This is still a lively subject of debate on our side of the Atlantic. There is a widespread perception, for example, that in the United States we apply a so-called 'consumer welfare' test, which takes into account only those efficiencies that are likely to be passed on to consumers in the form of lower prices. In Canada, the Competition Tribunal in *Superior Propane* recently rejected this test, opting instead for a 'part total welfare, part wealth distribution weighting' test, which it held was mandated by the Canadian statute.[7] Under this test, the Tribunal would

[5] Frederick Jenny, 'Competition and Efficiency', in *Antitrust in a Global Economy*, 1993 Corporate Law Institute, Fordham U School of Law, 194 (B Hawk, ed, 1994).

[6] Mario Monti, above n 4.

[7] *Commissioner of Competition v Superior Propane, Inc*, CT 98/02 (Competition Tribunal, 4 Apr 2002) (Reasons and Order Following the Reasons for Judgment of the Federal Court of Appeal dated 4 Apr 2001), available at: <http://www.ct_tc.gc.ca/english/cases/propane/0238a.pdf>.

approve a merger even if it is likely to result in higher prices, so long as the cost savings exceed what economists call the 'deadweight loss' from any reduction in output plus any negative wealth distribution effect on poor consumers.

In practice, our test is less of a pure 'consumer welfare' test than is generally thought. While we give greater weight to those efficiencies that will be passed on to consumers through lower prices in the near term, footnote 37 to the Guidelines, which was added as part of the 1997 revisions, makes it clear that we 'also will consider the effects of cognizable efficiencies with no short-term, direct effect on prices' where we think those efficiencies will ultimately redound to society's benefit.[8]

The Bell Atlantic/NYNEX merger is a good example of a case where the Division declined to challenge a merger even though a strict price test might have lead to a contrary result. In that case, the Division concluded that while the likely price effects of the efficiencies were small, the efficiencies themselves were so likely and so large and the possible anticompetitive effects so speculative that we should clear the merger nevertheless. Subsequent history has proven the Division right. A retrospective study by one of the merger's critics, AARP, found that the Bell Atlantic/NYNEX merger did, in fact, deliver very substantial cost-savings that surpassed even the parties' projections, as well as a 'marked improvement' in service quality.[9]

We have agreed with the European Commission to make this subject a priority of our joint US/EU merger working group. We are very much looking forward to working together in this critical area.

II. FIDELITY REBATES

Fidelity rebates are rewards or discounts given to customers who purchase all or a specified portion of their requirements for a given product or service from a dominant firm. In Europe, the Commission and the European Court of Justice have come close to establishing a per se rule against fidelity rebates granted by a dominant firm, the only exceptions being short-term discount programs and volume discounts that are cost-justified and open to all customers on equal terms.[10]

[8] US Department of Justice & Federal Trade Commission, Horizontal Merger Guidelines § 4, reprinted in 4 *Trade Reg Rep* (CCH) ¶ 13,104 (1992, revd 1997), s 4.

[9] Scott C Lundquist and Scott A Coleman, *Promises and Realities: An Examination of the Post-Merger Performance of the SBC/PACIFIC Telesis and Bell Atlantic/NYNEX Companies*, AARP Public Policy Institute, 9 (1999).

[10] Carles Esteva Mosso and Stephen Ryan, *Article 82—Abuse of a Dominant Position*, The EC Law of Competition (Jonathan Faull & Ali Nikpay, eds, 1999), 178.

In the United States, by contrast, we tend to view any reduction in price by a leading firm as moving prices toward the competitive ideal so long as the resulting prices are not below cost. We have generally refrained, therefore, from challenging discount programs like these under our antitrust laws.

This difference in approach is illustrated most starkly in the treatment of Virgin Atlantic's complaint about British Airways' incentive system for travel agents, which gave agents extra commissions in return for meeting or exceeding the previous year's sales of BA tickets. The European Commission found BA's incentive program to be an abuse of dominance.[11] By contrast, when Virgin sued BA on the same theory in the United States, the trial court granted summary judgment for BA and that judgment was affirmed on appeal.[12]

This is another area where a transatlantic dialog may be useful. While Europe's per se approach may unnecessarily discourage some procompetitive discounting, there are some in the United States who view the approach of the US courts as too laissez faire.[13] These opposing views are now being litigated in the Third Circuit in *LePage's v 3-M*.[14] Fidelity rebates will also be the subject of an OECD roundtable next month in Paris. This is clearly an area that will benefit from putting the best minds on both sides of the Atlantic at work together in developing a policy that balances the potential anticompetitive risks against the potential efficiency benefits and thereby promotes consumer welfare and economic progress.

III. PREDATORY PRICING

The US law on predatory pricing has been reasonably clear at least since the Supreme Court decided the *Brooke Group v Brown & Williamson* case in 1993.[15] There the Court held that to be found predatory, conduct must satisfy a two-part test: (1) the allegedly predatory price must be below an appropriate measure of cost, and (2) there must be a dangerous probability that the alleged predator will be able to recoup its losses through monopoly prices once its rivals exit the market.

The European Court of Justice has adopted the first leg of the *Brooke Group* test, but has expressly declined to adopt the second leg, holding that

[11] *Virgin/British Airways, Case No. IV/D-2/34.780, Commission decision of* 14 July *1999.*

[12] *Virgin Atlantic Airways LTD v British Airways PLC*, 257 F.3d 256 (2d Cir 2001).

[13] See Willard K Tom, David A Balto, and Neil W Averitt, '*Antocompetitive Aspects of Market-Share Discounts and Other Incentives to Exclusive Dealing*', 67 *Antitrust LJ* 615 (2000). See also Dennis W Carlton, '*A General Analysis of Exclusionary Conduct and Refusal to Deal — Why Aspen and Kadak Are Misguided*', 68 *Antitrust LJ* 659 (2001).

[14] *LePage's, Inc v 3M*, 277 F.3d 365 (3rd Cir 2002).

[15] *Brooke Group LDT v Brown & Williamson Tobacco Corp*, 509 US 209 (USNC 1993).

recoupment is not a necessary element of predation under Article 82.[16] In addition, whereas most US courts have held that the appropriate measure of cost is average variable cost, the ECJ left open the possibility of finding prices above average variable cost but below average total cost predatory if they are 'part of a plan for eliminating a competitor.'[17]

We view recoupment as an essential element of the test because, as the Supreme Court has said, 'cutting prices in order to increase business often is the very essence of competition.'[18] There are many legitimate, procompetitive reasons for charging prices that are below cost, and there is no rational reason to deny consumers the benefits of lower prices in the absence of any realistic prospect for recouping short-term losses through later supracompetitive pricing.

In the United States, we are also chary of relying on subjective intent as a basis for antitrust liability. As Judge Easterbrook has put it very colorfully, we expect firms to want 'to crush their rivals if they can.'[19] Happily, in finding that Deutsche Post had engaged in predatory pricing in the market for business parcel services last year, the European Commission did not rely on subjective intent but instead adopted an 'avoidable' cost standard, which looked only at the incremental or variable costs Deutsche Post incurred in providing these services, rather than at average total cost.[20] That approach is very similar to the approach we have taken in our *American Airlines* predation case, which is now before the Tenth Circuit Court of Appeals.[21]

IV. THE ESSENTIAL FACILITIES DOCTRINE

The fourth area in which we see a potentially significant difference between US and EU law relates to the use of the so-called 'essential facilities' doctrine to compel access to a dominant firm's facilities. While the essential facilities doctrine originated in the United States, we have construed the doctrine very narrowly, limiting it largely to regulated utilities and joint ventures, out of fear that its overbroad application would both chill incentives to invest and innovate and require antitrust agencies to undertake the uncomfortable task of having to regulate the terms of access.[22]

[16] *See Tetra Pak Rausing SA v Comm'n*, Case C-333/94P [1996] ECR I-5951 (1996).

[17] *AKZO Chemie BV v Comm'n*, Case C-62/86, [1991] ECR I-3359 (1991).

[18] *Brooke Group*, 509 US, at 226.

[19] *AA Poultry Farms, Inc. v Rose Acre Farms, Inc*, 881 F.2d 1396, 1401 (7th Cir 1989).

[20] *United Parcel Service/Deutsche Post AG*, Case No COMP/35.141, Commission decision of 20 March 2001.

[21] *US v AMR Corp*, 140 F.Supp.2d 1141, (D Kan 27 Apr 2001).

[22] Gregory J Werden, '*The Law and Economics of the Essential Facility Doctrine*', 32 *Saint Louis University Law Journal* 433–79 (1987). See also Phillip Areeda, '*Essential Facilities: An Epithet in Need of Limiting Principles*', 58 *Antitrust LJ* 841 (1989).

For this reason, there are no cases in the United States applying the essential facilities doctrine to require the compulsory licensing of intellectual property. Instead, in dealing with antitrust challenges to refusals to license intellectual property, our courts have generally applied what we call the 'Colgate' doctrine to hold that refusals to deal are lawful 'in the absence of any purpose to create or maintain a monopoly.'[23]

This issue is currently a hot topic of debate in the United States due to the seemingly conflicting decisions of the Ninth Circuit Court of Appeals in *ITS v Kodak*[24] and the Federal Circuit in *CSU v Xerox*.[25] Both cases involved the issue of whether a manufacturer of photocopiers could refuse to license its parts to rivals in the aftermarket. The Ninth Circuit held that while a refusal to license was presumptively lawful, it could be challenged if the reasons proffered for the refusal were 'pretextual,' inviting an inquiry into the defendant's subjective state of mind, which is something we generally try to avoid. The Federal Circuit expressly rejected the Ninth Circuit's approach for just this reason and suggested, in dicta, that a refusal to license should be found unlawful under the antitrust laws only if it were part of a tying arrangement designed to extend the patent monopoly into other fields or if the patent were invalid, a test which some have argued is too restrictive.[26]

A similar debate is ongoing in Europe as a result of two cases, *Magill* and *IMS*, applying, or attempting to apply, the essential facilities doctrine to intellectual property. In *Magill*, the ECJ ordered television stations in Ireland to license their program listings to a competitor seeking to create a single guide for all channels.[27] In *IMS*, the Commission concluded preliminarily that IMS had abused its dominant position by refusing to license to its competitors in Germany its copyrighted 'brick structure'—a system for dividing the country into geographic units for collecting data on pharmaceutical sales.[28] On appeal, the Court of First Instance (CFI) suspended the Commission's interim decision. Supporters of the application of the essential facilities doctrine in these cases have argued that they both involved 'extraordinary circumstances' in that the copyrights in question did not

[23] *US v Colgate & Co*, 250 US 300 (1919).

[24] *Image Technical Services, Inc v Eastman Kodak Co*, 125 F.3d 1195 (9th Cir 1997).

[25] *CSU LLC v Xerox Corp*, 531 US 1143 (2001).

[26] A Douglas Melamed and Ali M Stoeppelwerth, '*The CSU Case: Facts, Formalism and the Intersection of Antitrust and Intellectual Property Law*', 10 *Geo Mason L Rev* (forthcoming 2002 at time of writing. See also R Hewitt Pate, '*Refusals to Deal and Intellectual Property Rights*', 10 *Geo Mason L Rev* (forthcoming 2002 at time of writing).

[27] *Radio Telefix Eireann/Independent Television Publications Ltd*, Case No C-241/91 P and C-242/91 P, Commission decision on 6 Apr 1995.

[28] *National Data Corporation/IMS Global Services*, Case No COMP/38.044, Commission decision on 3 Jul 2001.

involve the kind of creativity copyright law is designed to encourage and that the decisions therefore should not undercut the incentive to invest and innovate. This raises the prospect of basing competition policy on whether we think the intellectual property rights at issue are worth protecting; this kind of ex post judgment cannot help but create uncertainty and reduce the incentive to innovate.

This is another area where we and the EU are both currently reexamining our existing policies. The Federal Trade Commission and we are holding a series of hearings on intellectual property and antitrust. On 22 May we will be having a session to take a comparative look at how these issues are handled in the United States and Europe and will have EU officials and European lawyers participating. In addition, we are considering forming a joint US/EU IP working group, similar to our joint merger working group, to coordinate our parallel reviews of our policies toward intellectual property more closely.

IV. MONOPOLY LEVERAGING

The final area of divergence is what we call monopoly leveraging in the United States — that is, using a dominant position in one market to gain a competitive advantage in another. Most US courts have held that it is not unlawful for a firm with a monopoly in one market to use its monopoly power in that market to gain a competitive advantage in neighboring markets, unless by so doing it serves either to maintain its existing monopoly or to create a dangerous probability of gaining a monopoly in the adjacent market as well.[29] My understanding is that under EU law, by contrast, it is an abuse of dominance for a firm that is dominant in one market to use that position to gain a competitive advantage in a neighbouring market in which it is not dominant even if the conduct is not shown to be likely to create a dominant position in the second market unless the dominant firm can show a legitimate business justification for its conduct.[30]

Our view, by contrast, is that, 'so long as we allow a firm to compete in several markets, we must expect it to seek the competitive advantages of its broad-based activity—more efficient production, greater ability to develop complementary products, reduced transactions costs, and so forth',[31] and that allowing it to do so ultimately benefits consumers. Again, this is an area that would benefit from a constructive transatlantic dialog over our differing approaches.

[29] See ABA Section of Antitrust Law, I Antitrust Developments 282–5 (4th edn 1997).
[30] See, eg, *Tetra Pack Rausing SA v Comm'n*, C-333/94P [1996] ECR I-5951 (1996).
[31] *Berkey Photo v Eastman Kodak Co*, 603 F.2d 263 (2d Cir 1979).

V. CONCLUSION

This has been a pretty exhaustive—and exhausting—tour of the areas in which we currently see potentially significant differences between our competition policies in the United States and yours here in Europe. My purpose in identifying these is to open up a more in-depth transatlantic dialogue, both to determine how real these differences are and to begin discussing whether and how we should try to bridge them. And that brings me back to the title of my paper. While there is value in convergence, convergence should not become an end in itself. Our goal is not convergence for its own sake, but rather convergence around sound competition policies. I hope we can all agree that sound competition policies should generally be those that best promote efficiency, economic growth, and consumer welfare. I also hope that we can reach agreement that in pursuing these goals our competition policies should embody the guiding principles we laid out in Capetown.

Again, I want to emphasise that we are not trying to dictate to anyone what the best appraoch to these difficult issues is. Given the differences in our economies, our legal traditions and systems, and our institutions, what works best for us may not be best for Europe. What I hope, however, is that we can at least agree on what our goals are and on what principles we should apply in developing administable legal rules. I would hope we could also agree to work together in designing the best possible rules for our economies in these very difficult areas where we are both still struggling to get it right..

The silver lining to the *GE/Honeywell* cloud is that it has opened up a much more substantive dialogue between Washington and Brussels, and I believe within Europe, over these important issues. I hope this talk contributes in some small way to moving that dialogue forward.

3. The Competition Appeal Tribunal and the Ordinary Courts

Sir Jeremy Lever, KCMG, QC*

The modernisation proposals put forward by the European Communities Commission continue to occupy the minds of competition lawyers throughout the European Union. The German Monopolies Commission believes that the proposals are so wrong, both as a matter of law and as a matter of policy, that if the Council adopts a new procedural Regulation in place of Regulation 4064/89 and the new Regulation has the features that have been proposed to date by the Commission, the German Government should challenge the validity of the new Regulation before the European Court of Justice. You can find the English language version of the Monopolkommission's 'Special Report' of October 2001 on its website <http:/www. monopolkommission.de> and Issue 7 of the European Competition Law Review which will be published later this year will contain a summary of that Report.

However, whatever the demerits of the Commission's proposals, there is now a strong probability that the Council will substantially implement them. It is therefore very important that we should seek to mitigate the defects of the new system and make the best of it and at the same time start to think about whether in the long term more radical reform may not be both desirable and practicable.

So far as the United Kingdom is concerned, an amendment that has been tabled to the Enterprise Bill in the House of Lords, if adopted, would significantly improve the position both immediately and, even more, when Article 81(3) becomes directly applicable in accordance with the proposed Council Regulation.

The amendment proposes that the Lord Chancellor and the Secretary of State (ie the Secretary of State for Trade and Industry) should have power to make Regulations that would enable the UK Courts to transfer to the Competition Appeal Tribunal competition issues that arise in private civil actions. The amendment would enable such Regulations to be drafted so as to allow for the greatest flexibility of procedure as between the court in which the private action has been commenced and the Competition Appeal Tribunal with the object of adopting the most cost-effective and expeditious means of disposing of the litigation.

* Monckton Chambers. Keynote speech delivered at the Second Annual Conference on International and Comparative Competition Law, at BIICL, May 2002.

If anyone here today can do anything to influence the House of Lords to adopt the amendment, I respectfully urge him or her to do so. The Enterprise Bill as drafted is simply perverse in this regard. It assigns to the Competition Appeal Tribunal jurisdiction to hear 'follow-on damage claims', ie claims for damages to compensate the claimant for an infringement of Articles 81 and 82 EC and Chapters I and II of the Competition Act 1998 where the infringement has already been established through public law proceedings.

But those are claims based on competition law that are least appropriate for determination by the Competition Appeal Tribunal. The ordinary courts are fully competent to quantify damages where liability has been established: it is a task that they perform the whole time; and the quantification of monetary compensation for loss caused by infringement of rules of competition law is no different in principle from the quantification of monetary compensation for loss caused by other breaches of legal duties. Indeed, the Competition Appeal Tribunal is actually a less suitable tribunal than the ordinary courts so far as assessment of damages is concerned; and use of the Competition Appeal Tribunal for the purpose will involve a dissipation of the scarce specialist resources of the Tribunal.

The civil cases where involvement of the Competition Appeal Tribunal is needed, and will be needed even more when Article 81(3) of the EC Treaty and the corresponding provision of the Competition Act 1998 become directly applicable, are cases where the substantive infringement has not already been established, that is to say by public law proceedings. Since the Tribunal will be the tribunal that determines, albeit on appeal from the Office of Fair Trade, precisely the same question of whether or not an infringement has been committed when the question arises in public law, it is extraordinary to deny to the ordinary courts the assistance of the Tribunal when the question arise in private law.

Despite my enthusiasm for the schema that the amendment that has been tabled in the House of Lords would make possible, I have to admit that the creation of an even better solution would require more radical changes. It is at this stage that what I shall say today becomes seriously heretical.

The great concern that has been expressed about the Commission's proposal that Article 81(3) should become directly applicable is based on a feeling that the provisions of Article 81(3) are not suitable for application by courts. A similar concern was voiced in this country in 1956 when the Restrictive Trade Practices Act was passed. That Act created a new superior court of record, the Restrictive Practices Court, over which a judge of the High Court or Court of Session presided, assisted by lay members. Agreements to which Part I of the Act applied needed to be justified, in accordance with certain conditions, as being not contrary to the public interest. The objection was raised that the justifiability of such agreements was not 'justifiable'.

The present controversy about the Commission's modernisation proposals has led me to revisit the issue of justifiability.

It is important here to note that courts decide questions in a way that is entirely different from the way in which decisions are taken by the Government, by Parliament, by commercial enterprises, by individuals in the course of their ordinary lives—in fact, different from the way in which almost all decisions are taken. It is only because we are lawyers that we take it for granted that the decisions with which we are concerned are decided in this unique way. But at least competition lawyers might be expected to question the use of court procedures. This is indeed particularly striking in the field of competition law where the self-same question will fall to be decided in one kind of way when the question arises as a matter of private law and in another kind of way when the question arises as a matter of public law.

In the former case, adversaries deploy evidence, in accordance with technical rules, and advance arguments before a court or tribunal which, in an essentially reactive fashion, picks, and chooses between, the material placed before it. In the latter case, the decision-taker investigates the situation under review in the way that the decision-taker regards as appropriate. If representations are made to the decision-taker by interested persons, the decision-taker may have a duty to consider those representations, indeed it may have a duty to permit such representations to be made and it will often be foolish, not to say unreasonable, if it fails to take the representations properly into account. But it is no sense in the position of a tribunal which, when the curtain rises at the commencement of the play, settles down to watch an essentially second-hand action unfold before it, almost certainly constrained by rules that require unity of time and place such as governed trench classical drama.

In other words, justiciability is about procedure: given the issue that has to be decided, is a curial or a non-curial procedure appropriate?

At present and in the foreseeable future, some competition law issues that ought to be decided by court procedures are, and will continue to be, decided non-curially and vice versa.

Thus, take the issue whether a number of businessmen met and agreed prices. If it is found that they did so, very large fines may be imposed—potentially much larger than any fine imposed by a criminal court. Yet, by adoption of the fiction that the fine under competition law is a non-criminal sanction, the powers to impose such fines are conferred in the first instance on competition authorities—ie, administrative agencies. If, but only if, the decision of the competition authority in such a case is seen as nothing more than an indictment, and there is then a real trial before a curial body, there can be no objection.

By contrast, certain issues that arise in competition law are wholly unsuitable for resolution using curial procedures. That is most obviously true of the application of Article 81(3) of the EC Treaty (and now of the corresponding provision of Chapter I of Part I of the Competition Act 1998). For some 30 years after the enactment of Council Regulation 17, the Commission of the European Communities itself insisted vehemently, and this case rightly, that the application of Article 81(3) was a task of a kind that could not sensibly be adopted by a court. The fact that it no longer suits the Commission to perform that task does not alter the truth of what the Commission said over a period of so many years.

It is significant that, in relation to at least a number of issues, the UK Competition Commission Appeal Tribunal (which is about to metamorphose into the Competition Appeal Tribunal), although statutorily endowed with 'full jurisdiction' when hearing appeals from the Director General of Fair Trading, has made it clear that it intends to exercise only an appellate and not a primary jurisdiction. With respect, I entirely agree that it is generally right to take that position. A necessary first step in the determination of many competition law issues, which by way of shorthand I will now call non-justiciable, is to get a decision from a competition authority—whether the Commission of the European Communities, the UK Office of Fair Trading or the German Federal Cartel Office.

If the amendment to the Enterprise Bill that has been tabled in the House of Lords is adopted, the situation in private actions will be much better than it would otherwise be; but it must be recognised that, when acting at first instance in relation to a competition issue transferred to it by the High Court or Court of Session, the Competition Appeal Tribunal will be performing a different task from what it will be doing when hearing appeals from the Director General of Fair Trading. The question before the Tribunal will often appear to be the same in both cases—for example, Is an agreement justifiable for the purposes of exempting it from the general prohibition of agreements that have has an object or effect the prevention, restriction or distortion of competition? But it is one thing to answer that question with the benefit of a decision by the competent authority; it is quite another thing to answer the question from scratch, relying entirely on curial procedures to do so.

It is such considerations as these that have led me to the conclusion that in the field of competition law, private law is no substitute for public law.

My conclusion about this is that, although the amendment that has been tabled in the House of Lords is not merely desirable but also necessary, we should then be considering a further reform. Under that further reform, it would be possible for complainants to the Office of Fair Trading to undertake to pay the costs incurred by the Office in processing the complaint if the Office were unwilling to take up the case of its own motion; under such a complaints procedure, the Office could also award to the target of the complaint its reasonable costs in the event of the complaint failing.

Under such a system, the Office could still decline to take up a complaint if, and to the extent that, it believed that the complaint raised issues that were better decided using court procedures rather than the Office's non-court procedures. And of course an appeal would lie in the ordinary way to the Competition Appeal Tribunal from a decision of the Director.

Finally to preserve a symmetry whereby justiciable issues were heard, first by a court and non-justiciable issues were decided, first by a competition authority, my further reform would enable the authority to apply to the High Court or Court of Session for a judgment that, for example, a number of competitors had been operating a cartel for which they should have been fined and on account of which they should be liable in damages.

In other words, whether one was concerned with the application of competition law as public law or as private law, the applicable procedure would depend on the nature of the particular issue that required determination.

So much for the broad canvas. But before I conclude, I should mention a few of a number of outstanding specific questions that need to be answered in connection with the Commission's modernisation proposals and that have as yet attracted insufficient attention.

First, how are leniency regimes to operate when the new Council Regulation becomes operative? Some national competition authorities have leniency regimes, others do not; and the regimes that do exist differ one from another—for example, the Office of Fair Trading operate different rules from those operated by the Commission of the European Communities. Moreover, in order to avail oneself of leniency rules, will it be necessary for an undertaking or its lawyers to call, with minimal delay, on every competition authority within the Community or will making a clean breast of it to the Commission in Brussels suffice?

Secondly, will the State, the competition authority of which handles the case, be entitled to keep the whole of any fine that is imposed? Quite apart from the potential scramble by national competition authorities to handle 'juicy' cases, the result could be both philosophically flawed and irrational in practice. Infringement of Articles 81 and 82 of the Treaty constitutes a wrong against the Community rather than against a particular Member State. It would be justiciable to allow the Member State of the competent authority that handled a case to keep a certain proportion of any fine as a 'handling fee' in the same way as Member States keep a proportion of the customs dues that they collect. As to the irrationality of the Member State of the handling competent authority retaining the whole fine, consider the case of the cartel in Member State 'A' that fixes the prices on sales to customers in Member State 'B'. Almost certainly the competition authority of Member State 'A' will be better placed than the competition authority of Member State 'B' to handle the case but it would surely be irrational for the resulting fine to swell the coffers exclusively of Member State 'A' and not at all those of the 'victim', Member State 'B'.

Thirdly, the national laws concerning 'legal professional privilege', 'secret professional', etc. differ from each other and from Community law as enunciated in the *AM&S* case.[1] Can we be confident that the Community rules will be applied by the national competition authorities in procedures initiated by them for the purposes of Articles 81 and 82 of the EC Treaty? Further, that they will not pass material that they have obtained thanks to the application of their national law to another national competition authority when the material in question, although not protected in the first country, is protected under Community law and under the law of the country where the recipient authority is located?

My final comment relates to the resources available to the national competent authorities, and more specifically to the Office of Fair Trading. I have stressed that in the field of competition law, private law is no substitute for public law. When the modernisation proposals are implemented, some work which under the present system would have been done, if at all, will fall to be done by the national competition authorities and the workload on the Office of Fair Trading, or at least the work that it ought to undertake, will again increase. While HM Treasury may be gratified by an increasing flow of fines into the public purse, the raising of revenue is not even a secondary object of competition law—indeed, in advocating the imposition exclusively of sentences of imprisonment on cartelist businessmen, an official at Directorate General Competition has argued that otherwise there may be a suspicion that the competent authority is interested in raising revenue rather than in furthering the proper objects of competition authority.

[1] Case 155/79 *AM&S v Commission* [1982] ECR 1575.

4. The Landscape after the New Regulation Implementing Articles 81 and 82

Kirti Mehta*

ADVOCATE GENERAL FRANCIS JACOBS

So it really is, I think, a great tribute to the Institute that they've put together this programme, and it's a great pleasure for me to open the conference. It only remains to me to welcome our first speaker, who's going to deliver the keynote address, and that is Mr Kirti Mehta, Director for Competition Policy and Co-ordination, and for International Affairs and Relations with Other Institutions, at the Competition Directorate-General of the European Commission. I take pleasure in calling upon him.

KIRTI MEHTA

It's a great pleasure for me to come here, because I happen to be an alumnus of this university and I received my degrees here; so it's a very important occasion. Today, I would like to bring you up to date and share with you some thoughts on what the competition law landscape would look like after the adoption of the new regulation implemented in Articles 81 and 82. Over the last few years the Commission has initiated and implemented a number of reforms in the competition field, all with a view to better protecting competition. These reforms represent considerable challenges to enforcers and legal advisers alike; we all have to adapt to new rules and new ways of applying them, and in particular the modernisation of Regulation 17 will bring fundamental changes to the way in which anti-trust rules are enforced in the Community.

It's already useful now to get used to the fact that the new system will become reality in the not too distant future. We hope that the new system will be in place at the beginning of 2004, so that we can all adapt to the new landscape. I deliberately use the word *we* because the Commission itself will also need to adapt to the reform; in particular, we must embrace a new world based on cooperation and sharing of enforcement responsibilities. New tasks will replace old ones, but I am confident however that the Commission will be able to meet these challenges and maintain a leading

* Director for Competition Policy Coordination, International Affairs and Relations with other Institutions, DG Competition, European Commission. Keynote speech delivered at the Second Annual Conference on International and Comparative Competition Law, at BIICL, May 2002.

role in developing Community competition policy and in ensuring its consistent application.

As one looks ahead, one of the main areas of change will be the relationship between the enforcement authorities in the Community. It is a fundamental element of the Commission's proposal for reform that the national competition authorities and the Commission shall create a network within which they will cooperate closely in the enforcement of Articles 81 and 82. Thus we will move from a system in which each authority applies its own body of law without cooperating much with its colleagues to a system in which there is close cooperation in the application of the same rules. It is I think difficult to over-estimate the importance of this shift and its impact on competition law enforcement in the Community. Cooperation will not only enhance the protection of competition, it will also result in a more predictable enforcement system overall.

At first sight it might seem a contradiction in terms to say that decentralisation will lead to more predictability; the opposite could be the case if the Commission had proposed nothing more than to decentralise the application of the rules. However, I believe we have done much more than that—decentralisation will be accompanied by an infrastructure linking the competition authorities and will be subject to a number of important co-operation mechanisms.

Let us look at case allocation and the question of forum shopping, since the first question that the network must address is the allocation of cases. The basic idea is that each individual case should be dealt with by normally a single competition authority that is well placed to do so. The starting point will be a new notice setting out indicative allocation criteria, which will give guidance to complainers. Given that the purpose of any enforcement action is to bring an end to infringements, the competition authority acting in the case should be one that can effectively address the competition problem at hand. It would therefore seem appropriate to take as the starting point the area in which the agreement or practice is implemented, and where it has effects on consumers. If an agreement or practice is implemented in a single member state, the competition authority of that member state is well placed to deal with that; it is able to prohibit it, and where necessary impose fines.

The case should therefore normally be handled by that authority. The national competition authorities may also be able to deal effectively with agreements and practices that are implemented in two or three member states. When more Member States are involved, the Commission must be considered best placed to act. As soon as a member of the network has received a complaint or started a case on its own initiative, it will inform the Commission and the other authorities of the case. It will form the general elements of that case, for example the names of the company involved, the products concerned, the alleged infringement and the geographical scope.

Following this information, the other members of the network will have a certain indicative period to examine whether they consider themselves better placed to deal with the case; if not, the case will stay with the authority that notified the network unless the facts subsequently change substantially, and the others would abstain from acting. If on the other hand another competition authority claims the case, the authorities concerned will discuss the matter and try to come to a common position. If they fail, the Commission can always resolve the dispute by itself dealing with the case. The proposed regulation provides that when the Commission opens the proceedings in a case, the national competition authorities cease to be competent to deal with it. In this system, the scope for forum shopping is limited. If for example a complainant is facing a competition problem on the German market, it would normally not be successful to complain to the French authority, because the latter could not help him. And even if such a complaint were made, the network would ensure that the case be re-allocated to the authority best placed.

Once the case allocation process is over, the competition authority dealing with the case will carry out its investigation, possibly with assistance from other members of the network; it will then make its assessment and either reject the complaint or issue a statement of objections. In the first case, it will inform the other competition authorities of its decision to close the case. In the second case, the formal cooperation mechanisms contained in the Commission's proposal take effect. Accordingly, the members of the network will receive a copy of the draft decision or statement of objections, and each member will be entitled to make comments and may also call a meeting of the advisory committee to discuss the case.

Moreover, the Commission has the power, as it has today under the new Article 6 of the proposal, to withdraw a case from a national competition authority and deal with the case itself. In a system based on co-operation, this goes without saying, that the Commission will only apply its power in cases where the envisaged course of action gives rise to significant problems of inconsistency. For the purpose of ensuring consistent application, it is essential however that this safety mechanism exists. In the network envisaged, the application of law by each individual member will be of common concern.

When you combine this element with the fact that all members are enforcement authorities that have the same essential mission, the network will be able to develop relatively quickly a common enforcement culture. The very fact of applying the same substantiative rule will in itself make an important contribution to consistent application. This is particularly so, since under Article 3 of the Commission's proposal, national competition authorities, when dealing with agreements capable of affecting trade between member states, would not be able to deviate from the common competition law standard of Community competition law.

Let me now turn to another area that has given rise to quite a lot of debate, namely the application of Articles 81 and 82 by the national courts. In the new system, the national courts will have two separate functions: first, they will review the decisions of the national competition authorities or hear cases that they bring, and secondly, they will hear cases brought by private individuals invoking the direct effect of Articles 81 and 82. It is particularly this latter function that has given rise to debate—indeed, when the Commission first made its proposal, many voiced the opinion that national courts would not be able to apply Article 81.3, and that decentralisation would give rise to serious problems of inconsistency and would also lead to forum shopping and mass litigation. Let me first say that the Commission attaches great importance to private enforcement. We fully subscribe to the view expressed by the Court of Justice in the recent *Courage* judgment, to the effect that private enforcement is very important from the point of view of increasing the deterrent effect of the Community competition rules. In fact, the concern can be that even in the new system there will be too little private enforcement, rather than too much. Modernisation certainly takes an important step in the direction of unblocking private enforcement by abolishing the Commission's exemption monopoly, and by giving to the national courts the power to apply 81 and 82 as a whole.

Even so, it is not obvious that many more private actions will be launched. Outside the field of hard-core restrictions, it can be both difficult and costly to substantiate a claim that a certain agreement or practice has likely anti-competitive effects. Proving significant market power normally requires detailed market analysis, which is often open to dispute. It is therefore difficult to assess the likelihood of success, which may reduce the incentive to bring the case in the first place. It is of more concern that national rules on damages often make it difficult for companies that have suffered from anti-competitive conduct to obtain effective reparation. This is so even when there is a clear proof of violation itself. The *Courage* case was an extreme example of such difficulties, given that the national law simply precluded the party to an agreement from claiming damages from the other party.

However, even in the absence of such clear obstacles, difficulties persist. For example, the application of general rules on damages to competition cases means that the plaintiff has to prove the loss suffered to a very high standard. In particular, in certain systems the plaintiff must show that the loss has not been passed on to his clients. Also, in the absence of clients' actions, it is not realistic for final consumers to claim damages for their loss.

These issues, we think, need to be further examined in order to consider how to improve the possibilities for claiming damages in competition cases. As indicated by the Court of Justice, this is an important aspect of effective enforcement. This is not to say that we should introduce rules on treble damages and the like, but certainly the time has come to take a critical look at the rules on damages as they apply in the field of competition law.

Turning to the application of Article 81.3 by the national courts, it is often argued that courts would be incapable of applying Article 81.3. From a competition law point of view, there is nothing extraordinary about this provision; it is essentially one that allows for the weighing of pro-competitive effect, efficiencies and so on of an agreement against the anti-competitive effects found in Article 81.1. This is no different to the assessment required under the US Rule of Reason, which has been applied by courts for decades. Article 81.3 is not an industrial policy instrument that allows the body applying it to accept restrictive agreements in pursuit of a host of other general interest aims. It is a competition instrument that allows restrictive agreements to be accepted when they fulfil the four conditions. They must produce economic benefits that outweigh the anti-competitive effects. Consumers must obtain a fair share of the benefits, the restrictions of competition must be indispensable for the attainment of those benefits, and competition must not be eliminative. When these conditions are met, the agreement is covered by the exception.

There is no discretion in this respect, and I think this is important, since we sometimes see the argument that the word *may* in Article 81.3 signifies a measure of discretion. That is not the case; it simply means that a power has been granted by the treaty, which must be exercised when the conditions are met. Agreements that fulfil conditions are pro-competitive and cannot be prohibited. This does not mean that analysis under Article 81.3 is necessarily simple; I think this comes over clearly from the Commission's case practice. It can be complex; but so can the assessment of whether or not there is restriction of competition under 81.1. We are working in a complex field of law, the Commission is well aware of this and of the need and the responsibility we have to provide guidance on the application of Article 81.3.

The Commission will also have to play its part in assisting in the training of judges if they should so wish; training is important with a view to ensuring that Articles 81 and 82 are applied consistently in the common market. We will work closely with member states to ensure that training programmes are made available before the new regulation becomes applicable. We have also provided in the proposed regulation that the national courts can come directly to the Commission and ask it for information or for opinion. Moreover, the Commission has proposed that it and the national authorities should have the power to make Friends of Court submissions to the national courts. Such powers already exist in for example Germany, and they allow the enforcement authorities to provide useful input to courts' hearing cases that raise important competition law issues. Given the public interest nature of Articles 81 and 82, it is only natural that the enforcement authorities have a right to express their opinion.

Finally, when considering the issue of consistent application, it is important to keep in mind that the Court of Justice has helped in the *Master Foods* case, that when the Commissioners adopted a decision in a case it is binding on the national courts in the sense that if they want to deviate from it, they have to make a preliminary reference. This ruling ensures that conflicts between the decisions of the Commission and the national courts are solved by the Community courts. Consistency is my preserve. The issue of forum shopping before the national court is sometimes presented as a problem. However, we believe forum shopping is adequately addressed in the regulation on jurisdiction in civil and commercial matters that has replaced the Brussels Convention. Under this regulation, as was the case under the Brussels Convention, the parties to an agreement can agree on what should be the proper forum, and thus avoid any issue of forum shopping. Moreover, cases brought by third parties are covered by the rules on torts, which provide that the action must be initiated before the courts relevant for the place where the harmful event occurred. In competition cases, that would normally be the place where the anti-competitive conduct has been implemented.

Let me say one word about criminalisation, a development that is on the competition law agenda in several member states. That is, there is no inherent conflict between these developments and the reform of Regulation 17. There is one issue, however, that merits some attention. Experience has shown that when combined with effective sanctions, leniency programmes constitute a very important weapon against cartels. The Commission has just revised its leniency programme in order to improve its efficiency. In order to maintain the efficiency of the leniency programmes, it is very important that they extend also to criminal sanctions, otherwise they will create a formidable disincentive to coming in under these programmes. If by claiming leniency for their company, individuals would expose themselves to prison sanctions, leniency simply would not be claimed, and cartel enforcement would suffer.

Finally, Mr Chairman, ladies and gentlemen, a few words about the relationship between modernisation and, in particular decentralisation envisaged by the Commission and international convergence in the field of anti-trust enforcement. The modernisation of reform is not hostile to global convergence. Since all the competition authorities in the Community will focus on the enforcement of Community competition rules and will co-operate closely in the application of these rules, the reform will greatly promote the creation of the common competition culture in Europe. In turn, this common culture will form an excellent basis for achieving further global convergence. Thank you very much. (Here follows applause).

ADVOCATE GENERAL FRANCIS JACOBS

Well, thank you very much, Mr Mehta. You've not only given us an excellent kick-off to our proceedings this morning, and given us on the very topical subject of modernisation and decentralisation, I think some genuinely new information and some new ideas, and much to reflect upon; you've also provided some valuable input into the sessions of the conference that will be looking specifically at the role of the national courts and the role of the national authorities in the implementation and enforcement of Community competition law. Mr Mehta has also kindly agreed to answer one or two questions if you have them, so I think this is really a very good opportunity to put just one or two questions on the subjects that Mr Mehta has addressed.

KIRTI MEHTA

One of the reasons why in our Europe agreements we have already foreseen that the candidate countries would apply *acquis communautaire*, and so, in other words, many if not all of the candidate countries have both an anti-trust authority and a state aid authority. So we apply both the anti-trust rules and the existing rules, and so I think many of them already have an authority, an administrative structure, that laws are in place. And of course as we change our *acquis communautaire*, they also develop. Certainly we will have a situation where we will have twenty-five rather than fifteen or sixteen enforcers, and that is why the network must work in the way that we are proposing in order to ensure consistency.

MICHAEL POPODAKIS

On the leniency notice, already we have some of the first cases under the leniency notice, and I notice that the Commission has some difficulties even clarifying for themselves what and how to deal with the applications for immunity or reduction of fines. Is there something more that you can tell us about the approach of the Commission at this early stage of the application?

KIRTI MEHTA

Well, I think that the case you have in mind has raised some particular issues, and so as we go from the old system to the new leniency notice, which provides for the Commission to be lenient more often, in other words to go more in the direction and come closer to how the system operates in the US, perhaps in the first few cases we will have a transition. But I would not like to discuss, because this is very particular in that case.

MICHAEL HUTCHINGS

It may be a question for our conference chairman rather than for you, Mr Mehta, but I think some of us are rather concerned about the implications of all these changes for the workload of the Court of Justice, partly with the expansion of the Community, but also with the expansion of the workload, including the expansion caused by the case, I think the week before last, possibly increasing the right of companies to bring direct actions. So I'd be interested in your comments, but particularly by reference to the workload arising out of the increased competition work.

KIRTI MEHTA

Certainly I would agree with you that of course the reform is a number that will have a very important beneficial impact on the enforcement of competition, and so we must make available the necessary resources and changes when required. Certainly also for member states, as you can see in the national courts, there's always a big debate on how can they deal with this case if there are a lot of cases? That means developing a system, making specialised courts and so on; our proposal doesn't deal with all that because I think one cannot put too much in a proposal. But I certainly agree with you that these are issues of great importance for the success of the reform. Thank you.

5. Trade and Competition Law

Professor John Jackson*

Unlike everyone else on this panel, I am not an expert on competition policy, I am mostly involved with trade policy and other matters of international economic law, except that of course in today's world, I think as ably brought out by all the previous speakers, you cannot escape the implications of competition and private actions that may be barriers to trade and really undermine the trade system.

Now there's a long history in the GATT, and a history preceding the GATT, of discussion in the context of the international trade organisation that never came into effect, of attention to competition policy—a whole chapter in that latter-charter that never came into effect. But there's been a great deal of controversy in recent years, and I will try to reflect a little bit, not in my own view but by way of explanation, some of the US observations that I perceive; and indeed the US approach generally, in government and in business, has been opposed to international initiatives regarding competition policy.

Now for many years, for the last ten or fifteen years at least, during the time in which I've been in touch with this subject in that connection, part of the argument has been, in fact maybe the strongest argument has been, there's no need: we can do this in other ways, we can do it with bilateral cooperation agreements that tend to be beamed below the radar screen of opponents and tend to work very efficiently in the background and I think there's a lot of truth to that, there's really no need for something broader, and of course even through the Seattle ministerial fiasco the US and Europe were really at loggerheads on this issue. I think—and then there's another view, that the WTO is overloaded, that the WTO is being given too much in the way of competence, and it really ought to stick to its original knitting, namely trade and border measures, and so forth. Now the fact is, the WTO is only overloaded because the governments have been so stingy as to resources for the WTO as an organisation; and that's really something of a scandal to be discussed elsewhere. The WTO could have competence here, because it already has competence in many other measures that are not just border or just trade related; we're seeing enormous attention to environmental measures for instance, etc. So I think that argument falls.

* Georgetown University. Speech given at the First Annual Conference on International and Comparative Competition Law, BIICL, May 2001.

Secondly, I think the argument that there's no need for something at the international level has really atrophied in the last couple years; we've really begun to see, as indeed reflected by all the talks this morning, a very strong worry about the dysfunction of the competition policy system in the face of the integration and globalisation and a number of different facets that of course Mr Hutchings brought out in his talk. So I think we are now confronted with the institutional question: what can be done? And many people have expressed ideas. If we assume that there must be something at the international level, of course the next step is, where do you put it, and how do you frame it? I'm very intrigued with Commissioner Monti's explanation, particularly the participation of non-government elements in the idea. Could you do that in the GATT?

Is the GATT too overloaded? Well, the first thing we can say is, the GATT and the WTO already have a lot of competition policy in it; I and others have done inventories of the clauses of the Uruguay Round texts, the thousand pages of treaty text in particular, and it covers two pages. There is just clause after clause, many clauses in the new services agreement, certainly intellectual property measures relate to competition policy and so on; so those who say we have to keep the GATT/WTO door closed to competition policy are too late—it's there. So we might as well recognise that. In addition, of course, we have I think the very able process going on of the working party set up after Singapore, which of course is essentially a global form already, because it has no particular mission to come up with rules or what have you; it's a study process, it's a culturisation process. And speaking of culture, incidentally, part of the problem in the United States, which some people might attribute to a turf war between the anti-trust parts of the government and the trade parts of the government, part of that difficulty is a cultural difference. And the anti-trust officials really are quite worried about the nature and inclinations of the trade officials, because they think the trade officials are going about their tasks in a way that undermines competition.

And that draws attention to something that's been implied or expressed, particularly by Mr Bellis, my colleague here; really, we could use a scrub of the trade rules in terms of competition, a real intense look at the ways in which the trade rules really undermine competition themselves, even though the trade officials would tend to blame private enterprise competition problems as undermining the trade system. So there's undermining in both directions.

So, a couple of quick points. First of all, as I said, the WTO already has much on competition policy in it; and we have to think in those terms, we have to understand that in whatever else is set up. Secondly, there has been talk about using the WTO because of the dispute settlement system; the dispute settlement system has been much admired, the GATT system before it was much admired and that drew attraction of both the services' interests in the electoral property interest. However, I think a strong argument can be made that the dispute settlement system of the WTO is not a good system for competition policy, at least yet. For one thing, the WTO system really cannot handle factual intensive cases; we've seen that in the Kodak-Fuji case, we see it in a number of other circumstances. There really are not adequate procedures for detailed examination of facts, and many of your competition cases seem to be extremely fact-intensive and in fact offer quite a bit of high-level economic analysis; and a lot of that is also absent in the WTO system.

Secondly, a dispute settlement system like that of the WTO depends on relatively precise rules; now we lack those in many respects, and that's part of the struggle going on in the jurisprudence, but to take a system that seems to be based on very broad principles, particularly US statutory clauses are very broad, and there's been many decades of exegesis on those, to take a system new and put it in this new context with a very broad mandate, means that you are delegating two or three individuals on an appellate body, for instance, enormous powers. And particularly, from what I'm hearing even from this panel, there is an enormous amount of discretion, the dependence on personalities and so on, and that's not the kind of thing I think you want to put in the hands of a dispute settlement system. So if you do something at the WTO level, it probably would be wise to do it in a way that it would not use the existing dispute settlement system at all, or those measures; or you could set up a so-called peace clause, like as not in agriculture; you could say for the first five years or ten years or hundred years, they should not use this.

In addition, there's a principle in the WTO called 'non-violation cases' that focus on cases for which there's no treaty violation but there's nullification or impairment; that's tremendously imprecise. And that has—the intellectual property measures have largely been exempted, at least preliminarily, from that kind of strand of thought; and certainly one ought to do something similar for the competition policy. So, I don't know where I am; I don't really have a recommendation. I like the idea of a global forum. Why do you want to create something new, separate, when we have existing institutions that might shelter it? Well, one of the reasons why, particularly when you're looking at the WTO, is that the WTO right now is suffering from enormous deficits, so-called democratic legitimacy deficits, of lack of transparency, lack of relationship with the different constituencies.

This may mean that adding competition issues may be less fortunate. One may be against any opening up of further differences there. Therefore, it might be wise to go elsewhere, or to set up something independent, leaving open the question whether in some future time, when the WTO seems more capable of handling some of these, of merging the subject into the WTO, but that's simply a wild idea, I have no really strong feeling about it at the moment, and I think I'll finish with that. Thank you.

Discussion from the First Annual Competition Law Conference—Globalisation of Trading

DAVID VAUGHAN

What I'd like to say in my contribution, really very much following on from Professor Jackson, is that clearly, I can well see strong arguments for forming some sort of board approach, a very light-fingered, or is that light-touch, approach to forming general principles of competition law, which could be adhered to by the majority of countries in the world. I'm very much in favour of that, and I'm very much in favour that it should be a light-touch, broad-touch, non-enforceable basis.

However, what my little contribution is really geared to is trying to encourage a little more bravery on the procedural side; it seems to be that competition law can be catastrophic in its effects upon people, one side or the other, and there's a lot to be gained and a lot to be lost out of winning or losing a competition case. In the United States, your freedom—in other cases, massive fines or prohibition upon carrying on business in the way you have always done, always thought you were entitled to. But on the procedural side, it seems to me that there is much more, or could be much more, common ground; Article 6 of the Human Rights Convention, 'Fair Trial', all those provisions, are now regularly applied by the European Court indirectly but effectively, in competition cases. And it would seem to me that although on the substance, a broad-brush, light-touch approach would be appropriate, on procedural grounds it seems to me that one should be very much braver and try and achieve broad principles of fair trial in a competition case.

Competition cases are not the same as other cases; they are not the same as criminal cases or the ordinary cases in national courts. They require a different approach—a different approach to evidence, a different approach to fact, a different approach to access to documents, a different approach to confidentiality of documents. It seems to me that it's well possible to try and draw up some broad guidelines on what one would expect out of a country that applies competition law in terms of the right procedures that should be approved. It would also seem to me that this would be something quite interesting for the United States, whose companies tend to get involved in competition cases in other countries; they should have a vested interest in ensuring that their companies are protected by the type of rights of defence that they would regard as their right to have in their own country, and which one would expect to have in Europe. It seems to me that this would be worthwhile. So my contribution, really, is to approve a lighter touch on substance, but to try and encourage people to be a bit braver on procedures. Thank you.

BARRY HAWK

Thank you very much David. Now before opening up the questions, I want to thank our panellists. Clearly, there's a broad variety of issues, concerns, fora—to deal with this. Now my own thought is, I wonder—if we're ever going to advance beyond the underworld of acronyms, which is still where we are, someone referred to turf-fighting within the US between the anti-trust bar and the trade bar, I don't know if the term turf-fighting is appropriate, but there's certainly a lot of jockeying going on in connection with this global competition issue and forum, what have you, among all kinds of groups: government, non-group, what have you. You sort of get lost—maybe we should advance this and identify concrete problems, not issues, not intellectually interesting things, but problems, and then try to prioritise the problems and begin to deal with, or see how one could deal with, certain important problems. Your institution or organisation may be totally different. Cartel in forms—problems either to the public, public authorities or problems to private—cartel enforcement is mentioned. When you hear the list, the list is fairly short of all the problems or the sets. Cartel enforcement is mentioned, which I presume would be primarily a discovery rather than an enforcement problem, ie prove a cartel, okay?

The other is merger control. Now merger control is a whole set of issues—everything from how do you avoid conflicting, how to converge, blah blah blah, or the other extreme, which I think maybe is solvable, is jurisdiction, which is a serious problem. Now with all the merger control around the world, just one very simple, practical, maybe intellectually very uninteresting problem is simply formulating the test, the threshold test based on local effects, when you have to notify a transaction, and secondly the threshold in remedies, but remedies get more complicated, right—I'm sorry—definition of the concentration. You have your thresholds—what are the thresholds—and secondly, what is this thing you're suppose to notify, which most of the time is easy but frequently is not. Is there still a joint control, blah blah blah. The Argentinean restaurant that has to be notified in Brussels because the joint parents, etc. There's a huge amount of transactions that are captured by merger control around the world, and a tremendous waste of public resources, okay? That's probably a problem, naively, if you've got a dozen, six, I don't know, some very small number of merger enforcement officials and lawyers who do merger work for a long weekend—there's a high likelihood that they would arrive at a model law, I'm absolutely convinced of that.

Now the hard part of the address is, what do you do with this model? At that point I don't care—I mean, if the WTO can get everybody to implement this international legislation, that's fine, if it's simple, I don't know. But that is, and I'll stop, that is an example of I think a very important problem that is capable of a solution so far as a model goes—that's maybe not all of it, because how do you get this international legislation? That is the trick, okay—but I think it's a solvable problem, maybe enforcement again. How do you prove that a cartel lends itself to reasoned discussion? Well, without further ado I'll probably open it up—I'll be instructed as to how long we're permitted to go. First question?

SIMON HOLMES

Yes, Simon Holmes from SJ Berwin. I'm not sure whether it's a question or a comment, but I'd like to pick up on a point that Rory made, which I think poses a challenge for the co-ordination of the substantive analysis of competition issues; and that's when Rory referred to the rather *ad hoc* development of ideas and policies through cases. Or rather, putting it in a positive way, the fact that the policy and ideas tend to develop in real-life, concrete situations rather than just through abstract thinking. Of course, it's much easier for an international forum to discuss abstract ideas than to actually coordinate things in concrete cases. Perhaps that lends itself—perhaps it throws us out of the question, seems to me that there are two alternatives there. Either you have greater co-ordination in those concrete cases, to try and arrive at some sort of international consensus in actually dealing with that case, whether it's a monopoly case or a merger, case; or you're going to have to see some sort of restraint by an individual authority in relation to that particular case in coming to a solution, while the debate is then taken forward at an international level and gets developed with a degree of international consensus. I wonder if anyone would like to comment on that.

RORY CHISHOLM

Well, I think clearly the idea of an international body exchanging ideas is a good one. I think most people who have spoken so far today, including the Commissioner, have favoured that; and so I very much agree with the first part. In terms of restraint—I'm not sure that'll work. I think that competition authorities like to restrain companies, but they don't like to be restrained themselves; and I think it would be politically difficult to see either individual countries or indeed the European Union handing over ultimate control on particular matters to an international body.

What I do think is possible, as I hope I indicated in the speech, is that such a body might be able to have cases referred to it, look at them, and produce a judgment. Now there might be no ultimate sanction from that judgment—you wouldn't be fining a particular country or jurisdiction for having reached a decision that this international body disagreed with—but I think it would have a strong effect. Some people dismiss the European Court of Justice because it takes so long to get cases there, and that's certainly true for businesses that things are very slow, and by the time you bring your case your merger is long since dead. But having said that, I get the impression that officials in the Commission do take seriously the European Court, not so much because it will change anything directly, but because it looks bad if the Court produces a ruling saying that their work was not good enough and was not done on a proper basis. In the same way, I think, regulators around the world would be sensitive to the rulings of any international body, and that would be its major benefit in that regard.

BRIAN SHER

Brian Sher from Linklaters Alliance. My question to the panel is, doesn't a case like *GenCorp* illustrate the need for a world competition authority? If I can just elaborate why I think that's the case, what we had in *GenCorp* was a global market, a commodity market where prices were quoted on international exchanges—a very homogeneous product. The effects of the merger were clearly felt at a global level, and the demand for platinum was largely in the United States, Japan and Europe, with only I think about 20 per cent of world demand being in Europe at the time. And yet, the only authority that assessed the merger was in fact the European authority—the European Commission. It was not assessed by the Japanese or United States authorities; and we had the situation where the European Commission officials were spending a not inconsiderable amount of time analysing the details of the Japanese jewellery market because that was a large segment of world demand and their role was to examine world demand.

So what we had there was the European Commission assuming the role of world policeman—I don't know whether that was done as the result of a discussion behind the scenes between the United States and the European Commission, a decision that the European Commission would see the case—but perhaps largely due to jurisdictional rules, the European Commission, assumed the role of world policeman and analysing segments of demand in other parts of the world. My question is, isn't this a rather random state of affairs, and isn't it also a rather unsatisfactory state of affairs?

DAVID VAUGHAN

My comment on that is, I like your reference to the 'behind the scenes discussion'. I don't know—I think it would be interesting to know, but one hopes that there is developing sufficient cooperation and comity between the various enforcement agencies. so that where a case like this comes up, they do agree amongst themselves which is the most appropriate body to proceed. Because it will be many, many years before there is any sort of global enforcement body; and while that happens, you either have multiplicity of enquiries by the Japanese, European, American authorities or from anywhere else round the world, which just leads to confusion, or you say, you hand control of the particular case, in a merger case, certainly, to one body, and that body then has sole jurisdiction to review that transaction.

JOHN JACKSON

We have a number of authorities represented here—I'd love to just take a vote on how many authorities are willing to give up their jurisdiction of a merger case to anybody else, (laughter) whether it's the WTO, Miami Florence, some new body. No hands? That's—the first is to limit the number of merger cases being reviewed, and that's the first step, that would be a great advance right there—and I'm curious of Rory's point, you said that politicians are capricious and regulators are capricious. The members of your appeal tribunal will not be capricious, I assume—why not?

RORY CHISHOLM

They'll all be capricious, but if there's a number of them, I suppose it'll average out and we'll get a sensible verdict.

CHAPTER FOUR

Mergers and Remedies—Papers and Discussion from the First and Second Annual Competition Conferences

1. The Commission's Review of the Tests of 'Dominance' or 'Substantial Lessening of Competition'?

Enrique Gonzalez Diaz*

Unfortunately we are in the process of examining the substantial number of contributions that we have received following the publication of the green paper; we have received over one hundred contributions, substantial contributions, very important contributions that we are intending to summarise and publish, and some of them will be put on our web site. However, by the fact that we don't have a final conclusion as to whether or not there is an objective need for a change of the test from dominance to substantial lessening of competition, I think that what I could say in this very short period of time is that before the Commission comes to the conclusion that there is a need to change the test, we have to be fully convinced that the existing test, that is the test of dominance as interpreted by the Court of Justice in a significant number of judgments up to now, is not adapted to cover or encompass the type of competition law problems that we are normally confronted with in dealing with mergers on a day-to-day basis.

I think that in conducting this exercise, we will have to look at the different types of transactions that are regularly reviewed by the Commission in merger proceedings; and essentially we have to distinguish between non-horizontal and horizontal mergers. We believe at this stage that as far as non-horizontal mergers are concerned, the dominance test is sufficiently adequate to deal with the type of problems with which we are confronted in the light of this type of merger.

I think that the problem is more with regard to horizontal mergers, because in the context of horizontal mergers, we have essentially the economic theory of the single dominant firm that is well established, and I don't think that there is even a question of whether or not there is a need to modify the test to better capture the implications of single dominant situations. I think that a more problematic area is the area of mergers in oligopolistic markets, and that in the context of mergers in oligopolistic markets we have I think to distinguish situations leading to collusion. I think that in the field of collusion the case law of both the Commission and the Court of Justice and

* Head of Unit, Merger Task Force, DG Competition, European Commission. Summary given at the Second Annual Conference on International and Comparative Competition Law, BIICL, May 2002.

the Court of First Instance is quite clear, the Commission under Article 2 of the Merger Regulations can conduct an analysis based on the collusive effects stemming from a transaction. Consequently I think that from that point of view there is necessarily a need to modify the test to tackle this type of situation.

And then the other part of the discussion, which I think is the more problematic one, is whether the Commission can, under the test of dominance, deal with mergers leading to anti competitive effects in oligopolistic markets, but in the absence of collusion. I'm essentially referring to what economists call one-shot equilibrium models, in which essentially, as a result of the reaction of a number of players in the market, or as a result of the elimination of competition between close competitors, competing brands or other forms of differentiation, the effect of the transaction will be to reduce competition, even in the absence of collusion between companies. We are in the process, internally and with the assistance of highly reputable economies, of revealing the economic implications of these transactions; and at the same time we are examining the potential adaptability of our test of dominance to this type of anti-competitive effect.

It is I think only after we have conducted this reflection, both economically and legally, that we will be in a position to tell whether or not our test is well-adapted to a proper enforcement of merger control, particularly in the context of oligopolistic mergers. I think that in any event the judgment of the Court of First Instance on 6 June on the Airtours case may have a significant impact on our thinking—or it may not, obviously we will have to wait for that, and Commissioner Monti, following the adoption of the judgment, will no doubt make the proper announcement as to whether or not the implications of the judgment as to deserve a modification of the test.

2. Remedies and Merger Cases: New Developments

Simon Holmes and Sarah Turnbull*

I. INTRODUCTION[1]

Over recent years, the Commission's practice in accepting remedies in merger cases has evolved rapidly. This paper sets out the procedure in remedies cases, summarises the Commission's recent Notice on Remedies which provides guidance on the Commission's practice, and examines recent key developments in remedies.

While the notice sets out the underlying principles, it should be noted that the Commission's practice in the remedies areas is evolving very fast and that in order to deal with the issues on a case-by-case basis the Commission must retain a degree of flexibility. In addition, the sheer number of merger cases involving remedies is

* SJ Berwin. Paper given at the Second Annual Conference on International and Comparative Competition Law, BIICL, May 2002.

[1] The authors would like to thank Mattia Pelligrini of the Remedies Unit, Merger Task Force, European Commission for his comments on an earlier draft of this paper. Of course all views expressed herein and any errors remain the responsibility of the authors.

growing at such a fast pace that it is becoming increasingly difficult to keep abreast of developments in this area.[2]

A. *Influence of US Practice*

The Commission has drawn on the experiences of the US Federal Trade Commission in remedies cases to define and develop its policy in this area. Mario Monti acknowledged in a speech[3] that the Commission's Notice was influenced by the US Federal Trade Commission's 1999 report on the divestiture process.[4]

The FTC is conducting an ongoing study to examine the effectiveness of divestiture remedies in merger cases. The FTC's study systematically reviews how buyers of divested assets have fared and aims to investigate whether there are reasons why certain types of divestiture fail to remedy competition concerns post-merger. The Report is based on the study of divestments from the period 1990 to 1994 and draws conclusions from the results of those cases. The Report suggests a number of provisions to be included in divestiture orders in order to provide increased assurance that the divested assets will be viable and able to compete in the market.[5]

The Report found that divestitures had generally succeeded in creating viable competitors. However, it also found that buyers do not have access to sufficient information to make properly informed purchase decisions.[6] The FTC has therefore altered its practice in examining divestiture orders to seek to ensure an improved balance in the bargaining positions between the merging parties and the buyer of the divested assets. In particular, the FTC is increasingly using hold separate agreements (to ensure that the merging parties do not damage the business in the interim period prior to divestment), crown jewel provisions (where an alternative more wide-reaching divestment will be imposed if the parties' preferred remedy does not work), and an increased role for trustees to audit the divestment process.[7] The FTC has also imposed increasingly short divestiture periods (in recent cases within 3 to 6 months of the consent agreement). The FTC is also more frequently requiring upfront buyers to ensure that there is an acceptable buyer and to reduce the possibility of the divested business being damaged in the interim period. The 'upfront' or 'fix-it-first' remedy means that the

[2] 30th Annual Report on Competition, 2000 at para 269.

[3] 'The Commission notice on merger remedies—one year after'; CERNA, Paris, 18 Jan 2002, SPEECH/02/10.

[4] 'A study of the Commission's divestiture Process' Prepared by the Staff of the Bureau of Competition of the Federal Trade Commission, 1999 (the 'FTC Report').

[5] See pages iv and v of the FTC Report.

[6] FTC Report at 8.

[7] FTC Report at 38.

merging parties bear the risk and have an incentive to identify a suitable purchaser and divest as soon as possible.[8]

The FTC has recently initiated a 'Best Practices Analysis' for the Merger Review Process[9] and is holding a series of public workshops on the US merger review process generally and on remedies.

There is a growing recognition in the EU and the US of the importance of *effective* remedies. There is no point in the authorities committing time and resources to reviewing a merger if the resulting remedy is a sham. It is crucial that a commitment package designed to remedy specific competition concerns, will operate successfully in practice. The FTC's paper recognised several issues in merger cases and the Commission aims to learn from the FTC's comments as well as from its own experience. Several of the FTC's practices summarised above are now used by the Commission including the increased use of trustees, upfront buyers and crown jewel provisions. These developments are examined further below. The Commission's practice in remedies cases can be expected to continue to develop and evolve to ensure *effective* competition.

B. Procedure and Timing in Remedies Cases

In the 12 and a half years from 21 September 1990 to 31 March 2002, conditions were imposed on 57 mergers after phase II and 89 mergers were cleared with undertakings after an extended phase I. This is of a total of 1,904 final decisions (18 mergers, or less than 1 per cent were prohibited).

In 2001, conditions were imposed in 8.5 per cent of phase I decision and 50 per cent of phase II decisions (compared with 1991: 5.5 per cent of phase I decisions and 60 per cent of phase II decisions)[10].

1. Test for Commitments

Phase I

Article 6 (1a) of the EC Merger Regulation ('ECMR')[11] enables the Commission to clear a merger in phase I where the parties offer commitments so that the concentration 'does not raise serious doubts as to its

[8] FTC Report, Section III, 39–40 'Innovations in More Recent Orders' and 42 Conclusions.

[9] FTC Press release 15 Mar 2002 'FTC initiates 'Best Practices Analysis' for Merger Review Process'.

[10] <http://europa.eu.int/comm/competition/mergers/cases/stats.html>.

[11] Council Regulation 4064/89/EEC.

compatibility with the common market'.[12] Recital 8 of Council Regulation (EC) No 1310/97 notes that commitments can be accepted in phase I 'where the competition problem is readily identifiable and can be easily be remedied'. Remedies offered in phase I must be straightforward and clear-cut in order to comply with the 'serious doubts' test and to remove the need for the Commission to conduct a full investigation. As examined further below, the Commission in developing its practice in this area and has begun to accept increasingly complicated remedies in phase I, including behavioural remedies (see for example *Masterfoods/Royal Canin*).

Phase II

Article 8 (2) ECMR enables the Commission to accept commitments in phase II to resolve any competition issues raised by the merger.[13] Recital 8 of Council Regulation (EC) No 1310/97 states that commitments in phase II must be '*proportional to and would entirely eliminate the competition problem*'.

2. *Timing*

The current timing for commitments is set out at Article 18 of Regulation 447/98:

Phase I commitments must be made within 3 weeks of the date of notification (Article 18(1)).
Phase II commitments must be made within 3 months from the Commission initiating phase II proceedings (Article 18(2)).

After parties submit undertakings, the Commission will conduct a review of the undertakings including market testing with third parties and comments from the Member States. As highlighted in Recital 8 of Council Regulation (EC) No 1310/97 'Transparency and effective consultation of Member States and interested third parties should be ensured in both phases of the procedure'. It is therefore crucial to respect the deadlines or the Commission may reject any late undertakings as out of time. Late undertakings may be a major factor leading to deals being blocked.

3. *Offering commitments late—the importance of market testing*

The importance of the time limits was highlighted by the Commission in the

[12] Art 6 (1b) ECMR.

[13] The test for remedies in phase II is that the concentration 'does not create or strengthen a dominant position as a result of which effective competition would be significantly impeded in the common market or in a substantial part of it' (Art 8(2) and Art 2(2) ECMR).

recent prohibition decision *Schneider/Legrand*.[14] The Commission warned in its press release announcing the prohibition:[15]

> Despite the scale and seriousness of the problems posed by the merger, Schneider Electric did not put forward in good time adequate undertakings to ensure that, following the merger, the conditions of effective competition would be restored [...]

After the expiry of the deadline for offering undertakings: 'the Commission could not accept any "last minute" undertakings unless it was able to establish immediately, without any possible doubt, that they would restore the conditions of competition'(emphasis added).[16]

In phase II, the deadline can be extended in 'exceptional circumstances', but this will only be possible where late undertakings are clear-cut and do not require further market testing. Exceptional circumstances were found in *Telia/Telenor*. The Commission accepted undertakings offered by the parties just outside the deadline in phase II due to the fact that the parties had to consult with the Swedish and Norwegian Parliaments before undertakings could be formally submitted. The package submitted was also sufficiently clear-cut for the Commission to be able to properly assess it. The Commission had already market tested the undertaking in phase I and noted that 'the fact that third parties had already submitted comments on a possible LLU [local loop unbundling] undertaking in phase one together with the clear-cut character of the proposed undertakings has enabled the Commission's services to conduct a full and proper assessment of the modified proposal, including adequate consultation with Member States and third parties'.[17]

In *Anglo American Corporation/Lonrho*[18] the Commission accepted revised undertakings offered outside the deadline in phase II due to 'exceptional circumstances'. In this case AAC had already submitted undertakings within the time period which were not acceptable but had then reconsidered and offered an acceptable undertaking within one week of the meeting of the Advisory Committee. The Advisory Committee had discussed and agreed a decision which contained the same terms as the

[14] *Schneider/Legrand*, Commission Press Release 'Commission prohibits acquisition of control of Legrand by Schneider Electric' IP/01/1393, 10 Oct 2001.

[15] Commission Press Release 'Commission prohibits acquisition of control of Legrand by Schneider Electric' IP/01/1393, 10 Oct 2001.

[16] In *TotalFina/Elf Aquitaine*, 9 Feb 2000 and Case COMP/M.1693 *Alcoa/Reynolds* 3 May 2000 the Commission accepted remedies offered after the deadline where it was satisfied that the commitments were extensive enough to remove all competition concerns and did not require further market testing (see para 130 *Alcoa/Reynolds*).

[17] Case COMP/M.1439 *Telia/Telenor*, 13 Oct 1990 at para 380.

[18] Case IV/M.754 *Anglo American Corporation/Lonrho* 23 Apr 1997.

revised undertaking.[19] The Commission therefore allowed AAC to give an undertaking on the same terms as those considered by the Advisory Committee. Member States and third parties had also had a reasonable time to submit comments on the revised undertakings.[20]

In contrast in *Volvo/Scania*,[21] the package of commitments submitted late was complex procedurally and would have required further market testing and consultation by the Commission.[22] The Commission noted 'procedural complexities inherently, and in particular when submitted at a late stage in the procedure, increase the difficulty in assessing the proposal's potential effects from a substantive viewpoint'.[23] Therefore, the new proposal did not remove all identified competition concerns in 'an obvious and clear-cut way'.[24] Similarly in *Airtours/First Choice*[25] the Commission refused commitments submitted late, arguing that there were no exceptional circumstances and that the package was unclear and required market testing.

Another recent example of modified remedies offered late which the Commission then did not have sufficient time to resubmit to a further market test is the *GE/Honeywell*[26] case. In that case, GE proposed a number of undertakings on the legal deadline for remedies (14 June 2001). These were considered by the Commission to be insufficient to resolve the vertical and conglomerate competition issues raised by the merger. Market testing also indicated that the assets which GE offered for divestment would not be a viable stand-alone business. The behavioural commitments offered were also considered to be extremely difficult to be effectively implemented by the Commission. GE then offered a further set of remedies two weeks after the deadline for remedies (28 June 2001). The Commission blocked the merger, rejecting these remedies. Not only were the revised remedies proposed at a very late stage in the procedure, the Commission also found them to be insufficient to deal with the competition issues and there remained concerns about effective enforcement of the remedies. The Commission was unable at that stage to conduct a further market test and

[19] The concentration had already been implemented and the draft decision of the Advisory Committee included measures under Art 8(4) ECMR.

[20] Case IV/M.754 *Anglo American Corporation/Lonrho* 23 Apr 1997 at para 125.

[21] Case COMP/M.1672 *Volvo/Scania*, 14 Mar 2000.

[22] The last date for commitments was 21 Feb 2000 and Volvo's new proposal was made on 7 Mar 2000 and the Commission noted 'there was nothing in the new proposal which Volvo could not have included in an undertaking submitted within the three-month time limit' (Case COMP/M.1672 *Volvo/Scania*, 14 Mar 2000 at paragraph 359).

[23] Case COMP/M.1672 *Volvo/Scania*, 14 Mar 2000 at para 360.

[24] Case COMP/M.1672 *Volvo/Scania*, 14 Mar 2000 at para 361

[25] Case No IV/M.1524 Airtours/First Choice 22 Sept 1999 at para 193.

[26] *General Electric/Honeywell*, 3 Jul 2001.

the revised remedies did not resolve the competition concerns in a clear and straightforward manner.[27]

The Commission's reluctance to accept remedies late is due in part to the continued importance of 'market testing' with third parties (customers, suppliers and competitors) in the Commission's assessment. In contrast with the procedure in the US, market testing plays an important and key role in the Commission's investigation of mergers.

The Commission's reliance on market testing has important implications for timing and also has given rise to criticism that the Commission relies too heavily on the views of competitors who are likely to have their own agendas (for example, purchasing assets in any divestment package, or trying to prevent their rivals from expanding in the market). The criticism is generally unfounded as it ignores the fact that the merging parties also have *their* own commercial agenda—getting their deal cleared! In the authors' experience, acting in equal measure for either the merging parties or third parties, the Commission receives information and arguments from all 'sides' and reviews it critically. If both the merging parties and third parties each feel the Commission is on the 'other side', then perhaps the Commission has struck a fair and 'neutral' balance!

In practice, the Commission shows considerable pragmatism in deciding whether to accept undertakings late. This was very evident in the *Alcoa Reynolds*[28] case where (out of time) the parties eventually offered essentially everything the Commission sought. Some Member States (eg Germany) objected that the parties' proposed commitments should be rejected as out of time.[29] Pragmatically, the Commission (supported by the UK) took the view that this was not the occasion to stand on the formal timing point (as the Commission got what it wanted) and the case-team worked hard to win round a majority of the Member States to their point of view.

Despite this pragmatism, submitting undertakings late in phase I is a major factor in cases going to phase II and submitting undertakings late in phase II is a major factor in deals being blocked. Note that, of the cases mentioned above, *Schneider/LeGrand*, *Volvo/Scania*, *Airtours/First Choice*, and

[27] See 'General Electric/Honeywell—An insight into the Commission's investigation and decision' Dimitri Giotakos, Laurent Petit, Gaelle Garnier and Peter De Luyck, Directorate General Competition, Directorate B, Competition Policy Newsletter, Number 3, Oct 2001, 5-13.

[28] Case COMP/M.1693 *Alcoa/Reynolds* 3 May 2000.

[29] The view of these Member States was that the parties should be required to withdraw their notification and re-file with the proposed remedies. Not only would this have delayed clearance of the deal by 5 or 6 weeks, it is not a practice which the Commission wants to encourage.

GE/Honeywell were all blocked after undertakings were offered late. One can, of course, argue that they would have been blocked anyway but the time at which undertakings are offered is undeniably a key factor.

C. *The Commission Notice on Remedies 21 December 2000*[30] *('The Notice')*

After 10 years of experience enforcing the Merger Regulation and the increasing number of conditional merger clearances with increasingly complex issues raised, the Commission set out details of its practice in accepting remedies under the Merger Regulation for the first time in a Notice adopted in December 2000. This Notice aimed 'to provide the business and legal communities with guidance and predictability on merger control policy in the European Union' and built on the Commission's experience in applying the ECMR. The Notice drew on the US FTC's experiences in remedies cases and was subject to a wide consultation exercise. Mario Monti stated 'This notice will, I hope, give companies the necessary and timely answers to the competition concerns. If and when this happens, the Commission will be happy to let deals sail through'.[31]

The Notice focuses on:

General principles for proposal and implementation of remedies;

Overview of main types of remedies accepted in merger cases to date;

Specific requirements for submission of remedies in phase I and in phase II; and

Major elements for implementing divestiture commitments.

The prime concern of the Commission is that 'Remedies must be clear-cut and entirely remove our competition concerns'.[32] Secondly, the Commission is keen that remedies can be implemented effectively and within a short period. The preference of the Commission is for structural remedies rather than behavioural commitments that require monitoring by

[30] Commission Notice on remedies acceptable under Council Regulation (EEC) No 4064/89 and under Commission Regulation (EC) No 447/98, 2001/C 68/03, adopted on 21 Dec 2000. Comments on the Notice include Andrea De Matteis 'The Commission develops its policy on merger cases: The New Notice on Remedies and its recent application' International Antitrust Bulletin, Fall/Winter 2001, 21 and Niels Christian Ersboll 'Commitments under the Merger Regulation' [2001]ECLR 357.

[31] IP/00/1525, 21 Dec 2000, 'Notice on merger remedies: how and when to cure dominance problems'.

[32] Speech by Mario Monti 'The Commission notice on merger remedies—one year after'; CERNA, Paris, 18 Jan 2002, SPEECH/02/10. See also Court of First Instance's judgment in Case T-102/96 *Gencor ltd v Commission*, [1999] ECR II-753, paras 313–30.

the Commission.[33] The preferred remedy is for a viable stand-alone businesses which ensure that 'competition is restored to the market either by the emergence of a new independent competitive entity or by the strengthening of an existing competitor'.[34]

It is for the parties to demonstrate clearly to the Commission that 'the remedy restores conditions of effective competition in the common market on a permanent basis'.[35] The parties must 'remove any uncertainties' about the type, scale and scope of the remedy and the likelihood of its successful, full and timely implementation by the parties; taking into account the structure and particular characteristics of the market in which the competition concerns arise including the position of the parties and other players on the market.[36]

II. RECENT DEVELOPMENTS

A. Enforcement Unit

In order to further develop consistent treatment and best practices in remedies, in April 2001 the Commission created an Enforcement Unit in DG Competition responsible for advising on the acceptability and implementation of remedies in merger cases.[37] The Unit holds regular meetings to discuss and compare experiences and developments in remedies cases to ensure consistency and best practice. Members of the Unit join the case-team on a merger case where remedies are being discussed with the role of providing guidance and ensuring consistency. A member of the Unit may be involved from the beginning of the notification or in pre-notification discussions (the enforcement team are all members of the MTF and continue to be involved in merger notifications irrespective of whether the case raises remedies issues). Alternatively, if the case-team does not include a member of the Enforcement Unit and remedies issues are raised, then an Enforcement Unit member will be 'parachuted' into the case-team.

33 At paras 9, 10 and 13 of the Notice. At Footnote 10 of the Notice—'Only in exceptional circumstances will the Commission consider commitments which need further monitoring: Commission Decision 97/816/EC (IV/M.877—Boeing/McDonnell Douglas; OJ L 336, 8.12.1997, 16)'.

34 Speech by Mario Monti, 'The Commission notice on merger remedies—one year after'; CERNA, Paris, 18 Jan 2002, SPEECH/02/10. See also the Notice at paras 9, 13, 14, 17 and 18. In 2001, 7 of the 13 cases cleared in phase I involved the divestment of a business and 1 the divestment of landing slots. In phase II, divestment of a business was the most frequently accepted remedy.

35 At para 6 of the Notice. See also paras 31 and 32 and n 38.

36 At para 7 of the Notice.

37 See further Speech by Mario Monti 'The Commission notice on merger remedies—one year after'; CERNA, Paris, 18 Jan 2002, SPEECH/02/10.

The influence of the team is becoming increasingly important particularly given the increasing complexity of remedies. The enforcement team has doubled in size since April 2001 (from 4 to 8 A Grade officials). As noted by Monti there is an 'absolute need for the partners in a merger which involves clear competition problems to give thought, at a very early stage in the project, to possible remedies and to enter into discussion without delay with the competition authorities'.[38]

The Enforcement Unit, headed by Wolfgang Mederer is currently developing best practice guidelines on remedies taking into account the experience of other national competition authorities in the EU and in the US and other countries. The Unit is also finalising a model for commitments and model texts for trustees' mandates. These guidelines and models will be published for third party comments shortly.

The draft model commitment is for a divestment of a business and deals with the parties obligations relating to the following key issues:

The Divested Business including: definition of the Divested Business; transfer of personnel (including appropriate incentive schemes to ensure key personnel remain with the Divested Business); customer list; Hold-separate obligations including duties of a Hold Separate Manager in order to assist in preserving the viability, marketability and competitiveness of the Divested Business until closing; ring-fencing of confidential business secrets of the Divested Business; non-compete clause for the specified customer list for a limited period (usually two years but will vary according to the nature of the business); non-solicitation clause; transitional arrangements for Divested Business to benefit from services from the merging parties;

The Divestment Procedure including: the First Divestment Period (usually 3 to 6 months) where the parties must find a suitable purchaser and enter a binding sale and purchase agreement (conditional on the Commission's approval); the Extended Divestment Period (usually 3 to 6 months) where, if the parties have not found a purchaser, the Divestment Trustee is given an irrevocable and exclusive mandate to sell the Divested Business at no minimum price (including a negative price); reporting obligations on the parties to keep the Commission and Trustee informed on a monthly basis on developments in divestment negotiations, on the data room documentation, the information memorandum (the Commission must give its prior approval to the information memorandum), and of the list of potential buyers who express an interest;

[38] Commission Press Release 'Commission prohibits acquisition of control of Legrand by Schneider Electric' IP/01/1393, 10 Oct 2001.

The Purchaser including: the purchaser standards (see further below at section 4), requirement to seek prior approval of the Commission of the Purchaser and the sale and purchase agreement;

Trustees including: appointment procedure with prior approval by the Commission; functions of the Monitoring and Divestment Trustees (see further below) and duties of the parties to keep the Trustees informed and to provide assistance (including providing offices on the parties' premises, managerial and administrative support, access to sites and financial support for corporate finance or legal advice);

The Review clause under which the Commission may allow extensions of the time period for divestment, changes to the Divested Business at a Purchaser's request, or modification or waiving the conditions and obligations in the commitments (in exceptional circumstances).

B. Role of Trustees

The Commission is increasingly requiring the parties to appoint Monitoring Trustees and Divestiture Trustees. Trustees will be appointed only subject to the Commission's approval and will usually be an investment bank, management consultant, accounting company or similar institution.[39] The Trustee's duties will be set out in a mandate approved by the Commission. As noted above, the Commission's Enforcement Unit is currently drafting a suggested standard model mandate to be used for Trustees, which will be published for comments shortly. The model mandate sets out the obligations of the Trustee in the divestment process and in monitoring compliance of the parties with the commitments. The Trustee will be subject to a variety of reporting obligations to the Commission on the divestment process including detailed monthly reports on actions taken and planned, meetings attended, any non-compliance of the parties, review of the divestiture process and of potential purchasers and its estimated timetable. The mandate also includes provisions relating to conflict of interests, remuneration, confidentiality, indemnity for Trustees and for termination of the mandate.

Trustees must be independent of the parties and in principle must not have any conflict of interests. The remuneration package must not affect the Trustee's independence and must not provide for a success premium linked to the final sale value of the Divested Business. The Commission will examine the links between the merging parties and proposed Trustees. In particular, it will look at the amount and nature of the work a Trustee has done/is

[39] Notice at para 55.

doing for the parties. In practice, the Commission seems to take a reasonably practical and flexible approach to this. Thus, while the Commission accepts that there are likely to be some such connections, it will be particularly careful to ensure that the relevant group/department within the Trustee has no conflicts of any sort.[40] Despite this, the Trustee's position is somewhat anomalous, or even schizophrenic. It is formally appointed and paid by the parties but it is required to accept instructions from the Commission and report to the Commission about the parties' behaviour and is forbidden to accept instructions from the parties. The Trustee may appoint its own legal or financial advisers (paid for by the parties) but there is a tendency for Trustees to look to the parties' advisers for guidance.

1. *Monitoring Trustee*

A Monitoring Trustee will monitor the parties' compliance with their commitments to keep the divestment businesses separate from the business to be retained. The hold-separate commitments are designed to maintain the independence, economic viability, marketability and competitiveness of the business.[41] The Monitoring Trustee's mandate deals with the task of supervising all measures to maintain the competitiveness of the business to be divested. This can be increasingly complex and involve daily input by the Monitoring trustee.[42]

2. *Divestiture Trustee*

A Divestiture Trustee[43] will oversee the implementation of the divestiture commitments, including supervision and reporting on the parties' efforts to find a suitable purchaser within a set period. The Divestiture Trustee will ensure that potential purchasers receive relevant information on the Divested Business through access to the data room documentation, the information memorandum and the due diligence process. The Divestiture Trustee will review whether potential purchasers are acceptable and will

[40] The current draft of the Commission's model Trustee mandate includes provisions prohibiting the Trustee during the mandate from taking any assignments which might lead to a conflict of interest with the merging parties, related undertakings, potential purchasers or competitors of the Divested Business without prior approval of the Commission. The draft model also requires the Trustee not to engage in any services to the parties or related undertakings without first obtaining the Commission's prior approval for a period of two years following termination of the mandate.

[41] Notice at paras 50–2.

[42] See for example Case COMP/M.2268 *Pernod Ricard/Diageo/Seagram Spirits,* 8 May 2001, which included a complex fire-wall structure for the parties managing brands to be divested in the interim period.

[43] Notice at paras 53–4.

report to the Commission on proposed purchasers and on the sale and purchase agreement. Where the parties do not find a purchaser within this initial set period (usually 3 to 6 months), the divestiture trustee will then be given an exclusive irrevocable mandate to dispose of the business within a specific deadline (usually a further 3 to 6 months) at any price (including a negative price), subject to the Commission's prior approval.

Rather than separate trustees, the Commission may appoint a single trustee to monitor the compliance of the parties with the hold-separate undertakings, the divestment undertakings and any behavioural undertakings. For example, in the recent clearance of *Masterfoods/Royal Canin*,[44] the parties committed to appointing a Monitoring Trustee responsible for monitoring all of the parties' obligations under the undertaking (which included various hold-separate, divestment and behavioural commitments).

C. *Increasingly Complex Sets of Remedies Including Behavioural Remedies*

Although the majority of remedies accepted by the Commission are in accordance with the principle that simple, straightforward divestments are the preferred solution, the Commission is ready to accept more complex packages when they provide an appropriate competitive solution.[45]

As noted above, conditional clearances are becoming increasingly complex with the Commission accepting more and more complex commitment packages including both structural and behavioural remedies.[46] Despite the Commission's stated preference for clear-cut divestments as a remedy, it continues to accept behavioural undertakings in suitable cases, whether as a supplement to a divestment package or where a divestment will not solve the competition issues raised by the proposed transaction.[47] Examples of behavioural undertakings are more common in new technology industries, air transport, media, telecoms and energy industries where access to networks or other facilities is necessary to ensure continuing competition. Access to necessary infrastructure or key technology has therefore been required as a remedy rather than divestment in several cases.[48]

[44] Case No COMP/M.2544 *Masterfoods/Royal Canin*, 15 Feb 2002.

[45] Speech by Mario Monti 'The Commission notice on merger remedies—one year after'; CERNA, Paris, 18 Jan 2002, SPEECH/02/10.

[46] The Commission's acceptance of behavioural remedies is not new, see for example Case COMP/M.877 *Boeing/McDonnell Douglas*, 30 Jul 1997.

[47] See paras 27 and 28 of the Notice.

[48] Access for competitors to Universal's films in Case COMP/M.2050 *Vivendi/Canal+/Seagram* 13 Oct 2000, access to roaming tariffs and wholesale services in Case M.1795 *Vodafone Airtouch/Mannesmann* 12 Apr 2000 and access to conditional access system and Kirch's pay TV services in JV.37 *BSkyB/Kirch Pay TV* 21 Mar 2000.

In considering remedies packages, it is important to bear in mind that the Commission is constrained by the tight timetable both in phase I and phase II that cannot easily be extended. This is in contrast to the significantly longer and more flexible deadlines in the US. The clear timetable is a great benefit of the EU system but may mean in certain very difficult cases that the Commission is forced to require a relatively simple clear-cut remedy where the other competition authorities such as the US authorities will have a longer period to evaluate more complex solutions.[49]

In phase I, remedies '*can only be accepted in certain types of situation. The competition problems need to be so straightforward and the remedies so clear-cut that it is not necessary to enter into an in-depth investigation*'[50] (emphasis added).

Despite this statement of principle, the Commission has accepted increasingly complex and innovative sets of remedies both in phase I as well as following in-depth phase II investigations. For example in *Nestle/Ralston*[51] the Commission cleared a merger in the pet food industry in phase I, with a complex licensing and rebranding package including an upfront buyer requirement combined with a 'crown jewel' remedy (see further below). In the recent Commission decision also in the pet food sector, *Masterfoods/Royal Canin*, the Commission cleared the merger in phase I subject to the divestment of a combination of assets (including an exclusive licence of certain brands for a limited period of time, requiring the purchaser to rebrand) consisting of a variety of brands from Masterfoods and from Royal Canin. The merger raised competition issues in France and Germany, but to make the divestment package viable, and to include a sufficient quality spectrum and offer critical mass, the package of brands to be divested is for the whole of the EU.

Further, the Commission also imposed certain behavioural restrictions on Masterfoods to ensure that a sufficiently strong purchaser will be able to integrate the assets into its own brand strategy and develop them (see further below on upfront buyer requirement). The behavioural commitment should also prevent Masterfoods raising barriers to entry.

The Commission has been accused of demanding remedies, which go further then is necessary to solve the competition issues raised and therefore using the merger clearance regime as 'industrial restructuring' or in order to liberalise markets. For example in *EdF/EnBW*,[52] EdF gave an undertaking to provide competitors with access to generation capacity located in France.

[49] For example Case COMP/M.1671 *Dow/Union Carbide*, 3 May 2000.
[50] Footnote 11 of the Notice.
[51] Case COMP/M.2337 *Nestle/Ralston Purina*, 27 Jul 2001.
[52] EdF/EnBW Commission press release 7 Feb 2001 IP/01/175.

In *Grupo Villar Mir/EnBW/Hidroelectrica del Cantabrico*[53] the Commission required EdF to substantially increase the commercial capacity of the Spanish French interconnector to 4000 MW to facilitate increased imports of electricity into Spain to remedy the existing collective dominant position on the Spanish wholesale electricity market which would have been strengthened by the merger.[54] Similarly, in the Commission's recent clearance of the acquisition of joint control of Hidroelectrica del Cantabrico by EnBW, EDP and Cajastur, the Commission cleared the deal subject to undertakings from EDF and EDF/RTE that they will increase the commercial capacity on the interconnector which delivers electricity across the Pyrenean chain from an existing 1,100 MW to around 4,000 MW.[55]

The Commission may require divestments beyond the affected product or geographic markets in order to ensure a viable divestment package which removes 'serious doubts'[56] and, in particular, in order to approve a clear-cut remedy in phase I. It is pertinent to note Götz Drauz's (Director of the Merger Task Force) comment in relation to *Unilever/Bestfoods*, 'Maybe they had to give away slightly more than they would have done had we gone to phase II but they got a good quick solution'.[57]

The importance of timing to the deal as a whole is a clear consideration for parties in offering remedies in *phase* I. If it is crucial to complete the acquisition in a short time period, and a phase I clearance is needed, the parties may have to consider offering a more wide-ranging divestment package to ensure that any 'serious doubts' are removed to avoid a full phase II investigation.[58] In other cases, avoiding a phase II investigation may be less important—perhaps because the US clearance is not expected for several

[53] *Grupo Villar Mir/EnBW/Hidroelectrica del Cantabrico* Commission press release 26 Sept 2001 IP/01/1320.

[54] On the suggestion that the Commission may be using merger control to assist in the liberalisation of markets, see Andrew Renshaw 'EC Merger Control: 2001 An overview of the main developments', November 2001 IBC's 8th Annual EC Competition Law Conference. See also the *Post Office/TNT Post Group/SPP*, Commission Press Release of 13 Mar 2001 IP/01/364.

[55] Case M.2684 *EnBW/EDP/Cajastur/Hidrocantabrico*, 19 Mar 2002.

[56] See Notice at para 17. Examples include Case IV/M.913 *Siemens/Elektrowatt* 1999, Case COMP/M.1578 *Sanitec/Sphinx* 2000, Case COMP/M1802 *Unilever/Amora Maille* 8 Mar 2000, Case COMP/M.1990 *Unilever/Bestfoods*, 28 Sept 2000. See also Case COMP/M.2277 *Degussa/Laporte*, 12 Mar 2001 Commission Press Release IP/01/352 where the divestment package included three manufacturing plants including products which did not raise competition concerns, as this was necessary to create a viable package to create an effective competitor.

[57] Rossella Brambilla 'Getting tougher: the Merger Task Force 10 years on', Global Counsel December/January 2000/01, 29–36 at 36.

[58] An example of this may be the *Rhône-Poulenc/Hoechst* merger where the parties agreed (inter alia) to divest certain agro-chemical products in phase 1. One can only speculate, but the parties might have been able to avoid this had they been prepared to submit to a full phase 2 investigation.

months. In these circumstances, the parties may be reluctant to offer up too much in phase I and be prepared to defend the merger without any commitments and/or offer of a smaller commitment in phase II. In other words, there can be a trade-off between the commercially optimum deal and the timing considerations: 'pay more now, or less later'. In addition, the development of the upfront buyer and crown jewel remedies (both of which were used in the phase I clearance of *Nestle/Ralston Purina)* have enabled the Commission to shift risk on to the parties—if the parties are sure that their proposed package is viable and will attract a suitable competitor, then they can take the risk (see further below).

Despite the increasingly complexity of remedies, it is important to bear in mind the key principle stated by Monti on several occasions—the solution cannot be more complex than the problem than the problem it is trying to solve.[59]

D. *Commission Will Reject Unsuitable Buyers*

As part of the Commission's approval of a divestment remedy, the Commission will require that the divestment package be transferred to a 'suitable buyer' within a specific deadline.[60] Generally, any purchaser will be subject to the prior approval of the Commission. The Commission will generally take around two to three weeks to approve a purchaser. This period may be longer where the Commission needs to market test the proposed purchaser. Parties will usually have informal discussions with the Commission on a range of buyers before submitting a final buyer to the Commission for formal approval. The Monitoring Trustee will also comment on the viability of any proposed buyer.

The Commission has set out a series of general '*Purchaser standards*' in its Notice:

> The purchaser is normally required to be a viable existing or potential competitor, independent of and unconnected to the parties, possessing the financial resources,[61] proven expertise and having the incentive to maintain and develop the divested business as an active competitive force in competition with the parties. In addition, the acquisition of the business by a particular proposed purchaser must neither be likely to create new competition problems nor give rise to a risk that the implementation of the commitment will be delayed.[62]

[59] Mario Monti 'The main challenges for a new decade of EC Merger Control', EC Merger Control 10th Anniversary Conference, Brussels 14-15 Sept 2000.

[60] Commission's Notice on remedies at para 19.

[61] Footnote 49 of the Commission's Notice states that the Commission does not accept seller-financed divestitures because of the impact this has on the divested company's independence.

[62] Commission's Notice on remedies at para 49.

The Commission may also impose further requirements on the purchaser specific to the business in question. For example, the purchaser in the *Masterfoods/Royal Canin* deal must have experience of *branded* (ie not just own label) petfood and relevant R&D facilities.

Where the viability of the divestment package is largely dependent on specific characteristics and the identity of the buyer, the Commission will require an 'upfront buyer' commitment (see further below).

The Commission has formally rejected the buyer originally proposed by the parties for the first time in the *TotalFina/Elf*[63] case. In this case the Commission cleared the merger conditional on the divestiture of around 70 petrol stations in France. In September 2000, the Commission rejected TotalFina's first proposed buyers because it believed that the proposal included buyers who did not have an incentive to bring sufficient competitive pressure on the merged company in the market for French motorway petrol sales. One of these proposed buyers has launched an appeal in the Court of First Instance.[64] TotalFina proposed a further set of buyers which was accepted by the Commission in May 2001.[65]

The Commission has become increasingly rigorous in vetting buyers of divestments. The Commission will now wish to see and approve a draft information memorandum prepared for the sale of the business to be divested and a list of potential buyers expressing an interest. It will then insist on seeing and approving the proposed buyer's business plan to ensure that the buyer intends to integrate the divestment package into its business and to operate as a viable competitor. In the US, to meet this concern, commitments have included a requirement for the merging parties to include a clause in the sale agreement for the divestment package for the buyer not to dispose of the divestment assets for a period of ten years. The Commission will also examine the sale agreement to verify that it complies with the commitments.

E. Upfront Buyer

The Commission has taken inspiration from the US practice of 'fix-it-first' remedies whereby in the US the parties must find a suitable purchaser for their proposed divestment package and sign a purchase agreement before

[63] Case COMP/M.1628 *TotalFina/Elf Aquitaine*, 9 Feb 2000.

[64] Petrolessence and SG2R operating jointly as Mirabellier appealed against the Commission's refusal to the CFI. Agip also appealed to the CFI but was then accepted in the second list of buyers proposed to the Commission and therefore dropped its case on 15 Feb 2001.

[65] Commission Press Release IP/00/1260 'Commission approves buyers for 70 motorway service stations belonging to TotalFina Elf', 7 Nov 2000.

gaining *approval* for their transaction. The Commission imposed an 'upfront buyer' commitment for the first time in December 2000.[66] This commitment required the parties to enter a binding contract to purchase the divestment package with a third party agreed by the Commission before the deal *closes*. The upfront buyer commitment is slightly different from the US style 'fix-it-first' in that the parties do not have to find a suitable purchaser and sign a sale agreement prior to gaining *clearance* for their acquisition, instead they must find a suitable purchaser and sign a sale agreement (in each case, approved by the Commission) before *closing* the transaction.

There is a clear preference in the US for fix-it-first style remedies that assist in ensuring that remedies are effective. The comparable EU 'upfront buyer' commitment is still fairly exceptional with only 4 examples to date (see further below). Upfront buyer remedies enable the Commission to shift the risk to the merging parties where it is unclear whether a divestment package will work (this may follow concerns raised by third parties in market testing as to the viability of the package or the existence of suitable buyers).

The Commission states at Paragraph 20 of the Notice that

> There are cases where the viability of the divestiture package depends, in view of the assets being part of the business, to a large extent on the identity of the purchaser. In such circumstance, the Commission will not clear the merger unless the parties undertake not to complete the notified operation before having entered into a binding agreement with a purchaser for the divested business (known as the 'upfront buyer') approved by the Commission.[67]

The four clearance decisions to date where the Commission has required an upfront buyer illustrate the types of situation where the Commission may require an upfront buyer:

1. *Where the Commission is concerned that the divested business may be weakened pre-sale*

In *Bosch/Rexroth* the Commission was concerned to ensure that the buyer was a strong competitor. Without a strong competitor, the Commission was concerned that Bosch would very quickly re-establish its position in the market. This was particularly because of Bosch's strong (and continuing) relations with the customers of the businesses to be divested and the possibility of persuading those customers to switch from the specific type of product being sold by the business being divested (radial piston pumps) to the specific type of product being retained by Bosch (axial piston pumps).

[66] Case COMP/M.2060 *Bosch/Rexroth*, 13 Dec 2000.
[67] Ibid.

2. Where the divestment package is not 'stand-alone' but is a combination of assets from the two parties merging and therefore it is difficult to assess the viability and attractiveness of the package

In *Masterfoods/Royal Canin*,[68] the divestment package accepted by the Commission included a combination of various brands from Masterfoods and from Royal Canin together with a Masterfoods' production plant. The Commission has required an upfront buyer before the deal can close. The upfront buyer requirement was imposed due to the difficulty of assessing the viability and attractiveness of the divestment package which is not stand-alone and the need to ensure that a sufficiently strong buyer can integrate the assets into its own brand strategy[69] (see further points 3 and 4 below).

3. Where the Commission is not convinced that the divestiture proposed will attract a buyer

In *Nestle/Ralston Purina*[70] the parties proposed the divestment in Spain of an exclusive licence in Spain for the Friskies family of brands and the Vital Balance brand (owned by Nestle) together with a factory. Any purchaser would have to rebrand after the exclusive licence. The Commission combined a requirement for an upfront buyer for the parties' preferred divestment with an alternative remedy if the parties did not complete the sale of their preferred divestment before closing the notified transaction—the so-called 'crown jewel' provision (see further section 6. below).

There was also some doubt, following market testing, whether the package proposed in the *Masterfoods/Royal Canin* deal would attract a buyer meeting the purchase conditions (see point 4 below).

4. Where the success of the remedy depends to a large extent on the identity of the proposed buyer

In *Masterfoods/Royal Canin* the Commission noted from the results of market testing with both competitors and customers that the transferability and viability of the divestiture package depended to a large extent on the identity of the purchaser[71]. The proposed buyer would need to have sufficient financial resources, R&D capabilities and a proven expertise in the branded pet food market. This was particularly due to the fact that the

[68] Case COMP/M.2544 *Masterfoods/Royal Canin,*15 Feb 2002.
[69] Ibid.
[70] Case COMP/M.2337 *Nestle/Ralston Purina*, 27 Jul 2001 at paras 67–9.
[71] Case COMP/M.2544 *Masterfoods/Royal Canin,* 15 Feb 2002 at paras 100–2.

divestment package included various assets from both Mars and Royal Canin located in several Member States. At the time of the clearance decision it was far from certain that a buyer would be found which (a) meets the stringent purchase conditions and (b) is willing to buy the whole package—or at least buy it at a price at which Mars is prepared to sell it. This illustrates the way in which an 'up-front buyer' remedy transfers the risk of a failed remedy to the merging parties.

In *The Post Office/TPG/SPPL*[72] the parties proposed an upfront buyer for TPG's Dutch subsidiary, TNT IM Netherlands, in order to create a viable competitor to the parties in the Netherlands for the provision of outbound cross-border mail services in the Netherlands. The success of the remedy depended to a large extent on specific characteristics of the purchaser.[73]

In this case, it was important to ensure that the purchaser would be able to run the divested business as a viable independent competitor after the transitional period (2 years when the purchaser would have access to TPG's network and know-how). It was therefore crucial that any purchaser was able to establish its own network for the upstream and downstream services temporarily provided by TPG. The purchaser would also have to be able to generate the necessary amount of mail volume that would enable it to purchase network services and which would enable it to sell its services at competitive prices globally. It was important that the purchaser could continue to offer mail distribution at as competitive prices globally as TNT IM Netherlands was able to prior to the merger. This would ensure that the purchaser did not lose its customer base and viability. Contracts for mail distribution are not long term and are not exclusive and customers can and will switch to service providers offering the best price/service package.

The Commission also imposed a particularly *short* divestiture deadline (three and a half months) for the parties to find an upfront buyer meeting these various conditions and for the Commission to approve the buyer, failing which the conditional clearance would not stand.[74]

In some cases, an up-front buyer requirement may be used as an alternative to a phase II investigation. In effect, the Commission says to the parties—unless you now agree to take the risk of finding a really effective buyer for your proposed divestment package (before closing the deal), we will have to take a more detailed look at the proposed merger in an in-depth phase II investigation.[75]

[72] Case COMP/M.1915, *The Post Office/TPG/SPPL*, 13 Mar 2001.
[73] Ibid, at paras 153–5.
[74] Ibid, at para 161.
[75] This appears to have been what happened in *Masterfoods/Royal Canin* (see above).

Furthermore, once the parties agree to the up-front buyer route, it puts them under a great degree of pressure. First, they cannot close the deal until they have had both the purchaser and the sale and purchase agreement approved by the Commission. Secondly, in practice, the Commission appears to insist that the parties select a single buyer of the Divestment Package for the Commission's final approval. Given the time constraints, this puts considerable pressure on the parties to only agree terms with a potential buyer that has a very good chance of meeting the Commission's purchaser standards.

F. *Alternative Divestiture Commitments—'Crown Jewel' Remedies*[76]

The Notice foresees the possibility, inspired by US practice, for the parties to have a period of time to attempt to divest their preferred divestiture package to a suitable buyer approved by the Commission, but failing that the Commission will require an equal or more extensive ('crown jewel') divestment. This will be used where the Commission is uncertain of the likelihood of a successful divestment, eg due to third party pre-emption rights or uncertainty surrounding the transferability of key contracts, intellectual property rights or employees.[77]

There have only been two cases to date where a 'crown jewel' remedy has been used: *Industri Kapital/Dyno*;[78] and *Nestle/Ralston Purina.*[79] The first case where the crown jewel remedy was used was *Industri Kapital/Dyno* where the Commission cleared the merger in phase II subject to several commitments. One of the commitments was to divest the formaldehyde and resin plant of Dyno in Kitee, Finland. If the parties did not divest this within a specified time period, Industri Kapital would then have to divest an alternative 'crown jewel' formaldehyde and resin plant of Neste (a company controlled by Industri Kapital) in Hamina, Finland. Industri Kapital, in fact, sold the Kitee plant[80] within the time period (ie the fall back on the 'crown jewel' alternative did not come into effect).

In *Nestle/Ralston Purina*, the Commission used the 'crown jewel' remedy to require the parties to divest a 'crown jewel' business (their non-preferred

[76] See paras 22 and 23 of the Notice and Monti's speech 'The Commission notice on merger remedies—one year after'; CERNA, Paris, 18 Jan 2002, SPEECH/02/10.

[77] The Commission accepted alternative commitments in cases prior to the Notice: Case IV/M.1453 *AXA/GRE*, 8 Apr 1999. See also Case COMP/M.1439 *Telia/Telenor*, 13 Oct 1999 and Case IV/M.1383 *Exxon/Mobil*, 29 Sept 1999.

[78] Case COMP/M.1813 *Industri Kapital/(Nordkem)/Dyno* 12 Jul 2000.

[79] Case COMP/M.2337 *Nestle/Ralston Purina*, 27 Jul 2001.

[80] This plant was sold to Ruetgers subsidiary Bakelite in Nov 2000 (see European Chemical News, Volume 73, No 1932).

divestment[81] which was a larger and more easily saleable package) if they did not sign a binding sale agreement for their preferred divestiture[82] by the time they closed the notified transaction. This was the first time that the 'crown jewel' remedy was combined with an upfront buyer and the first time that the 'crown jewel' was the package actually divested by the parties.

G. Proposals for Reform—The Green Paper[83]

1. Stop the Clock

The Commission's Green Paper on the Merger Regulation proposes to introduce a 'stop the clock' provision in phase I and phase II providing an additional 20–30 days in the timetable to allow further discussion and market testing which will operate only at the parties request.[84] This will consist of:

an additional 10 to 15 days for the parties to find 'an appropriate solution'; and

a further 10 to 15 days for the Commission to conduct market testing of the 'solution' and prepare a draft decision for the Advisory Committee.

The Commission will have a discretion in Phase I to refuse a request to stop the clock.

It is, at present, unclear exactly how this would work in practice and in particular whether parties will need specific justifications in order to stop the clock.

Nevertheless, the Commission is to some extent, restricted by the short time frame set out in the Merger Regulation and the proposed 'stop-the-clock' provision should allow the Commission and the parties extra time which may be needed in complex cases. The advantage of fixed and certain deadlines in the EU, has to be weighed against the fact that this may sometimes result in more extensive or more simplistic remedies in order to resolve the competition problems raised within the EU deadlines. This is to be compared with the situation in the US where flexible timing for Second Request investigations enables the competition authorities to construct

[81] The 'crown jewel' divestment was the 50 per cent shareholding of Ralston Purina in the Spanish joint venture with Agrolimen SA (Gallina Blanca Purina JV).

[82] The preferred option was the divestiture of Nestle's family brand of Friskies pet food products and Vital Balance in Spain by an exclusive licence of the brands and a restriction on the merged entity using the brands for an additional period (overall nearly 8 years).

[83] Green Paper on the Review of Council Regulation (EEC) No 4064/89, COM(2001) 745/6 final, 11 Dec 2001.

[84] At Section F, paras 203–21.

more complex remedies but means that parties are uncertain as to the likely timing for a clearance decision. Specified periods for each of phase I and phase II, combined with a 'stop the clock' option for the parties, is potentially a welcome compromise between European rigidity and US uncertainty. It is to be hoped, however, that this option is not overused: if it is busines', demand for timely clearances will be undermined.

2. *Commission to make 'suggestions' for remedies*

The Commission is seeking comments on the proposal that the 'Commission should take a more active role in identifying the measures that it deems necessary in order not to oppose a notified concentration': ie that it should make a 'suggestion' for remedies.[85]

This would meet concerns raised that it is sometimes difficult for the parties to anticipate the remedies required by the Commission at early stages in the transaction. The Commission suggests discussion of remedies by the parties at the earliest possible opportunity. A key criticism here is that parties may be forced to offer remedies at a stage where the Commission has not made its competition concerns clear. Goran Grosskopf, Chairman of the Tetra Laval Group and Henri Lachmann, Chairman and CEO of Schneider Electric SA, both of whom have had mergers prohibited by the Commission, have stated in response to Monti's suggestion that parties discuss remedies with the Commission at a very early stage in the project that: 'this presupposes clear objectives and a transparent merger process in which the Commission's concerns are conveyed early on, enabling parties to understand what remedies may be required'.[86] Karel Van Miert (the previous Commissioner for Competition) responded in defence of the European Merger process that 'the procedure set out in the European Union's merger control law is one of the most transparent in the world [...] The Commission not only makes its decisions public. It also details its concerns to the parties several times during the procedure. The parties can then reply both in writing and orally'.[87]

In practice, where legal advisers have good relations with the Commission, and are sensitive to the indications given, the parties should understand the Commission's concerns at an early stage in the notification process. This means that in some cases, following careful dialogue with the Commission, a remedies package may in fact be largely agreed during pre-notification discussions enabling the Commission to approve even complicated remedies

[85] At Section F, para 221.

[86] 'Think again, Mario' The Financial Times, 6 Dec 2001.

[87] Karel van Miert's letter to the Financial Times 'Carry on, Mario: EU merger policy is the envy of the EU', 11 Dec 2001.

packages within phase I. With a member of the Enforcement Unit on the case-team, this should further assist the parties and their legal advisers to understand what may be required and therefore to construct satisfactory remedies at an early stage. The Enforcement Unit's best practice guidelines on remedies and model texts for commitments and trustees' mandates should assist parties in drafting remedies. Further, the Commission is at present considering publishing guidelines on its practice in approving merger cases.[88]

III. CONCLUSION

The key aim of competition authorities in merger cases is to ensure that remedies packages enable *effective* competition to remain or be restored to the market following a merger. The Commission has rapidly developed its practice in this area, drawing on the US FTC's experiences. Transparency has improved following the publication of the Commission's Notice in 2001. The area of remedies can be expected to continue to develop rapidly with the Commission examining increasingly complex mergers and building on its experience. The Enforcement Unit will assist this process and ensure consistency in the Commission's practice. The model standard commitment and trustees mandates soon to be published for comment by the Enforcement Unit will also assist parties in structuring suitable remedies. The use of up-front buyer packages and crown-jewel provisions is a useful development in enabling the Commission to shift some of the risk of a remedy to the parties to ensure that a suitable buyer can be found or that the package is a viable stand-alone business. The stop-the-clock proposals in the Green Paper should enable the Commission to maintain the certainty of the Merger Regulation's time-table whilst providing some additional flexibility in timing to investigate remedies in complex cases.

[88] See press article James Kanter of Dow Jones Newswires: '*EU's Monti to clarify Merger Rules—Seen within next year*' 4 Apr 2002.

3. *GE/Honeywell* and *Tetra/Sidel*: Complements, Substitutes, and Theories of Exclusion in EC Merger Control

Derek Ridyard*

This paper discusses two key merger control cases of 2001, involving *GE/Honeywell* and Tetra Laval/Sidel (*Tetra/Sidel*).[1] Both deals were blocked over concerns that the post-merger firm would, by exerting leverage across two or more separate product markets, exclude rivals and thereby create or strengthen a dominant position. We consider the economic concepts behind these 'new' economic theories of exclusionary effects and how those concepts were applied in the two cases.

I. *GE/HONEYWELL*—EXCLUSIONARY EFFECTS THROUGH A COMBINATION OF COMPLEMENTS

The facts of the *GE/Honeywell* case are complex and cannot be fully appraised in a short review article. However, the essence of the theory against the merger lies in the fact that it brought together a series of businesses that were *complements* in the economic sense of the term. For example, GE's aero engines and Honeywell's aircraft avionics systems are complements since an aircraft manufacturer would need to buy both engines and avionics in order to build a new aircraft.[2]

Complements are defined in economic theory by their *negative cross-price elasticity*. If the price of aero engines were increased unilaterally, that would make it less commercially attractive to make new aircraft, which in turn would reduce demand for avionics systems. Thus, an increase in the price of engines would reduce demand for avionics systems.

This is the opposite of the situation that typically arises in horizontal merger cases, where *substitute* products are brought together under common ownership. The relationship between two competing aero engine suppliers, for example, is one of substitutes, defined by a *positive cross-price elasticity*. If GE raised the prices of its engines unilaterally, that would

* NERA. Paper given at the Second Annual Conference on International and Comparative Competition Law, BIICL, May 2002.

1 *General Electric/Honeywell*, Case COMP/M.2220 (2001), and *Tetra Laval/Sidel*, Case COMP/M.2416 (2001).

2 There were a number of complementarities between GE and Honeywell, including those between engines and starters, and lease finance and avionics. There were also some straight horizontal overlaps.

cause some customers to choose Rolls-Royce aero engines instead, thus increasing demand for Rolls-Royce engines. The possible harmful effects of a merger between two competing producers can be understood in the context of these cross-price effects. In a merger that brings together important substitutes, the firm in question can benefit from the fact that an increase in the price of one brand will raise demand for the other. In this way the positive cross-price elasticity between the merging products relaxes the pre-merger incentive to keep prices low.

Applying the same logic to a merger between suppliers of complementary products such as GE/Honeywell, we ought to predict a post-merger reduction in prices, since by reducing price for one product, the post-merger firm could boost demand for the other product that is now under common ownership. Whereas pre-merger GE obtained no benefit from boosting Honeywell's sales of avionics, post-merger that effect would be of benefit to the enlarged GE group. In an industry such as commercial aerospace, where incremental sales carry high price-cost margins, this could (under certain conditions) give a significant incentive for post-merger price reductions.

This likelihood of post-merger price reductions is fully acknowledged by the Commission in the *GE/Honeywell* decision, but, controversially, it is interpreted as an argument against the merger using the following chain of predictions:

First, because of the complementary relationship of the merging firms' products, the post-merger firm would, as predicted by economic theory, tend to reduce prices post-merger. Indeed, in order to get the maximum benefit from the negative cross-price elasticity between the complements, the offer of post-merger price reductions would have been made conditional on the customer buying a package of GE's engine and Honeywell's avionics—ie it would take the form of a discount on the 'bundle' of GE/Honeywell products.

Second, rival suppliers of engines and avionics would find it unattractive or impractical to respond (eg through merging or forming selling consortia) by offering their own competing 'bundle'.

Third, the result of the above would be for rivals of the post-merger firm to lose sales volumes to the more aggressive bundled prices of GE/Honeywell. This loss of rivals' sales volumes would result in their being unable to finance and sustain investment in new product development, which would over time cause them to exit the market, or at least to become less vibrant players.

Fourth, as a result of the above chain of events, the merger would ultimately have the effect of strengthening GE's dominant position in the supply of aero engines, allowing it to raise price and harm customer interests.

This chain of events represents the steps necessary under the *GE/Honeywell* case in order for the combination of complementary products to result in an anti-competitive, exclusionary effect. The chain of events is speculative, but it cannot be ruled out on *a priori* grounds, and a number of recent articles in the economic literature give some legitimacy to the theory.[3] The Decision does at least have the merit of spelling out the theory of the case with more clarity than in some of the previous portfolio power and leverage cases.[4]

The *GE/Honeywell* decision has attracted numerous commentaries. Some have questioned whether the Commission is right even to consider advancing a case based on the premise that the post-merger firm will reduce prices, but most have accepted some variant on the framework laid out above and focused their attention on whether the specific facts of the commercial aerospace industry can really support this set of post-merger predictions.

II. *TETRA/SIDEL*—EXCLUSIONARY EFFECTS THROUGH A COMBINATION OF SUBSTITUTES

The *Tetra/Sidel* case shares some features with the *GE/Honeywell* decision. It also resulted in a merger being prohibited despite the fact that most of the businesses of the merging firms lay in separate product markets, and on the grounds that bundling and related post-merger practices would result in the 'leveraging' of market power from one market to another.

The key difference between the two cases is that, whilst *GE/Honeywell* is essentially a merger in which the parties' businesses were complements, in *Tetra/Sidel* the parties' respective main businesses were selling products that were substitutes for one another. Tetra, as is well documented, is the dominant player in the carton packaging market, whilst Sidel is the leading player in the provision of equipment used to make PET bottles.[5] The two Article 82 cases in which Tetra has been involved have concluded that competition for Tetra's carton business from PET bottles is not strong enough to provide a constraint on Tetra's carton market dominance, but at the margin there is undoubtedly some degree of substitution between these types of packaging. If Tetra were to increase its prices for cartons and

[3] See, for example, Choi and Yi, 'Vertical Foreclosure with the Choice of Input Specifications', in *Rand Journal of Economics*, Vol. 31, No. 4, pp 717-743, and Nalebuff, 'Competing Against Bundles', in *Incentives, Organization, and Public Economics*, Oxford University Press (2000).

[4] See Coca-Cola/Amalgamated Beverages, Case IV/M.794 (1997), and Guinness/Grand Metropolitan, Case IV/M.939 (1998).

[5] The Decision puts Tetra's share of carton packaging systems at around 65 per cent. Sidel, meanwhile, is described as the leader in PET packaging systems, but not as enjoying a dominant position.

carton packaging machinery, that would be good news for suppliers of PET bottle machines such as Sidel, since at the margin this would tip the balance of choice for some customers away from cartons and towards PET.

In the *Tetra/Sidel* decision, the Commission argued that the merger would create a dominant position in the PET packaging market because Tetra/Sidel would find ways to leverage Tetra's carton packaging monopoly onto the PET packaging market. According to para 359 (e) of the decision, this would be achieved by some combination of discounts for customers buying a 'bundle' of Tetra and Sidel products, along with 'rebates' and 'price wars' designed to harm Sidel's PET rivals and thus make them less viable competitors.

However, since the main packaging products sold by Tetra and Sidel are substitutes, not complements, it is worth questioning how and why this merger was supposed to change behaviour. In the *complements* case of *GE/Honeywell*, the post-merger incentive to compete more vigorously on price is (at least in theory) well established. But by the same token the combination of Tetra and Sidel's *competing* businesses ought to weaken the incentive to compete on price. Pre-merger, Sidel already has an incentive to try to 'dominate' the PET packaging market and, subject to the constraints posed by competition rules, might contemplate doing so by aggressive rebates and sales techniques designed to squeeze rival PET suppliers from the market. But following the logic of the GE/Honeywell decision the merger with Tetra ought to reduce that incentive since efforts to drive prices down in the PET packaging market would now have the additional effect (not previously taken into account by the independent Sidel) of increasing the competitive pressure on Tetra's cartons business.

If in *GE/Honeywell* we are asked to believe that the combination of *complements* will make GE and Honeywell compete more aggressively on price, by the same logic it must be predicted that the combination of *substitutes* in *Tetra/Sidel* would encourage the post-merger firm to compete less aggressively on price post-merger as the parties came to recognise the spill-over effects caused by their competing behaviour in each others' markets. Thus, the Commission's theory of exclusionary effect in the *Tetra/Sidel* case lacks the basic merger-related motivation that is present in the *GE/Honeywell* case. For this reason its exclusionary effects story is inherently less convincing.[6]

In other respects, however, the *Tetra/Sidel* decision has more to commend

[6] There are theoretical models of monopoly leveraging and predation that can apply to products that are not complements, but the Commission did not specify any such models in the Tetra/Sidel decision.

it. Almost hidden, later in the decision, is a further theory about the strengthening of Tetra's dominant position in carton packaging systems which does relate the merger appraisal to the fact that the deal brought together suppliers of substitute products.

Recall that two Article 82 cases have concluded that Tetra enjoys a dominant position in carton packaging.[7] In economic terms, this means that competition between rival carton packaging suppliers has been found not to impose an effective constraint on Tetra. In such circumstances, it is well established in economic theory that the profit-seeking monopolist will raise price until the next closest competitive constraint starts to bind. Thus, when dealing with pre-existing dominance in a merger case it becomes critically important to identify and understand what constitutes the next closest substitute outside the dominated market.

The Commission decision paints a plausible account of how it is PET packaging that provides this next closest constraint.[8] Consequently, the combination of Tetra's dominant carton packaging business with Sidel's leading position as a PET packaging supplier gives a conventional horizontal concern with the Tetra/Sidel merger. The oddity is that this horizontal concern has been buried deep in the decision because of the Commission's efforts to develop a leverage effects theory of the case. Yet the aspect that makes the leverage argument unconvincing—the fact that the two parties supply competing not complementary products—is the very factor that gives weight to the horizontal concern.

III. IMPLICATIONS AND CONCLUSIONS

The exclusionary effects theories advanced in the *GE/Honeywell* and *Tetra/Sidel* cases make an interesting basis for comparison. In *GE/Honeywell*, the Commission has adopted a theory of the case that relies on a long chain of possible post-merger events, but in which the theory of post-merger harm to competition is based on some potentially legitimate (if very theoretical) models of imperfect competition. The main controversy of the *GE/Honeywell* decision surrounds the facts of the industry, and in particular whether the somewhat speculative predictions on which the exclusionary effects story are based really could be sustained with sufficient certainty to justify the prohibition.

In *Tetra/Sidel*, the Commission has again tried to develop a story of post-merger exclusion through bundling, but has built that story on shaky

[7] This proposition appears to have been accepted by Tetra in the course of the merger proceedings.

[8] See paras 392–400 of the decision.

foundations. Whereas in GE/Honeywell the complementary nature of the parties' businesses gives a prediction of post-merger price reductions that sets in motion a chain of events that could eventually harm competition, in *Tetra/Sidel* that basic starting point is missing. Applying the logic used in the Commission's GE/Honeywell story, the Tetra/Sidel merger should have made life easier, not harder, for rival PET packaging suppliers. The paradox of the *Tetra/Sidel* decision is that the Commission appears to have been so intent on developing its exclusionary effects theory that it has almost overlooked a conventional horizontal effect—the danger that Tetra's dominant position in carton packaging would be strengthened if it bought out the most potent rival in the adjacent *but competing* PET packaging sector.

Taken together, the two cases raise a number of concerns with the Commission's ability to apply new economic theories of exclusionary effects in a sufficiently critical manner. The *Tetra/Sidel* decision in particular shows the Commission favouring an exclusionary effects theory that does not seem well supported, even when there exists a conventional horizontal overlap that potentially raises genuine concern. Neither decision makes life easier for firms and their advisers in trying to predict which direction the Commission will take next.

Clearly, exclusionary effects theories are now a part of the regulatory landscape for European mergers, and observers of European competition law will appreciate that exclusionary effects concerns seem to receive a more sympathetic hearing in Brussels than in other jurisdictions. However, as the range of theoretical models of possible exclusionary effects grows, the obligation on the Commission to spell out its theory carefully, and to test that theory critically against the facts, becomes more important than ever.

4. Allocation of Jurisdiction in European and National Merger Control—The Multiple Filing Issue Revisited

Dr Cornelis Canenbley*

I. INTRODUCTION

- Clear-cut allocation of jurisdiction between the Commission and Member States authorities is of crucial importance to merging companies;
- mergers are time-sensitive and any delay or uncertainty in establishing which authority has jurisdiction can be highly detrimental;
- jurisdiction debate is, therefore, one of the key issues raised by the Green Paper;
- current regime has not achieved its objective of conferring Commission competence over those cases which—as far as their substance is concerned—have a Community dimension. If there were reliable and predictable criteria for the definition of the relevant geographic market in each individual case, the best yardstick for the delimitation between national and European merger control would be, whether a merger affects markets broader than a national market or a national market which is in the process of opening up to a European market (eg due to liberalisation of a regulated industry, such as telecom, energy, etc.);
- multiple filings give rise to a number of difficulties in terms of length of process, costs and legal certainty for entities involved;
- Commission, therefore, proposes to introduce automatic Community competence over cases subject to multiple filing requirements in three or more national jurisdictions.

II. THE CURRENT DIVISION OF COMPETENCE

A. *Article 1 of the ECMR—Concentrations with a Community Dimension*

The EC Merger Regulation ('ECMR') is based on the 'one-stop shop principle'. Under this principle, embodied in Article 21 of the ECMR, once a

* Freshfields Bruckhaus Deringer, Brussels. Paper given at the Second Annual Conference on International and Comparative Competition Law, BIICL, May 2002.

transaction has triggered the application of the EMCR, the national authorities of the Member States are generally precluded from applying their national merger legislation to the transaction. If the transaction has a Community dimension, filing with the Commission is mandatory. The two exceptions (which in reality are rather fine-tuning than exceptions) to the one-stop shop principle are set out in Articles 9 and 21 (3) of the ECMR.

1. *Jurisdictional Test under Article 1 (2) of the ECMR*

- ECMR applies only to 'concentrations with a Community dimension', regardless of whether the parties are domiciled within the Community and whether or not the transaction is to be implemented within the Community.
- The test for the existence of a 'Community dimension' triggering the duty to file the transaction with the Commission is designed to ensure that only large-scale acquisitions, mergers and joint ventures which significantly affect trade within the Community are caught.
- The concept depends on the respective turnovers of the undertakings concerned only, regardless of whether the effects of the transaction will be felt within the Community. (Controversial issue not to be dealt with in this paper is the question of whether international law requires a separate test of 'effect' if the turnover thresholds are met. Most common scenario: establishment of a joint venture in third countries with no or minor sales into the EEA, where the parent companies meet the turnover thresholds of the ECMR.)
- Under Article 1 (2) of the ECMR, a concentration has a Community dimension where certain thresholds are met:
  - the aggregate worldwide turnover of the parties exceeds €5 billion; *and*
  - the Community-wide turnover of each of at least two parties exceeds €250 million; *unless*
  - each of the parties achieves more than two-thirds of its aggregate Community-wide turnover in one and the same.

2. *Article 1 (3) of the ECMR*

Since March 1, 1998, the ECMR also applies to smaller concentrations which have a significant impact in at least three Member States, if:

- the aggregate worldwide turnover of the parties exceeds €2.5 billion; *and*

- the Community-wide turnover of each of at least two parties exceeds €100 million; *and*
- in each of at least three Member States, the aggregate turnover of all the parties exceeds €100 million; *and*
- in each of the three Member States mentioned above, the turnover of each of at least two parties exceeds €25 million; *unless*
- each of the parties achieves more than two-thirds of its aggregate Community-wide turnover in one and the same.

B. *Referrals back to Member States*

- The ECMR contains mechanisms for Member States requesting back from the Commission concentrations having a Community-dimension.
- Under Article 9 (2) of the ECMR the Commission, upon request of a Member State, may refer a notified concentration to the competent authorities of the Member State concerned, if
  - a concentration threatens to create or strengthen a dominant position as a result of which effective competition will be significantly impeded on a market within that Member State, which presents all the characteristics of a distinct market.
  - The Commission must refer a notified concentration to a national authority if a concentration affects competition on a market within the Member State, which presents all characteristics of a distinct market and which does not constitute a substantial part of the Common Market.
  - Most recently, the Commission has upon the request of the FCO referred to the Bundeskartellamt a joint venture by which Connex Verkehr GmbH, a subsidiary of the Vivendi group, and Deutsche Nahverkehrsgesellschaft mbH plan to offer local public transport services in Saxony, Germany. Earlier on the Commission had referred the two major gasoline cases (BP/Aral and Shell/DEA) to the FCO, which cleared both cases after divestiture commitments had been given.

C. *Article 22 (3) of the ECMR—Referrals to the Commission*

Since the ECMR entered into effect, Article 22 (3) of the ECMR has allowed individual Member States to request the Commission to review concentrations which do not have a Community dimension.

1. Single Request (the 'Dutch Clause')

- Prior to its amendment which took effect in 1998, Article 22 (3) aimed to 'help out' Member States that did not yet dispose of national merger control rules by allowing them to ask the Commission to step into their shoes.
- A single request has been made only 4 times—once by Belgium, once by Finland and twice by the Netherlands; none of these countries had a merger control legislation in place when making the request.
- Now that all Member States except Luxemburg have introduced national merger control legislation, the possibility of a single request under Article 22 (3) is of only very limited scope.

2. Joint Request

- The possibility of a joint request has been introduced by the 1998 revision.
- Joint referrals were intended to help:
  - strengthening the application of ECMR in cases with cross-border effects;
  - strengthening the one-stop shop principle;
  - alleviating the problem of multiple filings.
- Only recently, the first two cases were jointly referred to the Commission:
  - *Promatech/Sulzer*—Case COMP/M.2698 (referred in December 2001 and February 2002 by competition authorities of Spain, Italy, the UK, Germany, France, Portugal and Austria);
  - *GEES/Unison*—Case COMP/M.2738 (referred in February and March 2002 by competition authorities of Spain, Italy, the UK, Germany, France and Greece);
  - The President of the Bundeskartellamt, Mr. Böge, stated in a press release concerning the Promatech/Sulzer merger: 'In view of the markets affected Europe-wide and the Community-wide significance of the project I consider an examination by the Commission rather than by the Member States to be desirable.'

III. THE GREEN PAPER ON THE REVIEW OF THE ECMR

A. The Commission's assessment of the jurisdictional thresholds under Article 1

Based on the 2000 Report and additional studies carried out meanwhile, the Commission, in its Green Paper, is of the opinion that the thresholds of Article 1 (2) of the ECMR as well as the 2/3 rule function satisfactorily and that—much to the surprise of the reader—there is, therefore, no need to amend the provision. A revision of the threshold levels would, in the Commission's view, not be well suited to dealing with the multiple filing problem.

However, the Commission finds that the current Article 1 (3) has not achieved its objective of conferring Commission competence over a substantial number of cases that affect three or more Member States:

- Article 1 (3) was currently very complex to apply (and to explain to clients) and rarely brought additional transactions within the scope of the Commission's jurisdiction, thereby avoiding multiple national filings.
- Based on the 2000 merger review statistics, the Commission states that only a small portion of such cases have fallen within the ECMR: in 2000, only 20 cases were notified under Article 1 (3), compared to 75 multiple notifications to three or more Member States.

B. The Commission's assessment of Article 22 (3)

In the Commission's view, 'the [1989] amendments in Article 22 (3) have proved even less effective than has Article 1 (3)'. The Commission sees the following procedural and operational weaknesses:

- difficulties to calculate the one-month period for submission of a request to the Commission, Article 22 (4);
- difficulties to foresee when the one-month period expires, Article 22 (4);
- no provision for suspending the applicable national deadlines pending a joint referral;
- discretion of the Commission whether or not to accept a referral request;
- longer waiting-periods than within the immediate one-stop shop system;
- discretion of each competition authority involved whether or not to request/accept a referral;
- conflict with one-stop shop principle: non-requesting Member States may pursue parallel procedures.

C. The Commission's 'Three Member States Proposal'

As a result of this (preliminary) assessment, the Commission has come to the view that the current Article 1 (3) should be replaced by a provision whereby notification to three Member States is seen as a reliable indication of the cross-border nature of a concentration, triggering the Commission's competence to review the case.

This proposal has already been made in the 1996 Green Paper—was at the time, however, regarded as 'second best solution' (behind a threshold reduction).

IV. DISCUSSION

A. *Discussion of the Commission's Three Member States Proposal*

The three Member States proposal is an attractive rule from several points of view, not least because it takes as its central criterion the multiple notification requirement which is the reason behind it, rather than a more arbitrary indicator such as turnover or market share.

There may be even more 'three Member States cases' than appear in the statistics since, in practice, parties may take the commercial decision not to notify in an EU jurisdiction, even where they might arguably be required to do so.

However, the three Member States proposal raises some significant concerns which, in the absence of the introduction of a significantly greater degree of uniformity of both procedural and substantive national rules, cast great doubt on its workability:

- practical difficulty to identify with sufficient certainty whether a filing is in fact required under national law;
- three Member States rule would necessarily create delay while the issue of jurisdiction is settled;
- monitoring compliance with such a rule would be complex.
- It would be necessary that all national laws operate on the basis of jurisdictional thresholds based on readily ascertainable and objective criteria. Similarly, the types of transaction requiring notification would need to be clearly defined in each national law.
- Several questions regarding legal security and control by the judicative body of the national authorities' decision arise:
    - Would merging parties be given the opportunity to appeal against an national authority's decision that it (and, therefore, the Commission) does not have jurisdiction?
    - Would the Commission have standing to intervene in any such appeal proceedings?

- Would the national authorities' decisions have binding force under Community law to protect companies from claims that they notified to the wrong authority?

B. *Discussion of the Referrals System*

The President of the Bundeskartellamt, Mr. Böge, rejects, therefore, the Commission's three Member States proposal and instead favours 'the referral of merger cases in both directions [...] in order to guarantee effective protection of competition. [...] The Member States affected should, on their own responsibility, and in the sense of the cooperation concept refer cases of Community-wide importance to the Commission, as in [...] Promatech/Sulzer.'

- However, if Articles 22 (3)-(5) are to remain in force, Guidelines on Article 22 are also needed. Article 22 (3) is certainly in need of clarification, as it is not even clear when a joint referral should be made.
- Even under an improved Article 22 (3) with clear Guidelines, the principal problem will remain: without harmonizing national laws no effective system of joint referrals of concentrations can be installed—and such harmonization is difficult to achieve in the short- to mid-term.
- Furthermore, serious doubts remain whether joint referrals are an appropriate means to solve the problem of multiple filings because referrals always involve an assessment by two or more competition authorities which has a negative impact upon
    - legal certainty (unclear which authority will finally decide);
    - timing (longer waiting periods);
    - costs (higher administrative burden, eg preparation of a Form CO in addition to national filings).
- Article 22 (3) may also create difficulties where national competition authorities have deadlines which expire before the jurisdictional question is resolved. Parties may be forced at least to start working on national and EU notifications in parallel, which is clearly inefficient if these notifications turn out not to be needed.
- In fact, many of the factors relating to different procedural and substantive rules of national law which were discussed above in relation to the proposed 'three Member States' threshold are also relevant in the context of joint referrals from 'the bottom to the top'.

V. CONCLUSION

I support the Commission's objective of avoiding multijurisdictional filings and of bringing more 'European' cases within its jurisdiction. Given the difficulties described above relating to the current application of Articles 1 (3) and 22 (3) and the legal and procedural problems which would flow from the introduction of the three Member States rule as well as an improved referral system, a lowering of the thresholds in Article 1(2) and the deletion of Article 1(3) would be the most sensible and appropriate solution. I believe that such a step would catch many of the transactions currently subject to multiple EU filings and, at the same time, mark a return to the simplicity of the ECMR in its original form.

5. Preserving Effective Competition without Preventing Change to the Competitive Landscape

Debra A Valentine*

As merger remedies become more complicated, competition agencies understandably strive to keep remedial rules simple and outcomes as administrably feasible as possible. But they need to keep in mind that the goal is to preserve effective competition not to prevent any change in the competitive landscape.

I. THE EASY PART OF MERGER REMEDIES

Merger remedies are more unidimensional, from a remedial perspective, than antitrust remedies that address unlawful conduct.

A. Merger remedies need not punish illegal conduct, as cartel fines and incarceration are designed to do.

B. Merger remedies ordinarily need not reverse the ill effects of unlawful conduct, since no ill effects will have occurred in notification and review systems that suspend consummation of the merger.

C. Merger remedies need not prevent the recurrence of the conduct of merging, insofar as future mergers may well be benign or even procompetitive.

D. All merger remedies must do is maintain competition in the marketplace and signal to firms as clearly as possible which combinations are likely acceptable and which ones are likely to lead to an undue increase in market power.

Second, most mergers are notified to authorities or, if they fall below merger thresholds, are still carried out in public. Accordingly, merger remedies need not grapple with what constitutes adequate deterrence and whether enhancing the severity of a remedy is necessary because so many violations are not detected or not successfully prosecuted.

Agencies have traditionally analyzed merger remedies according to a relatively straightforward standard.

A. Merger remedies are generally designed to preserve the level of competition that existed in the market just prior to the merger, without,

* O'Melveny & Myers LLP Washington, DC. Paper given at the Second Annual Conference on International and Comparative Competition Law, BIICL, May 2002.

whenever possible, sacrificing any efficiencies that the merger achieves. Given that merger enforcement is prospective, agencies can easily assess what the current state of competition is in the marketplace.

B. That remedial competitive baseline is easier to assess than in unlawful conduct cases. In conduct cases, the goal may well be the same—restoring competition to where it would have been but for the unlawful conduct—but it often is far more difficult to determine what the state of competition would have been.

1. What the market would have looked like is clearly the focus of significant disagreement in the Microsoft case in the US.

2. Indeed, in rapidly changing high tech markets, it may often be impossible to restore competition to what it would have been absent the unlawful conduct, or even to determine what a competitive market would have looked like.

II. THE PROBLEM WITH AN EASY STANDARD

The standard that the competition agencies have relied upon in designing remedies—that consumers should benefit from the same degree of competition after the merger as before the merger—is relatively easy to define and administer but somewhat flawed in concept. The definition is a zero delta concept—the remedy should ensure that the HHI does not change.

A. The case law reflects a slightly different remedial standard: 'The key to the whole question of an antitrust remedy is of course the discovery of measures effective to preserve competition.'[1] Preserving competition does not necessarily mean maintaining it at exactly the same level as previously existed. A remedy that allows for a slightly increased HHI may well effectively preserve competition.

B. And the standard for challenging a merger is whether its effect 'may be substantially to lessen competition, or to tend to create a monopoly.' This standard does not require mergers to maintain competition as it existed before the merger. Ironically then, the standard for achieving a merger remedy—a settlement—is more difficult for parties to meet than the standard for what parties must demonstrate when a merger is challenged in court.

[1] *United States v EI du Pont de Nemours & Co*, 366 US 316, 326 (1961).

III. THE TRUTH WITH THE EASY STANDARD—EVEN EASY IS HARD

Even with this straightforward, albeit slightly aggressive remedial standard, merger remedies often remain difficult to design in practice.

A. Over the course of the 1990s remedies in general became stronger, particularly in non-merger cases.

1. Cartel fines increased in 1990 from $1 million to $10 million for corporations and from $ 100,000 to $350,0000 for individuals.

2. Moreover, the Comprehensive Crime Control Act and Criminal Fine Improvements Act of 1994 enabled the government to seek twice the gains from the illegal conduct or twice the loss to victims that the cartel occasioned. This justified the $100 million fine against Archer Daniels Midland Co and the $500 million fine against Hoffmann-LaRoche.

3. Imprisonment became a more frequently used remedy.

4. In non-merger cases, the FTC began resorting to remedies beyond a mere cease and desist order and, for example, obtained $100,000,000 in disgorgement of ill-gotten gains from Mylan for its illegal monopolisation of the critical input into a generic drug.

B. In the case of mergers, remedies became most noticeably more sophisticated, which makes them more difficult to design and administer.

1. Merger remedies also became stronger whenever the FTC believed that procedural rules for reviewing mergers had been violated. See, eg, The Hearst Trust (civil penalties for failing to provide relevant 4(c) documents and divestiture and disgorgement to remedy illegal monopolization)[2]; and Blackstone Partners (civil penalty for not providing relevant 4(c) documents). This is because not providing required information to enable agency review undermines the integrity of the whole merger review system.

2. Merger remedies may also become stronger insofar as the current Administration has indicated a desire to challenge already consummated mergers, as it is doing in MSC Software and intends to do in the health care sector. This could potentially require unraveling deals to an extent not engaged in for decades.

Both the US and EC express a strong preference for structural remedies, but there are instances in which structural remedies simply cannot accomplish the job.

[2] *United States v The Hearst Trust et al*, Civ No 1:01CV02119 (DDC 11 Oct 2001); see also *FTC v The Hearst Trust, et al*, Civ No 1:01CV00734 (DDC Dec 2001).

A. Even structural remedies of divesture require difficult issues of how much of a going business—staff, supplies and customer relationships—must be divested.

1. These issues do not necessarily fall within the traditional role of enforcers.

2. Businessmen, trustees or even sectoral regulators are likely better positioned to determine which assets and how many assets are needed to create a viable competitor that is capable of replacing the competition lost due to the merger.

B. Critical to designing an effective remedy is a relative degree of information symmetry between the remedy designer and the merging parties, since the merged firm has no incentive to create an effective competitor.

1. But enforcers and buyers often lack the depth of knowledge of the industry that the merging parties have.

2. Buyers occasionally underestimate the amount or kind of assets they will need and overestimate their ability to compete against the established players going forward.

3. Competition agencies do not want to constantly monitor remedies to redress any information asymmetry.

4. For these reasons, the past Administration often insisted that any divestiture arrangement include entire business units and identified up-front buyers who had business plans in place for operating the divested assets as well as adequate resources to implement those plans.

C. The current Administration is likely to somewhat moderate this policy and not insist as frequently on up front buyers, particularly if a relatively discrete ongoing business is being divested.

D. When structural remedies do not suffice—and they often do not when networks or intellectual property are involved and access is at issue—remedies can become very complicated.

1. In these cases, even when enforcers adopt regulatory or behavioral fixes, they should model their remedies to the extent possible on market behavior and mechanisms.

2. For example, in AOL-Time Warner, AOL and the first ISP on its cable system negotiated their carriage agreement; that agreement was approved by the FTC; and future carriage agreements for additional ISPs were to be modeled on that agreement or any agreement that AOL's ISP was able to negotiate for carriage on others' cable systems.

3. Enforcers must take care that the remedies they adopt do not destroy incentives to innovate.

E. Accurately targeted remedies, particularly ones involving access, take time to negotiate.

1. It is unlikely that the EC could ever have arrived at the remedies the FTC adopted in Time Warner-Turner or AOL-Time Warner, given the EC's immutable five-month review period.

2. For this reason, the Green Paper's proposal for stopping the clock offers clear advantages for achieving more precisely targeted remedies and for achieving more similar remedies on both sides of the Atlantic when appropriate to the competitive issues at stake.

Convergence in substantive standards and remedies goes hand in hand.

A. While the approaches of the US and EC to remedies seem to be converging at an analytic or conceptual level, it is important that we also be pushing towards the same substantive standards for reviewing mergers or we will end up adopting inconsistent and potentially conflicting remedies.

B. Unless the US and EC authorities do arrive at the same remedies when addressing comparable competitive problems, we will be imposing unnecessary regulatory burdens on transactions.

6. The Commission Should Accept its Proper Responsibilities

Joseph Gilchrist*

My conclusions are quite simple: the Commission should accept its proper responsibilities, having defined the distortions of competition or the impediments a merger is likely to create, it should identify the remedies necessary to achieve an equilibrium position. Secondly, the way that remedies are negotiated, particularly in second-phase cases, should be put on a simplified, transparent basis, possibly under the chairmanship of an independent person to adjudicate and arbitrate between the Commission and the parties.

Thirdly, market testing should be revisited; and let me as a final conclusion also cross swords with Simon and Debra on the last comments about more flexibility, stopping the clock and all the rest of it. One of the beauties of the present system is that there is a fixed timetable and parties can work to that; and I think it's a matter of making the present system work rather than trying to change the system. Stopping the clock is a very dangerous idea.

Let me get back to the beginning. At the moment, the onus for remedies is put on the parties; in that situation, the Commission is disregarding the principle of *égalité des armes*, which already applies to many areas of competition policy, because the parties and the Commission are not in an equal position when it comes to negotiating remedies. All the cards are in the hands of the Commission, particularly if the Commission plays with closed cards; the parties have to play with open cards, foot forward, one proposal after another, to meet the Commission's objectives.

Now this is not based in fact in law; it is based on a very odd interpretation of the merger regulation, because there in Article 8 Paragraph 2, it says 'following modifications by the undertakings concerned'. It doesn't say that it's the parties who have to actually put up the commitments that they have to carry out ideas; they have to carry them out. So my thesis is that the Commission should identify the necessary remedies. Having identified, the parties can then basically do a calculation: Is the pain worth the profit, or do we pull out of this deal, because that's then the alternative. In most cases, they'd probably still go ahead; as we see, the vast majority of second-phase cases end up in modifications to the merger and very often companies are perceived to burn up shareholder value.

* FIPRA. Paper given at the Second Annual Conference on International and Comparative Competition Law, BIICL, May 2002.

Now when it comes to the actual negotiation of the remedy, what I think is necessary is to avoid the sort of salami tactic and also the time factor in the present system, where there are a series of negotiations in most cases. Each time a little bit more is put on the table; the pot is increased and there is no immediate solution.

'The thought of death', Dr Johnson said, 'focuses the mind wonderfully.' And if you compress the negotiation of remedies, and by this second stage of the procedure everyone is pretty conversant with all the facts of the case. The Commission states what it wants; the parties state what they're willing to give, whether it be 80, 90, or 100 per cent of what the Commission's stated, but the meeting is chaired by an independent person. The possibility for this already exists in the new mandate of a Hearing Officer; he is invited to comment on the remedies and whether they are proportionate to the competition problems that have been identified. So all the mechanisms are in place; it's a matter of determination by individuals and a desire to put the thing right.

The final point, keeping within my six minutes. Once a negotiation has come up with a solution, it seems to me only fair that the Commission should give its support, because it is the Commission, after considering all the evidence submitted to it by third parties, by interested parties, information on member states and so forth, it's the Commission who's drawn up and defined the problems. Under what I'm proposing it would define the necessary remedies. After this, what is the use of the market test?

Member states in any case are in close touch and continuous and constant liaison with the Commission, and they have an opportunity, in advising the Committee, to comment on the measures proposed. At this stage, and I do consider from experience over many years that third parties have made their position clear, and they are not going to be moved from what they want. But then the Commission should accept its responsibility, open transparent negotiations are possible within the existing time frame, which is one of the great strengths of the merger system in the European Union Also, revisit market testing.

7. Behavioural Undertakings and the Restoration of Effective Competition in Merger Cases

Ian Rose*

I. INTRODUCTION

Under the EC Merger Control Regulation (the 'ECMR'), the European Commission (the 'Commission') must prohibit a concentration which creates or strengthens a dominant position as a result of which effective competition would be significantly impeded in the common market or in a substantial part of it.[1] The parties to the transaction may however seek to alleviate the competition concerns by offering commitments ('remedies') to the Commission. These must be shown by the parties to the merger, to the satisfaction of the Commission, to restore conditions of effective competition in the common market on a permanent basis.

The most common remedies are 'structural' in nature, involving the divestment of parts of the businesses being combined, although there may be 'behavioural' aspects to a divestment remedy, such as the appointment and activities of a 'hold-separate trustee' pending divestment. The Commission is, however, generally reluctant to accept behavioural remedies unless they have a structural effect on the market concerned and in most cases, any behavioural remedies that are agreed will form part of a package that includes structural remedies.

Despite this general approach, which is supported by case law, the Commission considers that behavioural remedies may be valuable in particular market circumstances, for example when divestments are impossible due to economic and legal reasons. Moreover, the Court of First Instance (the 'CFI') has stated that the granting of access to essential facilities on non-discriminatory terms is a remedy that could be capable of preventing the creation or strengthening of a dominant position and could consequently be acceptable.[2]

This paper outlines the general principles that the Commission applies in

* Watson, Farley & Williams. Paper given at the Second Annual Conference on International and Comparative Competition law, BIICL, May 2002. The author thanks Robert Eriksson of Watson, Farley & Williams for his help in the writing of this article. This is an article for general discussion. Reliance should not be placed nor decisions taken on the basis of its contents without specific advice.

[1] Article 2(3) of Council Regulation 4064/89/EEC on the control of concentrations between concentrations (OJ 1990 L257), as amended.

[2] Case T-102/96 *Gencor v Commision* [1999] ECR II-753.

accepting behavioural remedies in merger cases and it reviews the relevant case law. The paper considers the circumstances in which behavioural remedies can be considered to restore effective competition and it concludes by considering whether a move from the 'dominance' test to a test based on the concept of a 'substantial lessening of competition' might render the concept of behavioural remedies more acceptable to the Commission than is currently the case.

II. GENERAL PRINCIPLES

The Green Paper on the review of the ECMR does not examine the issue of behavioural remedies as such, although it does discuss the procedure of submitting and negotiating remedies.[3] However, the issue of behavioural remedies is covered by the Commission's Notice of 2 March 2001 on remedies acceptable under the ECMR and Commission Regulation 447/98 (the 'Remedies Notice'), which the Commission published to offer guidance on remedies.[4]

According to the Remedies Notice, parties proposing remedies must show that, once implemented, those proposed remedies will eliminate the creation or strengthening of the dominant position identified by the Commission. The parties must show clearly, to the satisfaction of the Commission, that the remedies restore conditions of effective competition in the common market on a permanent basis. Remedies must be capable of being implemented effectively and within a short period, and they should not require additional monitoring once they have been implemented.

The Commission takes the view that the most effective way to restore effective competition where a proposed merger threatens to create or strengthen a dominant position, apart from by prohibition, is by divestment. In 2001, the vast majority of the competition concerns that arose in merger cases were addressed by means of divestments.[5] Of the 13 cases that were cleared conditionally in Phase I, seven involved a divestment of a business or businesses and another one involved the divestment of landing slots.[6] Of the ten

[3] Green Paper on the Review of Council Regulation (EEC) No 4064/89, COM(2001) 745/6 final, 11 Dec 2001.

[4] Notice on remedies acceptable under Council Regulation (EEC) No 4064/89 and under Commission Regulation (EC) No 447/98 (OJ 2001 C 68).

[5] XXXIst Report on competition policy, 2001, European Commission, p 66, para 296.

[6] COMP/M.2602 *Gerling/NCM*; COMP/M.2574 *Pirelli/Edizione/Olivetti/Telecom Italia*; COMP/M.2300 *YLE/TDF/Digita/JV*; COMP/M.2396 *Industri Kapital/Perstorp (II)*; COMP/M.2286 *Buhrmann/Samas Office Supplies*; COMP/M.2277 *Degussa/Laporte*; COMP/JV.54 *Smith & Nephew/Beiersdorf/JV*. The notification involving divestment of landing slots, *United Airlines/US Airways*, was later withdrawn due to antitrust objections in the US.

cases cleared in Phase II, the divestment of a business or businesses was the most frequently accepted type of remedy.[7]

In addition to divestment, other types of remedies may be accepted by the Commission that are more 'behavioural' in nature, such as termination of exclusive agreements or ensuring that competitors have access to necessary infrastructure or key technology. The Commission has not, however, generally accepted behavioural remedies, and where they have been accepted, such remedies must be capable of preventing the creation or strengthening of a dominant position. This approach was confirmed by the Court of First Instance (the 'CFI') in *Gencor v Commission*.[8]

III. COMMUNITY CASE LAW ON BEHAVIOURAL UNDERTAKINGS

A. Overview

The Commission has accepted behavioural undertakings under certain circumstances. In the *Fiat Geotech/Ford New Holland* decision from 1991, the Commission decided not to oppose the transaction after Fiat undertook to terminate an exclusive dealing arrangement with a nationwide association of Italian agricultural machinery distributors and to send letters to the association members notifying them of the right to terminate these arrangements.[9] Fiat also agreed to enter into distribution agreements only with individual distributors covering their respective areas and to conform these agreements to EC competition rules. However, the *Gencor* case and the Remedies Notice have refined the principles that apply to the acceptance of proposed behavioural remedies.

In *Gencor v Commission*, the CFI reaffirmed that the Commission was required to prohibit a merger where it created or strengthened a dominant position, even if the undertakings concerned pledged themselves *vis-à-vis* the Commission not to abuse that position. The CFI held that even where it may be easy to check compliance with such a commitment, a mere commitment not to abuse a dominant position could not be allowed, since the purpose of the ECMR was to prevent the creation or strengthening of market structures which are liable to impede significantly effective competition in the common market. The CFI further held:

[7] XXXIst Report on competition policy, 2001, p. 66-67, para. 296-297; Cases referred to: COMP/M.2033 *Metso/Svedala*; COMP/M.1915 *The Post Office/TPG/SPPL*; COMP/M.2139 *Bombadier/Adtranz*. In four cases the parties gave a commitment to sell shareholdings in other companies: COMP/M.2530 *Südzucker/Saint Louis*; COMP/M.2533 *BP/E.ON*; COMP/M.2420 *Mitsui/CVRD/Caemi*; COMP/M.1853 *EdF/EnBW*.

[8] Case T-102/96 *Gencor v. Commission* [1999] ECR II-753.

[9] IV/M.9 *Fiat Geotech/Ford New Holland*, para 30.

[T]he commitments (...) must enable the Commission to conclude that the concentration at issue would not create or strengthen a dominant position (...). The categorisation of a proposed commitment as behavioural or structural is therefore immaterial. It is true that commitments which are structural in nature, such as (...) the sale of a subsidiary, are, as a rule, *preferable* from the point of view of the [ECMR]'s objective, inasmuch as they prevent once and for all, or *at least for some time*, the *emergence or strengthening of the dominant position* previously identified by the Commission and do not, moreover, require medium or long-term monitoring measures. Nevertheless, the possibility cannot automatically be ruled out that commitments which prima facie are *behavioural*, for instance (...) to make part of the production capacity of the entity arising from the concentration available to third-party competitors, or, more generally, to grant access to essential facilities on non-discriminatory terms, *may themselves also be capable of preventing the emergence or strengthening of a dominant position.* (Emphasis added).

The *Gencor* case has served as a basis for the approach to behavioural remedies and 'established the principle that the basic aim of commitments is to ensure competitive market structures'.[10] The importance of the case in setting the parameters within which behavioural remedies could be acceptable is illustrated by the reference to it in the Remedies Notice, where the Commission repeats the CFI's wording:

According to the Court, commitments which are structural in nature, such as the commitment to sell a subsidiary, are, as a rule, preferable from the point of view of the Regulation's objective (...).

B. Where divestment is impossible

Although structural remedies, particularly divestments, are the preferred type of remedy, they must be economically and legally possible. In *Boeing/McDonnel Douglas*, the economic impossibility to divest a business that, if divested, would have removed competition concerns, was an important factor for the Commission in approving behavioural undertakings, although in combination with structural undertakings:[11]

In the absence of any interest on the part of Airbus to acquire DAC [Douglas Aircraft Company], but also in the absence of any interest of other companies to enter this market through an acquisition of DAC, it is *highly unlikely that a buyer could be found for DAC*. A commitment on a *divestiture* would *not therefore have resolved the competition problems* resulting from the horizontal effects. (Emphasis added).

It is worth noting however, that the circumstances in the case also were specific on a political level. The US Department of Defence and Department

[10] Remedies Notice, para 9.
[11] IV/M.877 *Boeing/McDonnel Douglas*.

of Justice, on behalf of the US Government, informed the Commission of three areas of concern. First, a decision prohibiting the proposed merger could harm important US defence interests. Second, despite any measures the Commission could impose on a third party purchaser, a divestment of Douglas Aircraft Company ('DAC') would be likely to be unsuccessful in preserving DAC as a stand-alone manufacturer of new aircraft, resulting in an inefficient disposition of whatever of DAC's new aircraft manufacturing operations that potentially could be salvaged by Boeing, and in the loss of employment in the United States. Third, any divestment of DAC to a third party that would not operate DAC as a manufacturer of new aircraft would be anti-competitive in that it would create a firm with the incentive and means to raise prices and diminish service in respect of the provision of spare parts and service to DAC's fleet-in-service, a large proportion of which was owned by US airlines.

In its Annual Competition Policy Report (2001), the Commission stated that although the majority of remedies accepted by the Commission were structural remedies and such remedies were 'the ideal solution', it had accepted remedies 'more complicated' than straightforward divestments.[12] As an example, the Commission gives the *EdF/EnBW* case, which was cleared after a Phase II investigation.[13] The package of remedies included three elements, of which two were not of an unusual type, namely, EdF undertook (i) to renounce the exercise of its voting rights in CNR, an electricity producer active in France, and to withdraw its representative from the CNR board of directors and no longer be involved in CNR's commercial policy and market conduct; and (ii) to divest its 24 per cent, co-controlling shareholding in WATT, which restored the *status quo ante* in Switzerland.

The third element was an undertaking by EdF to provide competitors with access to generation capacity located in France in the form of 'virtual' power plants and back-to-back agreements to existing co-generation power purchase agreements. The contracts for the virtual power plants would be awarded through an open, non-discriminatory public auction, open to both utilities and energy traders.

In the *EdF/EnBW* case, the Commission found that a divestment was impossible, as the divestment of power plants could not be envisaged due to economic and legal reasons (relating to nuclear power plants in particular), since new entrants were unlikely to take the risks involved in acquiring a plant. Although admitting that the highly specific circumstances of the *EdF/EnBW* case meant that the lessons that could be drawn from it perhaps

12 XXXIst Report on competition policy, 2001, p 67, para 300.
13 COMP/M.1853 *EdF/EnBW*.

were limited, the Commission said in its Annual Competition Policy Report (2001) that it showed that the Commission was prepared to accept non-standard remedies when circumstances demanded them and when there was sufficient time in the merger control procedure for it to do so. This implies that such remedies would be agreed only where the case goes to Phase II.

C. Recent cases

Behavioural remedies were considered by the Commission in two recent cases that achieved general notoriety, namely *GE/Honeywell* and *Tetra Laval/Sidel.*[14]

In *GE/Honeywell,* General Electric offered, in addition to a number of structural undertakings, three significant behavioural undertakings. First, the parties submitted a non-compete agreement with the purchaser of an engine series, according to which GE would abstain from purchasing corporate jet aircraft on a speculative basis for operating leasing purposes concerning corporate jet engines. Second, GE proposed that it would abstain from bundling GE and Honeywell products (Avionics, Non-avionics or Aircraft Engine Products or Services) unless a competitor took similar action, and this would be ensured through an arbitration scheme.

In the third proposed behavioural undertaking, GE offered to hold GE Capital Aviation Services ('GECAS'), the aircraft leasing arm of General Electric, as a separate legal entity and to conduct its dealings with Honeywell on an arm's length basis. Compliance would be monitored by an independent expert. Furthermore, GECAS would not condition its purchases on the incorporation of Honeywell avionics and non-avionics equipment and GE Capital would not finance purchasers or operators of aircraft for the inclusion of Honeywell avionics and non-avionics equipment. GECAS would also not influence the selection of avionics and non-avionics equipment by its customers and would select its competitors' avionics and non-avionics products when it purchases aircraft for leasing purposes.

In response to the proposed remedies, the Commission held the following:

> *Apart from* the fact that the commitment relating to corporate jet engines is *purely behavioural*, it cannot be accepted (...). The undertakings (...) are *purely behavioural* and as such cannot constitute the basis for a clear elimination of the said concerns. The legal separation of GECAS does *not affect* its *management* and thus its *control remains in the hands of GE*. It cannot be expected that such separation will prevent GECAS from exercising the commercial strategy of GE. For the rest, the

[14] COMP/M.2220 *General Electric/Honeywell*; COMP/M.2416 *Tetra Laval/Sidel.*

undertaking on GECAS remains a *pure promise* not to act in a certain manner. Such a promise is in contrast with the Commission's stated policy on remedies and with the purpose of the [ECMR] (...). Moreover, the proposed undertakings can be expected to require a *significant amount of monitoring work on the part of the Commission.* (Emphasis added).

The decision confirms that the Commission is generally of the view that purely behavioural remedies on their own cannot constitute the basis for an elimination of the concern that a dominant position is created or strengthened, unless control of management is affected. Moreover, the Commission said in relation to an added structural component to the proposed remedies, that is, to divest 19.9 per cent. of the voting rights in GECAS, the Commission stated that '[a]lthough a structural component was added to the undertaking (...)', it could not constitute the basis the for a clear elimination of the said concerns, as the undertaking regarding GECAS still remained 'purely behavioural in nature'.

In *Tetra Laval/Sidel*, the Commission considered two proposed behavioural remedies as insufficient to resolve its concerns. Tetra Laval had proposed to hold Sidel separate from Tetra Pak, together with the confirmation of undertakings previously given in proceedings relating to alleged infringements of Article 82, to address the concerns of the Commission that the merged entity would be able to leverage its dominant position in carton packaging to gain a dominant position in PET packaging equipment. In response, the Commission repeated its approach in *GE/Honeywell* and declined to accept purely behavioural commitments or pure promises not to act in a certain manner, since they did not address the permanent change in the market structure created by the notified operation that caused concerns.

D. Access to essential facilities as a remedy

The granting of access to essential facilities on non-discriminatory terms was recognised by the CFI in the *Gencor* case as a remedy that could be capable of preventing the emergence or strengthening of a dominant position and therefore be acceptable. Merger decisions in which behavioural remedies have been accepted include those directed at ensuring access to essential input, or precluding discrimination in the grant of such access.[15] However, the remedies offered in these decisions have generally included structural remedies alongside the behavioural remedies.

[15] COMP/M.1439 *Telia/Telenor*; IV/M.190 *Nestlé/Perrier*; IV/M.468 *Siemens/Italtel*; IV/M.877 *Boeing/McDonnel Douglas*; IV/M.938 *Guinness/GrandMetropolitan*; IV/M.950 *Hoffmann-LaRoche/Boehringer Mannheim*; COMP/M.1795 *Vodafone Airtouch/ Mannesmann.*

In *Telia/Telenor*, the merging parties offered a package of undertakings, including both structural and behavioural remedies. The behavioural part of the undertakings consisted of local loop unbundling ('LLU'), that is, the parties allowing competitors access to their respective local access networks in order to provide any technically feasible services on non-discriminatory terms. The parties would be obliged to report to the Commission and the national telecommunications authorities with regard to compliance with the LLU commitment. The Commission stated that the comments it had received did not raise concerns that the remedy proposal would be ineffective and the Commission said that it would greatly reduce the competitive concerns identified for the various telecom services. It would also, by granting new entrants the ability to establish a unique customer relationship with their clients, assure that the merged entity would remain subject to at least the same degree of competition which was faced by each of Telia and Telenor prior to the proposed merger.

It is important to note that this behavioural remedy formed part of a package. In particular, it was found that the main beneficiaries of the LLU remedy were likely to be the larger business users and the divestment of the parties' cable-TV activities was designed to complement the LLU remedy, by enabling new owners of the cable-TV networks to compete with the parties' telecommunications networks on the various telecommunications markets for residential users and small businesses, who were less likely to benefit from LLU.

Another decision in which the Commission viewed a remedy relating to access to supplies as satisfactory, albeit in conjunction with structural remedies, was the case of *BP/E.ON.*[16] In this case, access to, and influence in, the relevant infrastructure would strongly enhance the market power of the new entity and divestment of an ethylene import terminal was not a viable option, as the terminal was not workable without inter-linked storage facilities and it was highly unlikely that an independent buyer was to be found. The Commission concluded that a commitment to provide access to supplies for certain ethylene customers removed the bottleneck infrastructure, which was under control of BP/Veba, allowing for competition to be restored. The remedies offered by the parties were assessed together and involved a divestment of certain shareholdings.

In *Hoffmann-LaRoche/Boehringer Mannheim,* the Hoffmann-La Roche Group undertook, in addition to a number of divestments, to give access through licences on non-discriminatory terms to the main DNA probe technology, the polymerase chain reaction (PCR) technique, for all *in vitro* diag-

[16] COMP/M.2533 *BP/E.ON.*

nostic applications, to all interested market participants. This ensured timely market entry and removed the Commission's competition concerns.[17]

In *Vodafone Airtouch/Mannesmann*, the parties offered non-discriminatory third party access to the merged entity's integrated network, so as to provide advanced mobile services to their customers, in addition to a de-merger of Orange. The undertakings covered exclusive roaming agreements; third party access to roaming arrangements; third party access to wholesale arrangements, standards and SIM-cards; and a set of implementing measures aimed at ensuring their effectiveness. Vodafone Airtouch also proposed to set up a fast track dispute resolution procedure in order to solve disagreements between the merged entity's group and third parties on third party access to roaming arrangements and third party access to wholesale arrangements, standards and SIM-cards. The provision of a roaming tariff and/or wholesale services would be made on a non-discriminatory basis between operators of the merged entity's group and other mobile operators. The non-discrimination principle would apply to both pricing and quality of the service.

The Commission stated the following in response to the parties' proposal:

> These undertakings appear sufficient to remove the competition concerns (...). [F]ollowing the implementation of these undertakings, third parties will be in a position to offer competing advanced pan-European mobile services thus preventing the emergence of a dominant position on the provision of these services. The undertakings will thus have *a structural effect on the market* in that they will make it possible to *preserve a competitive structure of supply*. The possibility to offer these services in competition with Vodafone will, in turn, also create the incentives for third parties to develop competing networks. (Emphasis added).

IV. CONCLUSION

The Commission, supported by case law, prefers structural remedies, normally divestments, in seeking to achieve the objectives of the ECMR. The Commission has recognised, however, that behavioural remedies may be valuable in particular market circumstances, for example when it is essential that undertakings grant access to infrastructure. However, the behavioural remedies must be capable of preventing the creation or strengthening of a dominant position. A mere commitment not to abuse a dominant position is not acceptable even where it is possible to monitor such a commitment after completion of the proposed transaction.

In particular cases, the Commission may accept other remedies where a

[17] IV/M.950 *Hoffmann-LaRoche/Boehringer Mannheim*, para 157 et seq.

divestment is impossible due to economic or legal reasons, such as the absence of any possible buyer for the business that the Commission would wish to see divested. In such cases, the Commission will nevertheless generally require a combination of structural and behavioural remedies.

The granting of access to essential facilities on non-discriminatory terms was recognised by the CFI in the *Gencor* case as a remedy that could be capable of preventing the creation or strengthening of a dominant position and that consequently could be acceptable. In *Telia/Telenor* however, the proposal concerning access to the local loop was approved by the Commission as an appropriate remedy together with divestments. In contrast, the Commission approved of undertakings in *Vodafone Airtouch/Mannesmann* that were mainly behavioural, but the Commission emphasised that they had a structural effect on the market in that they would make it possible to preserve a competitive structure of supply.

The Commission has not until now given any indication as to whether it would be more open to behavioural remedies if the substantive test under the ECMR were to change from the 'dominance' test to a test based on the concept of a 'substantial lessening of competition' (the 'SLC test').

It might be expected that if there is a change from the dominance test to the SLC test, the policy on remedies would have to undergo a review, because the policy is linked to the substantive test, in requiring that the remedies offered must enable the Commission to conclude that the concentration in question will not create or strengthen a dominant position. As the SLC test does not specifically require the creation or strengthening of a dominant position, behavioural commitments could conceivably be more acceptable under the SLC test than under the dominance test. However, it is not certain that a change of the substantive test from the dominance test to the SLC test will occur. If it does occur, then this discussion will have to be revisited.

8. Substantive Analysis under the EC Merger Regulation: Should the Dominance Test be Replaced by 'Substantial Lessening of Competition'?

Professor Richard Whish*

On 11 December 2001 the European Commission published its *Green Paper on the Review of Council Regulation (EEC) No 4064/89.*[1] In this wide-ranging document the Commission discusses a number of possible alterations to the provisions of the EC Merger Regulation ('the ECMR'): separate sections deal with jurisdictional, substantive and procedural matters. The shortest of these sections is the one that discusses the substantive test under the ECMR, but it contains perhaps the most interesting and important question of all: has the time come for the test based on the creation or strengthening of dominance, contained in Article 2 of the ECMR, to be replaced by a 'substantial lessening of competition' test ('the SLC test'), which is the standard to be found in many other jurisdictions, including for example the US, Australia and Canada. This paper will examine the arguments against and in favour of this possible change, and will conclude that such a reform would indeed be desirable.

I. PROLIFERATION OF SYSTEMS OF MERGER CONTROL

An obvious but important point is that the number of systems of merger control in the world has increased rapidly in recent years: there are currently at least 60 countries that enable mergers to be investigated and controlled,[2] and further laws are in contemplation in other jurisdictions. Equally obviously the proliferation of such laws poses a challenge to businesses and their advisers and to competition authorities: the need for multiple filings, the existence of different notification requirements, investigative procedures, time limits, rules on confidentiality and disclosure of information and the varying substantive standards of analysis can impose a substantial burden on firms, add to transaction costs, complicate the task of regulators and affect the outcome of cases. A considerable amount of time and energy has been expended on these issues in recent times, in particular with a view to minimising differences in procedures and filing requirements and to the encouragement of cooperation between competition

* Professor of Law, King's College London.

1 COM(2001)745/6 final.

2 See for example Rowley and Baker *Merger Control: The International Regulation of Mergers and Joint Ventures*, 3rd edn (London: Sweet & Maxwell, 2000).

authorities.[3] Less attention has been given—at any rate in the public debate—to the possibility of achieving harmonisation of the substantive grounds for the review of mergers. It may be that there has been a perception that it would be easier to achieve convergence in relation to procedural matters than substantive ones; it is possible, however, that the reverse is the case.

II. THE SUBSTANTIVE GROUNDS FOR THE REVIEW OF MERGERS CAN BE DIVIDED BROADLY INTO THREE GROUPS

Broadly speaking, the substantive test for the control of mergers in different jurisdictions can be divided into three groups: the public interest group, the substantial lessening of competition group and the dominance group.

A. *The public interest group*

Some systems of merger control have a 'public interest' test for determining which mergers may be prohibited or require modification. An obvious example of this is the current law in the UK.[4] In a merger investigation, section 69 of the Fair Trading Act 1973 requires the Competition Commission to consider whether the merger 'operates, or may be expected to operate, against the public interest'. Section 84 of the Fair Trading Act 1973 provides that:-

> the Commission shall take into account all matters which appear to them in the particular circumstances to be relevant and, among other things, shall have regard to the desirability—
>
> (a) of maintaining and promoting effective competition between persons supplying goods and services in the United Kingdom;
>
> (b) of promoting the interests of consumers, purchasers and other users of goods and services in the United Kingdom in respect of the prices charged for them and in respect of their quality and the variety of goods and services supplied;
>
> (c) of promoting, through competition, the reduction of costs and the development and use of new techniques and new products, and of facilitating the entry of new competitors into existing markets;
>
> (d) of maintaining and promoting the balanced distribution of industry and employment in the United Kingdom;

[3] For a summary, see Rowley 'The internationalisation of merger review: the need for global solutions' in *Merger Control: the international regulation of mergers and joint ventures 2002* (Global Competition Review, 2002).

[4] See IV below on the proposed amendment of UK law, which will abandon the public interest test in favour of the SLC test.

(e) of maintaining and promoting competitive activity in markets outside the United Kingdom on the part of producers of goods, and of suppliers of goods and services, in the United Kingdom.

While it is true to say that, in practice, the Competition Commission in the UK is almost entirely concerned, in its investigations, with the issue of competition, section 84 itself does not give pre-eminent importance to competition, and it would be possible, as a matter of law, for the Commission to take into account other matters such as, for example, public security, regulatory concerns or environmental considerations.[5] In India, the Companies Act 1956 in conjunction with the Securities and Exchange Board of India Regulations 1997 empower the Government to restrict certain transactions that would be prejudicial to the company acquired or to the public interest. Furthermore many countries that proceed basically on the basis of harm to competition (whether expressed in terms of dominance or SLC) nevertheless provide that a merger may be prohibited (or permitted), notwithstanding the competition analysis, for overriding public interest reasons.

B. *The substantial lessening of competition group*

Many jurisdictions apply a 'substantial lessening of competition' test. Under US law, s 7 of the Clayton Act 1914 provides that mergers are prohibited where the effect of an acquisition 'may be substantially to lessen competition, or to tend to create a monopoly'. In Canada, section 92 of the Competition Act 1985 establishes as the substantive test whether a merger or proposed merger 'prevents or lessens, or is likely to prevent or lessen, competition substantially'. Section 93 of the Act sets out a series of factors to be taken into account in making this assessment. Under section 50 of the Australian Trade Practices Act 1974 as amended:

A corporation must not directly or indirectly:

(a) acquire shares in the capital of a body corporate; or

(b) acquire any assets of a person;

if the acquisition would have the effect, or be likely to have the effect, of substantially lessening competition in a market.

In South Africa, s 12A of the Competition Act 1998 requires the investigating authority to consider whether or not a merger 'is likely to substantially prevent or lessen competition'; factors to be taken into account in making this assessment are set out in section 12A(2). It should be acknowledged that

[5] On the merger provisions of the UK Fair Trading Act 1973, see Whish, *Competition Law*, 4th edn (London: Butterworths, 2001), ch 22.

these formulations of the SLC test are not identical, but they do possess a common core.

C. *The dominance group*

Article 2(3) of the ECMR contains a test based on the concept of a dominant position:

> A concentration which creates or strengthens a dominant position as a result of which effective competition would be significantly impeded in the common market or in a substantial part of it shall be declared incompatible with the common market.

Many Member States of the European Union have followed this example, as have a number of those States in the 'queue' for accession. The dominance standard is the most common one to be found in the laws of European countries.

III. SUBSTANTIVE CONFLICT BETWEEN COMPETITION AUTHORITIES IS RELATIVELY RARE

Despite the fact that there are different tests for the scrutiny of mergers, it should be stressed that substantive conflict between competition authorities as to the outcome of particular transactions is relatively rare. Cooperation between the competition authorities in the EC and the US, for example, is now a fact of daily life: if anything the degree of cooperation has probably been greater than could have been imagined in the early 1990's, when the first US/EC Cooperation Agreement was entered into.[6] There are numerous other examples of inter-agency and international cooperation.[7] A great deal of attention, including press and electronic media coverage, is given to the few occasions on which there is real friction between competition authorities; obvious examples of tensions between the EU and the US were *Boeing/McDonnell Douglas*[8] and *GE/Honeywell.*[9] In the *Boeing* case the FTC in the US reached a majority decision not to oppose the merger, while the European Commission seemed likely, at one point, to prohibit it in its entirety; in the event commitments to modify the transaction were offered to the Commission with the result that it was given conditional clearance. No such solution was found in the case of *GE/Honeywell*, where a genuine conflict occurred between the Department of Justice in the US and the

6 See Whish 411–13 on the US/EC Cooperation Agreements.

7 Ibid 409 ff; see also Rowley (n 3 above).

8 Case IV/M.877 OJ [1997] L 336/16.

9 Case COMP/M.2220, on appeal Cases T-209/01 and 210/01 *Honeywell International Inc v Commission* (judgment pending).

Commission in Europe. However the few exceptional cases in which there has been conflict of this magnitude ought not to obscure the fact that a very large number of cases are successfully completed without any friction between the US and the EU, and that conflicts between other jurisdictions are also quite rare. A mature view would be that, no matter how sophisticated the machinery for cooperation between the EU and the US, or between any constellation of other competition authorities, there will always be exceptional cases where there is genuine disagreement as to the appropriate outcome of a particular case. It might be added that the disagreement in *GE/Honeywell* does not appear to have arisen from the different substantive tests of US and EC law, but rather from the appropriate application of those tests: there would have been disagreement even if both authorities had been applying the SLC test or if they had both been proceeding on the basis of dominance.

IV. IS THERE A NEED FOR SUBSTANTIVE CONVERGENCE?

The fact that substantive conflict has been relatively rare may be taken to suggest that there is no real need for convergence of the substantive grounds for merger review; it may be that it is a mere matter of semantics that distinguishes the two tests. If the reality is that competition authorities around the world in practice share the same belief: that merger control is essentially about ensuring that market structures will not be rendered uncompetitive as a result of changes in the control of firms; and if they are able in the majority of cases to reach outcomes that do not result in serious conflict, notwithstanding the different substantive provisions of their laws, there is clearly an argument that convergence is not necessary and that it would not actually achieve any difference in outcome. The Bundeskartellamt in Germany held a conference in October 2001 with university professors which concluded precisely this.[10] According to this view, attention should instead be focussed on those many procedural issues, referred to above, that complicate the efficient and expeditious handling of cases. However, the European Commission's Green Paper on the ECMR presents an important opportunity to visit the question of substantive convergence; and the fact that the UK Government has announced its intention to replace the public interest test contained in the Fair Trading Act 1973 with the SLC test, rather than the dominance test in the ECMR, adds to the sense that now is an appropriate time to consider the possibility for reform.[11]

[10] For a summary of the discussion, see <http://www.bundeskartellamt.de/discussion_papers.html>.

[11] See *Mergers: A Consultation Document on Proposals for Reform* DTI/Pub 4308; *Mergers: The Response to the Consultation on Proposals for Reform* URN 00/805;

There are, of course, several arguments in favour of the retention of the dominance test in the ECMR: the introduction of merger control in the EU has, in general, been a remarkable success, and the European Commission has been able to adapt the concept of dominance to a wide range of different factual situations thrown up by cases under the ECMR. However it is also the case that many arguments can be advanced in support of the SLC test. The following sections rehearse the arguments in favour of the two different tests and propose that the SLC test should be adopted as the substantive standard under the ECMR.

V. ARGUMENTS FOR THE RETENTION OF THE TEST OF DOMINANCE

- **The test of 'dominance' has a long antecedence in Community law**

The expression 'dominant position' was first used in the ECSC Treaty on coal and steel of 1951, and then again in Article 82 of the EC Treaty of 1957. Article 66(7) of the ECSC Treaty, the forerunner of Article 82 EC, established a rule for the prevention of the abuse of 'a dominant position shielding [firms] against effective competition ...'. Article 82 of the EC Treaty prohibited '[a]ny abuse by one or more undertakings of a dominant position ...'. Article 66(2) ECSC required prior authorisation of certain mergers which would give to the undertakings concerned 'the power ... to determine prices, to control or restrict production or distribution or to hinder effective competition in a substantial part of the market ...'. The EC Treaty did not contain specific rules on mergers. It is interesting to note in passing that the term 'dominant position' was not used in the ECSC Treaty in connection with the control of mergers, but rather in relation to the prevention of abusive behaviour: an important reflection as we consider whether the substantive test for mergers under the ECMR should now be detached from the dominance test used in Article 82 EC.

- **There is a considerable body of jurisprudence on the meaning of 'dominant position'—*Continental Can v Commission, United Brands v Commission***

By the time that the ECMR was adopted, the ECJ had developed a considerable body of jurisprudence on the meaning of 'dominant position' under the ECMR. The ECJ, when it heard its first appeal on the application of Article 82 by the Commission in *Europemballage Corpn and Continental Can Co Inc v Commission*,[12] held that, when identifying a dominant posi-

Productivity and Enterprise: A World Class Competition Regime Cm 5233 (2001), ch 5; clause 19 of the Competition Bill currently before Parliament in Ireland proposes the SLC test for Irish merger control: see <http://www.gov.ie/oireaahtas/frame.htm>.

[12] Case 6/72 [1973] ECR 215, [1973] *CMLR* 199, para 32.

tion, the delimitation of the relevant product market was of crucial importance. The classic definition of dominance itself remains the one given by the ECJ in *United Brands v Commission*:[13]

> 38 . . . The dominant position thus referred to by Article [82] relates to a position of economic strength enjoyed by an undertaking which enables it to prevent effective competition being maintained on the relevant market by affording it the power to behave to an appreciable extent independently of its competitors, customers and ultimately of its consumers.

These two judgments established the foundations on which the law and practice on dominance have subsequently been based. It is not surprising that, when drafting the ECMR, the decision was taken to harness the experience already gathered under Article 82 and thereby to set some limits upon the discretion of the Commission in the operation of the new law. Instead of adopting a wholly-new standard in the ECMR, such as the SLC test, the benefit of more than 25 years of case-law was made available to the Commission and the Community Courts in applying the new legislation.

- **The ECMR has been in effect now for more than 11 years, and a considerable decisional practice has been generated**

The ECMR entered into force on 21 September 1990, and the Commission has established a considerable decisional practice under it. By the end of February 2002, the Commission had adopted no fewer than 1948 decisions under the ECMR.[14] Several important judgments have been handed down by the Community Courts, on substantive matters, such as collective dominance, as well as procedural ones. There is an obvious argument, therefore, that this evolutionary process—from the Treaty of Paris of 1951, through Article 82 of the Treaty of Rome of 1957, to the ECMR as it is being applied in 2002—should not now be interrupted by departing from the dominance standard and changing to something as novel—in terms of Community law—as the SLC test. It is clearly the case that the test of dominance in the ECMR has not inhibited the Commission from tackling a wide range of different issues: its decisions deal not only with the 'simple' case of single firm dominance arising from a horizontal merger. The Commission has also developed the doctrine of 'collective dominance', to capture, for example, cases in which firms would be able to benefit from 'tacit collusion' in relation to prices and output following a merger; the Community Courts

[13] Case 27/76 [1978] ECR 207, [1978] 1 CMLR 429; the ECJ has used the same formulation on several other occasions, eg in Case 85/76 *Hoffmann-La Roche v Commission* [1979] ECR 461, [1979] 3 *CMLR* 211, para 38.

[14] See <http://europa.eu.int/comm/competition/mergers/cases/stats.html>.

in *France v Commission*[15] and *Gencor v Commission*[16] have confirmed that the ECMR does indeed apply to collective dominance. 'Range effects' or 'portfolio power' have been found to fall within the substantive test of the ECMR, where a merger would confer on the merged entity the ability to supply complementary products to customers in a way that might foreclose competition.[17] 'Indirect' effects can be controlled, where a merger does not result in an accretion of market power, but where the merged firm, for example, might be able to deter market entrants, for example by raising their costs of entry.[18] Vertical mergers can be controlled under the dominance test as well as horizontal ones: several vertical mergers have been prohibited outright where the Commission foresaw serious foreclosure effects.[19] It seems, therefore, that in the hands of the Commission the test of dominance has proved to be sufficiently supple that it can be adapted to new circumstances as required: no doubt the test of dominance is capable of further 'evolution' as different cases arise in the future.

- **Many domestic systems of merger control in the Member States have adopted dominance as the substantive test**

A different point is that many of the Member States, as well as the aspiring accession States, have adopted a system of merger control that applies the dominance standard for substantive control. In doing so, these countries have taken their lead from the EU model, and it may appear to be somewhat odd if the Commission were now to recommend to the Council of Ministers that it should abandon the dominance test in favour of one based on SLC: quite apart from the argument based on principle—which is the better test?—the politics of abolishing at Community level the very test that numerous States have recently adopted into their domestic law may be sensitive.

- **The ECMR test requires both the creation or strengthening of dominance and a significant impediment to competition in the common market before a merger can be prohibited**

An argument in favour of Article 2(3) of the ECMR as it currently stands

15 Cases C-68/94 and 30/95 [1998] ECR I-1375, [1998] 4 *CMLR* 829.

16 Case T-102/96 [1999] ECR II-753, [1999] 4 *CMLR* 971.

17 See eg Case No IV/M.938 *Guinness/Grand Metropolitan* OJ [1998] L 288/24, [1997] 5 *CMLR* 760; Case No COMP/M.2220 *GE/Honeywell.*

18 See eg Case No COMP/M.1439 *Telia/Telenor* OJ [2001] L 40/1, [2001] 4 *CMLR* 1226; Case No COMP/M.1630 *Air Liquide/BOC/Air Products.*

19 See eg Case No IV/M.469 *MSG Media Service* OJ [1994] L 364/1; Case No IV/M.993 *BertelsMann/Kirch/Premiere* OJ [1999] L 53/1, [1999] 4 *CMLR* 700, on appeal Case T-121/98 *Taurus Beteiligungs GmbH v Commission* (judgment pending); Case No IV/M.1027 *Deutsche Telekom/BetaResearch* OJ [1999] L 53/51, [1999] 4 *CMLR* 700, on appeal, as in Case T-121/98 (judgment pending).

is that, as drafted, it imposes a strict standard on the Commission: not only must it show that a dominant position will be created or strengthened as a result of the merger, but it must go further and show that 'as a result ... effective competition would be significantly impeded ...'. To those that fear that a SLC test would give the Commission too much discretion to prohibit, or require modifications of, mergers, the current test is preferable: establishing dominance is a threshold, but is not a ground, in itself, for prohibition; there must also be a significant impediment to competition. According to this view, the existing test is preferable to the vagueness of the SLC test, which would appear to give the Commission greater power to intervene than it currently has. It should be pointed out, however, that it is not entirely clear whether, as applied, the second limb of the test does have this constraining effect upon the Commission.

- **It would not be appropriate to introduce some of the jurisprudence in the US on substantial lessening of competition which has clearly been too interventionist**

Some opponents of the SLC test argue that it is undesirable to switch to the US standard for merger control. Some cases, such as *Brown Shoe Co v US*,[20] have been the subject of considerable criticism, although current US practice has evolved considerably since that decision; and anxiety has been expressed that the adoption of the SLC test in the ECMR would mean that evolving doctrine in the US would inevitably influence practice in Europe.

VI. ARGUMENTS FOR SUBSTITUTING THE SUBSTANTIAL LESSENING OF COMPETITION TEST FOR DOMINANCE

Notwithstanding the arguments set out in the previous section for the retention of the dominance test in the ECMR, there are many points that can be made in favour of its replacement with one based on SLC.

- **The substantive test for the control of mergers does not need to be linked to Article 82**

The point has been made above that, at the time that the ECMR was adopted, the decision was taken to make use of the experience gained under Article 82 in framing the substantive test for merger control. However, it is important to understand that it is not a necessity to link the tests under the ECMR and Article 82 together: indeed, it has been pointed out that the ECSC Treaty did not use the language of dominance in its treatment of mergers. To put the point another way, the purpose of merger control is not to prevent future abuses of a dominant position: rather, the reason for

[20] 370 US 294 (1962).

providing powers to prohibit or require the modification of mergers is to ensure that the structure of a market will not be rendered less competitive after a merger than before. Of course, the maintenance of effective competition will reduce the possibility of future abuses of dominance, but that is a beneficial consequence of, and not the reason for, merger control. The point was made by the CFI in *Gencor v Commission*:[21]

> the main objective in exercising control over concentrations at Community level is to ensure that the restructuring of undertakings does not result in the creation of positions of economic power which may significantly impede effective competition in the common market. Community jurisdiction is therefore founded, first and foremost, on the need to avoid the establishment of market structures which may create or strengthen a dominant position, and not on the need to control directly possible abuses of a dominant position.

The key point made in this passage is that merger control is not intended to control future abuses. The fact that the CFI talks of the need to avoid the establishment of uncompetitive market structures 'which may create or strengthen a dominant position' is understandable, given the vocabulary of Article 2(3) of the ECMR as it is currently drafted; however the Court's meaning would not have been any different if it had said that the reason for merger control is to prevent mergers which would result in 'market structures in which competition will be significantly lessened'.

Not only is there no logical or necessary link between the substantive test for mergers and the control of abusive behaviour, there is much to be said for detaching the two tests from one another. Such a detachment could serve the useful purpose of making clearer that merger control is about maintaining effective competition in markets, and not about predicting future abusive conduct. Furthermore, detaching the test in the ECMR from Article 82 could help to prevent developments under the ECMR from 'contaminating' the application of Article 82, a point that will be considered further below in relation to the doctrine of collective dominance.[22] There does not appear to be any legal impediment to the SLC test in Community law: a change to the 'substantial lessening of competition' standard would not require a revision of the EC Treaty, only of the ECMR; the ECMR is based on Article 308 (ex Article 235) of the Treaty as well as Article 83 (ex Article 87), and is not directly linked *as a matter of law* to Article 82.

- **The SLC test has a common-sense resonance**

If the purpose of merger control is to ensure that markets remain competitive, rather than to anticipate future abuses of dominance, it would seem

[21] Case T-102/96 [1999] ECR II-743, [1999] 4 *CMLR* 971, para 106.
[22] See 71–2 below.

that a test based on SLC has much to commend it, as opposed to the dominance test in Article 2(3) of the ECMR. Not the least of the attractions of the SLC test is its common-sense resonance: will a merger substantially lessen competition? This is more obviously meaningful than the test of creating or strengthening a dominant position. The expression 'dominant position' is not a term of economics: although the Community Courts and the Commission have tried to give this expression an economic meaning, it is not one to be found in the economics literature. The term 'dominant position' is a legal construct, written into the Treaties of Paris and Rome and subsequently carried over into the ECMR. It is the concept of market power that is well-known to and used by economists, and it would be preferable to adopt a SLC test that focuses upon this phenomenon.

- **The SLC test can be solidly rooted in economics**

The SLC test, if adopted, should and could be solidly rooted in sound economics. Intervention should be possible only where a merger would enable firms, individually or collectively, to exercise market power with the result that they would be able to raise prices over a substantial period of time in a way that would be privately profitable to themselves and harmful to consumers. Clearly a debate would be needed as to the precise form of words that would capture this phenomenon—as noted above, there are several variants of the SLC model—but the legislation would be written with this concept in mind. It should be added that a 'substantial lessening of competition' test should not be regarded as the converse, in Article 81(1) terms, of a non-appreciable restriction of competition. According to the Commission's new *Notice on Agreements of Minor Importance*,[23] horizontal agreements do not appreciably restrict competition where the parties' market share is below 10%, although this indulgence may not be available for 'hard-core' restrictions such as price fixing and market sharing; in the case of vertical agreements the relevant threshold is 15 per cent. These thresholds are not appropriate for the analysis of mergers, where one is concerned with future market structure.

One anxiety about a move from the dominance test to SLC is that this will give the Commission greater discretion than it has at the moment under the dominance test: that it will result in more mergers being prohibited (or modified) as a result of Commission intervention; and that the 'flexibility' of the concept will create greater uncertainty for the merging parties and their advisers. Related to this point is the controversial issue of the powers of the Commission in relation to mergers and the extent to which the CFI is able to exercise credible and effective judicial review of its decisions. The

[23] OJ [2001] C 368/13.

latter point is beyond the scope of this paper, and is one that, no doubt, will be considered in depth during the debate over the reform of the ECMR: suffice it to say here that this is a major issue that needs to be addressed, whichever substantive test is used for merger cases. The previous point—that the SLC test could give the Commission too much discretion and power—is, of course, also one of great importance. The SLC test, if it is introduced, must be framed in such a way that parties and their advisers will be able to predict how it will be applied in practice by the Commission. This is precisely why the test must be soundly rooted in economics. The words 'substantial lessening of competition' will not be sufficient in themselves to capture the policy underlying merger control and to give it practical expression. The legislation, and any accompanying *Notice* or *Guidelines* (which will certainly be necessary), must spell out the purpose behind the SLC test, the objectives that are intended to be achieved and the factors to be taken into account in the analysis of cases; and it will be necessary to explain how a series of issues—most obviously unilateral effects, coordinated effects (tacit collusion), indirect effects, potential competition, 'portfolio' and 'range' effects, vertical mergers, efficiencies and failing firms—will be dealt with; furthermore it would be important to provide guidance on the notion of 'substantial', in particular to explain how accretions of market shares will be regarded where a merger will lead to an increase in a market share that is already large. The SLC test should not come into effect until clear guidance on all of these issues is available. In drafting such guidance, the Commission would have available its substantial decisional practice under the ECMR: the fact that it has been deciding cases under the dominance standard does not render the experience and knowledge acquired over the past 12 years irrelevant under a SLC test. Furthermore, the Guidelines adopted in other jurisdictions—notably the US, Canada, Australia and New Zealand—will also be invaluable in preparing the way for the SLC test in the EU.

- **'International' mergers and the desirability of convergence of substantive standards**

Major international transactions are normally reviewed by numerous competition authorities around the world. Transactions such as *Glaxo Wellcome/SmithKline Beecham*, *GE/Honeywell* and *Hewlett Packard/Compaq* are of interest to the competition authorities in the US, the EU and many other countries. For firms involved in substantial transactions such as these, the jurisdictional question is not only whether a merger has a Community transaction, in which case a notification to the European Commission is required, or whether instead the Member States should be notified, but also whether non-EU filings are necessary. Many (most?) of the non-EU systems of merger control apply the SLC test to mergers; where such cases have a Community dimension there could be real benefits if the European Commission were to apply the same substantive test to the transaction as other major non-EU competition authorities do under their laws. Convergence on the part of EU law in such cases would not entail any conflict with Member State laws which, *ex hypothesi*, would not be applicable as a result of the principle of the one-stop shop[24].

As a general proposition, the harmonisation of merger laws is desirable where possible; it may in practice be easier to achieve harmonisation of substantive standards than to bring about convergence in relation to procedural matters.

- **It is possible that the Commission is already applying the SLC test**

The Commission has been finding 'dominance' in some cases under the ECMR at market shares below 40 per cent, and even below 30 per cent. The 15th Recital of the ECMR, which does not have legal force but which gives a strong signal as to the way in which the Commission should proceed in the analysis of mergers, states that where the combined market share of the undertakings concerned in a concentration does not exceed 25 per cent in the common market or in a substantial part of it, this is an indication that the concentration is compatible with the common market. However, dominance has been established above the 25 per cent threshold but where the predicted market shares were quite low: for example, in *REWE/Meinl*[25] at 37 per cent; in *Hutchinson/ECT/RMPM*[26] at 36 per cent; and in *Carrefour/Promodes*[27] at less than 30 per cent. The Commission also looks for possible 'indirect effects' that would arise from mergers, and sometimes concludes that dominance will be created or strengthened without any accretion of market share. For example in *Telia/Telenor*[28] the Commission was concerned that the merged entity would have an increased ability and incentive to eliminate actual and potential competition from third parties, to bundle products across a wider geographical area and to leverage sales. In *Air Liquide/BOC/Air Products*[29] the Commission was concerned that the merged entity would have an unparalleled distribution network in Europe, which would have given it additional power to deter others from market entry. Where the Commission investigates mergers in the 'new economy' it may wish to take commitments to overcome the possibility of 'transient dominance' while a new market becomes established and while existing barriers to entry are reduced. For example, in *VodafoneAirtouch/*

24 Concentrations that have a Community dimension in the sense of Article 1 ECMR are not subject to domestic merger control by Member States, subject to the possibility of an Art 9 reference in some limited circumstances.

25 Case No IV/M.1221 OJ [1999] L 274/1, [2000] 5 *CMLR* 256.

26 Case No IV/M.1412.

27 Case No COMP/M.1684.

28 Ibid, paras 155–67.

29 Case No COMP/M.1630.

Mannesmann[30] commitments were accepted for a period of three years which, effectively, would give third parties access to the merged entity's pan-European mobile telephone network.

Decisions such as these reveal the flexible way in which the Commission has adapted and applied the dominance test in Article 2(3) of the ECMR, with the consequence that many more transactions have been found to give rise to problems of dominance in recent years than was the case in the (understandably fairly cautious) early cases under the Regulation. One interesting question that arises from this is whether the Commission, in practice, is already applying a SLC test, albeit that it must write its decisions on the basis of dominance? Where the Commission is cooperating with the US (and other SLC jurisdictions) in an international case, it is understandable that the desirability of avoiding conflicting decisions would incline it, where possible, to reach the same outcome under the dominance test that other jurisdictions would achieve applying the SLC test. It is interesting to reflect upon whether the Commission, in a case based on Article 82, would have reached findings of dominance in the cases referred to above. There is, surely, a possibility that, when applying the ECMR, the Commission is reaching findings of dominance that it would not have reached under Article 82: in other words, there is already, *de facto*, a detachment between these two provisions, but one that is obscured by the use of the same word in each provision. If this is indeed the case, the argument for a real detachment—by having manifestly different standards for each phenomenon—is strong.

- **The SLC test is better than the use of 'collective dominance' for dealing with the problem of coordinated effects**

A particular area of difficulty under the ECMR (and under Article 82) has been the concept of collective dominance.[31] The Commission and the Community Courts have struggled for many years—with, it should be said, a reasonable degree of success—to develop such a concept under each of these legal provisions. There is no doubt that both the ECMR[32] and Article 82[33] apply to collective as well as to individual dominance, and the ECJ's judgment in *Compagnie Maritime Belge* seems to regard the concepts as having the same content in each case. This means that, in the case of the ECMR, the Commission is able to take action in relation to mergers that

[30] Case No COMP/M.1795.

[31] On this issue generally see Whish, ch 14.

[32] *France v Commission*, n 15 above.

[33] Cases C-395/96 and C-396/95 *Compagnie Maritime Belge NV v Commission* [2000] 4 *CMLR* 1076.

will create or reinforce a situation in which firms, post-merger, will be able to behave in a parallel manner without colluding in the sense of Article 81(1).[34] However, the fact that some success has been achieved in relation to collective dominance does not overcome the fact that this concept remains one of great difficulty. It is not an economic concept, but a legal construct that has grown by extension from the notion of dominance itself; there have been many problems in understanding precisely what it means, in particular over the issue of 'economic' and 'structural' links;[35] and there is confusion surrounding the Commission's decision in *Airtours/First Choice*, in particular as to the need for a retaliatory mechanism in order to discipline undertakings within the position of collective dominance and as to the possibility of unilateral behaviour on the part of collectively dominant undertakings: indeed it is difficult not to believe that the Commission, in this case, was *de facto* applying the SLC test. Furthermore, it is not clear that it is appropriate that firms that would be considered to be collectively dominant for the purposes of the ECMR, where the Commission's concern is future market structure, should also be held to be subject to Article 82 for this reason: this, however, would appear to be the consequence of the ECJ's judgment in *Compagnie Maritime Belge v Commission*.[36] There is a danger here that the evolving jurisprudence of the Community Courts and the decisional practice of the Commission in relation to collective dominance under the ECMR will enlarge the jurisdictional scope of Article 82 in an inappropriate manner; and that cases brought under Article 82 may have an adverse effect on merger analysis. This, therefore, is another argument in favour of detaching the law and practice of the ECMR from that under Article 82. The SLC test seems to be better suited to the problem of coordinated effects than the dominance one: indeed it was for this reason, in particular, that the UK Government preferred SLC to dominance when proposing the current amendments to UK merger control.[37]

- **Can collective dominance capture all cases that are of concern to a competition authority?**

A further point about the concept of collective dominance is that it would appear to be directly related to the problem of parallel behaviour in markets: will a merger enable firms to coordinate their pricing, production or investment decisions without actually infringing Article 81(1)? However, it can be questioned whether this notion of collective dominance is capable

[34] The Commission prohibited outright the mergers in Case No IV/M.619 *Gencor/Lonrho* OJ [1997] L 11/30, [1999] 4 CMLR 1076 (upheld on appeal, n 16 above) and Case IV/M.1524 *Airtours/First Choice* OJ [2000] L 93/1, [2000] 5 CMLR 494 (on appeal Case T-342/99, judgment pending) on the basis of collective dominance.

[35] See Whish, 488.

[36] See n 33 above.

[37] See the policy documents cited at n 11 above.

of capturing all cases of concern in terms of the future structure of markets. Where a merger leads the market from four to three, or three to two, players, the adverse consequence of this is not, or is not only, that this could lead to tacit collusion; in this situation, the market may end up being less competitive than it was, irrespective of whether there would be parallel behaviour between the remaining players. Collective dominance, as it is currently understood and applied, would not capture this situation; the SLC test would.

VII. CONCLUSION

Having weighed these arguments for and against the SLC test, my conclusion is that SLC provides a more principled approach to merger control than dominance, and that there would be merit in detaching the test for mergers from the law on unilateral abusive behaviour. Given the current review of the ECMR, there is a real opportunity to make this amendment, which would provide benefits in the handling of major transactions through the harmonisation of international standards. If such a changer were to be made, Member States and acceding States would have to choose whether to amend their domestic laws accordingly. However it would be necessary to have a clear and justiciable test of what is meant by a substantial lessening of competition: 'substantial' for this purpose must mean something more than 'not unappreciable' in the sense of the *de minimis* doctrine under Article 81(1). The SLC test should not be introduced until clear guidance has been produced, and consulted upon, as to the practical application of the new standard. The purpose of a change to the SLC test would not be to increase the margin of appreciation of the Commission, nor to 'capture' more mergers than at present, but to apply a better test than the test of dominance.

Discussion from the First Annual Competition Law Conference—Can the Authorities Cope with Multi-Media Mergers?

MARK HOFMAN

Mark Hofman, from Nomura. Just reverting briefly to this point about behavioural remedies and where there's portfolio effects—I was very interested by Mario Siragusa's point that he thought that these should be dealt with by the behavioural undertakings. I suppose this is really addressed to the regulators on the panel, but would they agree with that general analysis, and would they go so far as to say that provided the parties give those types of undertaking, that the regulators wouldn't therefore be justified in say, blocking a merger, simply because there weren't those effects?

ANDREW WHITE

Well, my general mantra is that the problems created by mergers are structural, and should have a structural remedy. Sometimes that isn't possible, but I think whenever a structural remedy is available, that's the right approach. If one has to revert to behavioural remedies, they're a lot less efficient—they are not resolving the problem, they are ameliorating it. But as I say, sometimes it has to be, and if it does have to be, then again, the competition authorities have a problem; they've got to, or may have to, find the resources to monitor and enforce those behavioural remedies, and they don't stop overnight. The monitoring and reinforcement may go on for a number of years, and if you're adding another set of behavioural remedies every six months, you're diverting more and more of your resources into that process. The answer, it seems to me when you have to have behavioural remedies, is to require that the parties to the merger meet the cost of monitoring and reinforcing them.

MICHAEL HUTCHINGS

Anyone like to comment on that controversial suggestion?

DEBRA VALENTINE

Well actually, this relates in ways both to his comment and a prior comment that Klaus made. The question is, you know, will the possibility for abuse be temporary; will it take hold and will a player truly become a monopolist in one of these emerging markets? I think I agree with Klaus that we can't just say oh well, it's all going to pass in five years. On the other hand, when enforcers impose remedies in this area, precisely because things are changing so quickly, I think they do have to be creative in terms of what they're doing; and one of the things that we did in *AOL/Time Warner* was to limit the duration of the order to five years, which is quite unusual. Most of our orders are 20 years. So in 5 years, if things really are different, or if the FCC has done things with compulsory access or not, this will all go away and you'll have to use traditional abuse—dominance monopolisation theories to get at things. And—that's enough for now.

RICHARD ECCLES

Richard Eccles, Cameron McKenna. I've just got a question arising from comments made by different members of the panel, about I think in particular the *AOL/Time Warner* and the *Canal Plus/Vivendi/Seagram* cases, as to whether you think the Commission was right to define the market as being on-line music delivery at the risk of over-simplifying, whether, as I think Mr White said, the Internet should be just seen as a form of delivery or distribution, and whether the music should have been more content-based than music-based. I'm thinking also in terms of the concerns that lay behind the need to, or the Commission's papers on the need to, legislate in the information society field, which was that digital and on-line facilities would make substitution of hard copies really very easy. Is there a sort of logic to say that therefore, in a merger control context you should look at the music itself rather than the on-line delivery form of it? I just wondered what you think.

ANDREW WHITE

I don't think I related my comment to *AOL/Time Warner*, particularly; what I was saying is that e-commerce, generally, is really a method of delivery to a variety of markets. And what impact e-commerce will have on those markets, it seems to me, will vary hugely; one of the areas where I think it may have a very big impact, it has had a big impact already and will have a bigger impact, is in music. But I think that's all I want to say on that—whether Stephen wants to add.

STEPHEN KON

I would make two comments, and both of them are actually relevant to other comments that have been made. Firstly, there's no doubt that if there is an application on the Internet that is the most likely to be successful, it's going to be music; but having said that, I think that with the current evidence, the jury is out with regard to the success of music on the Internet. It's a little bit like WAP technology as well. I think that even if one goes back to the time of the *AOL/Time Warner* merger, there was a perception that perhaps music was going to be a lot more successful in a shorter period of time than it has proved to be on the Internet. It goes back to the points that have been made concerning the difficulties of predicting how these markets are going to develop. I do have a lot of sympathy with Richard's point as well, which is that there is clear substitutability between music on the Internet and indeed one of the things, of course, in terms of things like the copyright collective that the music industry particularly concerned about in precisely that, and the need to have effective protection because it is seen simply as taking away sales from traditional forms of selling music. So I think—I'm sorry it's not the answer to your question other than to say I think it just demonstrates all the problems we've been talking about.

CHAPTER FIVE

Banking and Financial Services—Papers and Discussion from the Second Annual Competition Law Conference

1. The Competition Commission Inquiry into SME Banking

Peter Freeman*

I. INTRODUCTION

The SME Banking Report[1] is a recent, major report by the Competition Commission ('the Commission') into one sector of UK banking. It was published on 14 March this year and discussions about its implications and the measures the Government wishes to implement are continuing.

The Commission concluded that the market for the supply of banking services to SMEs was not working fully effectively; they found a concentrated structure, barriers to entry and a reluctance of customers to switch between suppliers. They found several pricing practices to be anti-competitive and, crucially, concluded that both prices and profits were excessive, although they limited this conclusion to England and Wales. The Commission recommended a number of 'behavioural' remedies. In addition, they recommended a 'transitional' pricing remedy under which the larger clearing banks should offer their customers either interest on business current accounts at 2.5 per cent below base rate, or free money transmission services, or a choice between the two.

The Government (the Chancellor of the Exchequer and Secretary of State for Trade and Industry acting jointly) accepted the Commission's recommendations in full and asked the Director General of Fair Trading to agree undertakings with the parties concerned. These discussions are still in progress.

It is not intended to say very much about the substance of the SME Report. Given that the period for bringing judicial review has not yet expired and that discussions on undertakings are in progress, there is obviously some considerable sensitivity. Instead, the objective of this paper is to consider how these complex monopoly inquiries work in practice and whether there are any lessons to be learnt from this Inquiry.

We shall begin by describing the present system for investigating complex monopolies and then consider how the SME Inquiry itself was conducted

* Solicitor, Head of EC and Competition Group, Simmons & Simmons. Paper given at the Second Annual Conference on International and Comparative Competition Law, BIICL, May 2002. This paper is intended to state the law as at 18 May 2002.

[1] 'The Supply of Banking Services by Clearing Banks to Small and Medium Sized Enterprises', Cm 5319 (2002), Published 14 Mar 2002.

and touch briefly on the substantive findings. We then ask whether things would have been different if this had been a 'market investigation' under the new Enterprise Bill proposals, and try and draw some conclusions.

A. Complex Monopoly Investigations

1. The Legal Analysis

The Government's Enterprise White Paper[2] described the complex monopoly law as 'a rigid structural framework . . . that is difficult to work with'.[3] In this age of economics, that may not strike a legal audience as necessarily a bad thing, but a closer examination may reveal genuine problems.

Essentially the scheme of the Fair Trading Act ('FTA') control of monopolies (which in one form or another extends back to 1948)[4] is to control the exploitation, against the public interest, of legally defined monopoly situations.

There are three stages to the analysis:

1. Is there a monopoly situation?
2. In whose favour does it exist? and
3. Does any act or omission by that person operate, or may it be expected to operate, against the public interest?

2. Monopoly Situations

'Scale' or 'structural' monopolies are distinguished from 'behavioural' or 'complex monopoly' situations. A scale monopoly is where at least one quarter of the services (or goods) of any description are supplied by one and the same person (including inter-connected bodies corporate). A complex monopoly, by contrast, is where that quarter is supplied by two or more persons (not being a group of inter-connected bodies corporate) who:

> whether voluntarily or not, and whether by agreement or not, so conduct their respective affairs as in any way to prevent, restrict or distort competition in connection with the supply of services of that description, whether or not they themselves are affected by the competition, and whether the competition is between persons interested as persons by whom, or as persons for whom, services are supplied.[5]

[2] 'Productivity and Enterprise: A World Class Competition Regime', Cm 5233 (2001), para 6.51.

[3] Ibid, para 6.51.

[4] Monopolies and Restrictive Practices (Inquiry and Control) Act 1948.

[5] Section 7(2) FTA. See Section 6(2) for similar a definition in relation to production or supply of goods.

3. *Identification of a Monopoly Situation—a Jurisdictional Test or a Judgment?*

The identification of monopoly is usually described as a matter of pure jurisdiction. It enables the Competition Commission to 'move on' to the substantive issue of whether the 'monopoly' enables the 'monopolists' to exploit it against the public interest.[6] There are some difficulties with this approach as the application of the test may also involve an assessment of competition.

The test is applied at two stages: first when the reference is made and secondly when the Commission conduct their Inquiry. At the first stage there is some justification for saying that what is needed is a simple, clear legal test, requiring no economic assessment. But the test is also applied by the Commission, who are asked in effect to confirm their own jurisdiction. It will come as little surprise that with one or two minor exceptions[7] the Commission have not refused to do so. Moreover, the test could by no means be described as clear, because it involves a degree of assessment of whether the relevant conduct 'prevents, restricts or distorts competition'. As the Commission themselves said in the SME Report, this 'inevitably requires an exercise of judgment'.[8] They went on to say that no court finding indicated 'that we could not or should not exercise our judgment in making that assessment'.[9]

Second, one might have expected a jurisdictional test to be approached first —in the order set by the FTA—before the issues of exploitation and detriment are addressed. But this need not be so; again, as the Commission said in the SME Report, in discussing the order of presentation:

> [The Conclusions chapter] first considers the reference and the background to it. It then considers the main issues we found to be relevant to two stages of our investigation, namely our finding as to whether a monopoly situation exists, and if so, whether any facts are found which operate or may be expected to operate against the public interest. These two stages are distinct. However, we found in this Inquiry that the underlying issues overlapped to a considerable extent.[10]

Indeed, it is clear the Commission used their assessment of competition in relation to the public interest to underpin their complex monopoly findings. This contrasts with the rather stricter approach adopted for example in the *Supply of Beer*[11] case in 1989 where the MMC said:

[6] See eg, Whish, *Competition Law*, 4th edn (London: Butterworths, 2001), 368.

[7] In *Roadside Advertising Services* (HC 1980–1, 365) the MMC looked critically at the definition of services specified in the reference. In *Television Broadcasting Services* (Cm 2035 (1992)) the MMC found no complex monopoly situation to be present.

[8] Cm 5319, para 2.438.

[9] Ibid.

[10] Cm 5319, para 2.1.

[11] Cm 651 (1989) paras 11.2–11.26, esp 11.16 and 11.25.

The finding of a complex monopoly does not mean that any practices... necessarily constitute facts which operate... against the public interest (11.25).

One is tempted to conclude that the legal gymnastics required to be performed here serve no useful purpose other than to introduce a false sense of legal discipline; that the test is neither straightforward nor purely factual; and that it does not in practice operate as a limit on the Commission's jurisdiction but instead provides a legal hurdle which must be, and virtually always is, successfully jumped as part of the investigation.

'In whose favour . . .'

The purpose of finding 'in whose favour' a complex monopoly situation exists is to distinguish between those whose conduct gives rise to the complex monopoly and those who benefit from it; they can be the same but equally they may differ.[12] Indeed, one of the justifications sometimes put forward for the complex monopoly régime is that it allows action to be taken against persons who are not 'part' of the monopoly.

The Commission must consider whether any action or omission by persons in whose favour the monopoly situation exists 'operates or may be expected to operate against the public interest',[13] and, in relation to remedying any adverse effects, only actions by Government departments and by the persons in whose favour the monopoly situation exists can be considered and relevant recommendations made.[14] In the SME Banking report the persons in whose favour the monopoly was found to operate were essentially the parent companies of the persons who were members of the complex monopoly group.[15]

'Whether any action or omission . . .'

As explained the Commission must consider whether any action or omission on the part of those benefiting from the monopoly operates or may be expected to operate against the public interest. These actions or omissions comprise 'facts'[16] and the Commission are further required to specify the particular adverse effects that these facts have or may be expected to have.[17]

[12] Section 49(2)(b) FTA See *Reg v The MMC ex parte Visa International Service Association* [1991] ECC 291 per Hodgson J. 'It is not in dispute that those persons (in whose favour the monopoly situation exists) may . . . be different from those persons forming the (complex monopoly) group. This is an important distinction . . .'. The Court of Appeal upheld the first instance judgment. See also *Films* (Cm 2673) [1994] and *Contact Lens Solutions* (Cm 2242) [1993] where the persons in whose favour the complex monopoly situation operated included the complex monopoly 'group' and other persons having a legal or economic connection with them.

[13] Section 49(2)(c) FTA.

[14] Section 54(3) and (4) FTA.

[15] Cm 5319, para 2.476.

[16] Section 54(3) FTA.

[17] Ibid.

This again is, to a degree, legal gymnastics. Readers of Commission reports may marvel at the elegant and somewhat dated phraseology which guides them through to the Commission's consideration of issues.

'. . .operates, or may be expected to operate, against the public interest'

When it comes to public interest, it is now the norm for this to be assessed by reference to the effect on competition. Section 84 FTA allows the Commission to do this, but does not require them to do so; in practice they concentrate on 'the desirability of maintaining and providing effective competition between persons supplying goods and services in the UK'.[18] The FTA allows them also to consider a wide range of consumer, efficiency, employment, technical progress and balance of payments issues.[19]

The competition test is itself very flexible. There is no requirement to find dominance or excessive market power, no need to fit within any formal definition of joint or collective dominance or to establish any given threshold of competitive structure or activity. The Commission are able to form their own view of the level of effective competition that it is desirable to look for, and as to how this may be assessed, and to take into account, in that assessment, whatever evidence they think fit.

In the SME Banking Inquiry the Commission made an adverse finding on efficiency (in relation to NatWest) and three other findings in relation to competition: one that the four larger banks charged excessive prices 'to an extent that would not be expected in a fully competitive situation', a second affecting the level of choice of services and a third affecting the level of information available to customers.[20] So this flexibility was used to the full, it might be said.

As to the evidence relied on, a crucial element in the SME Inquiry was the Commission's assessment of bank profitability, to which we will return.

4. *Remedies*

The framework of the Act also provides for remedies. The Commission *must* consider what action (if any) should be taken to remedy the adverse effects it has found and *may* make recommendations for such action.[21] The action may *either* be by Ministers or public authorities or by the beneficiaries of the monopoly situation.[22]

When it comes to the Government's powers to apply remedies, the FTA requires the appropriate Minister (normally the Secretary of State but in the

[18] Section 84(1)(a) FTA. [19] Ibid. [20] Cm 5319, para 2.512.
[21] Section 54(3) FTA. [22] Section 54(4) FTA.

SME Banking case the action was taken by the Chancellor and Secretary of State jointly) to take into account the Commission's recommendations[23] and any advice received from the DGFT under sections 86 and 88 FTA. Section 86 covers advice with respect to the report.[24] Section 88 covers the situation where the DGFT has been asked to investigate the possibility of undertakings and advises the Minister that no undertakings are likely within a reasonable time. The Act gives the Secretary of State wide order making powers under Parts I and II of Schedule 8 FTA but does *not* require the Secretary of State to adopt the Commission's remedies. Accordingly, Ministerial remedies can be identical to the Commission's recommendations, or they may be lesser or greater, or the Minister may do nothing.

If he does take action it must be 'for the purpose of remedying or preventing the adverse effects specified in the report':[25] and must be by reference to the facts found by the Commission that operate or may be expected to operate against the public interest and to the particular adverse effects these facts have or may be expected to have.[26]

In effect, the Commission *proposes* remedies; the DGFT *advises* on them and the Secretary of State *disposes*. In so doing, he is free to do what he likes,[27] provided that if he takes any measures they must be directly addressed to the facts and adverse effects identified in the Report. The current policy is to follow, so far as possible, the views and recommendations of the competition authorities.[28]

5. *Undertakings and Orders*

In practice most remedies take the form of negotiated undertakings; the DGFT is responsible for monitoring their effectiveness. Undertakings are negotiated with the DGFT but given to Ministers.[29] Undertakings are enforceable by civil proceedings as if they were an order; an order is enforceable (under section 93) not by criminal proceedings but by civil proceedings at the behest of any individual and by the Crown by injunction; directions pursuant to an order can be enforced in the courts.

[23] Section 56(3) FTA.

[24] For this to apply the report has to be on a reference which the DGFT himself could have made (section 86(2) FTA).

[25] Section 56(2) FTA.

[26] See section 56(1) and (2) FTA and *R v Secretary of State for Trade & Industry, ex parte Thomson Holidays Ltd* (1999) (unreported) (Times Law Report, 12 Jan 2000).

[27] Including further consultation (see *Carbonated Drinks*, Cm 1625 (1991)).

[28] See, eg, Cm 5233 (2001), para 3.3.

[29] Although Ministers can themselves conduct the negotiations. See: *Supply of Beer*, Cm 651 (1989).

6. *Process*

The Commission are free to set their own procedure and have done so (see the Chairman's Guidance in particular).[30] In essence they proceed by making initial requests for information and holding meetings, either in public or privately, to ascertain facts. They then prepare a list of provisional public interest 'issues' which they circulate to the parties and also publish. They do the same for a provisional 'complex monopoly finding'. They receive written submissions and hold private 'hearings' with the main parties in which they put questions to the parties and transcribe the discussion. They table hypothetical remedies in the same way and hold hearings. Increasingly, these three aspects are approached together. The Commission do not put provisional conclusions to the parties and their current practice is not to disclose their conclusions or discuss them with the parties. Instead the parties are required to comment on and correct so called 'put back' material, which is the descriptive parts of the report in draft form together with the Commission's summary of the parties' own evidence.

Complex monopoly investigations frequently take from one to two years; they consume much time, effort and resources, for Government and the parties alike. I will return to this point later.

7. *Excisions*

As part of the 'put back' process the Commission seek to identify confidential material that the parties wish to see excised from the report. Generally the Commission excise very little from the version they send to Ministers and pass the parties' requests to the DTI for consideration prior to publication informing the parties they have done so.[31] This can be a vexed issue as the DTI's practice is not to discuss possible excisions with the parties prior to publication. The result is that the parties have no way of knowing in advance whether their requests for excision have been accepted by the DTI.[32]

8. *Appeals*

There is no appeal. The actions of the DGFT or Ministers in making a reference, the Commission's report and any subsequent ministerial action are all subject to judicial review. This is a discretionary remedy requiring the leave of the court; the generally accepted grounds for review are procedural

[30] 'Chairman's Guidance to Groups on Procedures', Feb 2000.
[31] The grounds are set out in sections 82 and 83 FTA.
[32] Although they are told what the Commission itself has excised (again after the event).

unfairness, illegality and irrationality. Despite efforts to make it so, particularly since the enactment of the Human Rights Act 1998, judicial review does not allow the merits of the Commission's findings to be tested in court. One can challenge whether they are rational, not whether they are right. We will return to this point.

9. *Complex Monopoly Inquiry under the FTA—Summary*

If we try to summarise the nature of complex monopoly investigations, the following points could be made:

- The legal framework and statutory language date back to 1948.
- The division of functions is in the classic pre-Competition Act style with the DGFT or a Minister making the reference, the Commission investigating and reporting; the Minister deciding on measures, and the DGFT monitoring effectiveness.
- It is uncertain whether 'complex monopoly' is a jurisdictional matter or a substantive (and pejorative) judgment. The term itself is often negatively perceived by the media and by financial markets.
- The legal framework is precise and requires the Commission and Ministers to identify specific persons and facts and limit their actions to relevant matters within that legal framework.
- In practice the régime is used in a purposive way to investigate market failure; but its concerns can stray beyond purely competition issues.
- The Commission set their own procedures; Ministers enjoy a wide discretion on remedies.
- There is the possibility of judicial review, but no appeal on the merits or correctness of the Commission's conclusions or of any subsequent Ministerial action.
- Complex monopoly investigations frequently take from one to two years; they consume much time, effort and resources, for Government and the parties alike.
- Perhaps for this reason, they are not well liked by industry.

II. THE SME BANKING INQUIRY

So much for the background; let us now examine the SME Banking Inquiry itself. It was in some respects unusual in that it followed closely after a more wide-ranging but non-statutory enquiry conducted for the Chancellor by

Mr. Don Cruickshank;[33] and the reference itself was made jointly by the Chancellor and the then Secretary of State, Stephen Byers. The DGFT was not a party to the reference, although the reference was of a kind the DGFT could have made.

A. How the Inquiry was Conducted

1. The Cruickshank Report

The Cruickshank Inquiry was a year long investigation covering most aspects of banking in the UK, initiated in November 1998 (in response to a difficulty perceived by the Chancellor as to the availability of credit for SMEs) and which finally reported in March 2000. The Cruickshank Report made a large number of recommendations in relation to banking and the regulatory framework; it made findings as to profits earned by banks and it discussed developing market conditions in personal banking. In relation to banking services for small business, however, it concluded that structural remedies may be needed and recommended that a complex monopoly inquiry be instituted immediately. This was done.

2. The Reference

The reference made on 20 March 2000 jointly by the Chancellor and the Secretary of State, was in fairly standard terms referring to 'the supply of banking services by clearing banks to small and medium sized enterprises'.[34] It is unusual for the Chancellor to make monopoly references and reflects the heightened interest being shown by HM Treasury in competition matters.[35] The Inquiry period was 15 months to 20 June 2001, later extended to 20 October 2001, a total of 19 months.

3. Definitions

The reference did not define any of the terms it used and the Commission drew up their own definitions.[36] Of greatest significance were the definitions of 'clearing bank', which the Commission defined by reference to membership of UK clearing schemes and 'SMEs', which they defined as enterprises having turnover up to £25 million pa. None of the banks under

[33] 'Competition in UK Banking', published in Mar 2000 by Mr Don Cruickshank, Chairman of the Banking Review Team. The findings on profitability are summarised in Cm 5319 Appendix 5.1.

[34] See Cm 5319 Appendix 1.1.

[35] The CC Report (Cm 5319) was presented to the House of Commons by the Chancellor himself.

[36] See Cm 5319 Appendix 2.1.

investigation provided services to a category of customers defined on this basis, which had implications for the provision of data and the application of any remedies.

4. Procedure

The Commission's procedure followed the following sequence:

- The issue of questionnaires (April–May 2000).
- Open Meeting (3 November 2000).
- Issues Letter (7 November 2000).
- 'Factual' Hearings with the parties (November–December 2000).
- 'Issues' Hearings with the parties (January–February 2001).
- Provisional findings on complex monopoly (5 March 2001).
- Remedies Letter (20 March 2001).
- 'Remedies' Hearings (May 2001).
- 'Profitability' Hearings (June 2001).[37]
- Extension of term (12 June 2001).
- 'Put Back' material (May–October 2001).
- Report (19 October 2001).

There was, of course, a great deal of additional correspondence, discussion, staff meetings and submission of material alongside the formal steps in the process. Material 'put back' for comment and correction, for example, was very substantial and the so-called 'market annex' and 'financial annex' (early drafts of chapters of the report) were put back for comment at a relatively early stage (Autumn 2000).

Adopting a pragmatic approach the CC did not proceed in a 'linear' manner (monopoly, issues, remedies) but combined the various steps. Thus, some remedies were canvassed at the Open Meeting in early November 2000. The provisional complex monopoly finding was not put to the parties until after the so-called 'issues hearings'; and public interest issues (profitability in particular), were being put to the parties alongside the consideration of hypothetical remedies.

[37] There is therefore at least one error of fact in Cm 5319. In Appendix 1.1 para 8 there is reference to three hearings held with the major banks. One bank at least attended four hearings. This error is probably not material to the conclusions.

5. Scale

The scale of a complex monopoly investigation is large, making the task of assimilating, assessing and publishing the results quite immense. The SME Report is in four volumes totalling nearly 1400 pages of text. The 'Summary and Conclusions' volume alone is 160 pages. And some of the print is quite small. The demands made on the Commission's staff team and on the parties under investigation were enormous, with literally hundreds of people working for months at a time. For someone involved from the outset in November 1998 to the present time (for the case is still continuing) we are talking of a campaign equivalent to the First World War—in length of time at least, if not in numbers of casualties and terrain captured. And there must be a cost. One newspaper estimated the total cost as £100 million.

6. Confidentiality

As the Cruickshank team found, the banks were willing to cooperate to a lesser or greater degree but only on condition that the information they provided was not published or otherwise disclosed to competitors or third parties. As the Commission's definition of the SME customer stream was generally not recognised by the main banks involved, information for the Inquiry had to be specifically generated and was not otherwise publicly available.

Confidentiality was a significant issue and the combined effect of the Commission's and the DTI's procedures gave rise to difficulty in this case.

Essentially, the approach of the Commission to excising confidential data from their report to Ministers[38] was that (1) if the material was necessary to understand their industries they would leave it in and (2) disclosure to Ministers did not constitute publication. Therefore, whilst all the banks claimed confidentiality for a large amount of data provided, the Commission largely contented themselves with noting these requests and passing them on, without substantive comment, to the DTI.

The DTI then processed the requests applying a three-stage test: first was the information private, second, would publication (in the Secretary of State's opinion) seriously prejudice their interests, and, third, would it not

[38] Under section 82 FTA, the CC must 'have regard to the need for excluding, so far as that is practicable, .. any matter which relates specifically to the affairs of a particular body of persons, whether corporate or uncorporate, where publication of that matter would or might, in the opinion of... the Commission, as the case may be, seriously and prejudicially affect the interests of that body, unless in their opinion the inclusion of that matter relating specifically to that body is necessary for the purposes of that report.'

be in the public interest to disclose it? As we were reminded in the course of correspondence with the DTI, the decision is the Secretary of State's decision and while the parties can make representations, they can do no more than that to influence the process. In particular, the DTI refused to disclose what was proposed to be excised on the grounds that this might give the parties a clue to the Commission's conclusions.

The issue here was not so much whether to dispute the Secretary of State's decision but more to guard against mistakes. With so much confidential data involved it was asking a lot of the DTI officials to get it all right. You might think that a discussion with the parties would prevent mistakes occurring—but this was not allowed.

One of the parties' difficulties is that whilst they have seen the 'put back' material in draft, and claimed confidentiality on that basis, they have not seen any draft conclusions so did not know how much of their confidential data was included in them. The Government's view is that they cannot be shown what will be excised even from the parts of the Report they have seen in draft as it might enable them to work out what data the Commission thought was 'necessary for the purposes of the Report'.

This is a particularly futile and arid source of dispute. The issue only arises because of the perceived need to keep everyone outside the Government circle completely in the dark as to the conclusions in the Report, until Ministers have made up their minds what to do with it. This is therefore an issue of transparency, to which we will now turn.

7. Transparency

Transparency is a constituent of fair procedure but it is not synonymous with it. The Commission conducted a process which was in many ways very transparent and they are to be commended for doing so. The main formal documents were published, the open meeting was a useful initial exposé of the issues, the parties generally knew what issues were being considered and what stage the enquiry had reached, and there was some sensitivity shown to the needs of financial markets and the banks' reporting season during the period of March–April 2001. But there remain two serious points.

First, transparency to the world at large is not necessarily fair to the parties. Banks are unfortunately not held in universally high public esteem and a blow-by-blow public account of what the Commission were doing to them might not be perceived as helpful to their interests. What matters for the parties is transparency to them, ie a clear idea of what points they have to answer.

Here, despite all the emphasis on transparency—the putting of issues to the parties and the writing of documents setting these matters out at great length—the parties are told in practice everything except the one thing they really need to know, and to that extent transparency is not in itself delivering a fair process.

B. *Fairness of Process*

1. *The essential ingredient*

It is all too easy to describe as unfair things that simply do not go one's way. But what the parties need to know in order to engage in an effective argument with the Commission is not so much what are the issues (although that is helpful) but what is the Commission's assessment of them. In other words, what is being made of the party's evidence and arguments? Are they being accepted or rejected? If rejected, then on what grounds? If on the basis of some other party's evidence, then what was that evidence? Can it be disclosed and what is the Commission's view of it?

The answer given by the Commission in the SME Inquiry, when faced with arguments of this kind, was essentially that they were based on a fundamental misunderstanding of the way the Commission approach their task; the Commission do not engage in dialogue with the parties; they are not required to debate the issues; they put them to the parties, receive and consider their response; what they make of them is for the Commission alone.

The response to which is, surely, that this is precisely the problem. We know that is how the Commission operate. The question is, should they operate in that way?

2. *Justifications for the present practice*

Two main justifications were put forward by the Commission in the SME Inquiry for not discussing their reasoning with the parties. First that they were not legally required to do so; second that to change their procedures would require a process of consultation and this could not be done in the middle of an Inquiry.

3. *The law*

The leading case is of course *Interbrew*,[39] which was decided in January

[39] *Interbrew SA & anr v Competition Commission & anr* [2001] EWHC ADMIN 367.

2001, at a crucial stage in the SME Inquiry. In the Interbrew case, which involved the judicial review of a Commission merger report, it was argued, amongst other things, that the Commission ought to share their conclusions with the parties. Moses J made it clear that he thought the FTA did *not* require the Commission to put conclusions, even in provisional form, to the parties, better to inform the submissions on the appropriateness of remedies. The case was decided on a different issue of procedural fairness and the judgment was not appealed.

It is important to distinguish between whether giving provisional conclusions is *required* by the FTA and whether it is *permitted*. It is clearly permitted; but the Commission set their own procedure and there is nothing legally to stop them from changing it in this respect.

4. *Consultation*

In the context of the Enterprise Bill, the Commission has now[40] expressed a willingness to provide the parties with provisional conclusions on the issues, before going on to consider remedies. Reaction to this proposal has generally been favourable, but there is no reason why it could not have been implemented earlier; also in itself it is no panacea. What is needed is not just a formal statement of provisional conclusions but a more general willingness on the part of the Commission to engage in a dialectic process rather than a purely inquisitorial one—to be willing to justify the position they propose to take as opposed to simply stating it and closing the discussion.

5. *The Importance of Appeals*

Why does the Commission's unwillingness to debate, rather than to dispose, matter so much? The answer is simple; there is no appeal against the Commission's conclusions on the substance of the issues they investigate. It is hard to overstate the importance of this. If the Commission get their analysis wrong and come to a flawed conclusion the only thing that suffers (apart from the parties' interests), is their own reputation for judgment and competence. The conclusions as such cannot be overturned and may then be relied on as the basis for future regulatory action.

We discuss judicial review below. The essential point is that the absence of appeal on the merits means that the Commission are able to conduct their inquiry in the way that they do: tabling of issues, receipt of submissions, inquisitorial 'hearings' and then the putting together of conclusions without debating them with the parties under investigation.

[40] See CC Chairman's Press Release of 26 Mar 2002 (21/02).

6. *Judicial Review*

There is only a limited amount that can be said on judicial review in relation to the SME Inquiry as time for leave is still running. More generally, however, the limitations of judicial review are these:

Illegality

The authorities must correctly apply the law; this is controlled by the courts and is an important safeguard and discipline. On the whole, though, the courts are reluctant to turn this ground of review into a means of interfering with the Commission's assessment.[41]

Error of fact or reason

A material error of fact on the part of the Commission could be the subject of review but the control is essentially over the process of reasoning and assessment of evidence rather than the judgment that is made on the merits; and the hurdle of irrationality is high.[42]

Unfair process

Here again the hurdle is high and a significant degree of unfair process is required, of a kind that might influence the result, for review to succeed; and there is no reason to think that the Commission are intentionally unfair, in the sense that this is interpreted by the courts— the parties are generally made aware of the issues before them. Indeed, since the Interbrew case, the parties are as aware as the Commission can possibly make them and in the SME case they received two long letters at a late stage in the Inquiry essentially to the effect of: 'Here is what we have put to you. If there is anything you think we have not put to you, please tell us.' The real value of this may appear rather elusive.

The Carsberg opinion

In the SME Inquiry there was one aspect of the process that was unusual, to say the least. Before announcing the Government's decision, and without any consultation with the parties under investigation, HM Treasury commissioned a report from Sir Bryan Carsberg, a former DGFT and more recently Chairman of the International Accounting Standards Board, to report on the Commission's methodology for assessing the banks' profitability. That report was published with the full report on March 14th. It

[41] See *South Yorkshire Transport* [1993] 1 *WLR* 23, and *R v MMC ex parte Visa International Service Association* [1991] *CCLR* 13.

[42] *R v Monopolies and Mergers Commission ex parte, Matthew Brown Plc.* [1987] 1 *WLR* 1235.

endorsed the Commission's approach in general terms although making it clear that the author would not necessarily always have come to the same precise conclusion.

Distorting effect

The fact that the only way of overturning the Commission's findings and recommendations is by way of judicial review has a distorting effect on the process itself. Without giving away too many secrets, it is known that advice given to regulatory authorities is essentially this: provided the issues in play are put to the affected parties in sufficient detail for them to comment effectively, provided all evidence received is fully and fairly considered, and provided that the process of reasoning by which the conclusions are reached is sufficiently described and is not obviously implausible, the courts will not interfere with the conclusions themselves. This tends to encourage emphasis on giving the parties the opportunity to comment, on gathering in and assimilating the evidence and on describing in considerable detail the process of reasoning leading to the conclusions. Indeed, the Commission's usual approach is to describe the evidence they have considered, review the arguments, particularly from the parties, and then simply to express their view.[43] They do this in the knowledge that a court will almost always defer to that view.

The Period between Report and Announcement

The Commission send their report to Ministers who deliberate and eventually publish it[44] with their conclusions. The time is also spent working through the parties' requests for excisions. The administrative timetable set for this process is ten weeks.[45]

In the SME case, the Report was sent out on 19 October 2001 and Ministers announced their conclusions some 5 months later on 14 March. During that time (twice as long as the 'normal' timetable) the Government commissioned the Carsberg report (in secret), worked through excisions (again in secret), received the DGFT's advice (again in secret) and, presumably, debated what to do, deciding in the end to adopt all of the Commission's conclusions and recommendations.

Whatever else can be said of procedure under the complex monopoly régime, this part of it is, from the point of view of common sense, amongst the least satisfactory. The obsession with secrecy combined with the refusal

[43] Eg, Cm 5319 paras 2.140, 2.145, 2.242 etc.
[44] Ie, they lay it before Parliament. See section 83 FTA.
[45] See 'Guidance on DTI Procedures for handling Monopoly References and Reports', para 7.1.

to consult prior to a final decision is unfortunate. Not only does it diminish those conducting the process, but it risks an ineffective or impracticable result when it comes to the remedies adopted. As we shall see this part of the process will go with the Enterprise Act, and for many this will not be a cause for regret.

C. Substance

There is not a great deal I can usefully say about the substance of the Report from an objective point of view. More time is needed to examine the conclusions and the evidence described in the Report. However, as and when the debate progresses, it will probably focus on the following points at issue:

1. The findings on profits and prices

The Commission's conclusions on profitability and prices are summarised in paragraph 2.431 of the report. These were essentially that:

- Between 1998 and 2000 the four largest banks earned excess profits from SME banking.
- Those banks set prices so that they more than adequately financed an efficient business such as would emerge under fully competitive conditions.
- Hence, the level of excess profits was a measure of excess prices.[46]
- There was 'good reason to believe' that these excess profits and prices derived from current accounts and deposit accounts within the liquidity management service supplied by the major banks.
- Excess profits resulted from lack of price competition.
- Excess profits were indicative of lack of price competition.
- A pricing remedy was needed to 'give the level of prices a decisive and significant shift towards competitive levels.[47]
- Discussion on these central findings is likely to focus on the following:
  —The period over which excess profits were earned (whether three years at a beneficial part of the cycle can be said to constitute relevant 'persistent' excess profits).

[46] See para 2.490. [47] See Cm 5319, para 2.563.

—How to set the standard of 'fully competitive conditions' by which the level of financing is assessed, other than by a process of circular reasoning.

—Whether excess profits can, at the same time, result from lack of price competition, indicate a lack of price competition and be the measure of the excess prices resulting from lack of price competition.

—The method used to assess profitability: in particular the measurement of capital, the allocation of capital to the SME business, the assessment of profits, adjustment to the bad debt ratio, the whole approach to cyclicality and the period over which profits should be measured; the assessment and allocation of costs; what is 'excess' or 'excessive' and the benchmarks (if any) used.

—The assessment of price competition: in particular the reliance placed on 'price parallelism', market structure, price discrimination, differentiation and negotiation as indicating lack of price competition; the significance attached to customer behaviour as regards switching between banks and shopping around for products.

—The assessment of barriers to entry and the weight attached to the prospects for new entry and the evidence of actual new entry.

—The appropriateness of the main remedy to address the excess profits and prices found; whether, in an essentially unregulated industry, it is feasible to regulate the price charged for one product within a relevant service market without affecting prices for other products within the relevant market, or in other markets; whether the further measures envisaged should this happen,[48] are realistic.

—Similarly, in relation to the pricing remedy, the sense of imposing a pricing requirement on the incumbent banks that was one of the main competitive offerings for new entrants.

2. *Other matters*

There is much else in the Report about service provision and quality and other customer/consumer orientated aspects. These are of great interest to suppliers and customers alike but the controversy they arouse in terms of competition analysis is perhaps less significant.

One aspect is worth noting. The Commission found that the low percentage of switching by customers between banks was a feature of the market

[48] See Cm 5319, para 2.597.

that restricted competition. Apart from what they saw as the banks' tendency to offer favourable terms to dissuade customers from switching, the Commission found that 'the clearing banks were not responsible for any other obstruction to switching'. The Commission nevertheless recommended a series of action to be taken by banks to assist switching but accepted that significant constraints on switching would remain[49]. One is left with the feeling that the Commission felt frustrated by what they perceived as the 'wrong sort' of customer behaviour.

3. *Structural issues*

Suffice it to say that the Cruickshank Report's original justification for the inquiry—the need to consider structural remedies—was rejected by the Commission. Such remedies are by their nature drastic[50] and in the SME case could in theory have consisted either of horizontal divestment (the severance of SME banking activities) or vertical (the severance of bank branches). The Commission paid little or no attention to the former. On the latter they quickly discovered the several paradoxes of bank branches; banks that have them would often prefer not to, those that don't, want them. Customers make patchy use of them until closure or disposal is threatened, at which point they wish to use them all the time. Given that their use is as much by personal as by business customers, the Commission prudently avoided this particular problem.

III. WOULD THIS INQUIRY HAVE BEEN DIFFERENT UNDER THE ENTERPRISE BILL PROPOSALS?

The complex monopoly régime's demise was announced in the recent White Paper[51] and for a fleeting moment it looked as if these wide ranging inquiries would be a thing of the past. However, this was not to be and the Government set out its plans for new system of 'Market Investigations' which are now contained in Part 4, Clause 123 onwards, of the Enterprise Bill.

In view of the modernising claims made for this new system, it is only reasonable to ask whether the SME Banking Inquiry would have been any different if carried out under this new régime, insofar as one can work out what it will be like.

49 See Cm 5319 para 2.519 to 2.532.
50 See *Supply of Beer*, Cm 651 (1989).
51 'Productivity and Enterprise: A World Class Competition Regime', Cm 5233 (2001).

A. Making the reference

The first, obvious, point is that the legal edifice of 'complex monopoly' is to be swept away. It is replaced by a power for the OFT to make a reference to the Commission if it:

> has reasonable grounds for suspecting that any feature, or combination of features, of a market in the United Kingdom for goods or services prevents, restricts or distorts competition in connection with the supply or acquisition of any goods or services in the United Kingdom or a part of the United Kingdom.[52]

So, instead of a group of persons 'so conducting their affairs' we now have 'any feature, or combination of features of a market'.

'Feature' means any conduct (whether or not in the market concerned) of suppliers and also of customers. It also means market structure.[53] 'Conduct' includes a failure to act (intentionally or not) and 'any other unintentional conduct'.[54]

There is no threshold of a quarter of services supplied.

The likely effect of these provisions is as follows:

- The making of a reference by the OFT means that it suspects that competition on the market is not working effectively.
- This may be due to market structure, conduct of suppliers and/or conduct of customers.
- 'Market Investigation' reference is a more neutral term than the 'complex monopoly' reference.
- The OFT will have made a substantive judgment on competition and must be able to demonstrate that its suspicions are reasonable. In practice the reference is likely to follow an investigation by its own Markets and Policy Initiatives Division.[55]

B. References by Ministers

One might have been forgiven for believing that Ministers were being removed from the application of Competition policy.[56] However by

[52] Enterprise Bill, Clause 123(1).
[53] Enterprise Bill, Clause 123(2).
[54] Enterprise Bill, Clause 123(2).
[55] Note also the new powers of the OFT to require attendance and testimony on oath. See Enterprise Bill, Clause 166(3) and (7).
[56] See the Secretary of State's Foreword to Cm 5233: 'Ministers will be taken out of the vast majority of monopoly and merger cases.'

Clause 124, if a Minister (normally the Secretary of State) 'is not satisfied' with an OFT decision *not* to make a reference, he/she may do so on the same grounds as the OFT ('reasonable suspicion' etc.). So what happened in the SME case (where the OFT initially declined to become involved in the Cruickshank process) could still happen, and 'the appropriate Minister' can mean the Secretary of State *or* the Secretary of State acting jointly with other Ministers.[57]

C. *The Investigation*

The main changes in relation to Commission investigations seem likely to be as follows:[58]

- The Commission must now decide (rather than 'conclude') whether the feature (or combination of features) prevents, restricts or distorts competition as the OFT suspected.[59] If they so decides then there is a consequential, 'adverse effect on competition'.[60]
- The Commission must also decide:
- Whether they should take action to remedy, mitigate or prevent the 'adverse effect on competition' and any 'detrimental effect on customers';
- Whether others should do so, and, in either case;
- What action they should take and what is to be remedied, mitigated or prevented.[61]
- 'Detrimental effect on customers' means higher prices, lower quality or less choice in any market, or less innovation in the investigated market.[62]
- The Commission must try and be as comprehensive as possible but in deciding what to do (as opposed to deciding whether there is any adverse effect on competition) the Commission may have regard to the effect of any action on any 'relevant customer benefit' of the market features they have found.[63]

[57] Enterprise Bill, Clause 124(5). This paper does not attempt to discuss the provisions for public interest intervention by the Secretary of State in market investigation cases pursuant to Clauses 131-145.

[58] Enterprise Bill, Clause 126.

[59] Enterprise Bill, Clause 126(1). There is no attempt to link this test with the corresponding test in Art 81 or the Competition Act 1998 although it is hard to see how, in practice, such a 'read-across' can sensibly be avoided.

[60] Enterprise Bill, Clause 126(2).

[61] Enterprise Bill, Clause 126(4).

[62] Enterprise Bill, Clause 126(5).

[63] Enterprise Bill, Clauses 126(6) and (7), respectively.

- A 'relevant customer benefit' is the converse of the detrimental effect already described and the benefit must 'accrue as a result' of the market features concerned within a reasonable period and be unlikely to accrue without the market feature.[64]
- So we have a whole new vocabulary of terms including:

—'market features (or combination of features)',

—'adverse effect on competition',

—'action to remedy, mitigate or prevent the adverse effect',

—'detrimental effect on customers',

—'relevant customer benefit'.

At first sight it would not appear that the construction and terminology of Clauses 123–7 indicate that the investigation of markets has broken free of legal complexity, if that was the objective. As before, the Commission will have to make their decisions using the right legal terminology and going through each step in the right order.

D. Procedure

This Commission, as before, will set their own procedure. The Chairman of the Competition Commission has said he intends to issue provisional conclusions, as a prelude to a discussion of remedies.[65] This is a welcome step, but it is not one that is guaranteed by statute and could be dropped if the Commission find it difficult to make it work. Also, as previously described, while the issuing of provisional conclusions will help make the remedies discussion more rational, this will not *in itself* make the Commission's process for reaching its conclusions either fairer or better. It may, however, be more difficult for the Commission to refuse to discuss their reasoning, once their provisional conclusions have been shared with the parties. In particular it will be difficult for them to refuse to consider how provisional conclusions could be changed if the parties provide credible arguments as to why they are wrong.

E. Time Limits

The overall time limit is two years from the date of the reference—but this

64 Enterprise Bill, Clause 126(8).

65 CC Press Release, 'Competition Commission Welcomes Enterprise Bill', 26 Mar 2002 (21/02).

limit can be amended by Order.[66] There is obviously concern that the process may be prolonged by the changes to the conduct of investigations, but the timetable seems generous enough and will certainly not limit the scope or scale of the investigation any more than at present.

F. Implementation

Unlike the present situation, this is for the Commission, who have a duty to remedy any adverse effect on competition that they have found.[67] In doing so they must decide consistently with their substantive findings unless there has since been a material change of circumstance or 'the Commission otherwise [have] a special reason for deciding differently'.[68]

Implementation is by interim and final undertakings and orders.[69] The intention appears to be to preserve much of the current framework save for the crucial difference that in the case of competition investigations, undertakings are given to, and orders made by, the Commission themselves.

So, unlike the present situation, undertakings to comply with remedy decisions would be negotiated with and given to the Commission.

The effect of this is likely to be profound; the Commission will have to move from an advisory to a decision making rôle, and the investigation is likely to become much more focused and sharp.

G. Appeals

Any aggrieved person may apply to the Competition Appeal Tribunal ('CAT') to review a decision of the OFT, Minister, Secretary of State or the Commission.[70] This includes a failure to take a decision and is clearly intended to be a right available to suppliers, competitors and customers alike.

This is the much vaunted 'new appeal procedure'.[71] It is indeed a right (ie without the need to apply for leave) to have a decision reviewed by a specialist tribunal and to that extent is to be welcomed. Appeal on a point of law lies to the Court of Appeal and beyond, but unlike the Competition Act 1998 this is not an appeal on the merits. The CAT must 'apply the same principles as would be applied by a court on an application for judicial

[66] Enterprise Bill, Clause 129.

[67] Enterprise Bill, Clause 130.

[68] Enterprise Bill, Clause 130(3).

[69] Enterprise Bill, Part 4, ch 3.

[70] Enterprise Bill, Clause 169(1).

[71] Eg DTI Press Release 'Hewitt Introduces Bill to Boost Enterprise and Prosperity for All' 26 Mar 2002 (P/2002/193).

review',[72] and the CAT may only quash the decision and refer it back to be taken again.[73]

So, as now, the decision of the Commission on the merits of the case will not be open to appeal and we have not really made much progress here. It seems hardly necessary to rehearse the anomaly by which the same CAT reviews the merits of Competition Act 1998 decisions, but not those that will arise under the Enterprise Act.

Institutional gymnastics would need to have been performed to avoid the situation of one part of the Commission being subject to review by another part. Under the latest proposals, it is understood that the CAT is to be formally separated from the reporting (now decision making) side of the 'Commission' with no common members or staff.[74]

So, on the question of appeal, there is in substance little change. Market investigations will not be subject to appeal on their merits.

IV. CONCLUSION

The following conclusions may be drawn from this brief examination of the SME Inquiry against the background of the imminent changes to the legal framework:

1. The background to the SME Inquiry was unusual, stemming from a non-statutory competition inquiry sponsored by H M Treasury. The political dimension was inevitably a factor throughout the Inquiry.
2. The Inquiry was long and complex—in the literal sense; there were serious issues of definition and data production and the Report itself was some 1400 pages long. Large resource demands were made.
3. The complex monopoly legal framework does not appear to have provided much methodological constraint; the same competition analysis underlay the monopoly and the public interest stages.
4. The conduct of the inquiry, although overtly transparent, displayed all the characteristics of a process subject to judicial review rather than to a merits appeal; the *Interbrew* case led to even greater emphasis on putting issues to the parties. No provisional conclusions were put to the parties and insufficient debate took place as to the development of the Commission's thinking.

[72] Enterprise Bill, Clause 169(6).
[73] Enterprise Bill, Clause 169(7).
[74] Enterprise Bill, Part 5.

5. On substance, the findings on prices and profits were coloured by a suspicion of circularity; the profit findings themselves relied heavily on the Commission's choice of baseline, and adjustments and allocations from the baseline. They were, in the literal sense, 'constructed'.

6. On remedies, the Cruickshank Report's justification for a complex monopoly inquiry—the possibility of structural remedies—was not pursued. The main (pricing) remedy raises difficult issues and does not have any obvious market-opening purpose or effect; consequently 'success' may be difficult to judge.

7. 'Market investigations' under the Enterprise Act will provide a different but still quite exacting legal framework with new, but not simple, terminology. The authorities will have responsibility for investigation, inquiry, decisions, remedies and implementation all within a statutory timetable. Provisional conclusions will be put to the parties but no greater degree of debate is promised. The right of appeal remains elusive, with judicial review continuing to dominate, in contrast to the Chapter I and II régime.

8. Overall, there is ground for some scepticism as to whether the new régime will offer significant improvements over the old. Market investigations will continue to be essentially the view of an expert but not uniquely expert body who conduct their business behind the shelter of substantive immunity. This remains an unsound basis for regulation. It is regrettable that the Enterprise proposals perpetuate this situation, which will inevitably have to be revisited at some stage in the future.

2. The German and British Models

Dr Thomas Jestaedt*

PROFESSOR JOHN VICKERS

Welcome to the session relating to competition in banking and financial services. This is of particular interest to me, and it's a pleasure to be invited to chair the session. Before I join the OFT a year and a half ago, I was at the Bank of England for a while; and I'm quite often asked what is the biggest difference between the Bank of England and the OFT. The answer is that the subject of banking and financial services almost never crops up at the Bank of England; this is not the case of the OFT, although both jobs involve setting interest rates, but that's another matter. So I'm going to be a keenly interested consumer at this session. The overarching theme of the conference is trends and tensions, and this is the session where the speakers are both trendy and tense—they're trendy because they're all using PowerPoint, and tense because they're not sure they know which buttons to press, but that's something we will observe in due course.

THOMAS JESTAEDT

I will be talking about the application of EU competition law—thank you for having a German speaker on that one. I think it was a famous US Supreme Court Justice who once said that anti-trust problems are like holes in your socks, you don't worry about them unless someone makes you take off your shoes. And the banking industry in Europe is, I think, still firmly wearing its shoes, because if we look at the cases in a very brief overview of three minutes, we see that in the 1980s we had the good old money transfer and payment system cases, which actually continued until today and there have been a few recent decisions. These cases dealt with issues such as customer fee arrangements, interchange fees, non-discrimination etc., and as you can see, they have arisen mostly in a national framework.

Mostly, the cases concern agreements among associations—the Helsinki Agreement, for instance, as the name says, concerns the French thinking, and so forth with the other ones you see listed here. These cases I would term rather technical, and obviously the core line that the Commission took in those cases in the 1980s was that anything relating to customer fee arrangements should be prohibited, and they also issued a notice in 1995

* Lovells, Brussels. Speech given at the Second Annual Conference on International and Comparative Competition Law, BIICL, May 2002.

that summarises the policy. Then there have been two recent cartel cases, both from the German-speaking part of Europe, and I should term them as transition cases. The first case was named after a street here in London but actually took place in the most exclusive restaurant in Vienna, and that is the Lombard Club case, which the Commission is presently reviewing and which, according to the Commission's findings, is a clear-cut case of price-fixing. So that was the transition to new membership for Austria, and actually these lunches in that famous restaurant had a long tradition going back to before Austria even joined the EEA.

And then we have the Euro Conversion Rates case, which was decided last year, which is the transition to the euro for certain German banks, which according to the Commission's findings had agreed on the same rates to charge for the euro conversion. We have 121 cases, merger control cases involving banks, but only two of them raised real issucs, and both cases involved national champions—the bank *Austria Credit Anstadt* case of 1997 and the Swedish case with SEB and FEB, I've abbreviated the names because they are too difficult to pronounce. This case, following the opening of the second phase, was abandoned by the two parties; the Commission saw a very strong position of the combined force in the Swedish retail market. And then we have what are really the core competition cases, and now we come to the area in which competition law is almost playing a core role, the area of State aid.

Here we have quite a number of cases, dealing mainly with public banks, and I would like to state, especially from the German perspective, that this is obviously a very important issue right now in competition policy application in Europe. The old cases, going back to the 1990s, concern the restructuring of the French, Italian and Spanish public banking sector, and obviously the most important case was Tredilione, which I think received a total of 120 billion French francs in subsidies over a number of years.

These are the more basic restructuring cases—a bank in financial difficulty claiming aid to restructure and in return for the aid, making a commitment to drastically reduce its capacity.

Following these basic cases, we see now a more refined application of the State aid rules in the German *Landesbanken* cases, which are also public banks, but which concern the assessment of capital injections into companies that were sound and not in financial difficulties, as were the French and Italian—not in the same situation as Tredilione, for instance—and the assessment of public guarantees that had been in existence for 200 years for the German public banks. The third line of cases, and in both cases I should say that the Commission found that State aid was present, in one case the Commission handed down a decision, and in the other one, in the

Landesbanken case, it reached a settlement with the German Government, which a few weeks ago said that this would be abolished over time, and there's a very generous transition period of 15 years.

Then we have the true general economic interest services cases, and obviously there is a text-book case of how you should do it, which is the UK Universal Banking Services Case. This case was notified and a very narrowly-defined general economic interest service was conferred onto the ultimate recipient of the State aid; it was approved by the Commission, the Commission had no problem, at least on reading the decision, in finding that this was compatible with the Treaty. The French *Livret Bleu* case was also a case where Commission ultimately accepted that the provision of this *Livret Bleu* service contained a public service that was capable of being compensated through State aid. So if we really try to summarise the EU approach, it's really case-by-base and incoherent. Why is that so? Because the first element, which is a kind of mixed economic and political argument, is the so-called 'specialness' of the financial services—you find a reference to that also in the Cruickshank Report, for instance.

Why are financial services special? Because of the special systemic risks—if one bank has difficulties, the entire system is affected, and therefore they create these solidarity mechanisms that later we will talk about. They are special because markets and services are still national—this may change after the euro introduction, but according to the decision in the merger field by the Commission, the markets are because of language frontiers and so forth still national. They are special because of the political interference that you see in the public banking sector and in other sectors.

Another very important aspect of why the Commission isn't able to apply competition law in the financial services as for instance one would do in the insurance sector, is the general economic interest exception in Article 86.2, and we are right now, especially with the spectre of fear of State aid, seeing really a changing of the tides in there. I have already mentioned the *Ferring* judgment, and here we'll not go into detail, where the European Court of Justice ruled that the mere compensation of the cost of a public service does not constitute State aid; this is a deviation from Commission practice and also from the decisions of the Court of First Instance, and Advocate-General Jacobs has just written a very interesting opinion on that in the *Gamo* case, to try to sort that problem.

Financial services are different because the Commission will often find that there is no appreciable effect on trade between member states, and also because markets are national, there will in general not be single dominance, so as long as the collective dominance theory was still under-developed, we didn't see any Article 82 cases, which I think is interesting, also for the UK decision and for the discussion in the UK which is to follow. So therefore, the EU leaves the core competition policy to the member states. And this is my last slide—it may be a somewhat provocative comparison of Germany, you could say the Continent and the UK—on different approaches to preventing or dealing with market failure in the SME and private customer segments, which I understand is one of the core subjects of interest.

Arguably, in Germany, we try to prevent that market failure through the public banking system, which is based on a very broad general economic interest exception; it obviously leads to a certain degree of over-banking and low rates on return, not only affecting the public banks, but as you may have seen Deutsche Bank also got downgraded a few days ago. This has its problems with the EU on the State aid side, and as I said, the German government has capitulated on this a few weeks ago. In the UK, apparently, the approach is to have only a very narrow economic interest exception, limited to the core services, such as evidences in the *Universal Banking Services* case; there is no over-banking, probably a higher profitability, but the market failure issues, to the extent there are such issues, are apparently addressed under national law. You can see, I mean you have two big member states where obviously the competition approach to banking appears to be rather divergent, and they both can co-exist under the European system, one probably better than the German one with the public banks' situation. Thank you.

3. Solidity and Competition

Professor Paul Dobson*

What I'd like to talk about today is essentially a follow-up to Nick Paul's discussion about competition and what is being increasingly seen as a regulated sector. It's a group of markets representing banking and broadly the financial services, and the examples I'm going to use today are predominantly British, but the issues that it raises are generic across other countries as well.

I think the aspect I want to focus on first is that of trends in terms of competition, and the immediate issue that one is concerned with is the pace of change and what's actually going on in terms of competition. It's been a sector that has witnessed great change in terms of its activity and the nature of that activity, but it is quite apparent that in some areas there has been, for want of a better term, some degree of ossification. That is, the general nature of the firms there, the incumbents, means that they haven't essentially changed a lot in terms of structure of the market, but some elements of the behaviour might have changed. I'll compare this aspect with what has been seen as more dynamic markets, but it's apparent that when you observe market ossification, there is a number of issues that drive that; clearly concentration processes are important, to do with the nature of efficiency, and I've suggested that's down to things like economies of scale, scope and density, and by density I mean necessarily a network that may support the industry, an example would be banking with local banks and outlets. Clearly there's a process of mergers and consolidation going on, but there's also been a degree of segmentation, where potentially firms have sought to differentiate themselves from rivals to head off outside competition.

Added to that, of course, are significant barriers to entry, expansion, mobility and potentially exit, and a lot of that has to do with the very fundamental nature of financial services; that the key aspect that greets you about them is the nature of asymmetric information. Consumers are just not very well informed about the nature of the product they're purchasing and the implications of it, and that tends to affect their behaviour. There are issues related to that about customer switching costs, the issue about how you can change providers and the incentives to do so, and they're not immediately easy for consumers to configure or determine. In those circumstances, reputation of firms matters enormously, because that's what builds consumer

* Loughborough University. Speech given at the Second Annual Conference on International and Comparative Competition Law, BIICL, May 2002.

confidence that's what allows a market to progress. The big issue facing any regulator in this sector is to ensure that there isn't market failure; that is, that the market doesn't just go into terminal decline because of poor reputation of firms or poor reputation of products offered. That then gives a role for the regulator in protecting consumers and also in developing the industry where possible; but in itself, that regulatory protection might protect the incumbent firms, and the whole structure might lead to some degree of ossification.

Now, there's been a lot of discussion about UK banking, we've heard from the second speaker about the issues relating to SME banking; but there's been a general concern that while there's been some degree of jockeying of positions in UK banking, there hasn't been substantial change. I've given here an illustration of rankings for the top ten UK businesses—notice this is by market capitalisation and not market share. There's been some jockeying, and there's obviously been some mergers going on; in fact, since the 2000 ranking there's been two further mergers involving Royal Bank of Scotland and NatWest and Bank of Scotland and the Halifax. There's been a coupled new entry because of demutualisation, but when you look beneath this, you actually see that there has in structural terms been quite a bit of change. Leaving aside the branches, you see that concentration has generally been falling in this market. So it's not necessarily an ossified structure; positions might be changing, but clearly there's something going on in the structure, and that also lends itself to the key observation that I really need to make, and that is, when authorities come to look at industries, there really must be the key emphasis on behaviour in the market, and that's most apparent in financial services because it's quite clear that even with very low degrees of concentration, you can still get ineffective competition—because if consumers are not willing to switch or change provider, then even firms with very small shares in the overall market can still obtain some degree of market power over their captive consumers. Equally, it can work the other way; when you have a market that appears to be highly concentrated, there can be a great degree of turbulence in the market and in the way consumers react, and accordingly, one can get intense competition. So it's not structure that's so fundamental in this market—it's actually behaviour.

So what drives behaviour, and what drives new developments? Well, one only has to look at the dynamics of markets, and I can identify four different categories that suggest that financial services, in some instances, lends itself to being very dynamic. First of all, there's been the impact of new technology; information technology is now the new basis for competing, it's driven on new developments in itself, and also new products, which I'll comment on in a minute, and we're seeing increasing use of e-commerce, which also opens up new opportunities and might also allow for new entrants coming in, specialising in an e-commerce background, breaking into these markets. Added to that we see new products; some are customised, and IT has certainly lent itself to that; the firms are increasingly in a position to offer customised products to consumers because information technology allows it, but as opposed to that, we're also seeing greater use of common standards, and here the regulator has a key role. Clearly if the regulator sees ineffective competition and potential market failure, then there is a role for the regulator to step in, offer a new platform, and I've given a coupled UK example—CAT standards for ISAs, stakeholder pensions and the like—and they give a new base or product for competition to occur.

We're also seeing new services, and it's already been mentioned before about the issue of one-stop shops. This is just a general process that appears to be going on, about conglomeration in the industry; we're seeing the arrival of financial conglomerates offering a wide range of services, and related to Derek Ridyard's comments concerning mergers, it does allow for itself potentially to raise issues about future portfolio power problems. New entry, of course, occurs potentially from cross-industry entry, and that leads to the issue of conglomerates; we're seeing also some evidence now of cross-border entry. Admittedly most of it is by acquisition, but it does raise the prospect that there could be new direct entry, which would complete with existing incumbents. What seems to be less apparent is *de novo* entry, brand new entry—this doesn't seem to be that apparent in many sectors, and it often goes back to those quite high barriers to entry based on reputation, time served in the market and consumer familiarity with financial brands. The opportunities for new firms exist because of new customers—we're seeing a greater degree of financial independence with individuals as consumers, we're seeing them move for example from occupational pensions across to private pensions. But there is, and still remains, an issue about financial awareness and understanding, and I, like everybody, read the Cruickshank Review with great interest to see what issues about our knowledge of even a very simple product like a savings account; it doesn't demand too much intellectual capital to work out what might be issues about your interest rates, charges for withdrawals and the like, but as you can see from just a simple illustration, consumers don't appear to be that well aware of exactly what's going on with their money.

Now take that a step further—that's a simple product, but imaging a complex product or what we call a credence product, where even having purchased it you still don't fully understand how it works, nor can you fully assess how that product is being monitored and looked after. Pensions are a classic illustration of that, and I'll come back to that in a moment. So I keep emphasising that a lot of the problems and issues in financial services and banking are about ineffective competition, driven by consumers' asymmetric information—they just don't know as much as the providers know.

So what are the ongoing competition concerns? I've given a few issues here—I should hasten to add that the examples I give are potential examples, I wouldn't want you to rush away and say there are cartels operating here, there and everywhere—but there are issues arising because of either regulatory involvement, which has encouraged firms not to directly compete, or the firms may have learnt themselves not to compete, and I give some illustrations of the kind of practices that could occur. Focal point pricing, segmentation, exclusivity ties—we've already in a previous talk mentioned the issue of polarisation, which is effectively a vertical restraint, a relationship between the adviser and the provider, and the possibility of informal networks operating. There are always issues for regulators concerned with the institutional restrictions, but of course in financial services it's not just a formal regulator that is subjected to statutory objectives, there's an awful lot of self-regulation going on as well; that's often at national level, and it doesn't lend itself typically to encourage cross-border activity when we witness different national standards and rules.

But I come back to my key point today, which is really about the nature of the products and the asymmetric information; for economists, we are fond of distinguishing between two forms of opportunistic behaviour. One we call 'pre-contractual', that is, before the product is purchased, and here there's a potential issue of adverse selection; consumers just choose the wrong product, and that can be down to relying on past performance indicators and reputation, rather than having any indication of future performance. We have various forms of potential mis-selling: pensions one week, and then the next week it's on issues to do with mortgages. There are also issues about post-contractual opportunism—that's how a product is managed after you've purchased it, and here I may use the illustration where there's been much public debate on pensions and life insurance, and there's also the issue of captive consumers—once they've purchased a product, there seems to be little escape from them. And what implications does that have for competition?

So what are the tensions? Well, there is always an issue about business versus public interest, and I read with great interest this week about the way that UK bank bosses had responded to accusations of excessive profitability; there will always be a debate about what excessive profitability means, but it did make me smile that the argument appears to be that it's okay to earn excessive profits if it allows pension funds to be built up, and one wouldn't want to destroy those in the present climate. Now I'm not going to use it as an argument in a court case, but it would be an interesting one to wheel out—the issue is more broadly about what's going on in the market in terms of dynamics. Who understands the market the best? Is it business, because as markets unfold they're there to take advantage of any opportunities and competition to spur on new development, or is it the role of the regulator to encourage new innovation and new developments, and avoid the market failures?

There'll always be that conflict between business and public interest, and in the UK there's added spice here, because we have a sector regulator and of course our own competition authorities as well. The second tension will always remain about jurisdiction; who seeks to regulate and monitor competitive activity? Increasingly we're seeing the issue about supranational regulation, in the role of the European Commission; we're seeing other international bodies like the Sell Committee and the like, setting the regulatory tone, and they'll always be there for potentially a tension between national interests and the need to encourage broader cross-activity such as promoting the internal market.

Finally, the thing I would like to finish on is about objectives. The work of the FSA, in this country at least, has come about through statutory obligations about taking and being aware of competition and promoting competition, but it's always struck me that there is potentially a conflict between promoting competition, which sounds distinctly like regulation, and promoting competition, which is the key activity of competition authorities. The FSA themselves have produced a possible concern about their own regulation and what its anti-competitive effects are, and I'm sure at the back you'll find this difficult to read, but this chart is from the FSA's own work about being aware of the potentially adverse effects of regulation, and here we just need to be reminded that for a competition commission, it needs to assess what is going on in the market in terms of forms' own behaviour, but also the regulator's involvement in, for example, establishing barriers to entry or discriminating in favour of incumbents over new entrants. And disentangling those two aspects can often be very difficult, not least because firms are prepared to play cat-and-mouse with regulators, which means that the regulator sets a new regulation and the firms manage to work around that regulation, and then we see new regulations. The great news for us in this audience is that there's an awful lot of work out there, both as lawyers acting for regulation, and I also expect to see much greater concern from competition authorities about the nature of ineffective competition in this very important sector.

4. The Single Regulator and Competition

Nick Paul*

I'm going to speak from a lawyer's perspective just for a few minutes, on some points on the impact of financial regulations on competition.

The first conclusion is that there is an inevitable risk with financial regulation, however well-intended, that it will have an unintended adverse effect on competition, that it won't deliver the consumer benefits that are anticipated, and indeed that it may well harm consumer interests. Recognising that risk, my second point is that this risk exists just as much where financial regulation is being agreed and set at the international level, which it increasingly is, including at the Community level; that risk is just as present there as it is when financial regulations are being set at domestic member state level. And thirdly, to make some comment on the way in which the UK has developed some techniques for attempting to resolve those tensions, which might perhaps be of interest to some other member states that do not have equivalent procedures. First of all then, just a brief word on the tensions themselves, and obviously the first one is the whole issue of international competitiveness, the often-cited example of course, now rather old, of the Eurobond market, which came to Europe because of fears of over-regulation in the US and the securities market. And another, more recent example of just how mobile some financial markets are, has perhaps been the recent influx into insurance underwriting, where a lot of the capital has been coming in not to Europe, not to Lloyds and to the London market, but into Bermuda. And then of course there's the effect on competition actually within the markets themselves—the cost burden that regulated firms have to pay, not so much just the fees they pay but the compliance costs that go with the system, and of course in this country a whole compliance industry has developed in response to financial regulation over the last ten years. And then, the barriers to entry—obviously, in this case, the threshold conditions that were set by FSA for any financial firm to enter the market, and other distortions, for instance through conduct of business rules, and the most topical and perhaps the most extreme example of that is perhaps polarisation, which I'll come back to later. Now of course, moving on then to the setting of international standards and in particular the whole EU programme and the financial services action plan, this of course as a measure is highly pro-competitive, it's all about making it possible for firms

* CMS Cameron McKenna, London. Speech given at the Second Annual Conference on International and Comparative Competition Law, BIICL, May 2002.

to sell across borders without having to comply with a myriad of different regulations in different member states.

Enforcement is the task of not only the single market directorate general, but also by DG competition, including areas such as clearing and settlement. But as I said at the start, there still does seem to me to be the inevitable risk that I identified at the start, and for a variety of reasons, we are now moving not only from prudential regulation onto harmonisation of conduct of business rules but in various markets that remain currently very different from one member state to the next.

Equally I think that the expectations and objectives of the regulators themselves may not be fully harmonised; perhaps all those regulators wouldn't share the obsession with the risk-based approach that FSA now has, through different perspectives. What is to be done about that? Well, just one point to mention: the Wise Men report on the securities industry proposed a framework of overarching principles or principles of good regulation, and these included the promotion of competition, innovation and international competitiveness, and there was discussion that this might even be adopted in the form of a regulation or treaty amendment.

Moving on then quickly to the UK position: of course a lot of work has gone into establishing this new regime in the UK under the Financial Services and Markets Act and our new single regulator. It's now very clear that will encompass virtually the whole of the financial services sector by the time we get to N3 in two years' time, everything will be regulated by FSA. And there are four ways in this new system in which this tension between setting rules and the effect on this competition are addressed, which I'd like to just mention briefly. They are: first of all the whole concept of a single regulator, secondly the statutory objectives and considerations that are set at the beginning of the act and dictate everything that FSA does, the use of cost benefit analysis, and finally, in reserve if you like, competition scrutiny of FSA by the OFT.

The single regulator itself is seen as being pro-competitive; FSA has produced some very interesting papers on this. It removes the previous possibility of selecting your regulator, which some firms have; it removes the possibility of regulatory arbitrage, and it enables FSA to look at issues such as if they see credit risk moving from the banking sector to the insurance sector, to question whether there isn't something quite right in the different capital requirements. Another factor has been, for example, the introduction of integrated credential source books right across all the sectors. The second thing, as I said, is the question of the statutory objectives right at the start of the act; FSA has set its statutory objectives, and those are combined with a whole series of considerations, essentially competition-related, which it must weigh in the balance, and there they are on the slide.

Now that sounds like perhaps not a very significant point, but I think it is, because if you see everything that FSA does now, literally everything is referenced back to these objectives and these considerations. Every consultation it does, every action it takes, is all referenced back. So what that is doing, is embedding the competition issues in the whole process of regulation. Thirdly, whenever FSA proposes to change a rule, it has to go to consultation; and as part of that process it has to produce a cost-benefit analysis, that is a requirement of the act. And there are some of the issues that the FSA has said that it will look at, and it is now using in publishing these cost-benefit analyses; people can now look and debate, in theory at least, the relative cost of the benefit to be achieved, and that is part of the consultation process before any rule comes into effect.

And finally, I suppose, the reserve power if you like, which is scrutiny by the competition authorities under the—which is embedded into the act, specific procedures in the act, which are summarised there in that slide. The point I would make here is that this really covers the whole ambit of financial regulation in the UK; the act itself says very little, although it's extremely long, essentially it says basically there will be an authority called the FSA and it will make a lot of rules on financial regulation, full stop, and that's how it works. So that means that all the rules, all the requirements—prudential, capital, conduct of business, everything—sits in the FSA handbook; and that is subject to ongoing scrutiny both as to its current state and changes, and the OFT has the primary role in undertaking that review. That extends also to other areas, such as the exchanges and indeed the listing rules.

What about OFT scrutiny of FSA? The point I would make, obviously, is a lot of regulation has now been set at the international level, and a lot of that is at the EU level. Once that is done, there is precious little the OFT can do about it; those international norms are set, hence my point at the beginning. A couple of areas that are topical at the moment, in this context, are polarisation and the N3 of general insurance intermediaries. Polarisation is a strange rule, perhaps looking back, that was introduced in the UK in the mid-eighties and essentially said that for package products there were only two forms of permitted distribution—either you sold your single product provider, or you had to advise on every single product that was available in the market. It was supposed to provide clarity to consumers.

That was attacked—the SIB rules as they were then were attacked by the OFT, the OFT has now supported the full abolition of the polarisation rules under the new procedures that operate, and there is a consultation going on by FSA as to that. So the whole scrapping of polarisation is now very much on the cards. What happened when they looked at the rule, as it was now operating, was that everyone had appreciated that this was a very severe restriction on competition from the beginning, but they found that it wasn't providing clarity to the consumer at all—the consumer was confused, and worse than that, in some cases, it was actually causing consumers to be sold the wrong product and certainly to select a very limited choice.

As I said, one other area is general insurance intermediaries, who come into statutory regulation, most of them for the first time in two years' time. That will pose interesting issues because there are a very large number of intermediaries that are not financial institutions essentially—businesses that sell general insurance as a secondary activity, and as they come into regulation, travel agents, retailers and so on—exactly what sort of system will operate? There are obvious issues there about barriers to entry when FSA sets the threshold conditions.

Discussion from the Second Annual Competition Law Conference—Competition Issues in Banking and Financial Services

HELEN FLETCHER ROGERS

This is a question really for the first two speakers, particularly Peter and maybe also John. It's about some of the remedies that are suggested in some banking report, and the decision not to go for structural remedies, and whether that indeed leads us into a world where we see very stringent regulation, actually, on the main High Street banks in the UK; as in order for regulators to make decisions on such things as access and pricing to bunched networks, then you come into problems with the vertically integrated structure of the banks, which if you look at the 1996 undertakings for Sky, has certainly posed the OFT plenty of problems in operationalising those. So I would ask the first three members of the panel whether they have any comments on that.

NICK PAUL

Structural remedies—well, I cut my teeth on the *Beer* case, which was a case of severe structural remedies, and I think it's always been held up as an example of how things become quite difficult to follow through. The temptation to do something drastic and to do something once and for all is very laudable intellectually, but actually, as we've seen in the beer industry it's not once and for all; and I see that Punch Taverns has pulled its float this morning over concern over prices. In relation to the particular SME report, I think it's fair to say that I've no idea what went through the Commission's mind at all, but there were major issues in looking to structural remedies in relation to branches, because branches are used by personal customers as well as by small businesses, and so you'd have a knock-on effect, there's no easy structural remedy. I think that's all I want to say, I try to avoid talking about the substance of the report if I possibly can.

DR THOMAS JESTAEDT

Well, my only comment is a very broad one—I find that pricing regulation as a remedy to lessen market failure, whether it exists or not, is always very ambitious, and I mean, without structural changes—I mean, it's difficult, I'm not aware of an institution in Germany or at EU level where that has succeeded. If you have a market dominance problem, which apparently was the finding, it's difficult to see how one could address this through pricing regulation, but maybe we will learn.

ALEX NOURRY

This is for Professor Dobson. If the main problem in these markets is really asymmetric information, rather than market structure, would that indicate that further consolidation within the market would be okay?

PAUL DOBSON

I find that very difficult to address, because it applies across a number of different markets that make up financial services and banking, so it's very difficult; but one of the issues clearly for consumers, is this balance between wanting a wide variety of products but understanding what that variety is, and there's always a challenge there. So the issue is, if you do get consolidation, does that mean a narrowing of variety, does that enable consumers to understand better what the nature of those products is? And would it increase accessibility to those products? I can see that there would be potential advantages in certain instances of consolidation because of efficiency improvements such as the one I've outlined. But equally I'm acutely aware that there's always another aspect, and that is the prospect of market power and even greater ways that firms can develop to avoid competition. So there will always be that tension, and there's no clear-cut case to make for either argument; but I can honestly see advantages coming from consolidation in certain instances.

NICK PAUL

But I suppose the other comment, the other thing that happens, is the idea of having products that are simplified, where one is perhaps less concerned with the competitive elements and more with the consumer, making sure that the consumer really can understand the products. I quote one example, for which I think one can never underestimate the potential for consumers not to understand the products, and I just quote my own situation, on my pension. Many years ago I had a look at some pension products and couldn't make head or tail of them, I have to say, without putting a lot of effort into it. I handed it to my secretary and said: I've got his small amount to invest, can you just select them for me please and put some money into them. They then changed the tax rules and I'm now stuck with those pension products for the rest of my life—that's what comes out in polarisation exercises, is that there's a very well-intentioned measure, but people just do not appreciate how difficult consumers find it to understand even very simple products.

PETER FREEMAN

Can I just add one comment here? I think the point about information symmetry is well taken, but several of the issues in the industry are effectively about services to businesses. Now there may be a lack of understanding the smaller down the business chain you go, but some of the customers of the banks are major businesses, and they really ought to have access to advice and knowledge that is able to make the exchange an equal one.

ALEX PLANT

Alex Plant from the Treasury. The question that emerged in my mind during Peter's talk, but I don't wish to go into the details of that particular case, but really it's a question for the panel generally, is whether they feel that the UK's provision in the Fair Trading Act to look at complex monopolies (and as will be brought forward in the Enterprise Act) is a useful tool in the kit-bag of the competition authorities. However, that's something that other member states might be considering, or indeed the alternative of whether, given the criticisms of the report, there's something more fundamental that would suggest is not useful.

PETER FREEMAN

Thank you, Alex—that is a large issue, and I'll answer it simply. I didn't get into, in my talk, the parallel universe of the Competition Act, which has different appeal systems and a different approach altogether, and has fines rather than price remedies. I'm on the record for many years as saying that these two processes need to be brought together, and it is actually anomalous in the modernisation and decentralisation world of the EC to have a wholly separate Fair Trading Act evolving a based system. There is provision I think in the EC system, which we're adopting in the parallel universe, for sector enquiries, and sector enquiries are clearly necessary; my point is that I don't think you have to have a completely different legal norm that actually governs them, and a different system of appeal. I have in mind the fact that the test under the new Enterprise Act will be whether there is prevention, restriction or distortion of competition, but Section 60 of the Competition Act will not apply to that; there'll be no equivalent provision, and there's no obligation to interpret those words into EC jurisprudence and practice. I'm sure everybody will, but it seems extraordinary really to keep the bifurcation so set in concrete.

DR DEREK MORRIS

Derek Morris—I ought to declare an interest, as Chairman of the UK

Competition Commission and Chairman of the report that Peter referred to. Clearly, as he said, we're still in the judicial review period, so I can't really comment on the substance of the report. I wanted to make a slightly broader point, and this is a point that is often seen as very straightforward for an economist, but I sense is actually quite difficult in some competition regimes. If you find, and I'm talking not necessarily about banking at all now—if you find in a market that pricing or pricing structures really are very similar, we all know that there are at least two quite different explanations for that. One is that it is highly competitive and that's why prices are very similar, and the other is that there is a degree of what economists call tacit collusion, although it doesn't involve any actual collusion at all. In general, there is a mutual understanding on the part of concentrated players, that they have a mutual interest in not competing too hard on price, and therefore prices remain similar. How do you distinguish between them? The only real answer is: at what level of profitability are those parallel prices emerging? And so increasingly, and certainly banks was obviously an example of this, in the UK competition authorities have been wanting to investigate the level of profitability.

I sense some resistance from the private market—private practitioners in this area, almost as if it's not proper to look at that area, and I'd be interested in what experience there is from other regimes around the world, of the appropriateness and indeed the practicality of using profitability as an important indicator of degree of competition. Finally, just while I've got the microphone—obviously I can't debate this with Peter, but I should just place it on the record, that I do not think the Commission would accept for one moment the notion that, and I think I'm quoting Peter here, that there was no transparency in the Commission's thinking in this particular case. On the contrary, there was a very protracted process of dialogue over many hearings and indeed extensions to the whole process, so that it could continue. And nor, I must say just for the record, that the analysis of profitability, to which my original point referred, was restricted to a very short-term period; many of the adjustments to which Peter referred were precisely to deal with the problem that one has to consider profitability, at least I believe that one has to consider profitability over a considerably longer period. But I would be interested to know what, if anything, is developing in other jurisdictions on this use of profit.

DR THOMAS JESTAEDT

Well, to be honest I mean, in an Article 82 inquiry, which this is to me, it's normally—I think it's the first time I've come across it, I must say—normally you ask where the costs are, and look at costs. The only thing that

I can think of right now is the other way round in a State aid context, when you inject money into a company and that company is not profitable, you would expect a higher return on your investment, and this is really at the European level now where I think you would look at profitability—for Article 82 I find that quite ambitious, and this is where I think we're going now.

PETER FREEMAN

Well really, looking at cost and looking at profit are not two separate exercises, especially when you've got capital-intensive structures; but anyhow, there may be other observations from the audience on that point or others. Any other comments or suggestions? Do you want to come in on this?

PROFESSOR JOHN VICKERS

Well, just to take up Derek Morris's point, which I don't disagree with, actually—there's a case of curious agreement here. I've no problem with using profitability as a measure—indeed, one of the criticisms of the way the old MMC sometimes used to operate was that the profitability analysis was divorced from the rest of the analysis, and one could never quite work out why it was there. I do think they're picking up my point about process—that it places a very heavy responsibility on the Commission, particularly as it moves to a decision-making role, to get the analysis right. The fact that this can't be anything other than a matter of judgment is a point. On transparency please, I hope I made it clear that I thought the Commission was enormously transparent on all kinds of things—I was trying to a subtle point, which is I think there is one issue where more transparency needs to be developed, and that's an evolving matter. I think these investigations will produce a more robust result if there is a debate with the parties during the process as to the provisional conclusions that are emerging—not the issues, not the remedies, but the actual way the Commission is thinking, and that may involve some numbers. I wasn't really trying to make any greater point than that.

MICHAEL HUTCHINGS

I think that perhaps unwittingly, Chairman, you may have distracted people from asking about tension between regulators and competition authorities. I think that this is an issue that does need to be addressed, and certainly not just in this industry—the other industry that it is soon to come under a large single regulator is communications, as it will now be called. I think that having looked briefly at the Communications Bill, there is a similar issue—

that Ofcom will be given concurrent powers with the OFT, but from the way it's written they appear to have pre-eminent powers in certain directions, but they certainly have full-scale competition objectives in what they're doing, in the same way that the Financial Services Authority does. This, to the mind of a practitioner, has obvious difficulties, and I should be very interested in hearing your particular comments. but indeed any other panellist's comments on that issue, which of course crosses different industries.

NICK PAUL

Yes, just one comment I'd make in connection with perhaps a slight difference when looking at that issue, and I may not have been entirely clear on this point. In the case of FSA, is it that the balance is struck, the objectives are consumer protection and market integrity, and then the competition issues are considerations, and they're the next layer down, they have to be weighed in the balance. So the primary role of FSA is not as a promoter of competition, that is a consideration that is built into consumer protection law and I think that may decide it.

PAUL DOBSON

I mean, as far as the Competition Act is concerned, your Ofcom point is not new in kind, because there are existing concurrency arrangements with sector regulators who have powers under that act, which sort out who does what. Of course no-one has a monopoly on the enforcement of that act, because there are private parties as well, who could really come into play, and I think the FSA context is a different one where, as Nick explained, you've got a rule-making power and there is, through that act, the competition scrutiny that can come in. That's different from the more horizontal concurrency type of arrangement, which I think certainly up until now seems to have worked pretty smoothly.

PETER FREEMAN

Well, we're not talking about communications, but there will be a slight change in that the Independent Television Commission, which I actually advise, has competition powers but not concurrent powers. So there will be a new situation, where competition in relation to television broadcasting will be under concurrency and under Ofcom in this situation. But I agree—the issue is not really very different—it is necessary to make the regulatory approach and the competition approach work together, and that applies across the board.

CHAPTER SIX

The Tensions Between Competition and Intellectual Property Rights—Papers and Discussion from the Second Annual Competition Law Conference

1. EC Competition Law Remedies and TRIPS: Limitations on the Use of Compulsory Licensing as a Competition Law Remedy

Jean-François Bellis*

In recent years, the European Commission (the 'Commission') has been taking a more aggressive stance in applying EC competition law to restrict the rights of holders of intellectual property rights. For example, investigations into the practices of IMS Health[1] and Microsoft[2] have recently raised the issue of when the Commission may rely on EC competition law to force intellectual property holders to licence their intellectual property rights to competitors. As intellectual property rights by their nature are designed to afford innovators the right to exclude others from exploiting their innovations,[3] these recent Commission investigations have raised the issue of what limits, if any, may exist on the ability of competition authorities to restrict the use of legal monopolies granted by intellectual property laws.

This paper considers one such limit. This paper will begin by briefly introducing the background to the issue of the conflict between intellectual property rights and competition laws, and subsequently discuss the possibility that international treaties governing intellectual property rights (in particular the WTO Agreement on Trade-Related Aspects of Intellectual Property Rights ('TRIPS' or the 'TRIPS Agreement')) can limit the use of compulsory licensing as a competition remedy.

I. THE ESSENTIAL NATURE OF INTELLECTUAL PROPERTY RIGHTS

Recognising the need to further developmental and technological objectives, nations have historically found it desirable to afford various protections to those who innovate by adopting laws that protect intellectual property rights. The essence of such laws involves the grant to the innovator of a right to exclude other from exploiting the innovation. Indeed, so

* Van Bael & Bellis, Brussels. Paper given at the Second Annual Conference on International and Comparative Competition Law, BIICL, May 2002.

[1] See, eg, Case COMP D3/38.044—*NDC Health/IMS Health: Interim measures* OJ 2002 L 59, 18. The Commission's attempt to impose interim measures has since been rejected by the European Courts. See Case C-481/01 P(R) *NDC Health Corporation*, judgment of 11 Apr 2002.

[2] See, eg, Commission press release of 10 Feb 2000, IP/00/141.

[3] See, eg, Commission Evaluation Report on the Transfer of Technology Block Exemption Regulation No 240/96—Technology Transfer Agreements Under Article 81 (Dec 2001) at ¶28.

strong is the importance attached to such rights that they have been recognised in international treaties such as the Paris Convention for the Protection of International Property, the Berne Convention for the Protection of Literary and Artistic Works, the Rome Convention for the Protection of Performers, Producers of Phonograms and Broadcasting Organisations, and the Treaty on Intellectual Property in Respect of Integrated Circuits. Moreover, during the 1986–94 Uruguay Round, intellectual property rights and the essential 'right to exclude' were included in the GATT-WTO system under TRIPS.

Thus, for example, the TRIPS Agreement obliges its Members to recognise the following exclusive rights:

> Authors of literary and artistic works protected by this Convention shall have the exclusive right of authorizing the reproduction of these works, in any manner or form. (Article 9(1) of the Berne Convention (1971), as incorporated by Article 9(1) of TRIPS.)
>
> The owner of a registered trademark shall have the exclusive right to prevent all third parties not having the owner's consent from using in the course of trade identical or similar signs for goods or services which are identical or similar to those in respect of which the trademark is registered where such use would result in a likelihood of confusion. (Article 16(1) of TRIPS.)
>
> The owner of a protected industrial design shall have the right to prevent third parties not having the owner's consent from making, selling or importing articles bearing or embodying a design which is a copy, or substantially a copy, of the protected design, when such acts are undertaken for commercial purposes. (Article 26(1) of TRIPS.)
>
> A patent shall confer on its owner the following exclusive rights:
>
> (a) where the subject matter of a patent is a product, to prevent third parties not having the owner's consent from the acts of: making, using, offering for sale, selling, or importing [footnote omitted] for these purposes that product;
>
> (b) where the subject matter of a patent is a process, to prevent third parties not having the owner's consent from the act of using the process, and from the acts of: using, offering for sale, selling, or importing for these purposes at least the product obtained directly by that process. (Article 28(1) of TRIPS.)

It can therefore be concluded that international law has recognised that the essence of intellectual property laws is to provide innovators with the 'fundamental right to exclude'.

II. THE CONFLICT BETWEEN INTELLECTUAL PROPERTY RIGHTS AND COMPETITION LAW

Notwithstanding the recognition of the fundamental right to exclude, however, international law does also allow for exceptions in certain special cases. One such exception that is the topic of this paper is the adoption of measures to remedy a violation of competition laws (the 'competition law exception').[4]

The competition law exception can create a conflict with intellectual property laws because intellectual property laws grant a legal monopoly to innovators over the innovation,[5] whereas competition law can allow for restrictions to be placed on companies that 'abuse' such a monopoly provision. Thus, although holding a legal monopoly will not of itself violate these laws, the practices adopted by an innovator with respect to his legal monopoly can fall afoul of anti-monopoly laws.

Article 82 of the EC Treaty sets forth the relevant laws for those holding a dominant position (including monopolists):

> Any abuse by one or more undertakings of a dominant position within the common market or in a substantial part of it shall be prohibited as incompatible with the common market insofar as it may affect trade between Member States.
>
> Such abuse may, in particular, consist in:
>
> (a) directly or indirectly imposing unfair purchase or selling prices or other unfair trading conditions;
>
> (b) limiting production, markets or technical development to the prejudice of consumers;
>
> (c) applying dissimilar conditions to equivalent transactions with other trading parties, thereby placing them at a competitive disadvantage;
>
> (d) making the conclusion of contracts subject to acceptance by the other parties of supplementary obligations which, by their nature or according to commercial usage, have no connection with the subject of such contracts.

Thus, for example, while a legal monopoly may be viewed as granting the innovator the right to determine its own selling price, Article 82(a) of the EC Treaty appears to allow the Commission to take action against innovators who would impose 'excessive prices'. Indeed, the Court of First Instance has suggested that excessive pricing claims may exist even against holders of intellectual property rights.[6]

[4] Other exceptions include, for example, the limited ability to impose a compulsory licence on pharmaceutical products for reasons of public health.

[5] Notwithstanding the fact that intellectual property laws grant a 'legal monopoly' over the innovation, the innovator may not actually hold a monopoly (or even dominant) position given that other products may compete with the innovation. This paper discusses only those innovators whose 'legal monopoly' also results in a *de facto* monopoly, or dominant, position in the relevant market.

[6] Case T-198/98 *Micro Leader v Commission* [1999] ECR II-3989. See also *DSD* [2001] OJ L166/1, where the Commission essentially concluded that DSD would be imposing excessive prices if it charged any fee solely for the use of its 'Green Dot' trademark.

Perhaps more importantly, the issue has also arisen as to whether competition laws can impinge upon the innovator's 'fundamental right to exclude'. In other words, can an innovator's refusal to license an intellectual property right constitute an abuse under Article 82 of the EC Treaty? As demonstrated by the Court of Justice in *Magill*[7] and recent Commission investigations of IMS and Microsoft, the answer appears to be a qualified 'yes': the exercise of an exclusive right by an innovator 'may, in exceptional circumstances, involve abusive conduct' for purposes of Article 82 of the EC Treaty.

III. AN ARGUMENT FOR THE LIMITATION OF THE USE OF COMPULSORY LICENSING AS A COMPETITION LAW REMEDY—CONFLICT WITH INTERNATIONAL LAW

In the absence of further clarification from the European Courts of what can constitute 'exceptional circumstances',[8] limitations under the EC Treaty concerning the Commission's power to correct an innovator's 'abusive' refusal to supply remains uncertain. Nevertheless, it would be short-sighted to focus solely on domestic laws, as limitations may also exist within the international sphere. In this regard, the adoption of TRIPS would appear to afford an additional limitation, at least in certain circumstances,[9] as TRIPS circumscribes the right of WTO Members to rely on competition law to impinge upon the fundamental right to exclude.

A. The Competition Law Exception in Intellectual Property Rights Treaties Prior to TRIPS—The Example of the Berne Convention

Prior to the adoption of TRIPS, a person examining a treaty governing the protection of intellectual property rights (such as the Berne Convention) would look in vain for a 'competition law' exception. However, a treaty's silence on the issue could be misleading. For example, the fact that the adopted text of the Berne Convention does not provide for a competition law exception does not lead to the conclusion that no such exception exists.

This follows from the recognition that the Berne Convention encompasses more than the literal text. In addition to this text, a proper interpretation of the Berne Convention must also consider various 'understandings' that

[7] Cases C-241/91P and C-242/91P *Radio Telefis Eireann and Independent Television Publications Ltd v Commission* ('Magill') [1995] ECR I-743.

[8] Ibid.

[9] The European Courts' recent case-law regarding the imposition of interim measures on IMS Health have not clarified this point.

form part of the Treaty,[10] one such understanding being that a 'competition law' exception did exist.

It is clear that during various revisions of the Berne Convention, parties to the Treaty understood that the rights granted to innovators did not conflict with the right of states to take anti-monopoly measures.[11] For example, during the 1967 Stockholm revision conference, the UK and New Zealand sought to introduce amendments to the Convention making it explicit that countries could enact legislation necessary 'to prevent or deal with any abuse, by persons or organisations exercising one or more of the rights in a substantial number of different copyright works, of the monopoly provision they enjoy'.[12] However, it was argued by others at the conference that the amendments were unnecessary, and the Report of the Main Committee I described the ultimate result:

> The Committee accepted, without opposition, the proposal of its Chairman that mention should be made in this Report of the fact that questions of public policy should always be a matter for domestic legislation and that the countries of the Union would therefore be able to take all necessary measures to restrict possible abuses of monopolies. Whereupon, the proposals of Australia and the United Kingdom relating to abuse of monopoly were withdrawn.

Thus, under the Berne Convention, anti-monopoly provisions could be used to impinge upon the intellectual property rights established therein, at least to the extent that they were 'necessary', as this term was understood by the parties to the Convention.

One of the significant developments in the TRIPS Agreement, however, was

[10] Of course, as private parties lack standing to directly invoke a violation of their rights under TRIPS, such limitations may only exist insofar as TRIPS Members allow such arguments to be made in domestic proceedings, or, alternatively, to the extent that the innovator is a national of a Member willing to make a challenge on his behalf.

[11] Art 31 of the Vienna Convention on the Law of Treaties provides that:

'1. A treaty shall be interpreted in good faith in accordance with the ordinary meaning to be given to the terms of the treaty in their context and in the light of its object and purpose.

2. The context for the purpose of the interpretation of a treaty shall comprise, in addition to the text, including its preamble and annexes:

(a) any agreement relating to the treaty which was made between all the parties in connection with the conclusion of the treaty;

(b) any instrument which was made by one or more parties in connection with the conclusion of the treaty and accepted by the other parties as an instrument related to the treaty.

3. There shall be taken into account, together with the context:

(a) any subsequent agreement between the parties regarding the interpretation of the treaty or the application of its provisions;

(b) any subsequent practice in the application of the treaty which establishes the agreement of the parties regarding its interpretation;

(c) any relevant rules of international law applicable in the relations between the parties.

4. A special meaning shall be given to a term if it is established that the parties so intended.'

[12] S Ricketson, The Berne Convention for the Protection of Literary and Artistic Works: 1886-1986 (Kluwer 1987) at 546–8.

to raise the status of the 'competition law' exception from an unwritten understanding to explicit provisions in the actual text of the agreement itself.

B. The Competition Law Exception in the TRIPS Agreement

As noted above, the TRIPS Agreement specifically covers the 'competition law exception'. In addition, the TRIPS Agreement also circumscribes the use of the 'competition law exception' to certain special cases.

1. Recognition of the Competition Law Exception

The TRIPS Agreement recognises the 'competition law exception' in three separate provisions. First, the existence of the exception is expressly noted in Article 8(2) (Principles) of the TRIPS Agreement:

> Appropriate measures, provided that they are consistent with the provisions of this Agreement, may be needed to prevent the abuse of intellectual property rights by rights holders or the resort to practices which unreasonably restrain trade or adversely affect the international transfer of technology.

Second, with regard to licensing practices, Article 40 of the TRIPS Agreement provides that:

> 1. Members agree that some licensing practices or conditions pertaining to intellectual property rights which restrain competition may have adverse effects on trade and may impede the transfer and dissemination of technology.
>
> 2. Nothing in this Agreement shall prevent Members from specifying in their legislation licensing practices or conditions that may in particular cases constitute an abuse of intellectual property rights having an adverse effect on competition in the relevant market. As provided above, a Member may adopt, consistently with the other provisions of this Agreement, appropriate measures to prevent or control such practices, which may include for example exclusive grantback conditions, conditions preventing challenges to validity and coercive package licensing, in the light of the relevant laws and regulations of that Member.

Finally, with respect to patents, the TRIPS Agreement expressly recognises that compulsory licensing may be necessary to correct anti-competitive harm:

> Members are not obliged to apply the conditions set forth in subparagraphs (b) and (f) where such use is permitted to remedy a practice determined after judicial or administrative process to be anti-competitive. The need to correct anti-competitive practices may be taken into account in determining the amount of remuneration in such cases. (Article 31(k) of TRIPS.)[13]

[13] Ibid, at 547.

2. Restrictions on the Use of the Competition Law Exception

As is apparent even from the provisions quoted above, despite expressly recognising a 'competition law' exception, TRIPS also expressly sets forth the limits on its use. In Articles 8(2) and 40 of TRIPS, the use of competition measures must nevertheless be consistent with other provisions of TRIPS. Moreover, Article 31(k) concerning the use of compulsory licensing for patents also sets forth specific requirements that must be followed when used to remedy a competition law violation.

The provisions of TRIPS also establish other limitations that apply to the 'competition law' exception. For example, TRIPS would appear to proscribe the use of compulsory licensing of trademarks for competition law violations. Article 21 of TRIPS provides that 'it being understood that the compulsory licensing of trademarks shall not be permitted'. Read in conjunction with Article 8(2), it would therefore appear that imposing a compulsory licence as a remedy for a trademark violation is therefore incompatible with TRIPS.

Left unresolved is the issue of whether compulsory licensing of other intellectual property rights may be used as a remedy for a competition law violation. On the one hand, it could be argued that the express inclusion of such a provision in the Articles concerning patents, as well as an express description of the requirements that must be followed, demonstrates that compulsory licensing for other intellectual property rights is incompatible with TRIPS.

A somewhat softer approach, however, is to interpret TRIPS to allow for compulsory licensing to the extent that it is not incompatible with other TRIPS provisions. However, as limitations and exceptions to the exclusive rights, the use of the 'competition law' exception to impose compulsory licensing remedies would need to meet the relevant tests set out in TRIPS for all limitations and exceptions.

For example, with respect to copyrights, compulsory licensing would therefore only be appropriate where it is confined 'to certain special cases which do not conflict with a normal exploitation of the work and do not unreasonably prejudice the legitimate interests of the right holder' (Article 13 of TRIPS). With respect to industrial designs, compulsory licensing would be permissible only when 'limited' and provided that it does not 'unreasonably conflict with the normal exploitation of protected industrial designs and [does] not unreasonably prejudice the legitimate interests of the owner of the protected design, taking into account the legitimate interests of third parties' (Article 26 of TRIPS).

C. *Conclusions on the Compatibility of Compulsory Licensing as a Competition Remedy with TRIPS*

Although the TRIPS Agreement does recognise that competition laws can be used to limit the exclusive rights of innovators, it nevertheless places restrictions on their application. In particular, with respect to compulsory licensing, such remedies are only expressly permitted in the context of patents and layout-designs of integrated circuits, and then only subject to specific conditions.

With respect to other intellectual property rights, the availability of compulsory licensing as a competition remedy is less clear. For trademarks, it would appear that there is a very strong case that compulsory licensing is never permitted. With respect to copyrights and industrial designs, on the other hand, compulsory licensing may be permitted, but only subject to certain express conditions.

IV. THE USE OF COMPULSORY LICENSING AS A COMPETITION REMEDY FOR COPYRIGHTS IS INCOMPATIBLE WITH TRIPS WHEN USED TO GRANT A LICENCE TO AN INNOVATOR'S COMPETITORS

Given recent practice, it appears that copyright is the intellectual property right that is currently most at threat from the Commission under EC competition law rules. Beginning with *Magill*, and continuing to current investigations into IMS and Microsoft, the Commission appears to have shown an increased willingness to override the fundamental 'right to exclude' others from works protected by copyright.

Moreover, the Commission has been applying its competition rules in a manner that goes beyond the *Magill* judgment. This has the effect of bringing the Commission's application of the competition rules into direct conflict with the TRIPS Agreement. In *Magill*, the Court of Justice permitted a compulsory licence because, *inter alia*, the conduct of the monopolists involved an ancillary market only and prevented the development of a new product for which there was consumer demand.[14] In contrast, the compulsory licence sought in IMS involved a direct transfer of the innovator's intellectual property right to a direct competitor. Similarly, Microsoft is alleged to have abused a dominant position by refusing to supply its copyright-protected works to those who would use the information to compete directly on the same market.

[14] See also Art 37(2) of TRIPS, incorporating these conditions to the 'non-voluntary' licensing of layout designs.

Such an expansion of the *Magill* judgment by the Commission is inconsistent with the requirements of Article 13 of TRIPS, which requires that:

Members shall confine limitations or exceptions to exclusive rights to certain special cases which do not conflict with a normal exploitation of the work and do not unreasonably prejudice the legitimate interests of the right holder.

In particular, the grant of a compulsory licence to a competitor would create a conflict with the innovator's 'normal exploitation of the work'. As interpreted by a WTO Panel:

[Members should be allowed to] limit the recognition and the exercising of [the reproduction] right, for specified purposes and on the condition that these purposes should not enter into economic competition with these works' in the sense that 'all forms of exploiting a work, which have, or are likely to acquire, considerable economic or practical importance, must be reserved to the authors (emphasis added by the Panel.)[15]

Thus, exceptions to the fundamental right to exclude would be permitted, but only to the extent that they did not enter into economic competition with the ways the right holders normally extract economic value from their rights.[16]

Interpreting a similar provision in the context of patents, another WTO Panel reached the same conclusion:

The normal practice of exploitation by patent owners, as with owners of any intellectual property right, is to exclude all forms of competition that could detract significantly from the economic returns anticipated from a patent's grant of market exclusivity (emphasis added).[17]

Although the Panel was reviewing the sections in TRIPS concerning patents, the quote is instructive as the Panel was interpreting language identical to that under Article 13 and was expressly equating patent rights to other IP rights.[18]

Indeed, in reaching the opposite conclusion from the Court of Justice in *Magill*, the Advocate General explained why he concluded that the compulsory licensing of RTE and ITP's copyrights would violate their 'normal exploitation':

[15] Cases C-241/91P and C-242/91P *Radio Telefis Eireann and Independent Television Publications Ltd v Commission* ('Magill') [1995] ECR I-743, at ¶¶53, 54, 56.

[16] United States-Section 110(5) of the US Copyright Act, Report of the Panel, WT/DS160/R, 15 June 2000 ('US-Copyrights'), at para 6.179.

[17] Ibid, at para 6.183.

[18] Canada-Patent Protection of Pharmaceutical Products, Report of the Panel, WT/DS114/R, 17 March 2000 ('Canada-Patents'), at para 7.55.

As regards the specific decision to require RTE and ITP to grant licences for their programme listings, I believe that the result set out above that [the Commission] decision is incompatible with Article [82] of the Treaty is borne out by Article 9(2) of the Berne Convention, in particular because an obligation to grant licences for the production of products which basically meet the same consumer needs as the copyright owner's product, and which are therefore in competition with it, will in my view 'conflict with a normal exploitation of the work.[19]

Although the Court of Justice did not arrive at the same overall conclusion as the Advocate General, it first felt necessary to expressly reject the application of the Berne Convention. The Court therefore did not contradict the Advocate General's Opinion that the compulsory licensing would have violated RTE and ITP's normal exploitation over their exclusive rights.

V. CONCLUSION

We have seen that the Commission's recent practice in applying EC competition rules has created a conflict with an innovator's 'fundamental right to exclude'. Moreover, by impinging upon this right, or, at the very least, by creating uncertainty over the existence of this right, it remains to be seen whether this practice will have a chilling effect on innovation in Europe.

However, it is short-sighted to consider only domestic limitations on the Commission's powers. As a Member of the WTO, the European Communities are bound by their international obligations under TRIPS, which, as we have seen, restrict the ability of authorities to impose compulsory licensing as a competition remedy when the licence would be given to the innovator's competitors to allow the competitors to enter into direct competition with the innovator. Such a limitation may prove to be a valuable tool to innovators based in a WTO Member State outside the European Community who can obtain the support of their governments to bring a challenge under WTO dispute proceedings on their behalf. Moreover, the existence of such a remedy to foreign companies could also have a follow-on effect for nationals of the European Community, who would otherwise find themselves at a competitive disadvantage vis-à-vis their competitors should the Commission apply its current interpretations only to domestic companies.

[19] Moreover, the TRIPS provisions on patents gives a further indication that compulsory licensing for purposes of remedying a competition law violation could not meet the 'normal exploitation' test. Art 30 of TRIPS concerning limitations and exceptions on patent rights provides a test similar to that for copyrights under Art 13 of TRIPS. That the test under Art 30 would not allow for compulsory licensing as a competition remedy is clear from the fact that compulsory licensing is included in Art 31, entitled 'other use', which concerns 'a use other than that allowed under Article 30.' If Art 30 allowed for compulsory licensing, Art 31 (and the strict requirements imposed) could be evaded.

2. The CSU Case: Facts, Formalism, and the Intersetion of Antitrust and Intellectual Property Law

A Douglas Melamed and Ali M Stoeppelwerth*

I. INTRODUCTION

We live in an age of innovation. Industries are being restructured, technologies are being transformed, and huge sums of money are being made, and lost, by entrepreneurs and investors.

The law affects all of this. Not surprisingly, therefore, the age of innovation has been accompanied by an almost unprecedented prominence of the two bodies of law that most directly affect these phenomena—antitrust law and intellectual property law. They are widely perceived to be in tension.[1]

Intellectual property law is said to want to create monopolies over products in order to encourage research and innovation. It looks at the conditions of wealth creation ex ante.

Antitrust law, by contrast, is said to be hostile to monopoly and seeks to maintain prices at competitive levels. In effect, it is said, antitrust law is concerned with conditions likely to enhance economic welfare ex post.

This is a false conflict. It reflects an overstatement of some aspects of intellectual property law and a misstatement of antitrust law. And it leads to mistaken legal rulings, such as *In re Independent Service Organization Antitrust Litigation*,[2] which held that a patent or copyright holder's refusal to license or sell its rights is essentially immune from antitrust scrutiny. This article analyzes that decision, argues that it is wrong as a matter of both law and policy, and attempts to draw broader lessons about the intersection of antitrust and intellectual property law.

* Partners, Wilmer, Cutler & Pickering in Washington DC. Mr Melamed was Acting Assistant Attorney General for Antitrust in the Clinton Administration. Paper given at the Second Annual Conference on International and Comparative Competition Law, BIICL, May 2002.

[1] See, eg, Willard K Tom and Joshua A Newberg, 'Antitrust and Intellectual Property: From Separate Spheres to Unified Field', 66 *Antitrust LJ* 167, 189–90 (1997); Donald F Turner, 'Basic Principles in Formulating Antitrust and Misuse Constraints on the Exploitation of Intellectual Property Rights', 53 *Antitrust LJ* 485, 487 (1984).

[2] 203 F3d 1322 (Fed Cir 2000) (hereinafter CSU), *cert. denied*, 121 S Ct 1077 (2001).

I. THE CSU DECISION

The facts of the case can be summarized briefly. Defendant Xerox manufactures, sells, and services high-volume photocopiers and laser printers.[3] Plaintiff CSU is an independent service organization (ISO) that competes with Xerox to service Xerox machines. In 1984, Xerox decided to discontinue selling parts used to service its copiers and printers directly to ISOs unless they were also end-users of the equipment.[4] End-users remained free to purchase parts directly from Xerox, to supply to ISOs any parts they bought and to use any service provider they wished. In 1994, as part of the settlement of a class action brought by end-users and ISOs, Xerox agreed to sell parts directly to ISOs and to license its diagnostic software to copier and printer end-users. The end-users were then permitted to employ ISOs as their agents to order and use the software. CSU opted out of the settlement and filed its own action against Xerox, challenging Xerox's previous refusal to sell parts and license software under section 2 of the Sherman Act.[5]

Xerox filed a motion for summary judgment, arguing that its unilateral refusals to sell patented parts and to license patented and copyrighted software were a lawful exercise of its intellectual property rights and were therefore immunized from scrutiny under the antitrust laws.[6] Although the district court initially denied Xerox's motion, it subsequently reconsidered and dismissed CSU's antitrust claim, holding that, if a patent or copyright is lawfully acquired, the acquirer's refusal to sell or license its patented invention or copyrighted expression cannot constitute exclusionary conduct under section 2, even if the refusal to deal impairs competition in more than one market and is motivated by a desire to exclude rivals.[7]

The Federal Circuit affirmed the district court's decision. While recognizing that '[i]ntellectual property rights don't confer a privilege to violate the antitrust laws,'[8] the court nevertheless held that, '[i]n the absence of any indication of illegal tying, fraud . . . , or sham litigation, the patent holder may enforce the statutory right to exclude others from making, using or selling the claimed invention free from liability under [section 2].'[9] Buttressing this holding, in the court's view, were (i) the fact that '[t]here is no reported case in which a court ha[s] imposed liability for a unilateral

[3] Id at 1324.
[4] Id.
[5] Id.
[6] Id.
[7] *CSU LLC v Xerox Corp*, 989 F Supp 1131, 1139 (D Kan 1997).
[8] 203 F3d at 1325 (citing *Intergraph Corp v Intel Corp*, 195 F3d 1346, 1362 (Fed Cir 1999)).
[9] Id at 1327. The court extended a similar exemption to copyright holders. See id at 1329.

refusal to sell or license a patent'[10] and (ii) section 271(d) of the Patent Act, which provides that '[n]o patent owner otherwise entitled to relief [for patent infringement] . . . shall be denied relief or otherwise deemed guilty of misuse or *illegal extension of the patent right* by reason of his having . . . (4) refused to license or use any rights to the patent.'[11]

The potential implications of this decision are troubling. Read broadly, its holding may be interpreted as standing for the proposition that (absent evidence of fraud, sham litigation or concerted conduct) no antitrust claim may ever be asserted on the basis of a firm's unilateral refusal to sell or license intellectual property.[12] Such a rule would conflict with longstanding precedent holding that, for purposes of antitrust analysis, intellectual property should be treated the same as any other form of property.[13] It would also effectively immunize from antitrust liability a dominant firm's decision to deny rivals access to inputs or facilities they need, merely because those inputs or facilities contain patented or copyrighted materials, regardless of the competitive effect of the denial.

II. LEGAL BASIS FOR IMMUNITY

Recognizing that 'the antitrust laws represent a fundamental national economic policy,' the Supreme Court has repeatedly emphasized that 'exemptions from the [Sherman Act] are strictly construed and strongly disfavored'.[14] Absent clear evidence that Congress intended to immunize

[10] Id at 1326 (quoting *Image Technical Servs v Eastman Kodak Co*, 125 F3d 1195, 1216 (9th Cir 1997)).

[11] Id (quoting 35 USC § 271(d) (1999)) (emphasis in original). In justifying its conclusion on the copyright issue, the court acknowledged that '[t]he [Supreme] Court has not . . . directly addressed the antitrust implications of a unilateral refusal to sell or license copyrighted expression' but relied on the Fourth Circuit's decision in *Service Training, Inc v Data General*, 963 F.2d 680, 686 (4th Cir 1992) (rejecting a claim of illegal tying supported only by evidence of a unilateral decision to license copyrighted software to some firms but not to others), and the First Circuit's decision in *Data General Corp v Grumman Systems Support Corp*, 36 F3d 1147 (1st Cir 1994), to the effect that, absent any evidence that the relevant copyrights were unlawfully obtained or 'used to gain monopoly power beyond the statutory copyright granted by Congress,' a copyright holder's refusal to sell or license its works does not violate the antitrust laws. *CSU*, 203 F3d at 1328–29.

[12] In its brief in the Supreme Court, the United States suggested that the decision need not be read so broadly and that the Court should not grant certiorari but should, instead, await further discussion of the issue in the lower courts. Brief of Amicus Curiae United States at 7–8, *CSU*, 121 S Ct 1077 (2001) (denying cert). The United States did state, however, that it was not prepared to support the decision if it were read broadly. Id. at 10.

[13] See, eg, *Antitrust Guidelines for the Licensing of Intellectual Property* §2.0 (1995) ('[intellectual property is] essentially comparable to any other form of property.').

[14] *Square D Co. v Niagara Frontier Tariff Bureau*, 476 US 409, 421 (1986). See also *Silver v NYSE*, 373 US 341, 357 (1963) ('[i]t is a cardinal principle of construction that repeals [of the antitrust laws] by implication are not favored') (quoting *United States v Borden Co*, 308 US 188, 198 (1939)).

the challenged conduct or that denying immunity could subject the defendants in a particular case to conflicting legal requirements, courts have uniformly rejected such defenses to antitrust liability.[15] The holdings in *CSU* and other similar cases, however, have either ignored or misapplied these well-established principles. As explained below, nothing in the text of the Patent or Copyright Acts or their legislative history reflects a clear Congressional intent to treat intellectual property differently for antitrust purposes from any other form of property, and there is no basis for concern that applying the antitrust laws to refusals to deal in intellectual property would subject intellectual property holders to inconsistent legal standards.

No statute explicitly provides that refusals to sell or license intellectual property are exempt from the antitrust laws or are to be assessed under antitrust standards that differ from those applicable to other forms of property. Proponents of an antitrust immunity must therefore argue for an implied immunity.

The *CSU* court and most of the other lower courts that have rejected antitrust claims based on refusals to license intellectual property point to language in section 154 of the Patent Act, which authorises a patentee 'to exclude others from making, using or selling the invention throughout the United States.'[16] That section, however, does no more than afford patent

[15] See, eg, *Nat'l Gerimedical Hosp and Gerontology Ctr v Blue Cross of Kansas City*, 452 US 378, 388–89 (1981); *Gordon v NYSE*, 422 US 659, 689–90 n14 (1975) (explaining that in *United States v Philadelphia Nat'l Bank*, 374 US 321, 350–52 (1963), 'two factors pointed against antitrust immunity: (1) congressional intent in the [relevant] act not to immunize activities from [the] antitrust [laws], and (2) the lack of conflict between the Bank Merger Act and Clayton Act standards'); *Strobl v New York Mercantile Exch.*, 768 F.2d 22, 27–29 (2d Cir 1985); *S. Pac Communications Co v AT & T*, 740 F.2d 980, 999–1000 (DC Cir 1984); *Phonetele, Inc v A T & T*, 664 F.2d 716, 729–30 (9th Cir 1981). See also *Finnegan v Campeau Corp*, 915 F.2d 824, 829 (2d Cir 1990) ('repeal by implication may only be found where there is a conflict between the provisions of the antitrust and [other applicable] laws').

[16] 35 USC § 154. See, eg, *Cygnus Therapeutic Sys v Alza Corp*, 92 F3d 1153, 1160 (Fed Cir 1996); *Genentech v Eli Lilly & Co*, 998 F.2d 931, 949 (Fed Cir 1993); *Miller Insituform, Inc v Insituform of N Am, Inc,* 830 F.2d 606, 609 (6th Cir 1987); *United States v Westinghouse Elec Corp*, 648 F.2d 642, 647 (9th Cir. 1981); *SCM v Xerox Corp.*, 645 F.2d 1195, 1204 (2d Cir 1981); *Intergraph Corp v Intel Corp*, 88 F Supp 2d 1288, 1292 (ND Ala 2000), aff'd, 253 F.3d 695 (Fed Cir 2001); *Townshend v Rockwell Int'l Corp*, No C99-0400SBA, 2000 WL 433505, at *11 (ND Cal 28 Mar 2000); *Crucible v Stora Kopparbergs Bergslags AB*, 701 F Supp 1157, 1162 (WD Pa 1988).

Although the rights granted to a copyright holder are narrower than those provided to a patentee, courts rejecting antitrust claims based on refusals to license or sell copyrighted material have similarly relied on language of the Copyright Act that gives copyright holders the exclusive right to distribute copyrighted works. See, eg, *Fox Film Corp v Doyle*, 286 US 123, 127 (1932) (referring to a copyright owner's 'right to exclude others from using his property'); *Data Gen Corp v Grumman Sys Support Corp*, 36 F.3d 1147, 1186 (1st Cir 1994) (interpreting 17 USC § 106 as providing that, if a copyright owner 'pleases, [it] may refrain from vending or licensing and content [itself] with simply exercising the right to exclude others from

holders the same rights as those enjoyed by owners of tangible property under common law.[17] Neither the general language in that section nor any other provision in either in the Patent Act or the Copyright Act compels the conclusion that Congress intended the exercise of those property rights to be exempt from the antitrust laws.[18] To the contrary, the Supreme Court has repeatedly rejected assertions of intellectual property rights as defenses to conduct that would otherwise be condemned under the Sherman Act.[19]

The *CSU* court and some commentators have also pointed to section 271(d) of the Patent Act, which was added by amendment in 1988, as statutory support for a finding of antitrust immunity.[20] On its face, however, the language of that section does not purport to address antitrust liability.[21] Moreover, the legislative history of the 1988 amendment makes plain that it was originally conceived not as an antitrust exemption for patent holders,

using [its] property') (citations omitted); *Tricom v Elec Data Sys Corp*, 902 F Supp 741, 743 (ED Mich 1995); *Advanced Computer Serv of Mich v MAI Sys Corp*, 845 F Supp 356, 370 (ED Va 1994); *Corsearch, Inc v Thomson & Thomson*, 792 F Supp 305, 328 (SDNY 1992).

[17] See *Kaiser Aetna v United States*, 444 US 164, 176 (1979) (right to exclude others is 'one of the most essential sticks in the bundle of rights that are commonly characterized as property'); *Cont'l Paper Bag Co v E Paper Bag Co*, 210 US 405, 425 (1908) ('patents are property, and entitled to the same rights and sanctions as other property'); *Consol Fruit Jar Co v Wright*, 94 US 92, 96 (1896) ('A patent for an invention is as much property as a patent for land. The right rests on the same foundation and is surrounded and protected by the same sanctions.'); 35 USC § 261 ('patents shall have the attributes of personal property').

[18] See Turner, above n 1, at 485 ('A patent or copyright is a species of property whose use and disposition are no more immune from scrutiny under antitrust law and other public policies than other forms of property.'); William F Baxter, 'Legal Restrictions on Exploitation of the Patent Monopoly: An Economic Analysis', 76 *Yale LJ* 267, 276 (1966) (describing language of the Patent Act as 'highly general').

[19] See, eg, *United States v Line Material Co*, 333 US 287, 308 (1948); *United States v New Wrinkle, Inc*, 342 US 371, 378–79 (1952); *United States v Paramount Pictures, Inc*, 334 US 131 (1948). See also *Broad Music, Inc v CBS*, 441 US 1, 19 (1979) ('the copyright laws confer no rights on copyright owners to fix prices among themselves or otherwise to violate the antitrust laws'). See also *United States v Microsoft*, 253 F.3d 34, 63 (DC Cir 2001) (en banc) (describing Microsoft's argument for a broad intellectual property immunity as 'border[ing] on the frivolous').

[20] CSU, 203 F.3d1322, 1326 (Fed Cir 2000); Philip E Areeda and Herbert Hovenkamp, *Antitrust Law* ¶704.2, at 123 (2001 Supp).

[21] See *Image Technical Servs v Eastman Kodak Co*, 125 F.3d 1195, 1214 n7 (concluding that, although section 271(d) 'indicates Congressional intent to protect the core patent right of exclusion,' its language does not preclude a finding of antitrust liability); *Grid Sys Corp v Texas Instruments Inc*, 771 F Supp 1033, 1037 n2 (ND Cal 1991) (holding that, '[o]n its face, section 271(d) relates only to the defense of patent misuse' and that 'Congress rejected an extension of this statute into the area of antitrust'). Far from supporting an argument for antitrust immunity, the language of section 271(d)—in particular, its omission of any reference to the antitrust laws—instead supports the conclusion that Congress must have intended not to create an antitrust exemption. In other instances, where Congress did intend to provide antitrust exemptions for intellectual property holders, it did so unambiguously. See, eg, 17 USC § 115(c)(3)(B) (authorising and immunising joint negotiations for royalties under compulsory license for 'mechanical' right to make and distribute records containing copyrighted musical works).

but rather as an effort to address certain judicial precedents that Congress thought subjected intellectual property owners to harsher treatment than that afforded to owners of other forms of property.[22] The bill was narrowed in conference by deletion of the market-power provision and restriction of the patent misuse provision to refusals to license and tying arrangements.[23] A review of the Congressional record discussing the 1988 amendment and subsequent related bills reveals a consistent Congressional intent to create a 'level playing field' under the antitrust laws for all forms of property—not to provide special treatment, or an antitrust immunity, for patent and copyright holders.[24]

[22] The original version of the bill to amend section 271(d) contained two sections. The first (section 101) would have eliminated the presumption in antitrust cases that ownership of a copyright or patent creates market power. See *S Rep* No 100–492, at 9–12 (1988) (criticizing the majority opinions in *United States v Loew's*, 371 US 38, 44 (1962), and *Jefferson Parish Hosp Dist No 2 v Hyde*, 466 US 2, 16 (1984), and emphasizing that proposed section 101 would 'require only that courts evaluate practices involving intellectual property rights under the same antitrust principles that are applied to practices involving other forms of property') (emphasis added). The second (section 201) provided that no patent owner could be 'deemed guilty of misuse or illegal extension of the patent right by reason of his . . . licensing practices or actions or inactions related to [the] patent, unless such [conduct] . . . violate[s] the antitrust laws.' See *S Rep* No 100–492 at 13, 17–18 (1988) (explaining that section 201 was designed to address the problem that, under current judicial precedents, misuse based upon 'alleged anticompetitive extensions of the owner's patent rights . . . may also be found where the patent owner's conduct has not violated the antitrust laws, has no demonstrated anticompetitive effect and has not even injured the infringing party who raises misuse as a defense').

[23] See 134 *Cong Rec* 32,471 (1988) (statement of Sen. DeConcini) (observing that, although '[t]he purpose of the legislation . . . remained the same throughout [the conference process],' the amendment ultimately enacted differed from the original bill 'in two important respects: First, the patent misuse doctrine is no longer reformed across the board, but only as it relates to refusals to license or use patents, and to tying arrangements[;] [s]econd, as the misuse doctrine is applied to tying, the generic antitrust violation standard adopted by the Senate has been replaced by a market power test'); 134 *Cong Rec* 32,295 (statement of Rep. Kastenmeier) (explaining that the amendment as modified by the House 'proceeds on the basis of consensus about two categories of misuse [refusals to use or license and tying arrangements] that the [Judiciary] Committee concluded should not be the subject of a rigid per se rule').

[24] See, eg, *S Rep* No 100–492 at 9 (1988) (stating that the purpose behind the Senate bill to amend section 271(d) was 'to clarify the law of patent misuse and to put intellectual property rights on an equal footing with other property with respect to the license, sale and other agreements concerning the distribution of property rights'). See also *S Rep* No 101–8, at 11 (1989) (in recommending passage of S 270, another effort to eliminate the market power presumption in antitrust cases involving intellectual property, the committee report indicates that the intended effect of the legislation is to subject intellectual property owners to antitrust liability 'to the same extent as owners of other forms of property'; the report emphasizes, however, that '[b]y eliminating the presumption . . ., the committee does not sanction anticompetitive arrangements for the distribution of, or refusal to distribute, intellectual property rights and innovative products') (emphasis added); 136 *Cong Rec* 31,411 (1990) (statement of Sen Leahy) (intended effect of eliminating market power presumption in section 270 was 'to level the playing field between intellectual property rights and other property implicated in antitrust litigation').

Significantly, in subsequent remarks supporting passage of section 270, Senator Leahy rejected as 'emphatically not the case' concerns that 'this legislation might elevate intellectual property rights to too high a level of protection, rendering the owner or licensor of intellectual

As further support for their position, proponents of the *CSU* decision cite language in some of the Supreme Court's older opinions that might suggest that a patent owner's exclusive rights are absolute and that refusals to license those rights are therefore beyond the reach of the Sherman Act. In *United States v United Shoe Machinery Corp*, for example, the Court stated that a patent confers on its owner 'the right to exclude others from the use of the invention, absolutely or on the terms the patentee chooses to impose' and added that the 'exertion of this right within the field covered by the patent is not an offense against the Anti-Trust Act.'[25] But the language used in these cases reflected the Court's contemporaneous view of all forms of private property, not special rules for intellectual property.[26] Neither *United Shoe Machinery* nor any other of the handful of Supreme Court cases containing similarly broad language concerned the issue of an intellectual property law defense to what would otherwise be an antitrust violation arising out of a refusal to license or sell intellectual property.[27] Those cases do not provide a legal basis for the *CSU* holding.[28]

III. POLICY BASIS FOR IMMUNITY

Not surprisingly, *CSU* and similar cases pay scant attention to the legal basis for an antitrust immunity and focus, instead, on notions of policy. These cases appear to be based on a belief that antitrust immunity is necessary in order to further the objectives of the intellectual property laws—in particular, in order to prevent the antitrust laws from undermining the incentives for innovation that the intellectual property laws are intended to

property rights effectively exempt or immune from antitrust challenge.' See 136 CONG REC 31,411–2 (1990) ('[t]his legislation does not knock antitrust plaintiffs out of the box; it merely requires them to come forward with evidence to sustain their market power claim').

25 247 US 32, 57 (1918).

26 See, eg, *Cont'l Paper Bag v Eastern Paper Bag Co*, 210 US 405, 425 (1908) (patents are 'entitled to the same rights and sanctions as other property').

27 United Shoe concerned lease restrictions. See also *Cont'l Paper Bag*, 210 US at 423–4 (patent infringement case in which defendant challenged patentee's non-use of the relevant patent; Court observed that the exclusive right of patent holders to make use or sell their inventions employs 'the language of complete monopoly' and that '[t]here has been no qualification ... of [that] right'); *Bement v Nat'l Harrow Co,* 186 US 70, 90 (1902) (challenge to exclusive dealing and resale price maintenance provisions in a license agreement in which the Court said that a patent owner's "title is exclusive, and so clearly within the constitutional provisions in respect of private property that he is neither bound to use his discovery himself nor permit others to use it.") (citation omitted).

28 See Marina Lao, 'Unilateral Refusals to Sell or License Intellectual Property and the Antitrust Duty to Deal', 9 *Cornell JL & Pub Pol'y* 193, 199 (1999) ('[t]he Supreme Cou . . . has never directly considered the legality of unilateral refusals to license a patent where the practice is used for monopoly leveraging purposes'); James C Burling, William F Lee & Anita K Krug, 'The Antitrust Duty to Deal and Intellectual Property Rights', 24 *J Corp L* 527, 534 (1999) ('the intersection of duty-to-deal antitrust analysis and intellectual property law remains virtually uncharted territory').

create.[29] This policy concern, however, rests on an insufficiently refined statement of the purposes of the intellectual property laws and a misunderstanding of the antitrust laws. There is, in fact, no serious conflict between them.

A. The Purported Antitrust/Intellectual Property Conflict

The goals of the intellectual property and antitrust laws are complementary, not inconsistent. As the Federal Circuit has recognized, although they serve the public in different ways, both bodies of law 'are aimed at encouraging innovation, industry and competition.'[30] A reflection of antitrust law's recognition of the importance of promoting innovation may be seen in the permissive stance it takes toward research and development joint ventures, as well as the more recent emphasis on 'innovation markets' in the agencies' enforcement guidelines.[31]

The mistaken belief that there is a conflict seems to derive from two erroneous premises. The first is that Congress, convinced that such a reward was necessary in order to induce a sufficient amount of innovation, intended by means of the patent and copyright laws to permit intellectual property holders to *maximize* the returns from their works.[32] On its face,

[29] See, eg, *Data Gen Corp v Grumman Sys Support Corp*, 36 F.3d 1147, 1186 (1st Cir 1994) (observing that 'the [patent] exception is grounded in an empirical assumption that exposing patent activity to wider antitrust scrutiny would weaken the incentives underlying the patent system, thereby depriving consumers of beneficial products); *SCM Corp v Xerox Corp*, 645 F.2d 1195, 1209 (2d Cir 1981) (imposing antitrust liability for patentee's refusal to license on lawfully acquired patent 'would severely trample upon the incentives provided by our patent laws and thus undermine the entire patent system'); *Image Technical Servs v Eastman Kodak, Co*, 125 F.3d 1195, 1217–18 (9th Cir. 1997) (recognizing that '[w]ithout bounds, claims based on unilateral [refusals to deal]' by patent and copyright holders 'will proliferate' and '[t]he cost of such suits will reduce [their] 'incentive . . . to risk the often enormous costs in terms of time, research and development") (quoting *Kewanee Oil Co v Bicron Corp*, 416 US 470, 480 (1974)).

[30] *Atari Games Corp v Nintendo of Am, Inc*, 897 F.2d 1572, 1576 (Fed Cir 1990). See also *Intergraph Corp v Intel Corp*, 195 F.3d 1346, 1362 (Fed Cir 1999) ('The patent and antitrust laws are complementary, the patent system serving to encourage invention and the bringing of new products to market by adjusting investment-based risk and the antitrust laws serving to foster industrial competition.').

[31] See Turner, above n 1, at 485 ('Antitrust gives wide latitude to joint research and development among competitors, it being recognized that joint ventures will often facilitate innovations which no individual firm participant could attain'); Robert Pitofsky, *Antitrust and Intellectual Property: Unresolved Issues at the Heart of the New Economy,* Speech at Antitrust, Technology and Intellectual Property Conference, University of California, Berkeley (2 Mar 2001) (noting that 'since the passage of the Sherman Act in 1890, there has been only one federal government challenge to a research joint venture'); 'Antitrust Guidelines for Licensing of Intellectual Property' (1995), reprinted in 4 *Trade Reg Rep* (CCH) ¶ 13,132.

[32] Cf *King Instruments Corp v Perego*, 65 F.3d 941, 950 (Fed Cir 1995) ('[T]he Patent Act creates an incentive for innovation. The economic rewards during the period of exclusivity are the carrot. The patent owner expends resources in expectation of receiving this reward. Upon

this notion is untenable; the limited duration of intellectual property (unlike tangible property, which can be owned in perpetuity), the patent misuse and copyright fair use doctrines and the well-accepted understanding that intellectual property holders have no special right to tie patented or copyright property to other property are just a few of the many ways in which intellectual property law makes clear that it is not intended to maximize returns to holders.

The legislative history also makes this clear. Congress has repeatedly emphasized that the rights conferred under the intellectual property laws are not unlimited, as well as the fact that the monopoly grant itself represents a compromise among competing policy interests.[33] Limitations on intellectual property rights reflect that the purpose of those rights is to induce innovation and that too much protection for intellectual property can retard innovation.[34] As several commentators have noted, overly broad intellectual property rights can retard innovation by, for example, inhibiting the development of improvement patents[35] and derivative copyrighted

grant of the patent, the only limitation on the size of the carrot should be the dictates of the marketplace.').

[33] See, eg, *S Rep* 100-492, at 2 (1988) (explaining that, '[b]y recognizing intellectual innovations as property, the [patent and copyright] laws provide inventors, as well as authors and other artists, with exclusive rights to the use of their inventions and original works *for a limited time*' and '[t]hese rights enable innovators to capture some of the economic rewards of their efforts') (emphases added); *Stewart v Abend*, 495 US 207, 228 (1990) (reviewing legislative history of Copyright Act and observing that 'although dissemination of creative works is a goal of the Copyright Act, the Act creates a balance between the artist's right to control the work during the time of copyright protection and the public's need for access to creative works.'); *Sony Corp of Am v Universal City Studios, Inc,* 464 US 417, 429 (1984) ('The monopoly privileges that Congress may authorize are neither unlimited nor primarily designed to provide a special private benefit [;] [r]ather, the limited grant is . . . intended to motivate the creative activity of authors and inventors by the provision of a special reward, and to allow the public access to the products of their genius after the limited period of exclusive control has expired.').

[34] The National Commission on New Technological Uses of Copyrighted Works (CONTU), established by Congress in 1974 to study the implications of computer and other new information technologies and recommend revisions to the federal intellectual property laws, emphasized in its report the fundamental principle that '[c]opyright should not grant more economic power than is necessary to achieve the incentive to create.' See Peter S Menell, *An Epitaph for Traditional Copyright Protection of Network Features of Computer Software, Antitrust Bulletin* 651, 709 (quoting CONTU Report at 12) (1998).

[35] See Carl Shapiro, *Navigating the Patent Thicket: Cross Licenses, Patent Pools and Standard Setting, Remarks Before National Bureau on Economic Research Seminar: Innovation Policy and the Economy* (Apr 2000) (transcript available at http://www.haas.berkeley.edu/Shapiro/thicket.pdf) ('With cumulative innovation and multiple blocking patents, stronger patent rights can have the perverse effect of stifling, not encouraging, innovation.'); Joseph Stiglitz, Speech at Opening of FTC's Hearings on Competition Policy in the New High-Tech, Global Marketplace, *FTC Staff Report* 6 (1995) ('some people jump . . . to the conclusion that the broader the patent rights are, the better it is for innovation, and that isn't always correct, because we have an innovation system in which one innovation builds on another. If you get monopoly rights down at the bottom, you may stifle competition that uses those patents later on . . . so the breadth and utilization of patent rights can be used not only to stifle competition, but also have adverse effects in the long run on innovation').

works (such as the recent sequels to *Gone With The Wind*).[36] It is, in short, only the beginning and not the end of the analysis of an intellectual property law issue to n that one outcome will provide greater or lesser returns to the intellectual property rights holder than another outcome.

The second and more important mistake made by proponents of the *CSU* result is their apparent belief that the antitrust laws are hostile to lawfully acquired monopolies and, therefore, that application of those laws will prevent the intended exploitation of intellectual property rights.[37] There is, to be sure, language in older antitrust cases suggesting that even legally obtained monopolies are to be 'tolerated, but not cherished.'[38] However, at least since the Chicago school began to influence antitrust policy in the late 1970's and 1980's, antitrust doctrine has crystallized around sound notions of economic analysis. It is now beyond doubt that antitrust law—whether it cherishes or merely tolerates monopoly—explicitly permits firms to charge monopoly prices and otherwise to profit from their lawfully obtained monopoly.[39] It does so for the same reason that intellectual property laws create property rights—to create and protect ex ante incentives for entrepreneurship, innovation and commercial success. That is what the antitrust laws mean when they say that one who gains a monopoly by 'skill, foresight and industry' is permitted to reap the fruits of the monopoly.[40]

[36] See generally Menell, above n 37, at 677 (arguing against interpreting the Copyright Act as providing protection for network features of computer software and cautioning that, '[i]n view of the cumulative nature of technological advancement, intellectual property law must be careful not to choke off secondary innovation by according excessive or unjustified protections for first generation inventions.').

[37] See, eg, *Axis v Micafil*, 870 F.2d 1105, 1111 (6th Cir 1989) (asserting that because '[p]atent laws grant a monopoly for a limited time in order 'to promote [innovation]" while the '[a]ntitrust laws, on the other hand, are designed to promote and protect competition in the marketplace,' the two legal regimes 'seek to further different and opposing policies') (citation omitted); *United States v Westinghouse*, 648 F.2d 642, 646 (9th Cir 1981) (noting the 'obvious tension' between the patent and antitrust laws: '[o]ne body of law creates and protects monopoly power while the other seeks to proscribe it') (citations omitted).

[38] *Berkey Photo v Eastman Kodak Co*, 603 F.2d 263, 273 (2d Cir 1979) (quoting *United States v United Shoe Mach Corp*, 110 F Supp 295, 345 (D Mass 1953); *aff'd per curiam*, 347 US 521 (1954)); see also *Olympia Equip Leasing Co v W. Union Te. Co*, 797 F.2d 370, 375 (7th Cir 1986) (discussing the evolution in opinion about the offense of monopolization); *SCM v Xerox Corp*, 645 F.2d 1195, 1205 (2d Cir 1981) (quoting language from *Berkey* and observing that '[t]he tension between the objectives of preserving economic incentives to enhance competition while at the same time trying to contain the power a successful competitor acquires is heightened tremendously when the patent laws come into play').

[39] *Blue Cross & Blue Shield United of Wis v Marshfield Clinic*, 65 F.3d 1406, (7th Cir 1995) (monopolist that has acquired and maintained its monopoly by lawful means 'can . . . charge any price that it wants, . . . for the antitrust laws are not a price-control statute'); *Olympia Equip Leasing*, 797 F.2d at 376 ('[a] monopolist has no duty to reduce its prices in order to help consumers') (citing *Berkey Photo*, 603 F.2d at 294); *USM Corp v SPS Technologies, In.*, 694 F.2d 505, 512–13 (7th Cir 1982) ('there is no antitrust prohibition against a patent owner's using price discrimination to maximize his income from the patent').

[40] *United States v Aluminum Co. of America*, 148 F.2d 416, 430 (2d Cir 1945).

That is also why antitrust law explicitly permits ancillary restraints that reduce competition ex post if they are reasonably related to a procompetitive venture and, thus, are procompetitive ex ante.[41]

B. *The Similar Approaches of Antitrust and Intellectual Property Law*

The similarities of antitrust and intellectual property law run deeper. Intellectual property law gives rights holders ownership of the intellectual property. When that property enables the owner to have monopoly power in an antitrust market, the effect of the intellectual property protection is to enable the owner to reap monopoly profits.[42] An intellectual property owner is not free, however, to engage in efforts to extend his monopoly beyond the terms of the statutory grant. Thus, for example, a patentee may not tie patented items to unpatented goods[43] or charge royalties past the term of the patent.[44] Such conduct is proscribed under the doctrines of

[41] See, eg, *Antitrust Guidelines for Collaboration Among Competitors* §3.2 (2000). See also, eg, Turner, above n 1, at 486 ('it is now established antitrust law that even dominant firms are not only free but are encouraged to innovate and retain the fruits of their innovations even though innovative success may tend to perpetuate their dominant position'); *Olympia Equip Leasing*, 797 F.2d at 375 ('[a] monopolist, no less than any other competitor, is permitted and indeed encouraged to compete aggressively on the merits') (quoting *Foremost Pro Color, Inc v Eastman Kodak Co*, 703 F.2d 534, 544 (1983)).

[42] It is sometimes said that intellectual property laws are intended to enable rights holders to earn monopoly profits. That is not entirely clear. The intellectual property laws are intended to confer rights of ownership, but there is no a priori reason to think that those laws were intended to favor innovations that enable the owner to obtain monopoly power. Moreover, while it is often the case that an intellectual property holder can be rewarded for the innovation only if it is able to charge a price in excess of marginal cost, it is by no means clear that conferring the reward of monopoly profits is optimal as a matter of intellectual property law. See, eg, Ian Ayres and Paul Klemperer, 'Limiting Patentees' Market Power Without Reducing Innovation Incentives: The Perverse Benefits of Uncertainty and Non-Injunctive Remedies', 97 *Mich L Rev* 985, 987 (1999) (arguing that 'unconstrained monopoly pricing is not a cost-justified means of rewarding patentees' on the ground that '[t]he last bit of monopoly pricing produces large amounts of deadweight loss for a relatively small amount of patentee profit' and is not necessary to induce innovation). In any event, because there is no general prohibition in the antitrust laws or elsewhere on a monopolist's reaping monopoly profits, intellectual property laws predictably have the effect of enabling the realization of such profits, regardless whether that was their purpose.

[43] See, eg, *Zenith Radio Corp v Hazeltine Research, Inc*, 395 US 100, 136 (1969) ('[a]mong other restrictions upon him, [patentee] may not condition the right to use his patent on the licensee's agreement to purchase, use or sell, or not to purchase, use or sell another article of commerce not within the scope of his patent monopoly').

[44] See *Brulotte v Thys Co*, 379 US 29, 33 (1964) (while 'a patent empowers [its] owner to exact royalties as high as he can negotiate with the leverage of that monopoly[,] . . . . use [of] that leverage to project those royalty payments beyond the life of the patent is analogous to an effort to enlarge the monopoly of the patent by tieing [sic] the sale or use of the patented article to the purchase or use of unpatented ones'); *Meehan v PPG Indus*, 802 F.2d 881, 886 (7th Cir 1986). These cases appear wrongly decided from the vantage point of contemporary antitrust analysis because deferring royalty payments probably does not constitute creation of additional market power. But even if these cases rest on an economic mistake, they embrace as

patent and copyright misuse, and the proscription applies regardless whether the intellectual property holder acts unilaterally or in concert with others[45] and even though the rewards to the intellectual property holder might in some circumstances be greater if there were no such proscription.

Antitrust principles are similar. Under the antitrust laws, a firm is free to charge monopoly prices and earn monopoly profits, but it may not engage in anticompetitive conduct to increase its market power.[46] Anticompetitive conduct not only reduces economic welfare in a static sense by enabling price increases and output reductions but also diminishes and distorts innovation—precisely the harm the intellectual property laws are intended to guard against.

Although there are differing ways of articulating the notion of anticompetitive conduct, there appears to be an emerging consensus in both the economics literature and judicial decisions that anticompetitive conduct is conduct that serves no legitimate purpose, or is itself unprofitable, and is undertaken in order to exclude or weaken competitors in anticipation of increased market power and resulting supracompetitive recoupment.[47] This principle is, of course, entirely consistent with cases that find tie-ins and

a principle of intellectual property law that one cannot use intellectual property to extend the power conferred by it beyond the statutory grant.

[45] See *Leitch Mfg Co v Barber Co*, 302 US 458, 463 (1938) (reiterating 'the rule [that] every use of a patent as a means of obtaining a limited monopoly of unpatented material is prohibited' and emphasizing that it 'applies whatever the nature of the device [ie, unilateral action or contract] by which the owner of the patent seeks to effect such unauthorized extension of the monopoly').

[46] *See Berkey Photo v Eastman Kodak Co,* 603 F.2d 263, 274 (2d Cir 1979).

[47] See, eg, *Aspen Skiing Co v Aspen Highlands Skiing Corp*, 472 US 585, 610–11 (1985); (upholding jury verdict for plaintiff in section 2 case because the evidence 'support[ed] an inference that [the defendant] was not motivated by efficiency concerns and. . . was willing to sacrifice short-run benefits and consumer goodwill in exchange for a perceived long-run impact on its smaller rival.'); *Advanced Health Care Servs, Inc v Radford Comm Hosp*, 910 F.2d 139, 148 (4th Cir 1990) ('if a plaintiff shows that a defendant has harmed consumers and competition by making a short-term sacrifice in order to further its exclusive, anticompetitive objectives, it has shown predation'); *Neumann v Reinforced Earth Co*, 786 F.2d 424, 427 (DC Cir 1986) ('predation involves aggression against. . . rivals through the use of business practices that would not be considered profit maximizing except for the expectation that (1) actual or potential rivals will be driven from the market, or the entry of potential rivals blocked or delayed, so that the predator will gain or retain a market share sufficient to command monopoly profits, or (2) rivals will be chastened sufficiently to abandon competitive behavior the predator finds threatening to its realization of monopoly profits.'); *United States v Microsoft*, 87 F Supp 2d 30, 38 (DDC 2000) ('If the defendant with monopoly power consciously antagonized its customers by making its products less attractive to them—or if it incurred other costs, such as large outlays of development capital and forfeited opportunities to derive revenue from it—with no prospect of compensation other than the erection or preservation of barriers against competition by *equally efficient firms, the Court may deem the defendant's conduct 'predatory"),* aff'd in part and rev'd in part on other grounds, 253 F.3d 34 (DC Cir 2001).

Some cases involving alleged refusals to deal have analysed the issues under the so-called 'essential facilities doctrine,' which is typically articulated in a way that does not explicitly

efforts to extend intellectual property beyond its statutory term to be a violation of the intellectual property laws.[48] In other words, both the antitrust laws and the intellectual property laws distinguish between earning monopoly profits, which property owners are entitled to do, and sacrificing profits in order to create additional power.

While unilateral refusals to deal are assessed under these same broad antitrust principles, successful challenges to unilateral refusals to deal have been very rare.[49] For one thing, except in cases involving evasion of regulation,[50] unilateral refusals to deal generally do not enable the defendant to obtain supracompetitive profits beyond those it would otherwise be able to obtain.[51] Further, there are often legitimate reasons for one firm's refusal to deal with another; the latter may, for example, be an opportunist, untrustworthy with trade secrets, or an unreliable shepherd of the former's goodwill. It is thus widely acknowledged that all firms, including monopolists, are ordinarily free under the antitrust laws to decide with whom and on what terms they will do business.[52]

In addition, courts and antitrust enforcers recognize that one can prudently condemn a refusal to deal only if dealing is demonstrably feasible and the terms on which dealing should be required can be readily ascertained.[53]

focus on whether the defendant sacrificed profits in order to create additional market power. See, eg, *MCI Communications Corp v AT&T*, 708 F.2d 1081, 1132–33 (7th Cir 1983), *cert denied,* 464 US 891 (1983). Plaintiffs rarely prevail under this doctrine, however; and it is, in any event, not inconsistent in substance with the standard articulated in text, at least in cases involving unilateral refusals to deal.

48 See, eg, Cite.

49 Eg, *Aspen Skiing*, 472 US at 601; *Otter Tail Power Co v United States*, 410 US 366, 372 (1973); *Lorain Journal Co v United States*, 342 US 143, 155 (1951); MCI, 708 F.2d at 1102–03; Cf. *Goldwasser v Ameritech Corp,* 222 F.3d 390, 397 (7th Cir. 2000) (although it may be 'exceedingly difficult' to establish the possession-of-monopoly-power element of a section 2 case, this task 'is a snap' compared to the challenge of proving predation or the unlawful maintenance of monopoly power); *Data Gen Corp v Grumman Sys Support Corp,* 36 F.3d 1147, 1183 (1st Cir 1994) ('Despite the theoretical possibility, there have been relatively few cases in which a unilateral refusal to deal has formed the basis of a successful Section 2 claim.').

50 See, eg, *Otter Tail Power Co v United States*, 410 US 366, 368 (1973); *United States v AT&T*, 524 F Supp 1336, 1347 (DDC 1981).

51 Although the facts bearing on the antitrust issues in the CSU case were not developed, it appears very unlikely that the plaintiff there would have been able to prove the requisite competitive harm. The problem with the decision thus appears to be not the result, but the rationale.

52 See *United States v Colgate & Co*, 250 US 300, 307 (1919); *Serv & Training, Inc v Data Gen Corp,* 963 F.2d 680, 686 (4th Cir 1992).

53 In principle, the defendant should be required to deal only at a profit-maximizing price, which will of course be above marginal cost. The reason is that the defendant is permitted to maximize profits and the antitrust offense requires proof that it chose not to do so. Cf *Berkey Photo, Inc v Eastman Kodak Co,* 603 F.2d 263 (2d Cir 1979), *cert denied,* 444 US 1093 (1980) (plaintiff is entitled to relief only from the illegal increment of defendant's conduct, not to a competitive price).

Thus, they have, for reasons of prudence or principle, generally insisted on either a prior pattern of dealing by the defendant, which can serve as a benchmark by which to measure the defendants' duty to the plaintiff,[54] or that the defendant be already subject to regulation by a government agency with the expertise and resources to determine appropriate terms of dealing and to monitor their implementation.[55]

And, of course, there are the other elements that must be established by an antitrust claimant, such as the requirement that the defendant be shown to have monopoly power, or a dangerous probability of obtaining it, in a properly defined antitrust market.[56] This obstacle should prove insuperable for many potential plaintiffs—particularly ISOs like CSU that usually will have to show that the defendant will be able to exercise monopoly power in a market for servicing equipment that is sold in a competitive market.[57]

There is, in short, no serious conceptual or policy conflict between intellectual property law and antitrust law—properly understood—that could justify an antitrust exemption for refusals to license intellectual property. Nor, especially in light of the infrequency of successful antitrust claims based on unilateral refusals to deal, is there any reason to believe that,

[54] Eg, *Aspen Skiing,* 472 US at 597. Some commentators have gone so far as to suggest that there can never be a duty to deal if the monopolist has not previously dealt with rivals. See Pitofsky, above n 30, at 6 ('a patent holder has no obligation to license or sell in the first instance').

[55] See, eg, *Otter Tail Power Co v United States*, 410 US 366, 372 (1973). A duty to deal was also imposed in *United States v Terminal RR Ass'n,* 224 US 383, 410–11 (1912), *Gamco, Inc v Providence Fruit & Produce Bldg, Inc,* 194 F.2d 484, 488 (1st Cir 1952), and *Associated Press v United States*, 326 US 1, 12–13 (1945), but those cases involved concerted action, not a unilateral refusal to deal by a monopolist.

[56] See *Goldwasser v Ameritech Corp,* 222 F.3d 390, 397 (7th Cir 2000) ('Few would say that the first element [of a Section 2 case] is easily proved: it is exceedingly difficult to prove market power, or monopoly power directly, and the conventional way of proving power by showing a given share of a properly defined relevant market can present vexing problems as well.'). Where the product or service to which access has been denied is alleged to be an essential facility, the plaintiff must also demonstrate an inability practically or reasonably to duplicate the facility. See *MCI Communications Corp v AT&T*, 708 F.2d 1091, 1132–33 (7th Cir 1983); *Corsearch, Inc v Thompson & Thompson*, 792 F Supp 305, 332–33.

[57] Unless the defendant manufacturer has a very high share of the overall equipment market, ISOs challenging a manufacturer's refusal to license diagnostic software or to sell patented parts will have to rely on 'lock-in' theory articulated in *Eastman Kodak Co v Image Technical Servs, Inc,* 504 US 451, 496–97 (1992), to define the relevant market and establish monopoly power. That theory requires a showing that the market is characterized by high information and switching costs and that, as a result, customers become 'locked-in' to one brand of equipment and competition in the primary equipment market does not discipline aftermarket pricing. Since Kodak, few plaintiffs have been successful in establishing market or monopoly power by this means. See, eg, *PSI Repair Servs, Inc v Honeywell, Inc,* 104 F.3d 811, 821 (6th Cir 1997); *Digital Equip Corp v Uniq Digital Techs, Inc,* 73 F.3d 756, 763 (7th Cir 1996); *Allen-Myland, Inc v IBM Corp,* 33 F.3d 194, 208 (3d Cir 1994). But see *Picker Int'l, Inc v Leavitt,* 865 F Supp 951, 960 (D Mass 1994) (plaintiff presented sufficient evidence to create a genuine issue of fact with respect to whether the relevant market was service for Picker's CT scanners).

absent an antitrust immunity, ex ante incentives for innovation would be reduced.[58]

There is one practical concern, though, that should be noted. By contrast to a gas station at the only exit off the highway or a restaurant with the best chef in town or any of the countless other tangible assets that can create market power, intellectual property can be replicated at virtually no marginal cost. Intellectual property that could be useful to a rival's business—the stuff of antitrust disputes—thus invites a request for a license. Refusals to license might therefore more frequently be provoked, and a regime that permitted antitrust remedies for such refusals might be expected to induce unfounded lawsuits and thus to impose a tax on the legitimate exercise of intellectual property rights.[59] If large enough, the prospect of that tax could diminish the kind of innovative activity the intellectual property laws are intended to induce.

Although there is some theoretical basis for this concern, at least absent compelling empirical support, it does not provide a sufficient basis to justify a special safe harbor for intellectual property. In the first place, especially given the increasing importance of network industries,[60] which are themselves obvious candidates for access demands, it is by no means clear that antitrust disputes about refusals to deal are especially likely to involve intellectual property. Moreover, while there have in the past been flurries of lawsuits in response to perceived changes in the law, antitrust challenges to refusals to deal have rarely succeeded; and the claims have rapidly subsided as claimants have come to understand the difficult burden they must meet. There is no reason to expect a different result in the intellectual property context.

[58] See generally, Turner, above n 1, at 489 (explaining the 'flaw in the supposition that any antitrust rules limiting the patentee's reward would have a significant effect on decisions to embark on inventive activity'). See also, eg, FM Scherer, *Innovation and Growth: Schumpeterian Perspectives* 216 (1984) ('no evidence' that compulsory licensing in antitrust decrees led to reduced development in R&D).

[59] See *Image Technical Servs.*, 125 F.3d at 1217–18 (observing that '[t]he effect of [antitrust] claims based upon unilateral conduct on the value of intellectual property rights is a cause for serious concern' because '[w]ithout bounds, [such] claims . . . will proliferate' and 'subject holders of patents and copyrights' to the 'cost and risk of lawsuits based upon the effect . . . of their refusal to sell or license').

[60] See generally, eg, Allan Murray, 'Intellectual Property: Old Rules Don't Apply', *Wall Street Journal*, 23 Aug 2001, at A1 (citing software and pharmaceuticals as examples of products 'whose primary value lies in intellectual property' and which 'drive today's economy'); Peter S Menell, 'An Epitaph for Traditional Copyright Protection of Network Features of Computer Software', *Antitrust Bulletin*, 651, 656 (Fall–Winter 1998) (observing that modern markets in which network effects are significant 'have taken on growing importance' and 'include interface specifications for computer operating systems, protocols for Internet communication, networks of automatic teller machines for banking, and broadcast standards for high-definition television').

IV. TOWARD A SYNTHESIS

If unilateral refusals to deal rarely violate the antitrust laws, it might be argued, subjecting unilateral refusals to license intellectual property to antitrust scrutiny is unlikely to have a big practical impact. So, one might ask, why the controversy? Why does the *CSU* decision matter?

The answer is that it matters on several levels. In the first place, some unilateral refusals to deal are very anticompetitive and damaging. The *AT&T* case was, after all, a refusal to deal case.[61] There is no reason to think that AT&T should have been permitted to engage in the conduct at issue there if only the interfaces used by MCI to connect with AT&T's network had been patented—especially since AT&T's market power was a result of its ubiquitous local network, not its interfaces.[62]

Second, the line between simple refusals to deal and other kinds of exclusionary conduct is hard to draw, and antitrust immunity will no doubt encourage firms to seek to expand the boundaries—and to do so by formalistic arguments that focus on how to categorize types of conduct rather than on their competitive affects. *Lorain Journal*, for example, involved a monopolist's refusal to deal in order to deter customers from dealing with the monopolist's rivals so that it could obtain a monopoly in another business.[63] And, while the *CSU* case purported to be narrowly decided and to acknowledge, for example, that tie-ins involving intellectual property are not immune from the antitrust laws, it is by no means clear how its rule would treat an arrangement in the form of a unilateral announcement of a refusal to deal policy that effects in substance a tie in (*eg*, a firm announces that it will license patented product A only to firms that also buy B from it).

Third, and perhaps most important, safe harbors distort business behavior. Antitrust counsel would advise an AT&T of today, for example, that it could immunize its anticompetitive refusal to deal from the antitrust laws by contriving to design its system so that firms like MCI that need access to its network would have to use patented or copyrighted interfaces that, under *CSU*, it may refuse to license. In that event, competition would be

61 *MCI Communications Corp v AT&T*, 708 F.2d 1081, 1132–33 (7th Cir 1983).

62 Id at 1133. It has been suggested that this problem could be avoided by 'distinguishing between cases in which the intellectual property right itself is the facility to which the plaintiff wants access and cases in which intellectual property rights exist but are incidental to the control of the facility itself.' H Hovencamp, M Janis, and M Lemley, *IP and Antitrust* ¶13.3 at 13–21 (New York, 2002). This distinction seems on its face rather arbitrary and invites difficult line-drawing disputes in some cases. It is not at all clear, for example, whether a competing manufacturer of personal computer operating systems that seeks interoperability with Windows wants access to the copyrighted software or to the network externalities (ie, the universe of users and applications) available to Windows.

63 *Lorain Journal Co v US*, 342 US 143, 149–50 (1951).

injured, and network design and innovation would be distorted and presumably diminished. In other words, the *CSU* decision, although intended to prevent the antitrust laws from reducing incentives for and thus distorting innovation, could itself have the effect of both distorting innovation and undermining competition.

The larger problem with *CSU* is that it is retrograde. For more than twenty years, from at least the Supreme Court's decision in *BMI*[64] through the recent unanimous *en banc* Court of Appeals decision in the *Microsoft* case,[65] antitrust law has moved away from the rigidities of formalism and legal issues, in favor of a fact-based analysis that applies rigorous economic principles to distinguish anticompetitive from procompetitive conduct. The *CSU* decision seems oblivious to this development and to the resulting convergence of antitrust and intellectual property law principles. Ironically, therefore, *CSU* in this respect disserves its own purported objective of protecting a coherent regime for the exploitation of intellectual property rights.

Some have suggested that there might be a middle ground, a kind of partial immunity from the antitrust laws for intellectual property. Two such hybrid approaches have been suggested. Neither is sound.

The first approach, picking up on language in patent and copyright misuse cases proscribing attempts to extend monopoly power beyond the terms of the statutory grant, asks whether the alleged injury to competition resulting from the refusal to deal is within the patent grant (eg, the market in which patented parts are sold) or outside it (eg, the service market, for which the parts are an input). In the former case, the monopolist's conduct would be immune from antitrust scrutiny; in the second, ordinary antitrust principles would apply.[66] There are a number of problems with this proposed compromise. First, it ignores the reality that patents are granted for inventions, not

[64] *Broad. Music, Inc v CBS*, 441 US 1 (1979).

[65] *United States v Microsoft*, 253 F.3d 34 (DC Cir 2001) (en banc), cert denied, 122 S Ct 350 (2001). The court relied on a broad, fact-based analysis and rejected arguments for formalistic rules including, among others, safe harbors for product design and intellectual property, a per se approach to software tying, mechanical rules for exclusive dealing-type conduct, and special rules for proving monopoly power in dynamic industries.

[66] See, eg, Ronald S Katz, Janet A Hart & Adam J Safer, *Intellectual Property v Antitrust: A False Dilemma*, SD 72 ALI-ABA 1 (1999) (suggesting that '[t]here is a simple formula that will ensure that the purposes of [the antitrust and intellectual property laws] are fulfilled[;] [w]here there is one market involved a patent and/or copyright holder has the exclusive right to exploit his invention[;] [h]owever, where two markets exist and the patent or copyright holder seeks to extend his 'legal monopoly' into the second market, antitrust liability is likely'); *Telecomm Technical Servs, Inc v Siemens Rolm Communications, Inc,* 150 F Supp 2d 1365, 1369 (ND Ga 2000) (indicating that, even after the Federal Circuit's decision in CSU, '[t]here is still room for a particular plaintiff to show leveraging by proving that the market in which the defendant refused to deal was outside the scope of the patent').

markets, and the difficulty of distinguishing, for market definition purposes, between a product and its components.[67] In addition, such a formalistic rule could create incentives for intellectual property holders to avoid otherwise efficient vertical integration in order to make sure that they stay in the safe harbor.[68] Moreover, as others have noted, this approach is inconsistent with the doctrine of contributory infringement.[69]

The second approach focuses on whether the refusal to deal was genuinely intended to protect intellectual property rights or was, instead, a pretext for some other, anticompetitive goal.[70] It is not clear what this means. If it means that a refusal to deal loses its antitrust immunity if it is 'anticompetitive' in the antitrust sense, it effectively nullifies the exemption; if it means 'anticompetitive' in a less technical sense, then it is based on a false dichotomy because the very purpose of intellectual property law is to permit the holder to reap the benefits of exclusive enjoyment, even if that means charging monopoly prices to customers and not sharing the property with rivals. Moreover, as the *CSU* court correctly noted,[71] any rule that turns on intent and motive—rather than the economic attributes of the defendant's conduct—is inconsistent with the trend of the modern cases,

[67] See *Intergraph Corp v Intel Corp*, 88 F Supp 2d 1288, 1292 (ND Ala 2000) ('the patent grant is a legal right to exclude, not a commercial product in a competitive market'); In re Indep Serv Org Antitrust Litigation, 989 F Supp 1131, 1135–36 (D Kan 1997) (emphasizing that '[t]he scope of a 'patent monopoly' is defined by the claims of the patent, not by the limits of what a court determines is the most analogous antitrust market and criticizing the Ninth Circuit's assumption in Image Technical Services 'that a single patent . . . can be equated with a single relevant antitrust market' because were such a view to prevail, '[i]nventors rarely could refuse to license their products without fear that they had not properly defined the relevant antitrust market or considered how the relevant markets may be defined in the future').

[68] Cf Daniel L Rubinfeld, 'Antitrust Enforcement in Dynamic Network Industries', *Antitrust Bulletin*, 1998 WL 16568457 (observing that 'a dominant firm will have a legitimate interest in innovating and entering into complementary product markets, since (among other things) this will enhance the value of [its] product' and that such integration may create real efficiencies).

[69] See, eg, Phillip E Areeda and Herbert Hovenkamp, *Antitrust Law* ¶704.1 at 114 (2001 Supp) (explaining that in *Dawson Chem Co v Rolhm & Haas*, 448 US 176 (1980), the Supreme Court 'explicitly read the doctrine of contributory infringement broadly to permit a patentee to enforce its rights in a process patent even when the effect was to create a monopoly in an unpatented product to which the process patent applied, notwithstanding the infringement defendant's claim that the impact was to extend the patentee's monopoly from the patented process to the unpatented product').

[70] See *Image Technical Servs*, 125 F.3d at 1219 (desire to protect intellectual property rights is a presumptively valid business justification for refusal to license, but the presumption may be rebutted by evidence that the justification is a 'pretext . . . to mask anticompetitive conduct'). Cf. *Data Gen Corp v Grumman Sys Support Corp*, 36 F.3d 1147, 1188 (1st Cir 1994) ('evidence that [the defendant] knew that developing a 'proprietary position' in the area of diagnostic software would help maintain its monopoly in the aftermarket for service of [its] computers' was not sufficient to rebut justification in the face of 'evidence that [Data General] set out to create a state-of-the-art diagnostic that would help to improve the quality of [its] service').

[71] 203 F.3d 1322, 1327–28 (Fed Cir 2000).

which focus on objective evidence, rather than inferences from inevitably ambiguous evidence of subjective intent.[72]

V. CONCLUSION

Although the hybrids discussed above are flawed, they suggest an important intuition—one that lies at the core of both intellectual property law and antitrust law. It is that one may enjoy the fruits of her lawfully obtained property, including whatever monopoly profits that property enables her to earn, but she may not sacrifice such profits strategically, by using that property in ways that serve no legitimate purpose (ie, one that neither benefits consumers nor promotes efficiency) in order to create additional market power. In other words, a firm, even a monopolist, can profit from its property (including its intellectual property) but has no legal entitlement to extend its power beyond the intellectual property grant or to create additional market power.[73] The *CSU* case erred in not recognizing this common intersection of intellectual property law and antitrust law, in not understanding how the rigorous economics and careful attention to facts of contemporary antitrust law ensures that it protects the legitimate interests of property owners, and in relying on formalistic distinctions—between intellectual property and tangible property, and between refusals to deal and other forms of exclusionary conduct—that disserve the interests of both bodies of law.

[72] See, eg, *Olympia Equip Leasing,* 797 F.2d 370, 379 (7th Cir 1986) ('We add, what has become an antitrust commonplace, that if conduct is not objectively anticompetitive the fact that it was motivated by hostility to competitors . . . is irrelevant.'); *Ball Mem Hosp, Inc v Mutual Hosp Ins, Inc,* 784 F.2d 1325, 1338 (7th Ci. 1986) ('"intent to harm rivals" is not a useful standard in antitrust'); *Barry Wright Corp v ITT Grinnell Corp,* 724 F.2d 227, 232 (1st Cir 1983) ('"intent to harm" without more offers too vague a standard in a world where executives may think no farther than 'Let's get more business,' and long-term effects on consumers depend in large measure on competitors' responses').

The intent test also appears to conflict with the Supreme Court's holding in *Professional Real Estate Investors, Inc v Columbia Pictures Indus, Inc,* 508 US 49, 64 (1993), that a copyright holder's intent in pursuing an infringement action is irrelevant so long as the copyright is objectively valid and enforceable. See Areeda and Hovenkamp, above n 69, ¶704.1 at 112.

[73] See generally, William F Baxter, 'The Definition and Measurement of Market Power in Industries Characterized by Rapidly Developing and Changing Technologies', 53 *Antitrust LJ* 717, 725–26 (1984) ('The basic principle is that the owner of a technology is entitled to the expropriation of all the consumer surplus under the demand curve for his invention' but not to use his invention to 'erect entry barriers' or to 'suppress rivalry between different technologies'.)

3. Essential Facilities and a Duty to License—IMS

Professor Valentine Korah*

I. INTRODUCTION

In Europe in the 1970s, the Commission, the European Court of Justice (ECJ) and the Court of First Instance (CFI) started requiring dominant firms to grant access to supplies of consumable goods, to fixed assets and intellectual property rights (iprs),[1] but this obligation has been curtailed by recent judgments. The duty to supply required by a recent controversial interim decision of the Commission in *IMS Health*[2] has been suspended by an interim order by the President of the CFI until that court gives judgment on appeal from the Commission.[3]

The economic disadvantages of requiring dominant firms to grant access are 1) that the incentive to the original investment is reduced, 2) the incentive to develop a second source, where this is practical, is reduced 3) there is no agreement as to how compensation for access should be assessed, 4) sometimes the essential facility cannot serve rival firms satisfactorily.

The case law in the EC has not sufficiently addressed the issues, although in *Oscar Bronner*,[4] Advocate General Jacobs argued that the doctrine

* Visiting Professor, Fordham University School of Law, Professor Emeritus of Competition Law, University College London, Visiting Professor College of Europe at Bruges. Paper given at the Second Annual Conference on International and Comparative Competition Law, BIICL, May 2002.

I wrote a longer article for 69 *Antitrust LJ* 801, of which this is a substantially shortened version of the middle part.

I am greatly indebted to Craig Flanagin, a JD student at Fordham, who provided research assistance far beyond anything that might reasonably be expected and who opened my eyes to the reasons why the incentive to the original investment is less important when the property right has become a standard as a result of the business practice of those using the standard.

1 *Chemioterapico Italiano SpA and Commercial Solvents Corp v Commission* (6 & 7/73), 6 Mar 1974, [1974] ECR 223, [1974] 1 *CMLR* 309, *CMR* 8209, *Hugin-Liptons Cash Registers and Business Equipment Ltd v Hugin Kassaregister AB* (78/68/EEC), 8 Dec 1977, OJ 1978, L22/23.

2 *IMS–NDC Health/IMS Health:* Interim measures, 3 July 2001, [2002] 4 *CMLR* 111, not published in OJ because it was only an interim decision. It is available on the Commission's web site.

3 T-184/01 R II, 26 Oct 2001, [2002] 4 *CMLR* 58. There was an earlier holding order until the Commission and competitors were heard in *IMS v Commission,* T-184/01 R I, 10 Aug 2001, [2002] 4 *CMLR* 46. The interim order was confirmed by the President of the ECJ, C-481/01 (P) R, on the ground that the President of the CFI enjoyed a wide discretion and had not made a manifest error.

4 *Oscar Bronner GmbH & Co KG v Mediaprint Seitungs- und Zeitschriftenverlag GmbH*

should be narrow in view of all these considerations.[5] His views were followed by the ECJ although its reasoning was less substantial. In three cases the CFI has narrowed the duty to supply or license.[6]

Intellectual property rights are national and most are limited to a single member state. So, in the early days of the common market, they were perceived as partitioning it. Moreover, in the early days of the Community there was considerable fear of patent monopolies which, under the influence of the ordo-liberal school of economics in Frieburg, were perceived as barriers to entry.[7]

The Competition department of the European Commission was served mainly by lawyers, who had not been brought up to think at the margin or *ex ante*. The need to avoid free riding and to encourage investment had limited influence on competition law until, with the creation of the merger task force from 1989, the officials in the Commission of the EC began to respect economists more.

Sometimes, intellectual property rights may protect innovation considered essential by competitors. In *Volvo v Veng*,[8] however, the ECJ ruled that the right to exclude was part of the specific subject matter of a design right, although it objected to a refusal to licence coupled to one of three practices: charging unfair prices, refusing to supply repairers or ceasing to supply spare parts for a model when there were significant numbers of vehicles still on the road.

The judgment in *Magill*,[9] however, gave rise to controversy. Three television stations transmitting to Ireland and Northern Ireland published their own weekly tv guides. When Magill published the first comprehensive guide covering the three stations, each successfully sued it for copyright infringe-

& Co KG and others, case C-7/97, 26 Nov 1998, [1998] ECR I-7817, [1999] 4 *CMLR* 112, [1999] CEC 53.

[5] Compare P Areeda, 'Essential Facilities: an epithet in need of limiting principles,' (1990) 58 *Antitrust Law Journal*, for an outstanding article recommending that the US law be limited.

[6] I discussed these and other cases more fully in 69 *Antitrust LJ* 801 and will not repeat here what I said.

[7] See David J Gerber, *Law and Competition in Twentieth Century Europe* (Oxford: OUP, 1998) Chapter VVV, 232–265. Between the world wars, the Frieburg school of economists and lawyers was hostile to Nazi ideas and, in pursuit of liberty, advocated the dispersion of both political and economic power. They did not advocate the abolition of intellectual property rights, but considered that patentees should be required to act as if they had no market power, which amounts to much the same thing as abolishing them. Their work was profoundly influential in the early years of the EC. There were more German officials than other nationalities in the competition department of the Commission.

[8] *Volvo AB v Erik Veng (UK) Ltd* (238/87), 5 Oct 1988, [1988] ECR 6211, [1989] 4 *CMLR* 122, *CMR* 14498.

[9] *Radio Telefis Eireann and Others v Commission* (C-241 & 242/91P), 6 Apr 1995, [1995] ECR I743, [1995] 4 *CMLR* 718, [1995] 1 CEC 400 (ECJ).

ment. The ECJ confirmed the Commission's decision condemning this as the abuse of a dominant position. It made clear that the circumstances were special and mentioned that there were no substitutes for the information about programs contained in the stations' guides. Without justification, the tv stations were preventing the emergence of a new product, which they did not provide and for which there was constant consumer demand, thereby reserving that market to themselves.

After the judgment, there was fear that the holder of an improvement patent might be entitled to a licence under the basic patent. Advisors on IPRs were very concerned.

The Commission has gone far in applying the doctrine of essential facilities. The first judgment where it used the term was *B & I v Sealink*.[10] The owner of the port of Holyhead planned to introduce a third service per day to Dublin during the Summer. Its competitor, B & I, which operated from another pier in the port, complained to the Commission that when the Sealink boats came in or left, they left a wash, and for 15 minutes B & I would have to cease loading or unloading. The Commission defined the market narrowly as the central corridor of sea routes between the UK and Ireland to the exclusion of Liverpool that was two hours sailing further on. It adopted interim measures requiring Sealink to cancel the third sailing.

This must have harmed consumers, who lost the extra sailing and, in the event, B & I did not use Holyhead, but introduced a sailing from Liverpool, which required two hours less on narrow winding roads from England![11] Granting access deprives the incumbent of property rights which were the fruit of investment and should not be done unless there is a real bottleneck downstream, as there was in *Commercial Solvents*.[12] Market definitions should not be too narrow, or the consumer interest served may be outweighed by the dynamic factors. Owners of ports, however, often are or recently have been in the public sector, so the dynamic factors may be somewhat less important.

In *Sea Containers v Sealink*,[13] the Commission required Sealink also to make facilities available to another new entrant. It has issued similar decisions requiring access to other ports.

[10] Interim measures, Case IV/34/174, 11 Jun 1992, [1992] 5 *CMLR* 255.

[11] Derek Ridyard, 'essential facilities and the obligation to supply competitors under UK and EC law,' [1996] ECLR 438. I am told, however, that this became commercially sensible only later when faster ferries were used, reducing the time of the extra sailing. Nevertheless, the question arises whether property should be interfered with when the need for access is short term.

[12] *Istituto Chemioterapico Italiano SpA and Commercial Solvents Corp v Commission* (6 & 7/73), 6 Mar 1974, [1974] ECR 223, [1974] 1 *CMLR* 309, *CMR* 8209.

[13] Interim measures, [1994] OJ L15/8.

There have, however, been four judgments narrowing the scope of the judgment in *Magill—Oscar Bronner*[14] by the ECJ and three by the Court of First Instance: *Tiercé Ladbroke v Commission*,[15] *ITT Promedia NV v Commission*[16] and *European Night Services and another v Commission.*[17] I shall not repeat here the discussion of the cases that I wrote for the Antitrust Law Journal,[18] although I will refer to them.

II. IMS HEALTH

The Commission has invoked the essential facilities doctrine in a controversial decision, *IMS Health*,[19] imposing interim measures that required a licence of a business method that a German court had held enjoyed data protection.

IMS is the largest supplier in the world of information on sales and prescription of pharmaceutical products. The data are used by pharmaceutical companies to allocate sales territories, develop incentive schemes for sales representatives and to inform their sales force about changes in the market, market shares, comparisons with earlier periods etc. According to the Commission IMS enjoys a dominant position in providing regional sales data for pharmaceutical companies in Germany.

IMS divided the German territory into 1860 zones or bricks. In each zone there were at least 4 pharmacies. This segmentation of the market enabled IMS to give its clients sales data broken down into useful, small geographic areas based on industry practice, while avoiding the identification of sales through individual pharmacies. German data protection law requires at least three pharmacies to be included in every zone and 4 or 5 are required to keep the structure stable.

The pharmaceutical companies who were familiar with patterns of trade commented on the maps prepared by IMS, but it contributed considerable work itself not only when it first established the system, but also in modi-

[14] *Oscar Bronner GmbH & Co KG v Mediaprint Zeitungs- und Zeitschriftenverlag GmbH & Co KG and Other* (C-7/97) 26 Nov 1998, [1998] ECR I-7817, [1999] 4 *CMLR* 112, [1999] CEC 53.

[15] *Tiercé Ladbroke v Commission*, T-504/93, Jun 12 1997, [1997] ECR II-923, [1997] 5 *CMLR* 309, [1997] CEC 812.

[16] T-111/96, 17 Jul 1998, [1998] ECR II-2937, [1998] 5 *CMLR* 491.

[17] Cases T-374, 375, 384 & 388/94, 15 Sept 1998, [1998] ECR II-3141, [1998] 5 *CMLR* 718, [1998] CEC 955, appeal from Commission decision, 21 Sept 1994, OJ 1994, L259/20, [1995] 5 *CMLR* 76, [1998] CEC 955.

[18] 69 *Antitrust LJ* 801.

[19] *NDC Health/IMS Health*: Interim measures, 3 Jul 2001, [2002] 4 *CMLR* 111, not published in OJ because the Commission ordered only interim measures. It is on the Commission's web site.

fying it subsequently, for instance by sub-dividing bricks and adding zones on the reunification of Germany.

Until 1999, IMS was the only firm providing regional sales data in Germany. Then two firms, NDC and AzyX, entered the market and tried to base the information they supplied on different zones, but discussions with customers showed that this would not be marketable since the zones would not correspond to the territorial divisions already in use by the pharmaceutical companies.

The new entrants then started using IMS's brick system, until sued successfully for infringement of copyright under legislation giving effect in Germany to the data protection directive[20] and IMS obtained an interim injunction. Whether such use infringes copyright is contested and under appeal,[21] but the Commission required IMS to grant a license until notified of the Commission's final decision. IMS is not required to license its marketing data, only the geographical basis on which it is arranged. The Commission decided that the new comers cannot compete in the market without using that basis which has become an industry standard.

The Commission's decision states (¶¶39 and 43) that it is not required definitively to establish infringement of article 82—it suffices for it to make out a prima facie case. It found (¶58) that IMS enjoyed a quasi monopoly over the German market for regional sales data services. Defining the market by reference to a hypothetical monopolist raising price by 5 or 10%[22] leads to very narrow markets. The Commission is confining the market to distribution—indeed, to one of four kinds of data. IMS enjoyed, however, a first mover advantage and there is empirical evidence showing that parties who establish a network or standard enjoy a continuing advantage in its utilisation.[23]

The Commission added that the refusal of access to the brick structure is likely to eliminate all competition in the relevant market and is not objectively justified. The use of the structure is essential as it has become an industry standard and there is no substitute. This extends *Magill*[24] in that

[20] Dir 96/9 of 11 Mar 1996, OJ 1996, L77/20.

[21] Commission's decision, ¶194. The result is unlikely to be available for some years. In the main copyright action, now between IMS and NDC, a reference was made to the ECJ under Art 234 on 20 Aug 2001 as Case C-418/01.

[22] The SSNIP test used for merger control in the US, and adopted by the EC Commission in its notice on the relevant market for the purposes of Community Competition Law, [1997] OJ C/372/3 ¶¶ 15–19.

[23] Flanagin, Monge, Fulk, 'the value of formative investment in organizational federations', (2000) 27 *Human Communication Research*, 69–93.

[24] *Radio Telefis Eireann and Others v Commission* (C-241 & 242/91P), 6 Apr 1995, [1995] ECR I743, [1995] 4 *CMLR* 718, [1995] 1 CEC 400 (ECJ), confirmed in *Bronner*, ¶40.

the refusal to license the tv listings prevented the appearance of any comprehensive guides. IMS was providing a service similar to that the complainants proposed to offer.

The Commission adopted an interim order requiring a licence. It certified that the complainants had made out a *prima facie* case, relief was urgently required and the refusal to licence would cause serious and irreparable damage to the complainants and intolerable damage to the public interest.[25]

190. . . . there is good reason to suppose that unless NDC is granted a licence to the 1860 brick structure its German operation will go out of business and that there will be intolerable damage to the public interest.

The Commission referred to the substantial investments made by NDC (¶191) one of the new entrants, but not to investment by IMS. It was also concerned that in the absence of licences the other competitor would also leave the market before the German injunction could be reversed, and that no one else would want to enter. IMS would be left as the only supplier. This would cause 'intolerable damage to the public interest' (¶195).

The Commission considered that IMS' legitimate interests would not be prejudiced since it would be able to charge fees for its licences (¶200). It did not, however, specify the criteria for settling the licence fees. Should they reflect the monopoly profit on the expectation of which IMS' original investment was made and which the data protection law was designed to induce, or should they be based on IMS' costs?[26] If the latter, I hope that a margin is allowed for risk, as the CFI implied in *European Night Services*.[27] If this is all IMS is allowed to charge it will, however, be prejudiced.

Instead of determining the criteria, the Commission required the parties to settle the royalties and, if they failed to agree within two weeks, they should

[25] ¶¶ 187 et seq of the decision. In *Camera Care Ltd v Commission*, (792/79R) 17 Jan 1980, [1980] ECR 119, the ECJ confirmed the power of the Commission to grant interim relief, provided that four conditions were satisfied).

'19. However, the Commission could not take such measures without having regard to the legitimate interests of the undertaking concerned by them. For this reason it is essential that interim measures he taken only in cases proved to be urgent in order to avoid a situation likely to cause serious and irremediable damage to the party seeking their adoption, or which is intolerable for the public interest. A further requirement is that these measures be of a temporary and conservatory nature and restricted to what is required in the given situation.'

The measure must also be in a form capable of appeal to the ECJ.

The focus on harm to the immediate victim of anti-competitive action was not unusual in 1980.

[26] The fees of the experts are to be shared by the parties. So, it seems that IMS is not to recover even the costs of granting the licence.

[27] Above n 18.

select experts to settle them on the basis of (unspecified) non-discriminatory, 'transparent and objective criteria' within two weeks of appointment (¶215). If they failed to agree, the Commission would fix the compensation.

IMS appealed against the decision to the CFI and requested suspension of the decision. It argued that the refusal to license did not amount to the abuse of a dominant position, that the central findings of fact contradict the findings of the German courts, that the measures were not conservatory and its right to a fair hearing had been infringed.[28]

The Commission's interim decision is giving rise to controversy on many points and the President of the CFI made an interim order that the duty to license be suspended,[29] confirmed after an oral hearing until the appeal from the Commission's interim decision is determined by the CFI on its merits.[30]

The President accepted the earlier case law holding that the Commission's power to adopt interim decisions was as extensive as its power to adopt final orders: the Commission may extend the law on article 82 in an interim decision (¶¶60–68). The Commission has only to establish a prima facie case of an infringement, but the appellant before the CFI, similarly, has only to establish a prima facie case, not a particularly strong one against a remedy that is only provisional: it need not establish manifest error (¶¶65–68). It suffices to establish serious doubts whether the decision was correct (¶¶75 & 90–94).

After considering *Magill* and the other case law carefully, he considered that there was at least a serious doubt whether there was a duty to license when the holder of an ipr was itself offering much the same product as the complainant requesting a licence.[31] At ¶54 of *Magill* the ECJ referred to three circumstances that made the case special: 1) the refusal prevented the appearance of a new product, 2) which the appellants did not offer and 3)

[28] *IMS Health Inc v Commission*, final interim order of the President of the CFI, Case T-184/01 RII, 26 Oct 2001, [2002] *CMLR* 58, ¶76.

[29] (T-180/01R) 10 Aug 2001, [2002] 4 *CMLR* 46. The President stated at ¶24 that there were important differences from the circumstances in *Magill*. The legality of the far reaching remedy depended on the meaning of 'exceptional circumstances'.

'IMS has made out a not unconvincing case that the Commission's measures were not merely conservatory' (¶25).

[30] T-184/01 R II, 26 Oct 2001, [2002] 4 *CMLR* 58. The President's final order on suspension was appealed to the President of the ECJ but he confirmed the suspension on the ground that there was no manifest error, and the President of the CFI enjoys a broad discretion. The Commission's final decision which could be adopted as early as 2002 may well be the next step and that may also be subject to appeal to the CFI.

[31] Id¶101 at ¶¶103 & 104, he contrasted ¶131 of *Tiercé Ladbroke v Commission*, T-504/93, June 12 1997, [1997] ECR II-923, [1997] 5 *CMLR* 309, [1997] CEC 812 with ¶41 of the judgment in *Bronner* above n 5.

for which there was continuing consumer demand. The Commission treated these circumstances as alternatives, but they seem on my reading of *Magill*, to be cumulative. The factors are connected by the conjunctive *and*. Nevertheless all three are treated by the ECJ as its first reason, the next two being the lack of justification and leverage into a connected market. Ownership of copyright was no justification.

The President of the CFI thought the issue should not be decided by an interim decision but left to the CF.'s final decision on the merits (¶105).

When balancing the interests of IMS against the interests of the complainants and the public interest, the President of the CFI considered that the respect for iprs reflected in Article 30[32] of the Treaty and the clear public interest served by the ability of IMS to

> enforce and profit from the specific subject-matter of its copyright in the 1860 brick structure, the inherently exceptional nature of the power to adopt interim measures would normally require that conduct whose termination or amendment is targeted by such measures fall clearly within the scope of the Treaty competition rules. (¶144)

He went on to refer to Jacobs AG's view in *Bronner* (¶58) that the primary purpose of Article 82 is to safeguard the interest of consumers rather than particular competitors (¶145) and confirmed the suspension of the obligation to grant a licence. He considered that the risk to consumers of NDC leaving the market was no greater than the risk dismissed by the Commission of IMS suffering irreparable harm. The decision to suspend was confirmed by the President of the ECJ.

III. COMMENT ON IMS

The Commission's interim decision to compel licensing raises several questions.

First, the Commission established that the brick structure was essential to new entrants by asking their customers, the pharmaceutical companies (¶193). We are not told the terms of these questionnaires, and the fact that the customers said they would not switch was to be expected. There would be costs in switching and at least temporary disruption, which they had an interest in avoiding. Moreover, the firms may be answering honestly, but are not taking responsible decisions about their reactions to refusal to grant a licence.

[32] Id ¶143. Quantitative restraints on trade between Member States may be justified on grounds of intellectual property rights.

The Commission, however, also considered the difficulties of establishing a different zonal system in ¶¶124–52. Its reasoning based on the difficulty of complying with data protection laws seem cogent. Given knowledge within the industry of data based on IMS' brick structure, any minor changes to the structure would result in information being available for less than three pharmacies. It seems that the pharmaceutical companies may well have been locked into IMS' system.

The question remains, however, whether any analysis in advance can be reliable. People think of new ideas when competition compels. Markets seem to be far more volatile that one can predict. The President of the CFI (¶128) accepted that there might be a change of mind.

Secondly, I am no more convinced than was the President of the CFI that the licence required by the Commission went no further than maintaining the *status quo ante*.[33] The newcomers had been able to enter the market only by infringing the copyright and *sui generis* right conferred in pursuance of the data protection directive. Copying would have rendered them liable to damages if the copyright were upheld. The Commission's order entitles them to use the brick structure legally.

Thirdly, if competition law is intended to protect consumers rather than competitors as is accepted by the President of the CFI[34] one might argue that the pharmaceutical companies should have protected themselves from a monopoly in supplying the information by contract when negotiating with IMS to devise its brick structure and required it to license any competitor that might wish to enter the market. Their failure to do so may indicate that IMS would not have taken the trouble to devise the brick structure without the expectation of the exclusive right to use it.[35] Competition law should not lightly be used to mend bad bargains or incentives to investment will be under mined.

[33] For interim relief, see generally CS Kerse, *EC Antitrust Procedure*, 4th edn, 230. The fifth edition is in preparation, but unlikely to be published until the Council has adopted a regulation to replace regulation 17.

[34] ¶145. The Commission is often more concerned than the United States agencies and courts about the exclusion of a competitor from a market. It states that its care is for consumers rather than for competitors, but attributes more importance to the number of existing competitors than is done in the United States, which attaches more importance to the need for appropriate incentives to investment.

[35] The decision does not state whether there was a change in the law protecting data bases. If there was no protection when the bulk of the investment was made by IMS, it would be expecting a lot to rule that the pharmaceutical companies should have protected themselves from exclusive rights that did not yet exist. Compare the judgment of the US Supreme Court in *Eastman Kodak Co v Image Technical Services, Inc*, 504 US 451, 119 LEd2d 265, 112 SCt 2072, (1992), where there was a change in that Kodak had originally made the spare parts available to competitors downstream.

The President of the ECJ, however, at ¶¶80–6 cited *Continental Can*

according to which Article 82 'is not only aimed at practices which may cause damage to consumers directly, but also at those which are detrimental to them through their impact on an effective competition structure.

In my view that phrase does not deny the primacy of consumer interest over that of competitors.

Fourthly, the President of the CFI did not address the point[36] that there are two new entrants to the market requesting compulsory licences and the Commission is requiring both to be licensed. Yet, in *Oscar Bronner*, the ECJ suggested that if another paper proprietor organised a second national distribution system in Austria, compulsory access to that of Mediaprint would not be required.

It did not state why. It is now established that dominant positions within the meaning of Article 82 may be joint.[37] It is arguable, that once a licence has been granted to NDC, it and IMS would be jointly dominant and no further licences should have been required. As a factual matter it may have been more likely that once a second newspaper proprietor organized a national delivery system in Austria, it would have been prepared to deliver papers of independent proprietors than NDC would have been to grant a sublicence to AzyX.

Even so, the ECJ has suggested that very dominant firms may be subject to a stronger obligation not to exclude their competitors.[38] Once NDC is licensed, IMS might no longer be considered sufficiently dominant.

It may be argued that, had another large publisher of newspapers started a home delivery system in *Bronner*, there would have been possibilities for the proprietors of those with a smaller circulation to obtain home delivery,

[36] It was not argued and the CF. has jurisdiction to consider only those questions of substance that are argued.

[37] *Compagnie Maritime Belge Transports SA v Commission* (C?395/96P), 16 Mar 2000, [2000] ECR I-1365, [2000] 4 *CMLR* 1076. ¶¶32–58.

[38] See Richard Whish, *Competition Law*, 4th edn 2001, pp 162.

In Compagnie Maritime Belge Transports SA v Commission, Id above n 112. Fennelly AG said:

'137. . . . Where an undertaking, or group of undertakings whose conduct must be assessed collectively, enjoys *a position of such overwhelming dominance verging on monopoly*, comparable to that which existed in the present case at the moment when G & C entered the relevant market, it would not be consonant with the particularly onerous special obligation affecting such a dominant undertaking to impair further the structure of the feeble existing competition for them to react, even to aggressive price competition from a new entrant, with a policy of targeted, selective price cuts designed to eliminate that competitor.' (my emphasis)

In confirming that selective price cuts not below average variable cost amounted to an abuse, the ECJ at ¶119 referred to the conference 'having a share of over 90% of the market in question and only one competitor.'

and that even if it licensed NDC, IMS would have been able to prevent sublicensing for the benefit of further competitors. It is by no means, certain, however, that with even two papers being independently delivered to homes throughout Austria, that either would have been prepared to deliver other papers, especially if they were competing. It was less likely that once one new comer had been permitted to use IMS' zonal system, it would have granted a sub-licence to the other.

Fifthly, the Commission's interim decision on the merits clearly extends the law further than the ECJ and CFI's case law can support. Should this be done in an interim decision imposing such a far reaching remedy? An interim decision is not always appealed and may remain in effect and strengthen the case law. The President of the CFI took the novelty of the decision into account when considering the balance of interest, rather than when considering whether the Commission had made out a prima facie case.

Sixthly, another point not addressed by the President of the CFI since he suspended the duty to license, was the method of determining the appropriate royalty. One of the reasons expressed by Advocate General Jacobs in *Oscar Bronner* for applying any doctrine of essential facilities narrowly was the difficulty of deciding on the compensation to be paid for access (¶69). Should the Commission require access without specifying the criteria on the basis of which the licence fees should be set? In many cases it has required access and never decided the basis of compensation.

Seventhly, both NDC and AzyX remain in the market although they have not yet achieved a compulsory licence. This must weaken the argument that such a licence is essential.

On the other hand, IMS clearly enjoyed a first mover advantage and was helped by its pharmaceutical clients to devise its zonal system. There is empirical evidence that the first firm to develop a standard may be able to exclude competitors for many years. An outsider to the litigation cannot tell whether access is really necessary. Markets are often more volatile than can be proved in advance. The Commission alleged that the zones amounted to a de facto industry standard and implied that that might sufficient to make the circumstances special within the meaning of the judgment in *Magill*. Whether IMS was informed of this argument only after it had answered the statement of objections is contested.

It is doubtful as a matter of policy whether the kind of information in the zonal system should be protected by either copyright or by a sui generis right. The value of the system lay not so much in the initial work by IMS as in the fact that it had become an industry standard. The value had been greatly enhanced by industry practice.[39] There was less good reason why others should be excluded. Exclusive rights were probably not necessary to induce the original investment.

There is growing concern on both sides of the Atlantic that that unduly wide iprs are being granted by legislation or by patent examiners, especially when new technology takes off and they do not understand how wide the rights being claimed are, and by specialist judges.

This raises the question whether competition law should be used ad hoc to qualify intellectual property rights (iprs) that are framed too broadly. The function of copyright is to induce artistic and other investment. The inducement assumes that the copyright will be enforceable. In my view, competition advocacy is more desirable when the extent of new iprs is being debated in the legislative process than ad hoc, after business has relied on the incentive. This is too wide a topic to be pursued in this paper.

If niche markets are selected as relevant, many facilities will be found to be essential. In *Oscar Bronner*, Advocate General Jacobs warned against a wide concept of essential facilities for reducing the incentive to the original investment, to duplicating it and requiring regulation over the price to be paid for access. The ECJ largely followed his opinion, but did not clearly articulate what amounts to an essential facility. The Commission's final decision on *IMS*[40] and any possible appeal from it are awaited avidly.

IV. CONCLUSION ON THE DUTY TO LICENSE

Both the CFI and the ECJ have been narrowing the doctrine of essential facilities by stressing the need for the firm controlling the facility to expect to earn sufficient remuneration to induce risky investment. Until 1998, few judgments under the competition rules mentioned the need to compensate for successful risks.[41] Commentators have welcomed the emphasis by both courts on the needs of consumers rather than on any particular competitor.

In *Magill*, the intellectual property rights were wider than are usually granted in Europe or elsewhere. In *Oscar Bronner*, Advocate General

[39] See the Comments of Mark Patterson of Fordham Law School at the conference in 2002 on International Intellectual Property Law and Policy, to be published as volume 8 by Juris Publications probably in 2003. A more detailed version was published on the Web site of the Department of the Federal Trade Commission, <http:/www.ftc.gov/opp/intellect/020418mark-patterson.pdf>.

[40] I am told that the Commission is still working on the case, and may adopt a decision, either to reject the complaint or to require access this year or next.

[41] The joint venture, ENS (cases T-374, 375, 384 & 388/94) [1998] ECR II-3141, [1998] 5 *CMLR* 718, [1998] CEC 955, appears to have been unsuccessful. After the decision, the parties dropped all the original routes, switching to one other.

Jacobs suggested (¶63) that this may be the reason why a compulsory licence was in effect granted. The rights in IMS were granted under a Community directive, and it might be difficult to override them on this ground.

The judgment in *Magill* has been narrowly construed in four recent judgments[42] and Advocate General Jacobs as well as the President of the CFI have stressed that the interest of consumers should be protected rather than those of particular competitors. The CFI's order in *IMS* casts grave doubt on the Commission's wide use of the doctrine. Sometimes the two policy objectives leave to the same result.

In my view the Commission's interim decision was wrong, because I do not think that competition rules should trump iprs, which will induce investment only if enforceable. The copyright may not be upheld by the court in Frankfurt, which has made a reference to the ECJ for a preliminary ruling. If it does, I hope the wide extent of data protection will be narrowed by legislation.

In my view, the essential facilities doctrine does and should have a continued role, especially in the context of regulatory control: the regulator of a particular industry has considerably more information and economic expertise than a court and is better placed to determine the compensation to be paid for access. Many nationalised industries have been privatised and their exclusive rights terminated, but they often enjoy the benefit of investments made at the public expense or when they were protected from competition by special or exclusive rights. The incentive to make the original investment may have been less important. Moreover, as Advocate General Bronner observed in *Bronner*, it may be more difficult for a newcomer to compete with an incumbent who invested at public expense.

The incentive to the original investment is more important when it is made in the private sector, and access should be required only in extreme circumstances when the incumbent has a strangle hold on an important market. As public sector undertakings are privatised and lose their exclusive rights, they continue to invest and incentives again become more important. It is vital that the Commission should not take unduly narrow markets and require access.

It is also important that before imposing such a drastic remedy, the Commission should establish the facts by clear and cogent evidence. Answers to questionnaires to customers may not be reliable, although more so than answers by competitors. I am concerned that when national courts

[42] *Tiercé Ladbroke*, above n 16, *ITT Promedia*, above n 17 ENS above n 18 and *Oscar Bronner*, above n 5.

and authorities take a larger part in the enforcement of Community law, access to facilities called 'essential' may be required too lightly. Markets are surprisingly dynamic and firms often find ways round apparent bottlenecks. The argument ex post that the market in question will be more competitive if access is required is so obvious that it may be hard to persuade institutions, some of which have not long been dealing with EC competition problems, not to intervene in order to preserve incentives to investment. It is better to have supply by a monopolist than no facility.

The decision in *Magill* is not shocking on the facts, but would be disturbing if lightly applied to situations where the intellectual property right is better justified. The next steps in the *IMS* litigation are eagerly awaited.

4. A Response to the European Commission Evaluation Report on the Transfer of Technology Block Exemption

Dr Amelia Fletcher*

I. INTRODUCTION

The European Commission is carrying out an assessment of the Transfer of Technology Block Exemption Regulation No 240/96 ('TTBE'). Its evaluation report was made available publicly for comment by 26 April 2002. The Commission will then consider all comments before identifying the most appropriate solution for a future TTBE regime.

As set out in the report, several factors suggest a comprehensive reassessment of the TTBE. The TTBE is currently form-based and legalistic, rather than based on the likely economic effects of IP licensing. Its use is limited by its rather narrow scope, which only covers certain types of exclusive licensing agreements. The benefit of the block exemption depends on a large number of formal requirements to be found in lists of 'white', 'grey' and 'black' clauses. It is highly focused on intra-brand competition, rather than inter-brand competition, and it is now inconsistent with other recently revised EC rules, such as Regulation No 2790/1999, the Block Exemption for vertical restraints (VRs). These various factors are summarised in the following table.

This paper sets out comments, which are broadly supportive, on the changes suggested within the Commission's Evaluation Report.

II. THE SPECIAL NATURE OF IP RIGHTS

In evaluating possible changes to the TTBE, the special nature of IP rights needs to be taken into account. Specifically:

A. *The important role played by IP rights in incentivising R&D and innovation.*

R&D can involve substantial sunk costs. These are incurred not only prior to any revenues being derived from the innovation but without any certain knowledge that the R&D will even be successful. In order to provide firms

* Chief Economist, Office of Fair Trading (OFT). Paper given at the Second Annual Conference on International and Comparative Competition Law, BIICL, May 2002. The views expressed are personal.

with an incentive to engage in this upfront, risky investment, there is clearly a need for successful innovators to make profits that lie above the short-term competitive level, for at least a period after the innovation.

B. The important welfare benefits that can be derived from licensing IP

Licensing IP can be very valuable, and it will usually be pro-competitive. It can facilitate the rapid diffusion of new innovations, it can reduce wasteful duplication of R&D activity, it can spur incremental innovations (further innovative developments based on underlying licensed IP), and because licensing can increasing the overall return to the innovating firm, the potential to license can help to incentivise the initial R&D. It can also generate downstream competition: indeed, a refusal to supply of a small technology input can have a disproportionate impact on the ability of firms to compete in the downstream market.

III. THE DISTINCTION BETWEEN EXPLOITATION AND EXCLUSION

Neither of the above points are, though, sufficient for competition authorities to wish to give the holders of IP rights carte blanche as to how to use them.

With respect to the first point—the benefits of *ex post* profits in generating *ex ante* R&D investment, a key distinction needs to be made between exploitation and exclusion.

On *exploitation*: Competition policy should not usually limit the returns being made by an innovating firm, at least during the period of legal IP rights protection.

On *exclusion*. However, this does not give an innovating firm the right to restrict, prevent or distort the development of effective competition in the market place, through its licensing practices, pricing practices, or otherwise. Indeed, because rapid innovation can lead to large social benefits, any practices by current IP holders, which might potentially restrict the success of future innovations, would be of particular concern.

IV. EVALUATING POSSIBLE CHANGES

In practice, there will often be a fine line between exploitation and exclusion. In evaluating possible changes to the TTBE, the test set out in the US DoJ/FTC *Antitrust Guidelines for the Licensing of Intellectual Property* can be adopted.

1. The DoJ test and using the right counterfactual

The DoJ/FTC Guidelines advance the principle that a licensing agreement may raise antitrust concerns *if it harms competition that would have occurred in the absence of the arrangement.*

To apply this test in assessing the TTBE, it is very important to use the right counterfactual. Restrictions will often be necessary for IP licensing to occur in the first place. That is, the relevant counter-factual to a specific licensing agreement, with particular restrictions, may not simply be the same license without the restrictions. Rather, it may be that the company would have issued no licence at all. And if this is the counterfactual, then a licence that imposes restrictions on the licensee is still likely to be pro-competitive.

Therefore, in trading off between pro-competitive benefits of licensing and any anti-competitive impacts of restrictions, it is necessary to take into account the likelihood that the benefits of licensing might not be obtained absent the restrictions.

2. 'Type 1' and 'Type 2' errors

In evaluating the TTBE, there will always be:

Type 1 errors: situations where the TTBE prevents (or discourages) licensing agreements that would have been pro-competitive; and

Type 2 errors: situations where the TTBE gives exemption to licensing agreements that are, on balance, more anti-competitive than pro-competitive.

Both sorts of these errors will tend to dampen innovation and competition. Clawback mechanisms can be built into the TTBE framework to limit the latter type of error. But there will always be some residual errors of both sorts. The art of designing the TTBE is to strike the right balance between types of error, but it is important to recognise that nothing is ever going to be perfect.

V. THE COMMISSION'S SUGGESTED TTBE: A MULTI-PRONGED APPROACH

The Commission's evaluation report contains a detailed discussion of the likely economic effects of a variety of types of IP licenses and specific license restrictions. The report then sets out a multi-pronged approach to the TTBE, which reflects this economic discussion, and is designed to strike an appropriate balance between the likely pro-competitive effects of licensing and possible anti-competitive effects of license restrictions.

The principle elements of the Commission's suggested approach are:

- *A distinction is made between non-competitors and competitors.*

  This is based on the view that agreements between non-competitors are less likely to give rise to serious economic concerns than agreements between competitors.

- *For non-competitors, a distinction is made for restrictions that relate to exploitation of the IP and those that do not.*

  This is, to some extent, based on the view that the restrictions that relate directly to the exploitation of the IP are likely to be the most crucial for the license existing at all.

- *Distinct tests, based on different dominance and market share thresholds, are then suggested for each category.*

  The use of dominance and market share thresholds is designed, on the one hand, to exempt a large number of IP licenses, which occur between firms with low market shares, where the competition implications are unlikely to be large, while refusing blanket exemption to licenses where there is a greater risk of detrimental impact.

- *The application of the TTBE will be constrained by limited form-based hardcore lists.*

  Certain restrictions will not be exemptible, even for licenses that would otherwise be covered by the TTBE. The intention here is to curb serious horizontal problems that might be associated with particular license restrictions. The most obvious of these is price-restrictions. As set out in the OFT's own draft IP Guidelines—relating to the Competition Act—pricing restrictions are always viewed as a hardcore, with strong justification required for individual exemption.

- *The focus of the current report is on the TTBE, but—as for vertical restraints—it is intended that these would be supplemented by detailed Guidelines.*

  This will be intended to give greater legal certainty even to firms whose IP licenses technically fall outside the TTBE.

VI. THE USE OF MARKET SHARE AND DOMINANCE THRESHOLDS IN INNOVATIVE MARKETS

In evaluating these various proposals, account is taken of the discussion and conclusions of a recent discussion paper on innovation and competition policy, carried out for the OFT by Charles River Associates.[1]

[1] *Innovation and Competition Policy*, by Charles River Associates, Mar 2002. OFT Economic Discussion Paper 3.

While it may not be easy to put into practice all of the policy recommendations made in this thought-provoking report, it is important in carrying out competition policy to recognise that:

- *It can be difficult to define markets, and so assess market shares, where innovation is rapid.*

  Where markets are continually changing, the past may not be a good guide to the future, even in terms of the delineation of the relevant market.

- *In rapidly changing markets, market shares can be a poor indicator of potential problems.*

  Small shares can *tip* into large ones, and large ones can erode overnight. In addition, in many innovation markets, sales will be made via bidding or negotiation, and indeed each customer may arguably be a market of its own. Shares can mean little in such markets.

- *It can be correspondingly difficult to prove dominance.*

  In particular, even if an innovating firm has (what one might call) 'short term' dominance in terms of an ability to price independently today, it is far from clear that it has 'long term' dominance in terms of its ability to maintain this position in the face of new innovations.

VII. THE DISTINCTION BETWEEN COMPETITORS AND NON-COMPETITORS

The Commission's suggested TTBE applies different tests, depending upon whether or not the licensee and licensor are competitors. This is in line with the US approach, which draws a clear distinction between the two situations. The proposed definition of non-competitors is set out at paragraph 125 of the Evaluation Report.

There are three interesting elements of this definition worth commenting upon.

(a) It applies not only to non-competitors of the normal vertical sort, but also non-competitors that would traditionally have been seen as horizontal

This seems appropriate, given the importance of complementary and 'blocking' IP rights in many innovative markets. There is little reason why such non-competitors should be treated differently from more traditional vertical relationships. Indeed, licensing of IP between horizontal holders complementary patents can have very similar benefits to vertical licensing.

(b) Parties to a licence will only be viewed as non-competitors if "the licence does not remove any competition which could have taken place between the licensor and the licensee absent the licence".

This is in line with both the DoJ/FTC test and with the underlying economics. Depending on the precise application of this test, it may also have the benefit that parties who are significant 'potential competitors' would be treated as 'non-competitors'. It would be appropriate to have a strong test of this sort, given:

- the breadth of the suggested block exemption for non-competitors (see below); and
- the risk that potential competitors in the upstream technology market could be deterred from innovating if there was a consequent risk of losing the BE (this risk would clearly be eliminated if such potential competitors were not covered in the first place).

However, this could potentially be a difficult test to apply in practice. In particular, it may be hard to show that the licensee would not have carried out R&D in order to enter the upstream technology market absent the licence.

(c) Parties to a licence may be viewed as non-competitors, even if they were competing prior to the innovation, if the innovation represents such a sweeping breakthrough that there would no longer be any competition absent the licence.

While the economic foundations for this condition are sound, it is important that this test is applied carefully. Will there be many examples of innovations that are sufficiently 'sweeping' to fulfil this condition with any great certainty?

In addition to the distinction between competitors and non-competitors, some thought could also be usefully given to whether a distinction should be drawn between licensees that resell the IP, in one form or another, and those that are end users. One might imagine, for example, situations where non-compete restrictions and tying could potentially be more detrimental to competition between technology suppliers when included in licenses to end-users than when included in licenses to downstream firms.

VIII. THE DOMINANCE THRESHOLD FOR *RELATED* RESTRICTIONS IN IP LICENCES BETWEEN *NON-COMPETITORS*

For non-competitors, the suggested TTBE makes a distinction between restrictions that are directly related to the exploitation of the IP—including exclusive territories, customer exclusivity, and field of use restrictions—and restrictions that are not.

The Commission suggests that a future TTBE could limit coverage of the directly related restraints with a dominance threshold. While it is not entirely clear from the Evaluation Report, presumably this test would relate to the existence, or not, of dominance in the market for the licensed technology, rather than the licensee's position in the downstream product market.

That the TTBE is limited by a dominance threshold is unsurprising, given that no block exemption can give certainty to dominant firms. The focus on dominance, as opposed to a lower market share threshold, is however inconsistent with the vertical restraints block exemption, where a 30% market share threshold for these sorts of restrictions is employed. That said, there are a number of strong arguments for a dominance, rather than a market share, threshold for such restrictions. These include the following premises:

- A view that high market shares derive from successful innovation and thus should not be penalised.
- A view that market shares at this level may mean little in terms of true market power.
- A view that licensing IP can generate more social benefits and a greater pro-competitive effect than other forms of vertical supply.
- A view that, at the same time, potential licensors also require more incentives (in the form of restrictions) to license than do more traditional vertical suppliers.
- A view that serious competition problems arising from these sorts of restrictions, when concluded between non-competitors, will tend to occur only where the technology licensor has a high degree of market power.
- A view that reserving the right to withdraw the TTBE provides further reassurance against serious competition concerns.

In this light it may be worth reiterating in the Guidelines (as stressed in the OFT's own draft IP Guidelines) that although IP law gives innovators a 'monopoly' over the relevant technology, this does not necessarily confer 'dominance' in a competition policy sense. In order to assess whether a particular IP right confers dominance in this sense, it is necessary to define the relevant economic market—which will include any substitute technologies that would be acceptable to potential licensees—and then to assess the strength of the party's position within this relevant market.

Other comments on this element of the TTBE relate to issues that are not discussed explicitly, but which the Commission will need to consider carefully before reaching a final judgement on the way forward:

- *Restrictions on passive sales.*

While it is not discussed explicitly, presumably the proposed TTBE will not allow restrictions on passive sales (which are allowed under the existing TTBE). This change would be appropriate, and would put the TTBE in line with the VRs BE.

- *Networks of agreements.*

The Evaluation Report does not discuss networks of agreements, or how these are to be treated under the TTBE. This is in sharp contrast to the VRs block exemption, where substantial focus was placed on this issue.

- *Two-way licensing agreements.*

The Evaluation Report does not make it clear whether two-way (ie bilateral cross-licensing) agreements would be covered under this element of the TTBE. While it seems reasonable to include such licence agreements between non-competitors, it is not clear how prevalent such agreements are likely to be.

- *Bilateral patent pools.*

The Evaluation Report also does not make it clear whether bilateral patent pools between non-competitors (eg complementary/blocking patents) would be covered under this element of the TTBE. There is some argument for inclusion, since patent pools will generally be pro-competitive so long as they are between complements and thus do not harm competition between patents that would have taken place absent the agreement. Not only do they potentially reduce transactions costs, but they may also reduce the overall price of the combined technology.[2]

However, there are also a variety of risks for competition associated with patent pools, even between complements. For example, there is a risk of foreclosure of actual or potential competitors of one or other technology in the patent pool. There would be an argument for excluding patent

[2] The overall price of two complementary technologies will tend to be lower when the technologies are sold together than when they are sold separately. The explanation for this is that, when sold separately, neither party takes account of the positive effect a further reduction in its own price would have on the sales of the other party. Thus, each party sets prices at a higher level than is jointly profit-maximising. When sold together, this positive externality can be internalised and the overall price will be reduced. This effect—which is analogous to the 'double marginalisation' issue in vertical markets—is sometimes referred to as the 'Cournot effect'.

pools from the TTBE, and instead providing detailed Guidelines on how they will be treated. Certainly, further work could usefully be done in this area before a final decision is made on this issue.

- Grantbacks and no-challenge clauses.

It is not clear where grantbacks and no-challenge clauses lie within the proposed TTBE framework. Are these viewed as related restrictions or not? And if viewed as related, is a dominance test right? This issue could usefully be given further attention.

IX. THE 30 PER CENT MARKET SHARE THRESHOLD FOR *UNRELATED* RESTRICTIONS IN IP LICENCES BETWEEN *NON-COMPETITORS*

For restrictions that are not related to the exploitation of the IP rights—such as non-compete clauses and tying—the suggested TTBE would include a 30 per cent market share threshold for non-competitors.

The Evaluation Report is not explicit as to which market this threshold applies. However, given the wording of the VRs block exemption, it presumably relates to the licensor's market share in the upstream technology market.

A clear benefit of this approach is that it is consistent with VRs BE. However, there are two concerns.

(a) It can be difficult to calculate market shares in technology markets.

As stated above, market shares can be particularly difficult to assess on technology markets. This is recognised in the DoJ/FTC Guidelines and an alternative approach is employed—which effectively involves simply counting up the number of independently controlled competitors in the technology market. This is clearly an imperfect approach, which anyway does not solve the problem that it can be hard to define relevant markets for highly innovative technologies. However, it may nevertheless be worth giving thought to this—or alternative—approaches, before finalising a TTBE.

(b) Tying and non-compete clauses raise greater competition concerns if there are risks of markets 'tipping', as in many technology markets.

If there are risks of tipping then a firm with a 30 per cent market share might potentially be able to tip this, or another related, market through the use of tying or non-compete clauses. This issue too could usefully be given further thought.

In addition to the thresholds discussed above, the Evaluation Report suggests that there might be a limited hardcore list of restrictions, even for the case of non-competitors. This would include "pricing constraints and certain territorial restraints", but would specifically not include a number of restraints that were previously viewed as hardcore restrictions: "quantity restrictions, certain customer restrictions and maximum and recommended prices". This is in line with the VRs block exemption, and seems a sensible approach. Such restrictions can raise important competition problems, even when included in agreements between non-competitors. However, this will usually only occur when the licensor firm is dominant in the technology, and the TTBE would not apply in such circumstances.

X. THE 25 PER CENT MARKET SHARE THRESHOLD ON IP LICENCES BETWEEN COMPETITORS

For IP licences between parties that are to any extent competitors, or would be competitors in the absence of the licence, the Commission has suggested a blanket TTBE up to a market share threshold of 25 per cent. This would contain a hardcore list for restrictions that directly or indirectly fix prices, limit output or sales, or allocate territories or customers.

This approach is similar to the 20 per cent 'safety zone' for licensing agreements between competitors incorporated in the DoJ/FTC Guidelines. No justification has been given for the use of a 25 per cent share limit rather than the US figure of 20 per cent. However, the 25 per cent limit seems reasonable.

The Evaluation Report is a little sketchy in terms of the detailed workings of its 25 per cent test, and leaves open a number of obvious questions in this regard. Specifically:

- *Does the 25 per cent limit relate to each of the licensee and licensor individually, or is it a 'collective' share figure?*

  A collective share test would be the more appropriate. Under the DoJ/FTC Guidelines, the 'safety zone' relates to a 20 per cent *collective* market share limit.

- *Which markets does the share limit apply to: the upstream technology market, the downstream product market, or both?*

  Under the DoJ/FTC Guidelines, the 'safety zone' test is applied to the specific market where the license might potentially have negative effects on competition. While this would seem appropriate in theory:

  (a) substantial thought would need to given on how to place such an effects-based rule within a formal EC block exemption; and

  (b) in doing so, the Commission should note that licences that primarily restrict competition in one market (say, the product market) can indirectly have the effect of restricting competition in another market (say, the technology market).

As such, it may be that any such rule within the TTBE would need to be complemented by detailed Guidelines on which market(s) the share limit would apply to for different types of agreements and restraints.

In addition, where the market share limit would relate to the technology market, it may be worth giving further thought to the difficulties of calculating market shares at this upstream level, and whether there might be an argument for accepting other tests, such as the US 'counting competitors' approach.

- Within the hardcore list, what sorts of restraints would be viewed as 'indirectly' fixing prices or limiting output or sales?

For example, it is well recognised that a cross-licensing agreement with royalty payments (as opposed to a lump sum payment) can facilitate collusion. But would any such agreement be black-listed? The accompanying Guidelines would need to provide substantial clarification of when restraints might 'indirectly' have the effect of fixing prices or limiting output or sales.

- How would networks of agreements be treated?

Networks of agreements are likely to raise substantially more concerns where agreements are between competitors than where they are between non-competitors. A network of restrictive licensing agreements *between competitors* could potentially have important negative implications for competition, even where the two firms involved in each individual agreement have a joint market share of below 25 per cent. That said, many IP markets are characterised by networks of licensing agreements between competitors that do not raise significant competition concerns. This area could usefully be given more attention before the Commission reaches a final view on the structure of any new TTBE.

- Would this element of the proposed TTBE cover bilateral cross-licensing?

Cross-licensing is, perhaps surprisingly, often an important driver of innovation. In markets characterised by cross-licensing, firms—whose real focus may be on supplying a product—will have an incentive to innovate in order to gain a bargaining chip in their negotiations to use the technologies of others alongside their own.

It is not entirely clear how bilateral cross-licensing would differ, in terms of its potential impact on competition, from a combination of two one-way IP licences between two competing parties. Would it really be appropriate to bring the latter under a TTBE while excluding the former? This would potentially simply force firms to write licences in a particular form, when the same result could be achieved—more efficiently—by allowing parties the flexibility to sign two-way cross-licensing agreements. That said, effective cross-licensing—however achieved—can have substantial detrimental implications for competition if there is a network of agreements, especially if each firm cross-licenses its technology to several other competing firms in the market, creating a lattice of agreements between competitors. As such, the issue of how to treat networks (discussed under the last bullet) is particularly important when dealing with cross-licensing agreements.

- Would this element of the proposed TTBE cover bilateral patent pools?

  While patent pools between complementary patents will tend to be pro-competitive, patent pools between competing patents will tend directly to reduce competition in the technology market, without any significant countervailing benefits. This may not raise substantial concerns if there were a single patent pool in which patents involved were jointly to account for less than 25 per cent share of the technology market, but competition could potentially be severely harmed if there were a network of such pools. Moreover, the effects would in this case be direct (as compared with the more indirect effects on competition of a network of traditional licensing agreements). This is an area that might be better covered by Guidelines, rather than the TTBE.

XI. MULTI-PARTY LICENSING

The Commission is considering whether it would be appropriate for the future TTBE to cover multi-party licensing. This would require an amendment of Council Regulation 19/65 which currently only allows coverage of licensing agreements between two parties.

The Evaluation Report does not make specific suggestions on multi-party licensing. The Commission has put out a tender asking for economic consultancy to review this issue further. However, this is likely to be an area for Guidelines rather than a block exemption, especially given the difficulties associated with patent pools highlighted above. Such difficulties can only increase for pools between more than two parties.

XII. CONCLUSIONS

In designing a TTBE, there will always be a trade-off between giving certainty to parties and the risk of allowing anti-competitive licenses to exist. However, there are major benefits to having a block exemption, not least in terms of streamlining post-modernisation enforcement of EC law.

The suggested approach in the Evaluation Report has broad similarities to the approach (Guidelines plus 'safety zone') taken in the US. The DoJ/FTC guidelines have now been in place since 1995, and are generally viewed as having been successful.[3]

That said, the DoJ and FTC are holding joint hearings on Competition and IP Law. The aim of these hearings is 'neither to rehash the Guidelines nor to critique them'[4], but rather to examine a variety of issues that may not be covered effectively by the Guidelines. Amongst the issues under discussion have been grantbacks, patent litigation and no-challenge clauses, package licences (including several patents at once), patent pooling, and standard setting.

The findings of the DoJ/FTC in these important hearings should provide valuable insights in developing EC Guidelines on these complicated issues.

[3] See Richard Gilbert and Willard Tom, 'Is Innovation King at the Antitrust Agencies? The Intellectual Property Guidelines Five Years Later', Apr 2001.

[4] Opening Day Comments by Charles A James, DoJ/FTC Hearings on Competition and Intellectual Property Law and Policy in the Knowledge—based economy, 6 Feb 2002 (<http://www.ftc.gov/opp/intellect/james.htm>).

5. Why Interference with IPRs Should Not be Treated as 'Exceptional' under the Competition Rules: Some Food for Thought

Stephen Kon and Sarah Turnbull*

I. INTRODUCTION

1. The relationship between competition law and intellectual property law has always raised intensive debate.[1] Whilst both areas of law are aimed at encouraging innovation to benefit consumers, the monopoly rights granted to intellectual property rights' owners have, on occasion, been considered to clash with competition aims. Over the last year, there have been several key developments in the competition—intellectual property debate, including major reviews and consultations into the complex inter-relationship by the EU, UK and US competition authorities. This review process is timely. Intellectual property rights ('IPRs') are increasingly a major aspect of industry's focus in all sectors. Licensing activities are becoming an essential activity and IPR holders are using complex business strategies to maintain and develop any market power provided by these rights.

2. Drawing the dividing line for competition law to intervene in IP cases is a difficult issue. Several jurisdictions are conducting reviews into the intellectual property and competition law paradigm and examining whether competition authorities need to develop new approaches to IP agreements and also to behaviour by dominant companies using IPRs. In particular, the EU Report evaluating the Technology Transfer Block Exemption,[2] the Draft OFT Guidelines on intellectual property rights and CRA's economic discussion

* SJ Berwin. Paper given at the Second Annual Conference on International and Comparative Competition Law, BIICL, May 2002.

[1] For extensive discussion on the IP-competition debate at EU level see Steven D Anderman *EC Competition Law and Intellectual Property Rights. The Regulation of Innovation* (Oxford: Oxford University Press, 1998) and I Govaere *The Use and Abuse of Intellectual Property Rights in EC Law* (London: Sweet & Maxwell, 1996).

[2] See IP/02/14 'Commission policy: Commission opens debate on block exemption for licensing agreements', 7 Jan 2002. Commission Evaluation Report on the transfer of Technology Block Exemption Regulation 240/96 Technology Transfer Agreements under Art 81. See also Paolo Cesarini and Luc Peeperkorn, *Review of the block exemption Regulation on technology transfer agreements* Commission's Competition Policy Newsletter, Number 1 Feb 2002 at 47–9.

paper, *'Innovation and Competition Policy March 2002'*,[3] evaluate many of the fundamental issues concerning the IPR competition law interface.[4]

3. Since the outset, there have been attempts in EU case law and practice to reconcile, or at least establish a balance between, the apparently contradictory objective of monopoly protection conferred by IPRs and the consumer welfare requirements of competition policy. Therefore, as early as 1966, in *Consten & Grundig v Commission*,[5] the European Court of Justice ('ECJ') sought to establish a distinction between the *existence* and *exercise* of IPRs and stated that the articles of the Treaty protecting intellectual property rights (Articles 30 and 295) are only designed to protect the existence of the IPR and not their exploitation. Much of this early case law, which culminated in the *Centrafarm* cases,[6] was inspired by a need for the ECJ to reconcile the national monopoly protection conferred by IPRs and the provisions of the Treaty, in particular Article 28 (ex Article 30) protecting the free movement of goods. The ECJ focused on where the reliance upon national IPRs is justified under Article 30 (ex Article 36). While the ECJ indicated that similar general principles should apply in reconciling the EC competition rules with national IPRs,[7] it was only in *Volvo v Veng*,[8] *Magill*[9] and, most recently in *IMS*[10] that the ECJ focused on the circumstances where the exploitation of an IPR may operate in a manner contrary to the objectives of the EC competition rules; this case law has led to a wider recognised general principle that it is only in *exceptional* circumstances that competition law should intervene with IPRs.

4. It is suggested that, the recent *IMS* proceedings before the Commission,

[3] 'Innovation and Competition policy' Economic Discussion Paper 3, Mar 2002, Report prepared for the Office of Fair Trading by Charles River Associates.

[4] See also the ongoing review process by the US FTC where a series of public hearing began in Jan 2002 on *Competition and Intellectual Property Law and Policy in the Knowledge-Based Economy*. See <www.ftc.gov/os/2001/11/ciphearingsfrn.htm> and Timothy J Muris, Chairman, FTC before American Bar Association, Antitrust Section Fall Forum, Washington DC, 15 Nov 2001, *Competition and Intellectual Property Policy: The Way Ahead*.

[5] Cases 56 & 58/64 *Consten & Grundig v Commission* [1966] ECR 299, Case 24/67 *Parke, Davis v Centrafarm* [1968] ECR 55 and Case 78/70 *Deutsche Grammophon v Metro* [1971] ECR 487. See futher Anderman, above at ch 2.

[6] Case 15/74 *Centrafarm v Sterling Drug* [1974] ECR 1147 and Case 16/74 *Centrafarm BV v Winthrop BV* [1974] ECR 1183.

[7] See, eg, Case 262/81 *Coditel II* [1982] ECR 3381.

[8] Case 238/87 *Volvo v Veng (UK) Ltd* [1988] ECR 6211. See also Case 53/87 *Maxicar v Renault* [1988] ECR 6039.

[9] Cases T-69/89 *RTE v Commission* [1991] ECR II-485, upheld by the ECJ Cases C-291/91 P *RTE and ITP v Commission* [1995] ECR I-743. See also Case C-7/97 *Oscar Bronner v Mediaprint* [1998] ECR I-7791.

[10] Case COMP/D3/38.044 *NDC Health/IMS Health: Interim Measures*. Commission Decision of 3 July 2001 which was provisionally suspended by order of the President of the Court of First Instance on 10 Aug 2001 in Case T-184/01R *IMS Health Inc v Commission*, confirmed by final order of the President of the CFI, 26 Oct 2001.

the Court of First Instance ('CFI') and the ECJ[11] in which, in the Second Interim Order on 26 October 2001, the CFI's President suspended the interim measures order by the Commission, *inter alia* on grounds that there was 'a serious dispute at the very least' as to whether 'exceptional circumstances' existed in that case capable of justifying the imposition of a compulsory licence,[12] only goes to emphasise the inadequacy of trying to address the IPR/competition law interface by reference to over-generalised principles, whether it be 'the existence or exercise of IPRs' or a definition of the 'specific subject matter' of particular categories of IPRs.[13] Concepts such as the 'essential function' of the IPR (or 'exceptional circumstances') may be tools in any overall assessment of whether the existence or exercise of an IPR may conflict with the competition rules; however, developments over the past 35 years since *Consten & Grundig* only go to show that it is a fundamental error to become a slave to any of these 'tests' or 'analytical tools'.

5. That is why, in approaching the application of competition policy in general and Article 82 in particular, it is suggested that the correct starting point must be the 'first principles approach' advocated by Steve Salop in his article in the Antitrust Law Journal in 2000;[14] that is, there should be an examination of the competitive effects of the conduct at issue. This means that in antitrust analyses, there should be a full evaluation of all the circumstances surrounding the grant of an intellectual property right, the nature of the right concerned and the market effects of the exercise of those rights. It is only on a case by case analysis that any conclusion can be reached.

6. It is therefore suggested that it is a fundamental error to immunise the very right itself (referred to in case law as 'the existence of the right',[15] 'the

[11] Case COMP/D3/38.044 *NDC Health/IMS Health: Interim Measures.* Commission Decision of 3 Jul 2001 which was provisionally suspended by order of the President of the Court of First Instance on 10 Aug 2001 in Case T-184/01R *IMS Health Inc v Commission*, confirmed by final order of the President of the CFI, 26 Oct 2001. In Mar 2001, Commission had sent a statement of objections to IMS Health alleging that it had abused its dominant position by refusing to grant competitors a licence to enable them to have access to its 1860 brick structure (Commission Press Release IP/01/365, 14 Mar 2001). The President of the ECJ upheld the CFI by order of 11 Apr 2002 (C-418/01 P (R) *IMS Health GmbH & Co OHG v NDC Health GmbH & Co*. The case is also being examined on preliminary reference from the Landgericht Frankfurt am Main Case C-418/01 *IMS Health GmbH & Co OHG v NDC Health GmbH & Co* (reference received by the ECJ Registry on 22 Oct 2001) OJ C3/16, 5 Jan 2002.

[12] See Order of 26 Oct 2001 at para 106.

[13] See, eg, Case 16/74 *Centrafarm & De Pijper v Sterling Drug* [1974] ECR 1147 and Case 238/87 *Volvo v Veng (UK) Ltd* [1988] ECR 6211 at para 8.

[14] Steve Salop: *First Principles Approach to Antitrust, Kodak and Antitrust at the Millennium*; *Antitrust Law Journal* Volume 68 No 1, 187.

[15] See, eg, Cases 56 & 58/64 *Consten & Grundig v Commission* [1966] ECR 299, Case 24/67 *Parke, Davis v Centrafarm* [1968] ECR 55 and Case 78/70 *Deutsche Grammophon v Metro* [1971] ECR 487.

specific subject matter of the right'[16] or 'the essential function of the right'[17]) from antitrust scrutiny; those issues are of fundamental importance in assessing whether, in any particular case, IP law and antitrust law are pursuing complementary or contradictory goals. As Timothy Muris noted in his speech to the American Bar Association in Washington in November 2001:[18]

> IP law and antitrust law both seek to promote innovation and enhanced consumer welfare. [...] IP law, properly applied, preserves the incentives for scientific and technological progress—ie, for innovation. Innovation benefits consumers through the development of new and improved goods and services and spurs economic growth. Similarly, antitrust law, properly applied, promotes innovation and economic growth by combating restraints on vigorous competitive activity. By deterring anti-competitive arrangements and monopolisation, antitrust law also ensures that consumers have access to a wide variety of goods and services at competitive prices.

7. Against this general background, this paper would make a number of observations in determining in particular how Article 82 and the general policy objective of avoiding monopoly abuse can be reconciled with IPR protection:

8. The existence of an IPR is a fundamental consideration in any competition analysis.

8.1 In evaluating alleged anti-competitive conduct and its likely market effects where IPRs are in issue, the principle that an IPR cannot in itself create a dominant position is relatively uncontroversial.[19] It is equally uncontroversial that an IPR can be a very important consideration in determining whether, in fact, within the context of a full economic evaluation, a dominant position exists.[20]

8.2 As the CRA study for the OFT pointed out, whether conduct is anti-competitive or not usually depends on the exact circumstances of a case; as CRA also points out, competitive issues that arise in dynamically

[16] See, eg, Case 238/87 *Volvo v Veng (UK) Ltd* [1988] ECR 6211.

[17] See, eg, comments of Advocate General Gulman in the *Magill* case.

[18] Timothy J Muris, Chairman, FTC before American Bar Association, Antitrust Section Fall Forum, Washington DC, 15 Nov 2001, *Competition and Intellectual Property Policy: The Way Ahead.*

[19] See Case 78/70 *Deutsche Grammophon v Metro* [1971] ECR 487 at paragraph 16 and Cases C-241 and 242/91P *Radio Telefis Eireann v Commission('Magill')* [1995] ECR I-743 at para 46; see also OFT 418 draft Guideline 'Intellectual property rights' at paragraph 3.3 and OFT 402 'The Chapter II prohibition' at para 3.15. See also US *Antitrust Guidelines for the Licensing of Intellectual Property*, 6 Apr 1995 at para 2 (b): 'the Agencies do not presume that intellectual property creates market power in the antitrust context'.

[20] See OFT 402 'The Chapter II prohibition' at para 3.15 and OFT 418 draft Guideline 'Intellectual property rights' at para 3.3: 'The Director General takes the view that ownership of an IPR will not necessarily create a dominant position. Whether or not dominance results from the ownership of an IPR will depend upon the extent to which there are substitutes for the product, process or work to which the IPR relates.' See also para 3.4.

competitive industries invariably involve exclusionary power rather than pricing power.[21] In these circumstances, the existence of IPRs must be a fundamental consideration in any assessment of whether, in fact, market power and dominance exists.

8.3 It is for this reason that the statement by the President of the ECJ of 11 April 2002 in IMS[22] that, 'it is clear from the case law that the exercise of intellectual property rights may be subjected to restrictions imposed under Article 82 only in exceptional circumstances', may be somewhat misleading; the existence of IPRs and their exercise should be examined in the same way as any other contractual or proprietary interest to determine whether there is anti-competitive behaviour.

9. A thorough assessment of the nature and scope of the IPR at issue must be made.

9.1 It follows from the principle set out above at point 8, that an important aspect of the assessment that needs to be undertaken is a *thorough assessment of the nature and scope of the IPR* or IPRs in issue.

9.2 After the Commission's decisions in both *Magill* and *IMS*, a debate was ignited as to the extent to which competition law should legitimately interfere with validly granted IPRs. However, the competitive assessment in both cases turned, to a material extent, on the *nature* of the IPRs in issue; in the case of *Magill*, a rather weak IPR which would not have qualified for copyright protection in many Member States and in *IMS*, a copyright which, on the facts, appeared to amount to a *'de facto industry standard'* (created with the assistance of industry) and which appeared to foreclose the market entirely to any effective competing structure.

9.3 Similarly, in the recent *DSD-Green Dot*[23] case, it was the precise nature and function of the Green Dot trade mark that was fundamental in the Commission assessing whether it was abusive that DSD customers had to pay fees corresponding to the volume of packaging bearing the Green Dot trade mark rather than fees corresponding to the volume of the packaging for which DSD was actually providing take-back and recycling services.

[21] See CRA OFT Economic Discussion Paper 3 'Innovation and competition policy' at para 1.3.

[22] Order of the President of the ECJ of 11 Apr 2002 in Case C-481/01 P(R) *NDC Health Corporation, NDC Health GmbH & Co KG* (appeal against the Order of the President of the CFI in Case T-184/01 R *IMS Health v Commission* [2001]ECR II-0000) at para 64. In *Oscar Bronner*, Advocate General Jacobs noted 'the right to choose one's trading partners and freely to dispose of one's property are generally recognised principles in the laws of the Member States [...] incursions on those rights require careful justification'.

[23] Case COMP D3/34493 Commission Decision of 20 Apr 2001, *DSD*, OJ L166/1, 21 Jun 2001.

9.4 Some of the fundamental issues currently proposed in the hearings being organised by the FTC on the role of IP and competition policy are illustrative of this need to undertake a case-by-case investigation into the nature and scope of exclusive IPRs that may be at issue in certain areas[24]. For example:

- 'Patent thickets'[25]—need for multiple licences from multiple patentees (cross licences and/or patent pools) in commercialisation of new technology—what is the effect on competition and the policy issues this raises—does this create difficulties for competitors to sell competing products?
- Settlement of patent disputes—are settlements being used to prevent or forestall competition and is patent litigation being used as a tool to deter competition?[26]
- Standard setting where the standard relies on IP—are attempts to influence development of standards for which a company holds IPRs anti-competitive, or should IP protected products be excluded from standard setting?[27]

9.5 None of these issues can be adequately addressed without a full investigation into the nature, scope and circumstances of grant of the

[24] See Federal Register Notice of Public Hearings *Competition and Intellectual Property Law and Policy in the Knowledge-Based Economy* <http://www.ftc.gov/os/ 2001/11ciphearings frn.htm.> See Timothy J Muris, Chairman FTC before the American Bar Association, Antitrust Section Fall Forum, Washington DC, 15 Nov 2001 *Competition and Intellectual Policy: The Way Ahead.*

[25] Described by Professor Carl Shapiro as 'a dense web of overlapping intellectual property rights that a company must hack its way through in order to actually commercialize new technology' in 'Navigating the Patent Thicket: Cross Licenses, Patent Pools and Standard-Setting' in *Innovation Policy and the Economy*, Volume I (Adam B Jaffe et al Eds, 2001) <http://haas.berkeley.edu/~shapiro/thicket.pdf>.

[26] The FTC has examined patent settlements between pharmaceutical companies in the context of drugs about to come off-patent and generics. The key concern here is that generic entrants are being paid not to compete, delaying generic drug competition. The FTC has also investigated conduct by branded manufacturers which may be aimed to delay competition, for example by listing additional patents in the Federal Drug Agency's 'Orange Book' shortly before their original patents expire, which then enables them to file patent infringement suits against generic drug firms about to enter the market. Patent litigation will mean an automatic 30 month stay on FDA approval of the generic drug (Hatch–Waxman Act). The FTC is conducting a study of the generic drug industry following the request of Representative Waxman and is examining conditions of competition, in particular in anticipation of brand name drugs with US sales of $20 billion going off patent between 2001 and 2005. (See further Timothy J Muris, Chairman FTC before American Bar Association, Antitrust Section Fall Forum, Washington DC, 15 Nov 2001 *Competition and Intellectual Property Policy: The Way Ahead*).

[27] See further Timothy J Muris, Chairman FTC before American Bar Association, Antitrust Section Fall Forum, Washington DC, 15 Nov 2001 *Competition and Intellectual Property Policy: The Way Ahead.*

relevant IPRs (ie, the 'existence' of the rights). A further example of the importance of the nature and extent of IPRs in any competition review is found in the current US IP licensing guidelines where in reviewing the competitive effects of any IP licence, the nature and extent of the IPR to be licensed will be examined. Thus, if a licensed manufacturing process or patented product does not represent an economic improvement over the available existing technologies or non-patented products and the patent is not a blocking patent, then a licence agreement between competitors would not be considered to involve a useful transfer of technology, or to lead to an efficiency enhancing integration of economic activity and may, according to the US guidelines, be challenged under the *per se* rule if it leads to price fixing, market or customer sharing or output restriction.[28]

9.6 It is suggested, therefore, that it is entirely appropriate for the competition regulators to look into the nature of the IPR in issue, the circumstances surrounding its grant and its innovative nature. The fact that such an investigation may overlap with the type of investigation undertaken by a patents judge in looking at claims concerning the invalidity of patents, trade mark registries in granting trade marks or national judges in looking at questions of copyright infringement should not, it is suggested, be seen as providing any reason for competition authorities to abstain from such investigations in assessing the position and effect of the relevant IPRs on competition and the maintenance of consumer welfare.

10. The grant and enforcement of an IPR in itself may be abusive—generics and the pharmaceutical industry.

10.1 Finally, since IPRs are essentially *exclusionary* rights which are enforced primarily before courts and specialist tribunals, it may be that the very facts and circumstances of the grant and review process of an IPR and its subsequent enforcement is a legitimate subject for review where it can be established that any of these are not working sufficiently to ensure that only true innovation is protected. For example, with increasing numbers of patents being filed year on year, there is a criticism that patents are being granted for trivial or non-existent improvements impeding competition in true innovation.

10.2 Clearly, as set out in Pat Treacy's paper, there is a need here to consider improvements to the IP enforcement procedures (relating to the grant and the challenge of IPRs—closer examination at grant stage,

[28] US *Antitrust Guidelines for the Licensing of Intellectual Property*, 6 Apr 1995—see Section 3.4 example 7 and Section 4.

simplifying oppositions and challenges to IPRs, quicker judicial scrutiny of IPRs to avoid lengthy IPR litigation). However, it is suggested that there will always remain a need for competition law to intervene to ensure that IPRs are not used in an anti-competitive fashion, for example, to protect a monopoly position where an IPR has slipped through the system and is not one which should warrant protection.

10.3 The case of generics and the pharmaceutical industry is a good example here. The pharmaceutical industry has recently provided a number of examples where antitrust authorities have expressed a willingness to investigate whether the grant, review or enforcement of IPRs may be operating in an anti-competitive manner.

- In an EU context, Mario Monti signalled, in a speech given in October 2001, that the Commission is currently looking at certain situations where patent monopolies may have been illegitimately extended by, for example, 'developing therapeutically equivalent versions of the patented product containing the same active substance or molecules' or 'developing up-graded versions of the patented product'[29]; in other words, the Commission is investigating the very circumstances under which patents or extensions of patents may come into being as potentially anti-competitive abusive conduct.
- In the *Biovail*[30] case in the US, certain procedures under the Waxman-Hatch Act in the US concerning introduction of generic competition on expiry of patent terms were condemned by the FTC in circumstances where a pharmaceutical company illegitimately listed patents in the so-called 'Orange Book' (Orange Book listings are not subject to a review process[31]) in order to extend patent term protections; the FTC has made it clear that it wishes to ensure that pharmaceutical companies do not create barriers to generic competition through strategic patent acquisition and through abusing the US regulatory framework.[32]

[29] SPEECH/01/450 Commissioner Monti, 'Competition and Consumer: the case of Pharmaceutical Products'; European Competition Day in Antwerpen, Astrid Park Plaza, 11 Oct 2001.

[30] FTC Press Release *Wrongful 'Orange Book' Listing*, 23 Apr 2002.

[31] Under the US pharmaceutical system, companies holding a New Drug Application ('NDA') are able to unilaterally list patents in the Orange Book. Such patent listing automatically triggers a 30-month stay excluding generic competitors from entering the market, regardless of whether the patent listed actually claims the branded drug approved under the NDA. The FDA views its role in listing patents in the Orange Book as 'purely ministerial' and there is no private right of action to challenge a patent listing under the US Food, Drug and Cosmetic Act. This enables pharmaceutical companies to list inappropriate patents in the Orange Book and gain a 30-month delay on generic drug entry.

[32] Bristol-Myers Squibb is under FTC investigation relating to alleged actions taken to delay generic competition for Taxol and Apotex has complained to the FTC about

- Similar competition action may prove necessary in the UK following a recent report of the UK National Health Service which suggested that pharmaceutical companies are increasingly using tactics aimed to extend the life of blockbuster patents by launching 'improved' versions of established products about to come off-patent and then withdrawing supplies of the original product to delay or prevent generic competition.[33]

10.4 Equally, the very enforcement of IPRs by IPR owners may, under certain circumstances, be evidence of abusive conduct. In US antitrust law, the concept of 'sham litigation' or 'predation through government process' as an antitrust violation where the action brought by a dominant firm cannot reasonably be considered as a legitimate attempt to establish rights has been recognised for some time. Thus in *Walker Process Equipment*[34] the Supreme Court held that the enforcement of a fraudulently obtained patent may violate section 2 of the Sherman Act, provided the other elements necessary to a section 2 case are present.[35] In the EU, Mario Monti's recent speech concerning the pharmaceutical industry[36] suggested that this is an area currently under investigation by the Commission. The CFI made it clear in the *ITT Promedia* case[37] that it is only in exceptional cases that the bringing of legal proceedings can constitute an abuse of a dominant position under Article 82. Nonetheless, the Commission, in the same case (without criticism from the CFI), identified that there may be abuse by the bringing of legal proceedings subject to two conditions:

(a) legal proceedings can only be regarded as an abuse if they cannot reasonably be considered to be an attempt to assert the rights of the undertaking concerned and can therefore only serve to harass the

GlaxoSmithKline's use of patents to restrict generic competition for Paxil—see Jacob Plieth 'Profit warnings' SCRIP Magazine, Feb 2002, 50. See also comments of Timothy J Muris on pharmaceutical companies use of IP, *Competition and Intellectual Property Policy: The Way Ahead*, 15 Nov 2001.

33 See article 'NHS warns on firms' delaying tactics' SCRIP No 2718, 6 Feb 2002 at3 which estimates that delaying tactics will cost the NHS some £140 million over the next few years.

34 *Walker Process Equipment Inc v Food Machinery & Chemical Corp*, No 13 Supreme Court, 6 Dec 1965.

35 See also Professor Bork comments on the case: 'pressing claims known to be without foundation for the purpose of stifling competition is a violation of Section 2 of the Sherman Act'; Bork, 'The Antitrust Paradox. A policy at war with itself' at ch 18—Predation through Governmental Processes, at 353.

36 SPEECH/01/450 Commissioner Monti, 'Competition and Consumer: the case of Pharmaceutical Products'; European Competition Day in Antwerpen, Astrid Park Plaza, 11 Oct 2001.

37 Case T-111/96 *ITT Promedia NV v Commission*, [1998] ECR II-2937.

opposing party. This must be examined in the context of the situation existing when the action in question is brought; *and*

(b) the proceedings must be conceived in the framework of a plan whose goal is to eliminate competition.

The nearest the Commission has come to applying the principle that the very enforcement of an IPR in practice may be abusive is its *Hilti*[38] decision. In that decision it found that actions to block or unreasonably delay the grant of a licence of right available under UK patent law were abusive.[39]

II. CONCLUSION

11. It is suggested that this brief analysis of IPR/competition related issues points to support the view that some of the analytical *'badges'* used to assess the interface between competition and IPR in EU competition law, such as distinctions between the existence and exercise of IPR rights or the current vogue for emphasising the exceptional nature of any antitrust intervention where IPRs are concerned are ill-conceived. Rather, the approach suggested by Steve Salop and reinforced in the recent CRA discussion paper for the OFT of focusing on the nature of the exclusionary behaviour in issue is vital to ensure that intellectual property rights do not result in disincentives or barriers to innovation.

12. By using badges such as 'exceptional circumstances', there is a risk that competition enforcers 'put the cart before the horse' and determine the consequences of a competition investigation (ie no or very limited intervention in IPRs) before undertaking a detailed antitrust analysis. It is worth recalling here the *Micro Leader*[40] case. In this case, the Commission dismissed a complaint from Micro Leader Business without examining the allegation of an abuse of a dominant position as it considered that the behaviour was a legitimate use of IPRs and could not be abusive. The CFI annulled the Commission decision, noting that the use of copyright to ban parallel imports from outside the Community could, in certain exceptional circumstances[41] amount to an abuse and therefore the Commission should

[38] Commission Decision *Eurofix—Bauco v Hilti*, 22 Dec 1987, OJ [1988] L65/19, Case T30/89 *Hilti v Commission* [1991] ECR II—1439 and Case C-53/92P *Hilti v Commission* [1994] ECR I-667.

[39] See also Commission Decision 87/500/EEC *BBI/Boosey & Hawkes* OJ [1987] L286/36 decision where the Commission appears to have accepted that Boosey & Hawkes' conduct of pursuing unjustified litigation in the UK for breach of copyright with the aim of delaying the launch of competing products might be abusive.

[40] Case T-198/98 *Micro Leader Business v Commission* 16 Dec 1999.

[41] The CFI referred to the *Magill* judgment here (Cases C-241/91 P and C-242/91 P, at 49 and 50).

have, at least, examined the complaint to see if there was such an abuse. Thus, the CFI has recognised the need to properly consider IPRs and their use, rather than jumping immediately to the conclusion that if a firm's behaviour involves an IPR, it is immune.

13. Rather, the proposed 'first principles' approach necessitates a full investigation including a detailed review of all the economic and factual circumstances surrounding the grant and review process and circumstances of enforcement of any IPR in order to identify any possible infringement of the competition rules. This approach recognises the benefits of competition law intervention to protect and promote innovation. No aspect of IPRs should gain immunity from the need for a full competition investigation in cases where there is evidence of anti-competitive exclusionary behaviour. This is not to suggest that IPR holders should fear that their rights will be annihilated by competition law but that all circumstances relating to the very existence of an IPR will be relevant to ensure that there are continued incentives to innovate.

6. Competition and IP: The Solutions

Pat Treacy*

I. INTRODUCTION

Competition law and intellectual property law are closely linked. They strive to achieve similar policy aims using differing routes, but are often perceived to clash. At a time when innovation and research and development are high on the policy agenda and there is renewed commitment on

* Bristows, London. Paper given at the Second Annual Conference on International and Comparative Competition Law, BIICL, May 2002.

the part of governments to the support of competition, the relationship between these key policies is bound to be the subject of close scrutiny. This is such a time. In the last six months we have seen the OFT publish its guidelines on IP, an OFT Economic Discussion Paper on Innovation and Competition Policy, an EU consultation document on the Technology Transfer Block Exemption, and the current hearings by the US Department of Justice and the Federal Trade Commission concerning Competition and IP[1].

The relationship can be an uncomfortable one, and the way in which it is approached in practical terms by competition authorities and by courts has differed over time. In simple terms, the nature of interrelationship is determined by the fact that whilst intellectual property law grants a limited 'monopoly' to rights owners enabling them to control the production and supply of goods incorporating their technology, competition law seeks to ensure free competition and a minimum of restraint on commercial activity. This dichotomy of approach can lead to practical (and theoretical) tensions. However, any consideration of such tensions must bear in mind that, whatever the differing approaches of competition policy and IP law, both competition law and intellectual property law have similar underlying policy objectives of encouraging technical development and consumer welfare.

The purpose of this paper is to set the scene for a discussion of some potential 'solutions' to the problems that may follow from the tensions that do arise. With that in mind, it explains briefly the nature of the relationship, the way in which IP and competition law currently coexist and touches on some possible solutions—to the extent that anything new is needed at all.

The solutions to the perceived 'problem' arising from the interrelationship between competition law and IP law may lie, at least in part, in a challenge to the perception of the two systems. If, as a starting point, it is recognised that competition law and intellectual property rights (IPRs) are not based on different value systems and should not be regarded as mutually antagonistic this may make a coherent approach more feasible.

One route to resolving the difficulties that can arise in practice from the application of the laws embodying IP and competition policies respectively may be through regarding the two areas of law as forming a set of 'checks and balances'. The focus of their interaction should be on enhancing consumer welfare by providing incentives to innovate, but also by ensuring

[1] The OFT IP Guidelines (OFT418) and the Economic Discussion Paper on Innovation and Competition Policy are both available on the OFT web-site: www.oft.gov.uk; the DG Competition Evaluation Report on the Technology Transfer Block Exemption is available at: <http://www.europa.eu.int/comm/competition/antitrust/technology_transfer/>; Information on the joint Department of Justice and FTC Competition and IP hearings, as well as speaker contributions, can be found at: <http://www.ftc.gov/ftc/antitrust.htm>.

that the benefits of innovation are shared and that IPRs are not used to unduly restrict further enhancements. In achieving this balance innovation must be protected and encouraged.

If properly understood, the conflict between IP protection and competition policy may be less of a problem than is generally thought and the difficulties faced by companies (and practitioners) with interests in both areas may be less intractable than they might appear. This paper considers whether a tension can really be said to exist between the two bodies of law.[2] It sets out examples where steps have been taken within IP law to solve some of the problems that can arise from the IP regime. Some aspects of the application of competition law to IP are then outlined, before the paper addresses the task of suggesting 'solutions' promoting a smoother interface between IP and competition. Others this afternoon will deal in more detail with specific areas in which the relationship between IPRs and competition law is most developed (and where most problems have arisen).

It is hoped that this paper will contribute to the overall debate concerning the relationship between competition and IP law. There is a 'dialogue of the deaf' that often exists between IP lawyers and competition lawyers and between apologists for both systems! The lack of informed dialogue contributes to the difficulties faced by those who have to wrestle with practical aspects of the relationship between these disciplines. Both competition law and IP law have a role to play in ensuring efficient outcomes and their respective roles, scope and limits ought to be understood, at least in a broad sense, by anyone who seeks to advise in these areas. The current consultation process being conducted by competition authorities in the EU, US and UK on the role of competition policy and IP rights ('IPRs') in supporting growth and technical development is welcome and, if it results in a broader understanding of the values (and drawbacks) of both, will be extremely valuable.

II. THE TENSION BETWEEN COMPETITION AND IP—OVERVIEW

At its core, the apparent tension between competition law and IPRs stems in large part from the perception that interference with IPRs through the competition rules is fundamentally inappropriate. Sometimes those who make this criticism start from a position of 'exceptionalism' for intellectual property rights and move from there to the oft-repeated criticism that any interference with IPRs for competition policy reasons will negatively affect

[2] The focus is on IPRs—notably patents and copyrights - which touch on technology transfer and innovation related issues. Trademarks, which typically address product differentiation issues are not focused upon.

the incentive and/or the investment plans of those seeking to innovate and then to obtain IPRs.[3]

Certainly, the justification for granting substantial protection to IPRs is readily familiar and widely accepted: to encourage and protect true innovation and to enable innovators to receive a reward for their efforts. It is envisaged that this in turn leads to greater innovation effort and to the wider dissemination of innovation, to the overall public good. However some fundamental issues can be raised. Should this justification be understood differently from the justifications underlying the protection of other property rights more readily familiar? Does the 'IPR justification' really mean that the IPR rights should not be interfered with, as is the case with other property rights?[4] Is investment in 'innovation' inherently more worthy of protection than other investments? Is this the case in some sectors (eg the 'new economy') and not in others?

It is worth recalling that some interference with property rights in our modern society is the rule rather than the exception[5]. It is commonplace to regulate the terms on which an owner of chattels disposes of his goods both under competition law and otherwise. Equally, in certain circumstances real property rights can be regulated or affected.[6] For IPRs to be more favourably treated than other property or ownership rights as a matter of principle would require a strong theoretical justification to support such a view[7].

In broader policy terms, when legislators turn their minds to the appropriate scope of an IP right, it appears that this is not the case. Under the TRIPS Agreement, it is expressly envisaged, for both patent and copyright, that the interests of third parties can be taken into consideration in restricting the scope of the privileges extended under either the patent or copyright, so

[3] Eg see Office of Fair Trading 'Innovation and competition policy' (Mar 2002), para 5.100, at 97: 'Imposing compulsory access conditions may reduce the return earned by the owner of the property right, and as a result may diminish investment incentives.' Here the view is couched in temperate and wholly unexceptional terms. Sometimes it is raised as a rationale for a blanket exception from the application of the competition rules for the exercise of IPRs.

[4] See USDOJ/FTC *Guidelines on the Licensing of Intellectual Property,* 3 of which state: '[F]or the purpose of antitrust analysis, the Agencies regard intellectual property as being essentially comparable to any other form of property'.

[5] Although it is true that the extent to which this is accepted varies from country to country.

[6] See, in particular, the 'ports' cases: *B&I Line/Sealink* [1992] 5 *CMLR* 255; *Sea Containers/Stena Sealink*, OJ 1994 L15/8; *Irish Continental Group v CCI Morlaix* [1995] 5 *CMLR* 177; *Port of Rødby*, OJ 1994 L55/52 [1994] 5 *CMLR* 457.

[7] In the context of EU law, Art 295 of the Treaty (formerly Art 222) is frequently cited as supporting the view that IP rights are 'protected' in some way from the full rigour of the competition rules. Leaving aside entirely the wider debate about the intended scope of Art 295, it is notable that it gives no support to any pleas of exceptionalism for *intellectual* property as opposed to any other form of property.

long as doing so does not unreasonably conflict with a normal exploitation of the IPR, and the legitimate interests of the IPR owner are not unreasonably prejudiced.[8]

There seems no general reason to believe that the granting of certain rights to exclude, which commonly form the core of IPRs, does not mean that duties cannot simultaneously be imposed upon the party holding those rights whether as a matter of law/jurisprudence or as a matter of policy. Those rights to exclude are granted to the innovator not solely for his benefit but also to secure greater benefits to society, as described above, by encouraging him, and others, to continue to innovate and invest. In principle, the results of such innovation and investment will benefit society as a whole and it is therefore accepted that the incentive to do so should not be interfered with. However, this benign paradigm may break down in certain circumstances. When it does, a corrective will be needed to ensure that the general policy justifications for granting protection to innovators as a matter of course, does not result in unforeseen and antithetical results with either particular or general adverse effects on welfare.

When such a breakdown takes place or is foreseen, a number of correctives might be appropriate, one of which may be the use of competition policy or competition law to restore the 'balance' between effort, incentive, reward and the distribution of benefits. The 'balance' referred to above might, for example, be skewed either by large 'system' effects (eg where a change in the nature of certain products or industries takes place or if a general change in corporate behaviour in a sector takes place that disturbs the previously accepted status quo[9]) or by individual actions of rights owners. As IP law and competition law both intend to promote consumer welfare it may be argued that competition law is in fact a particularly good candidate to act as a check and balance when the widespread grant and enforcement of IPRs has particular unforeseen consequences.

[8] See Arts 13 and 30 TRIPS. Art 30—Exceptions to Rights Conferred—states:
Members may provide limited exceptions to the exclusive rights conferred by a patent, provided that such exceptions do not unreasonably conflict with a normal exploitation of the patent and do not unreasonably prejudice the legitimate interests of the patent owner, taking account of the legitimate interests of third parties.

[9] For example it might be considered whether the increased use of patents to form 'thickets' in industries with high degrees of technical interdependence is such a change or see the legislative response of the US, through the Hatch–Waxman Amendments, to particular problems arising in the pharmaceutical industry. For a discussion of the patent 'thicket' issue, see Carl Shapiro, Navigating the Patent Thicket: Cross Licenses, Patent Pools, and Standard-Setting (2001), available at <http://www.ssrn.com>.

A. *When might a general 'problem' arise in the IP field?*

As mentioned above, such a 'problem', or a situation where careful analysis is required, might occur in a particular industry sector where, for example, the way in which patents apply and the way in which they may be used as a strategic tool in all the circumstances of the industry, differs from the traditional or classic model. An understanding of the different ways that IPRs, especially patents, are used in various industries is important. This background is helpful in understanding both the general 'problems' that may arise from industry wide shifts in behaviour and also the opportunities that IPRs can represent for companies engaging in conduct that will upset the 'balance'. The focus here is on patents because they are recognised as providing the most effective barrier against competitors, at least when compared to other IPRs. The IT and the pharmaceutical industries provide interesting examples of different strategies in the obtaining and use of patents.

Most undertakings of any size in the computer industry operate a policy of seeking to obtain a significant number of patents each year. Each of the key players in the industry holds portfolios of hundreds or thousands of patents.[10]

The large number of patents (more of which are constantly being granted) which result in part from this strategic choice, together with the interoperability/interconnection requirements prevalent in the IT industry, mean that it is almost impossible to manufacture any computer component without the likelihood of some other undertaking's patents being infringed. Furthermore, the nature of new technologies (not only computer hardware) is often such that each new product must build upon numerous previous patents rather than start from scratch. These factors mean that cross-licensing on reasonable commercial terms is the norm within the IT industry. Such licences are generally for the mutual benefit of the parties, enabling each to offer a wider range of products than it would otherwise be possible. This also benefits society as a whole by widening the range of products available, maintaining the speed of innovation and ensuring a competitive market. Patents are thus normally used as valuable commercial assets in a highly interdependent industry, not to kill off suppliers or commercial collaborators, or to exclude others, but to achieve a win/win agreement in which both parties achieve freedom to operate in a rapidly evolving market. Whilst this differs from some traditional models of patent exploitation it

[10] A list of the top patent owners can be found at <http://http://www.ipo.org/Top300-2001.htm>; for 2001, eg, IBM was awarded 3411 patents in the US, thereby attaining the number one spot. In total IBM currently holds around 37,000 patents world-wide, including 20,000 in the US.

can be an efficient way of achieving benefits for the innovator and ensuring that those benefits are disseminated.

However, it should be noted that the extensive patent portfolios of large undertakings can in certain circumstances (for example when combined with a position of real strength in a core product or technology) be used as extremely effective weapons. Such weapons may include patent 'mine-fields'. The existence of these minefields and the fear, uncertainty and doubt which they can sow in the minds of competitors and their customers mean that it may be extremely difficult for a smaller undertaking (sometimes a new entrant) to 'cross' a larger undertaking with such a patent minefield—even if the smaller undertaking believes there is no merit whatsoever in, for example, a claim that interfacing components infringe a valid patent right of the incumbent.

In contrast to the computer industry (where each saleable product may infringe literally hundreds of patents and individual model lifespans are extremely short), the pharmaceutical industry uses patents quite differently. There, single patents are much more likely entirely to cover the active ingredient in a saleable product. There is little or no interdependence and each commercially successful invention will represent enormous research and development costs. In addition, many successful drugs will have a lifespan which exceeds the 20 year life of the patent. Broad cross licensing arrangements or industry licences are far less common. Undertakings are more likely to reserve the exploitation of their invention to themselves. Licences are granted typically only in territories where the patent owner has too limited a presence to market the product effectively.

If litigation about the validity or infringement of a pharmaceutical patent occurs, it can generally be resolved before the patent protection becomes irrelevant (as pharmaceutical products do not become so rapidly obsolete and generally only a very limited number of patents are relevant or may need to be examined). In the case of IT, this may not necessarily be the case for the reasons outlined above.

From the above rather simple account of the different uses (and possible effects) of patents, which can lead to wholly different patenting and enforcement strategies, it can be seen that a simple assessment of the way in which rewards are obtained through patents will not easily capture either the strategic background or the possible effects of particular behaviour. A thorough examination of all the circumstances will be necessary to identify the likely effects of any given course of conduct and whether those effects are overall pro-innovation or anti-competitive and whether as a consequence the behaviour should be prevented or whether, on balance, the conduct in question does not have a sufficiently serious effect on competition to justify intervention. The above account of patents in the IT and pharmaceutical industries should make it evident that 'per se' approaches to the relationship between IPRs and competition policy are dangerous whether the bias is always pro-patent or always pro-competition. A consistent bias one way or the other risks unnecessary repercussions for both industry and the consuming public.

III. COMPETITION AND IP: COMPLEMENTARY APPROACHES?

Although a 'per se' approach may itself be dangerous, it is clear that both IP legislation and competition law can work in complementary fashion to attain similar goals. There has been some recognition that either the scope or the exercise of IPRs should in some circumstances be controlled. In some circumstances specific 'IP' provision has been made; in others competition law and policy will be the preferred or, for reasons of history and practicality, only possible route.

For example, the problems that can arise from the 'blanket' granting of IPRs with (often) relatively limited or no scrutiny as to the achieved justification for, or effects of, such a grant have been recognised under IP law for sometime. For some more recently introduced rights, these problems have resulted in specific provisions of a 'competition' nature in the IP legislation itself.

This section is not intended to be exhaustive. Its purpose is to demonstrate that the potential problems identified above have been explicitly acknowledged by legislators. It first sets out some examples from various pieces of IP legislation where potential 'competition' problems have been expressly dealt with, *as a matter of IP law*, before looking at the application of competition law in those areas where no express provision has been made. It focuses on steps taken to lessen any conflict between competing interests and to limit, or make explicit, circumstances in which it is necessary to resort to competition law instead of IP law.

A. *IP legislation on anti-competitive behaviour*

As a general proposition, owners of IPRs are given considerable room for manoeuvre when it comes to the exploitation of their rights. However, taking the UK as an example, certain concerns about the possible effects of wholly unfettered freedom are nevertheless addressed by its IP legislation, which acknowledges the needs for some limits on the freedom of IPR owners.

As an example, before their recent repeal Sections 44 and 45 of the Patents Act 1977 concerned contracts relating to patented products. They provided for the nullity of certain restrictive conditions within such contracts. Section 44 rendered automatically void tie-in clauses in licences. Section 45 allowed either party to a licence concerning a patent or patents which had expired to terminate the licence to the extent that the contract related to the subject-matter of the expired patents in question. An infringement of Section 44 of the Patents Act meant that a patentee could not enforce his patent in the UK. Interestingly, not only was the patentee prevented from enforcing his rights against the 'victim' of the tie, but also against third parties.

These two sections have now been repealed by section 70 of the Competition Act 1998. At the time of the entry into force of that Act, the view was expressed that general competition legislation provided the appropriate mechanism to deal with any particular problems arising from provisions of this sort. This seems to reflect a view, on the part of the legislator, that IPRs should not be regarded as exceptional and that, whilst it might be possible to deal with particular IP related difficulties by specific provisions, it is more appropriate to deal with such problems in a uniform way[11].

B. Compulsory Licensing Provisions

In addressing the problems that can sometimes arise from the existence and rigorous exercise of IPRs, compulsory licensing is a possible remedy or solution that is considered (and applied) from time to time.

It is worth noting that, as a general matter, compulsory licences may be regarded as a possible remedy *either* under the IP rules *or* under the competition rules. Despite the availability of this remedy under IP law to deal with specific problems, as discussed below, compulsory licensing under the competition rules has been heavily criticised, principally because imposing such a licence seems to contradict the principle of freedom of contract that is at the core of most modern legal systems (see the opinion of Advocate General Jacobs in Oscar Bronner for a consideration of this issue[12]). Compulsory licensing is also criticised as undermining the essence of an IP right. It is argued that the whole point of such a right is the right to exclude others, and that a compulsory licence cuts across the fundamental purpose of the right, and undermines the incentive that flows from the grant of such rights.

[11] In the EU, it is also competition law that deals with the potential effects of such provisions. For example, see also the EU Technology Transfer Block Exemption (Regulation 240/96) and its recitation of certain black listed terms. Several continental jurisdictions likewise are opposed to any attempt to extend patent 'power' outside the strict limits of the granted patent although this appears to be regarded mostly as a matter of patent law.

[12] *Oscar Bronner v Media Prints* [1998] ECR I-7791.

Despite these arguments, which certainly indicate that compulsory licences should be ordered only sparingly, both IP and competition law have explicitly recognised that circumstances may exist where such a remedy is appropriate. The key difficulty is determining what those circumstances may be. Both systems recognise potential difficulties and the need for possible solutions. Both systems also recognise the need to act with circumspection to preserve the balance between incentive and reward.

1. UK Patents Act 1977.

Compulsory licences may be applied for under the Patents Act 1977 ('the 1977 Act') Section 48 and Section 48A. Section 48(1)(a) of the 1977 Act provides that at any time after the expiration of three years[13] any person may apply to the comptroller for a licence under the patent. Subject to Section 48A, if he is satisfied that any of the relevant grounds are established, the comptroller may order the grant of a licence to the applicant on such terms as he thinks fit.[14]

Section 48A of the 1977 Act provides the relevant grounds for an application under section 48, where the proprietor of the patent is a WTO proprietor:[15]

where the patented invention is a product, that a demand for the product in the United Kingdom is not being met on reasonable terms;[16]

that by reason of the refusal of the proprietor of the patent concerned to grant a licence or licences on reasonable terms[17]

(i) the exploitation in the United Kingdom of any other patented invention which involves an important technical advance of considerable economic significance in relation to the invention for which the patent concerned was granted is prevented or hindered;[18] or

[13] Though the Comptroller has the discretion to extend this period under s 50(2)(a) of the 1977 Act.

[14] The Patents Act 1977, s 48(2)(a).

[15] A proprietor who is (a national of) domiciled in a country which is a member of the WTO or has a real and effective industrial or commercial establishment in such a country. 48B sets out the grounds in respect of patent whose proprietor is not a WTO proprietor.

[16] The Patents Act 1977, s 48A(1).

[17] Ibid, s 48A(2). The court must make a careful consideration of all the surrounding circumstances, including the nature of the invention; the terms of the any licences already granted; the expenditure and liabilities of the patentee in respect of the patent; and, the requirements of the purchasing public. Importantly, when looking at royalties, it has been held that there is 'no necessary relationship between cost price or selling price (and the royalty which a patentee is entitled to ask'. The best test of whether a royalty is reasonable in amount or the reverse is: how much are manufacturers who are anxious to make and deal with the patented article on commercial lines ready and willing to pay?': *Brownie Wireless Co Ltd's Applications* (1929) 46 RPC 457, 473 per Luxmoore J.

[18] Under this sub-section, no order shall be made unless the comptroller is satisfied that that the proprietor of the patent for the other invention is able and willing to grant a reciprocal licence on reasonable terms. The Patents Act, 1977 s 48A(4).

(ii) the establishment or development of commercial or industrial activities in the United Kingdom is unfairly prejudiced.[19]

It is notable that these grounds are essentially based on market effects or effects on competition. The underlying thrust is that, if the benefits of the patent are not in some way being 'shared' with society, whether through working the patent fully or by enabling someone else to do so, then steps may be taken, on 'society's' behalf to force some disgorging of those benefits. In this regard Section 51 of the Act is also relevant. Although it has not been used yet, this section enables a Government Minister to apply for a licence under a patent, or to seek an entry in the register that licences are obtainable as of right, in each case when a report of the Competition Commission has been laid before Parliament under the responsibility of the Minister. Such a Competition Commission report can be based on a monopoly reference or a competition reference, in which case the report has to establish either that a monopoly situation exists or that a person is engaged in anti-competitive practice, respectively, and that either the monopoly or the practice operates or may be expected to operate against the public interest.

By way of further example, the Biotechnology Directive, as incorporated into UK law, provides for possible compulsory cross-licensing between patents and plant breeders' rights. Articles 12(1) and (2) of the Directive provide that:

- Where a breeder cannot acquire or exploit a plant variety right without infringing a prior patent, he may apply for a compulsory licence for non-exclusive use of the invention protected by the patent inasmuch as the licence is necessary for the exploitation of the plant variety to be protected, subject to payment of an appropriate royalty.
- Where the holder of a patent concerning a biotechnological invention cannot exploit it without infringing a prior plant variety right, he may apply for a compulsory licence for non-exclusive use of the plant variety protected by that right, subject to payment of an appropriate royalty.

Again, the general theme becomes clear: ensuring that products emerge on the market to the benefit of the consuming public is of interest under the IP laws. Specific provisions have been incorporated in particular pieces of IP legislation reflecting this goal. Those provisions will apply where particular circumstances require action.

[19] When an application is made on this ground, not only must it be proved that there has been a refusal to grant a voluntary licence but also that such refusal is the cause of the unfairly prejudiced establishment or development.

2. Other IPRs under UK law

Compulsory licences are also available for other rights, specifically copyright, in particular circumstances:

- Where a copyright comprises broadcast schedules and a person wishes to reproduce those schedules;[20]
- Where a work is a sound recording and the proposal is to broadcast it or include it in a cable programme;[21]
- Where copyright had lapsed but has been revised under the Duration Regulations;[22]
- Where the work is a document embodying a design which was in existence on January 1, 1989 and therefore subject to transitional provisions;[23]
- Where the Secretary of State has made an order regarding the lending of works;[24]
- Where a copyright work is included in a broadcast which is re-transmitted by cable under a statutory requirement but beyond the original broadcast area;[25] and
- Where the work is of 'enemy origin'.[26]

In addition, and similar to Section 51 of the Patents Act, a Minister is able to apply for a licence under certain rights, or seek an entry in the register that licences are obtainable as of right, as a result of the Competition Commission producing a report detailing anti-competitive practices or the abuse of a monopoly position. This mechanism is available for the following rights:

- Copyright[27]
- Design[28]
- Database right[29]

[20] Broadcasting Act 1990, s 175–176 (reacting specifically to the circumstances which gave rise to the *Magill* cases).
[21] Copyright Designs Patents Act (CDPA) 1988, ss 135A-H.
[22] Duration of Copyright and Rights in Performances Regulations (SI 1995 No. 3297), reg 24(1).
[23] CDPA 1988, Sched 1.
[24] CDPA 1988 s 66.
[25] CDPA 1988 s 73(4).
[26] The Patents, Designs, Copyright and Trade Marks (Emergency) Act 1939 (c 107), s 2.
[27] CDPA s 144.
[28] CDPA s 238.
[29] Copyright and Rights in Databases Regulations 1997, SI 1997/3032, Sch 2, para 15 (database right)

It can be seen that, in the context of specific IP legislation, legislators have had no general difficulty in recognising that there may be circumstances (some clearly market related and some not) in which the grant of an IP right, including the 'core' function of exclusion, may be reviewed and interfered with. This is explicit recognition of the fact that in some circumstances the specific policy objectives that lead to the granting of a limited monopoly may be outweighed by other, more fundamental, requirements.

C. Building Pro-competitive steps into the IP laws

In addition to including specific provisions in IP legislation to deal with particular IP issues, as discussed above, legislators (particularly in Europe) have begun to include more general provisions in IP legislation, explicitly to deal with competition/consumer welfare concerns. It is evident that provisions to benefit third parties can be introduced to limit the scope of certain IPRs and that the need for such provisions has been recently acknowledged. By addressing through such provisions certain activity deemed desirable, and/or by specifying and mandating access to material which is recognised as being necessary in order to compete, the legislator is able to lessen the apparent conflict with the competition laws by addressing potential anti-competitive concerns within the IP laws.

Examples of this specific legislative approach are evident in recent EU Directives providing for new IPRs (eg the database right) and those indicating that old rights apply to 'new' types of material (eg computer software).

1. Treatment of Interface Information/Introduction of 'Pro-competitive' Privileges

The EU Software Directive is perhaps the best example of legislation in which the Community has explicitly considered, at the legislative level, the policy balance between the protection of intellectual property rights (and thus the provision of incentives to the inventor in the public interest) and the principle that competition should be protected (also in the public interest).[30]

For example, the recitals to the Software Directive deal with the problem of neighbouring/ancillary products in a specific sector and explain the need for the creation of a specific statutory exception for certain conduct intended to achieve interoperability in limited circumstances:

[30] Council Directive 91/250/EEC of 14 May 1991 on the Legal Protection of Computer Programs: OJ 1991 L 122.

Whereas, nevertheless, circumstances may exist when such a reproduction of the code and translation of its form ... are indispensable to obtain the necessary information to achieve the interoperability of an independently created program with other programs;

It has therefore to be considered that in these limited circumstances only, performance of the acts of reproduction and translation by or on behalf of a person having a right to use the copy of the program is legitimate and compatible with fair practice and must therefore be deemed not to require the authorisation of the right holder;

Whereas an objective of this exception is to make it possible to connect all components of a computer system, including those of different manufacturers, so they can work together;[31]

A similar approach can be found in the Designs Directive. Its recitals specifically state that:

...technological innovation should not be hampered by granting design protection to features dictated solely by a technical function;... whereas, likewise, the interoperability of products of different makes should not be hindered by extending protection to the design of mechanical fittings...[32]

Accordingly, Article 7 of the Directive provides that:

A design right shall not subsist in features of appearance of a product which are solely dictated by its technical function.

A design right shall not subsist in features of appearance of a product which must necessarily be reproduced in their exact form and dimensions in order to permit the product in which the design is incorporated or to which it is applied to be mechanically connected to or placed in, around or against another product so that either product may perform its function.

2. *Express Recognition of the Applicability of the Competition Rules*

Leaving aside the ways in which EU legislation has, in some circumstances tailored the scope or enforceability of 'new' IPRs where necessary to protect certain wider policy goals, EU legislators have also been careful to indicate in such legislation that IPRs are subject to the general application of the competition rules. The following paragraph is commonly part of the recitals included in such Directives:

Whereas the provisions of this Directive are without prejudice to the application of the competition rules under Articles 85 and 86 of the Treaty;[33]

[31] See Recitals 21–3.

[32] See Recital 14.

[33] This language can be found in the Database and Computer Program Directives. See also Recital 18 of the Designs Directive and Recital 17 of the Proposed Software Patents Directive.

Other Directives, including the Software and Database Directives are especially clear on the potential applicability of Article 82. The Software Directive states:

> Whereas the provisions of this Directive are without prejudice to the application of the Competition Rules under Articles 85 and 86 of the Treaty if a dominant supplier refuses to make information available which is necessary for interoperability as defined in this Directive.

Similarly, the recitals in the Database Directive make it clear that, although intellectual property rights have a public interest role, that cannot exclude the countervailing policy interest in the maintenance of adequate competition and the development of new ancillary products:[34]

> Whereas in the interests of competition between suppliers of information products and services, protection by the sui generis right must not be afforded in such a way as to facilitate abuses of a dominant position, in particular, as regards the creation and distribution of new products and services which have an intellectual, documentary, technical, economic or commercial added value; whereas, therefore, the provisions of this Directive are without prejudice to the application of community or national competition rules.[35]

Principally, this recital refers to the sui generis right as set out in Article 7 and the exceptions to that right set out in Articles 8 and 9. It is noteworthy that, under Article 16 of the Directive, the Commission is obliged to examine the application of the sui generis right, including Articles 8 and 9, and verify whether the application of this right has led to abuse of a dominant position or other interference with free competition which would justify appropriate measures being taken, *including* the establishment of compulsory licensing arrangements.

With regard to patents, it is important to note that the very recent proposal for a Directive on Software Patents suggests that in the event that patent rights are exercised in abusive way, compulsory licenses may be available as a remedy, as well as possible recourse to competition law. The proposed Directive specifically recognises:

> Patent protection allows innovators to benefit from their creativity. Whereas patent rights protect innovation in the interests of society as a whole; they should not be used in a manner which is anti-competitive.[36]

[34] Directive 96/9/EC of the European Parliament and of the Council of 11 Mar 1996 on the Legal Protection of Databases: OJ 1996 L 77.

[35] See Recital 47.

[36] See the Proposal for a Directive on Software Patents, Recital 8.

D. *The role of Competition Law*

It has therefore been accepted that, in certain circumstances, the overall balance between the interests of the IPR owner and those of 'society' must be adjusted. The above examples are of specific statutory provisions where express provision is made. Given that position, and the view set out above about the complementary goals of IPRs generally and competition policy, it may be that the role of competition law should be recognised as providing another, more generally applicable, route to address such problems where there is no specific legislative provision or where a problem arises, with significant adverse effects, not specifically foreseen by legislation.

As with specific IP provisions to deal with these issues, it will only be in unusual situations that it would be appropriate to exercise the general power of competition policy to intervene. For example, it is important to stress that issues on compulsory licensing, as such, currently arise under EU competition law only in instances where there is a question of substantial market power. Where this is the case Article 82 of the Treaty may mean that a refusal to license IPRs, or certain forms of exercise of IPRs, will be unlawful. In those circumstances a variety of possible remedies may be ordered. In some instances a compulsory licence, or an obligation to negotiate a licence on fair and reasonable terms may be the most appropriate remedy. The question of the correct remedy, will be one for careful consideration in the light of all the surrounding facts.

1. *The current position*

It has been argued that the Community Courts are of the view that particular care needs to be taken by the competition authorities in requiring those who own IPRs to grant access to them to third parties. Commentators have referred to *Volvo*,[37] *Magill*[38] and *Oscar Bronner*[39] as authority for that view. All of those cases are certainly authority for the proposition that, in the field of IPRs (as for other rights) mere refusal to license (like mere refusal to supply) will not constitute an abuse under Article 82. However, in the field of IPRs, as for other property rights, a refusal to license, like a refusal to supply or a refusal to grant access, will constitute an abuse in certain circumstances and, where that is the case, proportionate remedies will be ordered. It also appears that the circumstances in which such an abuse may occur have not been exhaustively defined in the jurisprudence of the European Courts, although this position is currently under review (see discussion of the *IMS* case below).

[37] *Volvo v Veng* [1988] ECR-6211.
[38] *RTE and ITP v Commission* [1995] ECR I-743.
[39] *Oscar Bronner v Media Prints* [1998] ECR I-7791.

Perhaps the most thorough recent consideration of the application of the principles of EC competition law to refusals to permit access to property, whether intellectual property or other, is in *Oscar Bronner*, where both the Advocate General and the ECJ reviewed the case law and its development thoroughly.

The Advocate General in *Oscar Bronner* carried out a thorough review of the issues relating to the balance between the protection of property rights, including the right owner's freedom to exercise those rights as he pleases, and the need to protect free competition. Jacobs AG concluded his review of the case law as follows:

> It is clear from the above rulings that a dominant undertaking commits an abuse where, without justification, it cuts off supplies of goods or services to an existing customer or eliminates competition on a related market by tying separate goods and services. However, it also seems that an abuse may consist in mere refusal to license where that prevents a new product from coming on a neighbouring market in competition with the dominant undertaking's own product on the market.[40]

Similarly the ECJ referred with approval to the judgment in *Magill* that:

> refusal by the owner of an intellectual property right, even if it is the act of an undertaking holding a dominant position, cannot in itself constitute abuse of a dominant position, but that the exercise of an exclusive right by the proprietor may, in exceptional circumstances, involve an abuse.[41]

Thus the European Court explicitly recognises the need to strike a balance between the goals of protecting IPRs (maintaining the incentive to innovate) while ensuring that they do not *in fact* harm the consumer interest (or the ability of others to compete and to innovate) in a way that is not justifiable. Where there are exceptional circumstances such as the foreclosure of a market, discrimination, or the extension of dominance into ancillary markets there may be an abuse, depending on the facts and on the extent of the effect on competition. The existence of IPRs is a factor in the assessment, but no more than that.

The ECJ in *Oscar Bronner* went on to give examples of the circumstances that might be 'exceptional' in the *Magill* sense so as to render a refusal to supply or license abusive. Those circumstances are set out in paragraph 40 of the judgment and can be summarised as follows:

- The product, service or right to which access is sought is indispensable for carrying on the business in question.

[40] *Oscar Bronner* Advocate General's Opinion, at para 43.
[41] *Oscar Bronner* ECJ judgment at para 39.

- The refusal of access prevents the appearance of a new product for which there is potential customer demand.
- The refusal of access is not justified by objective considerations.
- The refusal is likely to exclude competition in a secondary/ancillary market.

If those four conditions are satisfied, current law holds that at least a prima facie case of abuse may be established. This does not seem to be a position that is either unreasonable or insensitive to the need to have due regard to the existence of, and rationale for, IPRs.

Whether the precise circumstances set out by the ECJ are the only circumstances that could justify intervention, and whether they are the right circumstances is an issue that would usefully repay further review. Recently in the *IMS* case, the Court of First Instance (CFI) has been asked to consider more closely how the previous so-called 'essential facilities' cases fit together, including whether the factors set out in *Bronner* should be interpreted as being cumulative or not and, by implication at least, whether they are exhaustive.[42] Whilst the outcome of this case is by no means certain, it is submitted that if the CFI accepts the invitation to clarify the law as has been requested, it may result in the loss of a degree of flexibility in this area of the law. This would be a shame, given the general thesis that it would not be beneficial to move the law closer to a 'per se' style of application when competition law in this area should focus on adverse effects on competition with a real flexibility of approach requiring a serious and in-depth review of relevant circumstances.

In the light of all the above, however, the fact that the ECJ has explicitly recognised the role of competition law in maintaining a 'balance' whilst stipulating that intervention by competition law is required only exceptionally, is welcome.

IV. COMPETITION AND IP—THE 'SOLUTIONS'

The discussion so far addresses the question whether there is truly a 'conflict' between the IP regime and competition law and policy. It appears, in fact, as if both IP policy and competition policy have recognised that specific difficulties may arise from the acquisition and exploitation of IPRs in certain circumstances and as if each is attempting to define a way in which the adverse consequences can be addressed.

[42] *IMS Health GmbH & Co OHG v NDC Health GmbH & Co* (Case C-418/01) is currently under consideration by the CFI. The issues in the case are treated in greater detail in the article by Nick Green QC, below at 285.

It is clear that only if there is a real conflict does the need to consider new 'solutions' arise. The possibilities for resolving any tension between the two areas of law can be split into two: contemplating change to (1) the IP laws; and/or to; (2) the competition laws.[43]

In the context of this conference, one purpose of any such exercise should be first to encourage thinking 'outside the box', and not to treat any aspect of the competition/IP relationship as being in principle inviolate. Such a fundamental examination is perfectly consistent with the underlying policy justification for both the IP laws and competition law. Both seek to promote consumer welfare—indeed for the intellectual property system, that is the entire raison d'être for its existence.[44] Accordingly, one focus should be on how the interaction/relationship between the two sets of rules might, all practical considerations aside, be improved, so as maximise the effect on consumer welfare. The fruits of that consideration can then inform a general review of possible ways of improving the working relationship between the two systems, as they currently stand, so as to achieve their common policy goal.

A. Amending the IP Laws/Enforcement Regime

The IP laws could be fine-tuned so as to prevent or reduce the need to turn to the competition rules to solve particular problems that can be foreseen or have arisen. Some examples of this might be:

- identifying further material, which, as with the treatment of 'interface information' under EU Computer Program Directive, should be considered appropriate for exclusion from the scope of protection;
- considering further exceptions (as is permissible under the international IP convention), which, like the decompilation provision under the EU Computer Program Directive, assist in achieving interoperability or other aims likely to be pro-competitive;
- addressing the situation where several rights structures apply to the same subject matter (eg patents and copyrights applying to computer programs); the concern is that, if this is not considered, the pro-competitive provisions of some areas of IP law such as copyright may be overridden through patent or other laws. Two examples of this have been included in recent EU legislation or proposals:

43 As, to the extent, already seems to be happening—see Section III above.

44 While competition law, at least in the EU may have other policy objectives such as territorial integration and the attainment of the single market.

- Article 6 of the Proposed Directive on Software Patents is intended to expressly preserve the application of the provisions of the Computer Program Directive concerning decompilation and interoperability.
- Article 6(4) of the Copyright and Related Rights Directive attempts to set out how copyright exceptions are envisaged to apply in the face of technological protection measures which are legally protected under the Directive.[45]

- Judicial scrutiny of IPRs potentially also stands to affect the scope and duration of rights, thus reducing the need to rely on competition law. In the United States, for example, the Supreme Court has agreed to hear two cases which, respectively, potentially stand to affect the scope of patents and the duration of copyright:
  - In *Festo*, the Supreme Court may reconsider the court-created doctrine of equivalents, which has a long history in U.S. patent law.[46] This doctrine was recently expressed by the Supreme Court in *Warner-Jenkinson* in 1997:

    > a product or process that does not literally infringe upon the express terms of a patent claim may nonetheless be found to infringe if there is 'equivalence' between the elements of the accused product or process and the claimed elements of the patented invention.[47]

  - In *Eldred,* the Supreme Court has agreed to review the constitutionality of the Copyright Term Extension Act of 1998, which lengthened the life of a copyright by 20 years.[48] Among other things, Eldred challenged the 1998 Act as violating the constitutional requirement that copyrights exist only for 'limited times'.
- Generally, if judicial scrutiny of IPRs were quick, thorough and relatively cheap, some of the potential difficulties—arising, for example from very aggressive patenting programmes or from 'threats' (however disguised) to litigate—might be resolved in that context.
- A more wholesale reconsideration of the foundations of the patent system might also be considered. For example, it might be asked whether it is appropriate to grant 20 year periods of exclusivity for patents in

[45] Unfortunately, both of these provisions raise more questions than provide answers. For example, it still is not clear how in practice legislators envisage certain users applying the available exceptions when faced with other areas of law which potentially overlap and restrict otherwise legal conduct.

[46] *Festo Corporation v Shoketsu Kinzoku Kogyo Kabushiki Co, Ltd A/k/a SMC Corporation and SMC Pneumatics, Inc*, cert granted 69 USLW 3673 (18 Jun 2001).

[47] *Warner-Jenkinson Co v Hilton Davis Chem Co,* 520 US 17, 21 (1997)

[48] *Eldred et al v Ashcroft*, case 01-618, cert. granted (Feb 2002).

some areas, or whether a more limited period is desirable from the perspective of enhancing consumer welfare.

- Other possible changes might be to increase the resources available to patent examiners, or to simplify oppositions or challenges to patents other IP rights.

As a matter of practicality, few (if any) of the above changes are likely to be welcome, nor would wholesale changes of this nature be a viable solution to all potential problems. However, acknowledging the fact that the current system is not without flaws and that its operation may give rise to unforeseen consequences may be valuable as it could lead to a more open consideration of the ways in which such issues could be addressed with minimal changes to the existing, widely accepted system of IP protection. One such route (as already explained above) would be through the appropriate use of competition law, which is addressed below.

B. Amending the Competition Rules

From the above, it can be seen that a pure 'IP' response to some of the problems that can on occasion arise from the way in which IPRs arise and operate is impractical and probably undesirable as a matter of complexity and legal certainty. Certainly, a wholesale overhaul of the IP system is unlikely and would be a disproportionate response to problems/issues that, despite their high profile, arise only relatively infrequently. That being so, it is suggested that competition law, with its complementary focus on consumer welfare is perfectly placed to deal in a flexible and proportionate way with the distortions that occasionally arise from the exercise of IPRs.

However, if this basic premise is accepted, competition law should not be applied to such complex issues in a mechanical fashion. For competition law, the key issue has perhaps more to do with improving legal certainty and with creating a coherent policy basis for intervention, ensuring that the system has the capability to react proportionately to the issues that face it. One aspect of the challenge is to review how the competition laws do (and should) apply to intellectual property and whether this applicability is understandable to the extent that it will allow commercial parties to plan their activities accordingly.

As such, three main areas for improvement could be considered:

(i) underscoring the point that in the majority of cases, competition law is not likely to interfere in the exploitation of IPRs; achieving this may require a change of emphasis and, possibly the adoption of a 'first principles' approach to the application of competition law (see section 2 below);

(ii) encouraging a better understanding of IPRs from the competition law perspective to enable the appropriate application of the law; and

(iii) clarification of how the law applies to companies which have IPR, including in the licensing context and, for companies with particular power (for example, those controlling a gateway) when that may fetter their freedom to act eg when the 'essential facilities' doctrine or some similar concept may apply to IPRs.

1. IPRs are largely free from the interference of Competition Law

It is important to underscore the point that competition law largely should not interfere with IPRs save in limited circumstances. In particular, when considering the terms of IP licences the following guidelines should be stressed with regard to 'vertical' and 'horizontal' arrangements:

- vertical arrangements (or arrangements between non-competitors): most forms of exercise should be permitted save for limited 'hard core/per se' issues—eg tying; price fixing.
- horizontal arrangements (or arrangements between actual or potential competitors): more careful scrutiny of potential effects and of market characteristics can be expected.

In terms of improving legal certainty, companies should be reminded that reliance may be placed on several EU relevant block exemptions. A coherent approach to the issues that arise should be continued, building on the considerable work already done in this field, as is likely to appear in the Guidelines accompanying any new TTBE.[49] Amelia Fletcher's paper pays particular attention to issues arising this context.[50]

In terms of the application of Article 82, it should also be stressed that the remedy of granting compulsory licences as a result of the application of the competition rules is rare and is likely to remain so. It is worthwhile to point out that the compulsory licence remedy is at least theoretically more readily available directly under the IP laws, certainly in the UK. This area has been considered more particularly by Stephen Kon.

[49] Guidelines already exist for vertical restraints and horizontal agreements: see Guidelines on Vertical Restraints [2000] OJ C291/1 and the Guidelines on the Applicability of Art 81 to horizontal co-operation agreements [2001] OJ C3/2.

[50] It should be noted that considerable concern has been expressed by commentators about the use of market shares as a threshold for block exemption in the IP field: See for example: Olivier Vrins: 'Intellectual Property Licensing and Competition Law: Some News from the Front—The role of market power and 'Double Jeopardy' in the EC Commission's New Deal' [2001] EIPR 576; and Bristows' comments on the review of the TTBE at <http://www.bristows.com>. The reasons for those concerns are touched on briefly below.

2. A 'new' approach?

In setting the parameters for the appropriate impact of competition law on IPRs, especially in the light of the challenges of the new economy, it is suggested that a focus on 'first principles' of competition law enforcement might be an appropriate starting point.[51] In this context, the 'first principles' approach centres on an examination of the competitive effects of the conduct at issue. This is appropriate because, stripped of its legislative and judicial accretions, the assessment of competitive effect is the true core of competition law. In some respects it might be argued that competitive effect is already the key issue and in principle that may be true. One difficulty which arises, however, is the extent to which it appears to be required that an examination of market definition and market shares is an essential prerequisite to the consideration of competitive effects at least in the EU. The traditional approach, at least in the context of most circumstances where the exercise of IPRs is at issue, first seeks to define the relevant market, and to assess the existence of market power or dominance, before considering whether particular behaviour is anti-competitive or has substantive adverse effects. Whether this is appropriate may repay closer examination.[52]

In the context of IPRs, and particularly in certain hi-tech industries, it is suggested that the 'first principles' approach with less immediate focus on market definition may assist in improving legal certainty to the extent possible in such fast moving industries. For example, such an approach would permit authorities to focus more on elements of competition other than price, including exclusionary or foreclosing behaviour which is of particular concern in certain industries. The approach will also require less rigid application of the existing rules and less reliance on listing 'per se' violations or on setting rigid criteria for the circumstances in which the law may intervene.

Consider the following examples:

- **Licensing of IPRs.** The argument is often made that 'any licence is better than none' in that the licence may permit competition which would not have taken place absent the licence. However, it is not difficult to envisage a licence which, whilst permitting another product to come onto the

[51] This approach has been advocated by Steve Salop and is discussed in the recent OFT Economic Discussion Paper, 'Innovation and competition policy', n 1 above; See Steve Salop, 'The First Principles Approach to Antitrust, Kodak, and Antitrust at the Millennium', *Antitrust Law Journal*, Vol 68(no.1), 187–202. OFT, op cit.

[52] The difficulties of applying market share tests in accessing the effects of conduct related to IPRs is discussed in the papers referred to above in n 50 above, in the OFT's recent Economic Discussion paper on 'Innovation and Competition Policy' and below, briefly.

market currently (thereby being 'pro-competitive'), also contains provisions which curtail the licensee's ability to innovate or may exclude it in the future. The effects of such licences should therefore nevertheless be subject to scrutiny under the rules, particularly in industries where dynamic competition and innovation are important.

- **Patent Pools/mutually exclusive cross-licences.** Under the traditional approach, such arrangements are subject to particular scrutiny when engaged in by competitors. However, the need for competitors to cooperate is much more widespread in the new economy, mainly because compatibility issues are likely to be so common with highly complex products. As such, the competition rules must not be mechanically applied lest pro-competitive benefits should be eliminated without good reason.
- **Licensing practices of dominant companies.** It appears from recent comments by the Commission that certain common commercial practices may be denied automatic exemption when engaged in by 'dominant' companies, and may indeed be effectively prohibited for such companies, given the expense and difficulty of obtaining specific clearance. It is not clear that there is a good policy justification for this automatic distinction which comes perilously close to penalising the mere fact of dominance, rather than actual abuse.[53]

3. A Better Understanding of IPRs by competition practitioners/enforcers

It is suggested that achieving a better understanding of IPRs whether by competition practitioners or the competition authorities would be of great benefit to improving the practical aspects of the interrelationship between IPRs and competition law. A better understanding of the true scope of IPRs, and of the extent to which either the existence or the exercise of specific rights in particular circumstances may be achieving or distorting the balance between incentive, reward and the public good, will lessen the chance that the rationale for IPRs in general will be treated as applicable in every circumstance when it comes to the application of the competition rules to particular rights. Of course it is not suggested that this desire for improved understanding should lead to a challenge to the rights themselves.

If, as is advocated under the 'first principles' approach, the focus of competition law and policy is to be on the actual effect on competition of specific rights in a specific context, both sides of the equation (the IP policy justification and the competition policy imperative) need to be applied and scru-

[53] And, generally, consider the perils of market definition and the calculation of market shares where IPRs are involved.

tinised equally thoroughly. It is therefore essential that an application of competition law in detail to the exercise of specific IPRs is based on a thorough understanding of the nature of the IPRs in question. Such an understanding would seem to include at least the following points in relation to patents:

- the number of patents granted in the industry field in issue—where there is a high number of patents, this would be relevant to considering, for example, whether a cross-licence between competitors is in reality procompetitive;
- what sort of 'product' the patent extends to: something entirely new, and covered in its entirety by a single patent or family of patents; a substitute; a complement; a protocol; an improvement; an interface; etc? This may be relevant to examining the likely effect of patent enforcement, the time scope of the innovation (and investment) involved; and possibly, the intent of the right holder in enforcing his rights, whether a legitimate exercise is involved or whether the right holder is attempting to leverage his position into a neighbouring market;
- whether patents cover the entire lifecycle of products/whether it is realistically possible to successfully challenge with new products in a commercially viable time frame—this could be relevant to the consideration whether a compulsory licence may be a necessary remedy;
- the commercial (as opposed to the theoretical) purpose of the company in question in obtaining and maintaining IPRs—whether it is largely to obtain freedom to operate or whether it is primarily to slow the process of innovation by other companies, including competitors.

Another consideration concerning patents might be to gain an appreciation of the strengths and flaws of the examination/granting process. It should be asked whether the complexity and number of patents being applied for in a certain field means that there is little chance that the national Patent Office, due to obvious constraints on its resources, is really capable of weeding out applications lacking merit. If this is the case, does it mean that primary reliance should be placed on the legal system to invalidate such patents through litigation? What role, if any, should competition law play when faced with an IPR lacking overall merit or, for example, with patent 'minefields'?

4. *A detailed consideration of the context*

Once violation of the competition rules has been alleged and its potential implications considered in the light of all the 'IP related' circumstances, it would be necessary under the 'first principles' approach to gain an understanding of the economic context in which the violation takes place.[54] For example, consideration of the following would seem to be highly relevant to making better decisions concerning the application of the competition rules to IPRs:

- The degree to which the industry in issue is subject to dynamic competition—a dynamic industry may warrant a more considered application of the competition rules and less reliance on 'per se' rules;
- Whether 'tipping' has occurred or may occur (this occurs when one standard becomes predominant in a market; eg the IBM PC versus Apple)—if an IPR holder is using his rights for reasons other than mainly obtaining remuneration for his innovation and is possibly seeking to block further innovation, it may merit closer consideration of the application of the competition rules;
- The extent to which the company is in control of critical assets, including IPRs—this may affect the rate of innovation and may merit closer consideration of the application of the competition rules;
- When dealing with high tech industries, it may be appropriate to focus on whether there are interoperability issues that may not be addressed through the particular IP laws (eg conventional patent law does not address this issue, unlike other more recent IPRs);
- Similarly, it should be ascertained whether there are standards issues and whether such standards are 'open' or 'closed' and how the IPRs at issue relate to these standards—for example, if a company has achieved market power or dominance by offering open access, and then removed those access privileges, there may be a much stronger case for mandating access under the competition rules.

In all, it should be stressed that in applying competition principles to IPRs it is important to encourage to all those involved look at the movie rather than to dwell on the snapshot. This is particularly the case for today's dynamic industries making up the 'new economy'.

5. Dominant Companies and IPRs

It is suggested that the 'first principles' approach or 'potential effect on competition first' approach could bring greater legal certainty to the application of the competition rules for dominant companies, including when

[54] See discussion above in Section 1 concerning patents in the hi-tech and pharmaceutical fields.

competition law should provide the remedy of compulsory licensing. This is because, under the suggested approach, one would look first at the alleged abuse and its possible overall effects on competition (perhaps using a minimal 'quick and dirty' market share 'sieve'), before asking how market definition and an assessment of market shares could assist in understanding the issues only when a prima facie case of potential serious harm has been established. This could be contrasted with the present approach under EU competition law, which assesses whether a particular behaviour is likely to be abusive only after the relevant market has been defined and, generally, after market shares have been calculated. If combined with a move away from 'per se' condemnation of particular conduct, this may relieve companies with apparently large market shares from some uncertainty.

Why may this approach be particularly appropriate in this area? In an environment where competition is primarily innovation driven and based on the introduction of new products and features and only secondarily based on price, most of the allegations and concerns about anti-competitive behaviour will relate to actions or agreements that threaten to exclude competitors or to tilt the playing field through the adoption of anti-competitive strategies. Indeed, such exclusionary behaviour may allow a firm to achieve, maintain, expand, or extend a genuinely dominant position.

It follows that, if the competition rules are not capable of being applied in a quick and flexible fashion, but instead require particularly unwieldy analysis focused on market definition and the assessment of dominance[55] before even considering a possible violation, a considerable degree of exclusionary conduct may go unchecked with the result that consumers will be harmed through a lesser degree of innovation or differentiation of products. This concern may be especially acute with companies already capable of exercising market power, but it is not *only* such companies that may be of concern. Equally, there will be circumstances in which particular conduct which is argued to be anti-competitive will quickly be deemed to be unlikely to have any significant adverse effect, given the surrounding circumstances, whatever the position of the company in question. Here also a review from first principles will reach this conclusion quickly, without the need to focus first, or extensively on complex issues of precise market definition and market share, in what may be a fluid market situation.

In this regard, it is important to consider the relationship between innovation, IPRs, and exclusionary conduct. As Professor Carl Shapiro points out, when 'innovation is king', IPRs play a prevalent role in any company's

[55] There has been some serious criticism of the use of market share tests and of the standard market definition models in circumstances where IPRs are pivotal.

competitive strategy, whether it is dominant or not.[56] For this reason it is likely that in many industries claims of exclusionary conduct will increasingly involve IPRs and will not necessarily be of concern only when engaged in by companies already dominant. This problem is currently not addressed by the focus on dominance as a pre-requisite for consideration.

Concerning the question of abuse, generally, the view under EC law has been that the mere enforcement of IPRs could not, without more, amount to an abuse. Stated so boldly, and without qualification, this is likely to mislead. Case law indicates that, in certain limited circumstances, the way in which a dominant company enforces and exploits its IPRs may amount to an abuse under Article 82. The 'without more' does not necessarily refer only to 'more' conduct on the part of the dominant company. Rather, it appears also to encompass the possibility that extraneous circumstances, such as general market conditions or the actual effects of the conduct in question, may be sufficient when combined with exercise to require remedy. For the reasons identified above, and throughout this paper, it is suggested that this basic approach is correct and that some exercises of IPRs should be corrected in some circumstances. As has been indicated in the section immediately above, to assist in a proper application of the competition rules in this area, however, attention should be given to the nature of the IPR in issue and the context in which it is applied, rather than to focus exhaustively on dominance where this is inherently difficult, the tests applied of questionable relevance or accuracy and the results often the subject of dispute.

In all, if, as suggested above, the real aim of competition policy is to avoid and/or to censure behaviour that has a serious adverse effect on competition—perhaps that is where we should start, rather than with a traditional analysis aimed first at a finding of dominance.

V. CONCLUSION

This is a good time to re-examine the fundamental nature of the relationship between the IP and competition policy areas. As Professor Shapiro has commented:

> In a world of bottlenecks, where interfaces, compatibility, standard and bottlenecks take on great significance, competition authorities cannot afford to stand on the sidelines just because innovation is rapid.[57]

[56] Carl Shapiro, *Competition Policy in the Information Economy*, in 'Competition Policy Analysis', Einar Hope, ed *Routledge Studies in the Modern World Economy*, 2000.

[57] Ibid.

IP laws continue to develop and to have resonance in a society where access to information is increasingly necessary (and information itself is valuable) and where systems/networks/interoperability requirements permeate key sectors. To reiterate a particular concern expressed above, it seems necessary to encourage discourse to gain further understanding of the dangers to the information society (and possibly other sectors) that may flow from an indiscriminate granting of IPRs that may be exercised without the possibility of review.

Competition law is also developing and, with IP laws, spreading into a global context.[58] For reasons given above, the present approach of EC competition law may not be far in practice from a sensible solution to ensure that the benefits for consumer welfare intended to arise from the granting of IPRs are not wholly captured by IPR owners through unforeseen consequences of the IP system (eg patent 'minefields' and the grant of patents on minor improvements that nevertheless provide a blocking capability in technologies where a high degree of interoperability is the norm). To achieve the policy goal of protecting the balance of incentive, reward and consumer welfare may require not a wholesale bonfire of accepted verities but:

- a revisiting of some accepted truths;
- an understanding of the complementary goals and natures of competition law and IP law;
- an acknowledgement that whilst competition intervention should be sparing, so as not to undermine incentives, equally the grant (often after limited consideration) of an IP right does not confer immunity from antitrust scrutiny but that some competition intervention may be not only acceptable, but welcome, in some circumstances; and
- an understanding of the drawbacks of excessive zeal in using 'market shares' as the principal guide in applying the competition rules and of the need to avoid the over/or under regulation that will result from too many 'per se' rules.

[58] For example, the revision of the EU Technology Transfer Block Exemption is bound to affect not only parties doing business globally, but will also shape the legislation of many countries outside the EU, in particular those aspiring to become full members of the Community.

7. Is *Magill* Dead?

Nicholas Green, QC*

My comments are largely directed at the recent decision of the CFI, ECJ and Commission re *IMS*, and I have three 'tense points' to make. The first tension may be expressed as follows: If the Commission is right in *IMS*, is *Magill* dead? The second tension is what I describe as the Animal Farm point, and the third tension is a problem with remedies, that may be summarised as follows: can an open door be shut? Let's take each of those points in turn.

First of all, if the Commission's right in *IMS*, what does that mean for intellectual property? As Val has explained, in *Magill* the court laid down a series of seemingly conjunctive requirements for Article 82 to apply—there had to be a new product, which was being denied in the downstream market, the licensor was not in that market, there was a consistent demand for the product, and there was no objective justification for the refusal to license. In *IMS*, the refusal to license was in the same market, and there was no evidence of a consistent demand being thwarted because *IMS* was providing the service, the product itself. So there was a substantial departure from the *Magill* criteria, assuming they were cumulative. It follows that if the Commission is right and the conditions are in fact disjunctive, then *Magill*, if not dead, is indeed very sickly.

The question is: is the Commission right? One has to go back to basic here; the exception that was laid down in *Magill* was described as an 'exceptional jurisdiction', it would only arise in exceptional circumstances, because the basic rule was that laid down in *Veng v Volvo*, which was that an intellectual property holder's rights were sacred and could not be encroached upon. And if you consider what the policy underlying the European Court's case law has been, it has been that intellectual property is recognised as being of value in the public interest, but that the treaty, which of course binds the courts in Article 295 as it now is, says that the treaty shall not prejudice systems of property ownership. Whether you like it or not, while the court recognises that IP falls within the scope of Article 295, that is also going to be one of the linchpins of the court's policy as the President and the CFI recognised. And thirdly, it's always necessary to reconcile the sanctity of intellectual property with competition law.

* Brick Court Chambers, London. Comments given at the Second Annual Conference on International and Comparative Competition Law, BIICL, May 2002.

So it seems to me that while the Court of Justice recognises the validity of *Veng v Volvo*, and that IP requires special treatment and indeed while the Court persists in recognising that Article 295 covers intellectual property, then it is going to be extremely difficult for the Commission to maintain a fair position—because if they do, you are simply treating intellectual property as if it were widgets, and a refusal to supply a widget is being treated in the same way as a refusal to license intellectual property. I've always viewed *Magill* as a remedy for a form of market failure, where there is a thwarted demand that is not being satisfied, and the licence order patentee, the intellectual property right holder, is failing in that respect and therefore the law steps in. That's the first tension—it's really what if the Commission turns out to be correct?

The second tension is the Animal Farm point, and this raises a slightly different question, which is: are all intellectual property rights equal? Everybody says well, in *RTE* we're dealing with a sub-species of copyright, it's a weak form of protection; in *IMS* we're dealing with copyright. It's probably easier to justify derogation from the sanctity of IP, where the rights concerned are, in relative terms at least, weak. However, where the category of IP is a stronger one, for example a patent, then perhaps different considerations apply; and I thought it was appropriate, given that this Chairman is chairing this session, to cite from a judgment of his in *Philips*, where he raises this point, and it's *Philips* in England in 1998 and the two common market law reports, Paragraph 66. The Chairman said there that although it is not necessary to decide the point for the purposes of this application, it seems to me strongly arguable that not all intellectual property rights are equal. Some are more equal than others; it is convenient and conventional to treat copyright, designs, topography rights, moral rights, confidential information, patents and trade marks as a group, but there are substantial differences between them. They last for different periods in respect of different types of subject matter, they are infringed by different types of activity, they're subject to different types of defences of exceptions. For example, the fair use defences in copyright law have no equivalent in patent law; and the compulsory licence provisions in patent law have no equivalent in copyright law.

In *Magill*, what was being considered was the right to the subspecies of copyright; it does not follow inevitably that *Magill* can be applied by analogy to a patent case. Now this was not, of course, a definitive conclusion in that case; but the observation is one that is worthy of very serious consideration, not least because recently, in ECJ and CFI cases on Article 82, the court has been at pains to emphasise the notion of a special responsibility, which is attributable to dominant undertakings. And you will know, for instance, the recent CFI ruling in *Irish Sugar*, where the court said that the height or the severity of that special responsibility depends on all the surrounding circumstances, including the legal context. And in the case of a patentee, the legal and indeed economic considerations include the cost incurred in obtaining the patent and the fact that the grant of the monopoly is for the very purpose of both rewarding the inventiveness and at the same time creating an ex ante incentive to others to do the same.

One can see I think in the context of a patent, that a derogation from that monopoly undermines to a far greater degree the public interest in both the reward and the ex ante incentive, both of these characteristics being of course interdependent. And it's also true to say, as the Chairman pointed out in the *Philips* case, that the patent system provides its own system of cheques and balances in the form of compulsory licensing regimes or prohibitions on tying, and in the defences it permits to otherwise infringing acts. I think it is a fair point for the Commission and the Court to consider in future cases, whether you can simply translate *Magill* to other, stronger forms of intellectual property.

The third and final tension that I wish to mention, which flows perhaps more acutely out of *IMS*, is the problem with remedies; and it's encapsulated in the question, can an open door be shut? If you open the door on compulsory licensing, pursuant to some form of expanded *IMS* doctrine, then you have to ask: is it fully open, is it only a little bit open, or is it somewhere in between? There are many alternatives that can be postulated, but let me give you very briefly, to conclude, three. Option A—once the door is open, it's fully open and can't be shut. In other words, a breach of Article 82 results in the evaporation of at least part of the intellectual property right; we know the notion of the existence and exercise, we hear have the evaporation of the right, because there is no longer the right to refuse a licence. The very specific subject matter and essence of the intellectual property right lies in its exclusivity, and that has gone. Your exclusivity is now turned into some form of monetary compensation through a licensing regime. But where does it end? If you have to grant one licence, do you have to grant five, do you have to grant ten? The first person who comes for a licence is willing to pay 100 euros per unit; by the time you've got ten licensees, the value of the licence has gone down to two euros per unit. How do you predict that at the outset? Is there any limit to the number licences that can or should be granted pursuant to some form of *IMS* doctrine? This solution seems to be improbable, because the specific subject matter of the IP is its very exclusivity; and to simply go that far, in my mind, is disproportionate and would run counter to Art 295.

Option B—it's only open to the first licensee, to the complaining or claimant licensee. This equally seems difficult, because it has an element of discrimination in it—why should the first person to complain get a license, or the person who is involved in litigation get a licence, but nobody else? And finally Option C—do you only open the door to the extent necessary to procure the abuse? If the abuse is starving demand for a new product downstream, the remedy is to grant only those licences that will in aggregate serve to satisfy that demand—but again, how do you calculate that at the outset? So in summary, it seems to me that many of the practical problems relating to *IMS* and indeed *Magill* remain to be resolved, and it's fair to say that the relationship remains very tense.

8. A Successful Legislative Approach

John Frank*

I may take a few minutes, as the 22nd speaker today, to talk about a particular case study of a solution where essentially a legislative approach was taken at the creation of the intellectual property right to address an intellectual property problem and a competition law concern, and to draw some of the lessons about the advantages of how the legislative approach worked successfully. Today's conference coincides with the launch of a major IP product, and just because the attack of the clones, it may not be relevant, you may not make the connection immediately but at the end of this I hope you'll see the connection between our parties and George Lucas.

Starting with the Council Directive, the Software Directive, from 1991, which started with a green paper in 1988 and then a 1989 proposed directive. Software was a new industry at the time; there were very different IP approaches across the Member States. In Germany, for example, whether or not you could claim a valid copyright under a Bern test you would find out once you went to enforce it, and it required that you were to be above average in creativity. It was a rather difficult standard to know at the outset, whether yours was going to be above average or below average as the court developed the test. So there was a need for harmonisation across the EU, and there was a clear decision made that the harmonisation would take place at a higher level of protection than some of the member states had recognised up until that point.

There were three key areas that were recognised to be important for IP protection for software; and the first one is reproduction, which is the obvious one, and we all know that even today the piracy rate for business software in Europe still remains at about 30 per cent. The second one may take some explanation, because it's not as commonly thought of; but it is the risk of imitation or unfair imitation in the software development. The third is related to the first, and it's counterfeiting, which is actually today a very substantial problem, with people manufacturing CD-ROMs that buyers pay good value for but in fact acquire no intellectual property rights with them. The imitation point deserves some explanation. Starting with some fundamental point that copyright extends to the expression of ideas, but you can't copyright the idea itself; and so when you think about competition in the

* Microsoft EMEA Services. Speech given at the Second Annual Conference on International and Comparative Competition Law, BIICL, May 2002.

software industry, the historical dynamics have been feature-for-feature matching, or I come up with a new idea and implement it and somebody else wants to do the same thing. And generally it's accepted that you can imitate—you can build your own feature, but so much of the work in the software industry goes into the engineering and the figuring out how to do it.

I'm trying to think of an analogy that will work. With software, you ship the product, you get the complete blueprints to it essentially, because the software works like your computer, in binary code. Now you write the software using a programming language in human readable form and a series of logical steps and calls, and then to make it run on the computer you put it through what's called a compiler, which turns those concept words into zeros and ones that the machine can read. And that's what you license to customers. Now a customer can effectively take those zeros and ones and recompile it, or reverse-engineer it, and turn it back into something that's not quite your source code, but something that's a close approximation, which is referred to as quasi-source code. With that quasi-source code you can study the engineering of exactly how they achieved their result; and once you know exactly how they did it, you know that's a way that works and so that's a path that I'll take for my development. So in the software industry the long debate had been whether or not this reverse engineering or reverse analysis, based upon decompilation, was fair competition or not; there was extensive litigation with IBM and I believe Fujitsu over copyright infringement around this, and it was a very hot topic in the industry.

And so, probably one of the concerns addressed in the software directive was how to prevent this unfair competition from studying exactly how you did it so you somebody else could in turn follow your steps to build their own—because after all, the idea is not protected, it's simply the expression, the exact words that you use, that enable you to create the effect you're trying to do in software.

At the same time, people recognised they wanted to protect against cloning; there was another argument that said look, I need to decompile because I need to get interface information to achieve interoperability. In 1984, of course, with the major case with IBM, the key issue was: are you disclosing the interface information so that I can build for example a memory product that will physically fit into the new IBM mainframes as you bring them to market, and for the physical connection where it plugs in, the conclusion was that it can't be copyrighted because that would prevent other people from making substitute products. So on your cell phone, the shape of the battery can't be copyrighted because somebody else can do that. There was in this morning's newspaper something about the ink cartridges for colour printers—again, going to this idea of can you prevent people, fairly or unfairly, from coming out with generic products in that space.

So this concept was very alive, but the 1989 Directive did not address this. The Commission simply said in their proposal that they would leave it to competition law to address, recognising that competition law would play a concern, but they weren't going to try to work this out. Now in response to some very heated criticism of this, the European Parliament did propose amendments to the Directive in July 1990, and just a few months later the Commission came out with an amended proposal that included an attempt to reconcile the prevention of cloning with the need to provide interface information. This was at the time the most heavily lobbied issue in Brussels, in 1991. There was broad debate, with industry polarised, and IBM probably taking the most extreme position against any decompilation, and then certain hardware manufacturers, including Fujitsu and Sony, taking a position in favour of a very broad right of decompilation. Eventually, after the debate continued for a while, there emerged a consensus in the centre; in effect Microsoft and Olivetti were the companies that staked out the centre ground, because we recognised just from a corporate point of view that we often need to make our products work with others, and so some decompilation right as a self-help remedy is important.

So in the final compromise that was reached, you could decompile but it was limited to four particular circumstances to ensure that it was really done in good faith and was not being done at the expense of destroying the incentive to innovate. So essentially it was a self-help remedy, but it was only available to you if the person hadn't previously disclosed the interfaces. This was going to create an incentive for people to really share the information and hopefully reduce the burden and the need to decompile. Secondly, you had to have made enough process in your own product to show in good faith that you knew how to get there, you just needed to get the interface information, you weren't trying to get all of the intellectual property of how they did it; and you could only look at interfaces indispensable for the independent work, and only for the purpose of interoperability, as defined in the directive. Again, interoperability is a very stretchy concept, but the Directive focuses on the concept of 'machine-readable' or 'machine-compatibility' as opposed to cloning.

So this four-part rest was resolved in 1991, and served the industry extremely well; in part because there was such a broad discussion about it, I think there's been a pretty stable consensus on it. The two protagonist groups, the trade association ESS and BSA in 1997 during the software directive review, concluded that there was no point in reopening this debate, it was too much effort the first time and the compromise worked well for everybody. However, it has been a stable consensus, and much to the surprise of the people who were active in working out the legislative compromise, there hasn't been private litigation on this. Everybody thought this was the one part of the software directive that was going to produce the most litigation. The answer to that has to be that industry has two parts: one, it's very hard to detect whether or not somebody's decompiled and studied inappropriately, but secondly, the compromise is the bright-line rule, people know exactly how to follow it. Competition law is not pre-emptive, but the open question is, guided by the analytical framework of the directive, you know, what further application of law—how does it fit in here? Those issues are not resolved.

Discussion from the Second Annual Competition Law Conference—Competition and IP: The Solutions

THE HON JUDGE NICHOLAS FORWOOD

That was a suitable final presentation to remind us that the interface between competition law and IP is one that does involve a lot of judgments, essentially by the legislator, who normally is the same legislator for the purpose of defining the intellectual property right and indeed for defining the application of the competition rules, which presuppose a certain idea of what is normal competition and what constitutes a distortion of normal competition. There are clearly a number of economic judgments there, and indeed one of the problems in the IP area has essentially been the problem of transition from a situation where national IP rights are nationally defined as the norm, and the Community legislator on the other hand has only acted in the area of trade marks and so on, and in that area, and contrary to what Mr Justice Laddie suggested earlier, I think the right way of reading the *Levis* decision is essentially as a decision by the Court of Justice that the trade mark directive as the Community legislator deciding how this trade-off between the differing interests should be resolved. You might like it, you might not like it; no doubt a reasonable legislator could have come to a different view, but essentially that decision was being made, whereas conversely, a lot of cases where the Court of Justice has intervened, particularly in the early days of the trade mark cases the *Centre Park* cases and so on, were precisely because one would still have the national content and the national aspects of the IP rights coming into conflict with the principles of the free market, and that just had to be resolved somehow. So it's finishing as we have what I think is a useful stimulus, I hope for the remaining fifteen minutes we have for questions, for those of you who have any for any of the panel. Do I see any hands rising? Yes—there.

ALEX NOURRY

Alex Nourry of Clifford Chance. The presentation was fascinating, but I was really struck by the logic of Stephen Kon's thesis, which seemed to be that competition authorities should have the right and the ability to reopen the issue of whether a particular IP right is legitimate or not. And if that was the case, isn't there a risk that you could be undermining the whole basis of intellectual property rights and increasing uncertainty and thereby increasing risks of retarding innovation?

STEPHEN KON

Yes, there is that risk, and it's a risk that clearly has to be thought about very carefully; but equally I think that if you don't allow the competition regulator that scope, it seems to me very difficult, it seems to me that you come back to the situation where you could easily argue that IPRs therefore are to all intents and purposes, and in terms of their nature, and in terms of the extent of the IPR, the circumstances surrounding their grant are immune from attack under the competition rules. And that seems to me to be an equally unsatisfactory state of affairs; I think that one should work on the basis that the competition authority or the national court, if such is the case, is going to undertake that analysis cautiously and is going to look at it based on the facts and on the evidence of the nature and the extent of that IPR right.

I think that whichever way you look at this problem, there's always going to be a risk that either competition policy will be undermined or the IPR right will be undermined; but it seems to me that to not allow that investigation to take place goes some way towards granting a very limited immunity to IPRs, and that seems to me to be an unsatisfactory state of affairs. Some of the circumstances that I've set out in the paper I've done, and which have been taken up for example by the FTC, and which it appears that the Commission are prepared to take up in some of the cases referred to by Mario Monti in his speech at the end of last year, concern that very fact, that unfortunately there will be circumstances where the grant process will be abused, and that can give rise to a competition infringement. It seems to me that it's perfectly legitimate, in those circumstances, for the competition authority to investigate that.

THE HON JUDGE NICHOLAS FORWOOD

Yes—if I can add an observation, I think that Amelia's paper reminded us, by looking at the block exemption, that nobody has any difficulty with the idea of competition law intervening in one particular way in which IP rights are exercised, that is through licensing, and involving those judgments, and it doesn't seem to be all that controversial that even in relation to the grant and exercise of the rights themselves otherwise than through licensing, there should be a base for competition law, albeit a limited one, that reflects the nature of the rights in question.

STEPHEN KON

Absolutely, and if I may just add to that, that's why I started by saying that I think some of these badges, which have been very usefully developed as you said within the context in particular of reconciling national IPRs and community competition law, but I think some of these badges can be used such as existence and exercise, to suggest that the very existence of the right is immune from consideration by the competition authorities, and in my view that cannot be right.

CORNELIS CANENBLEY

Thank you. I'm slightly confused, and I want to be absolutely sure whether we talk about the protection of intellectual property, or whether we talk about the control of its exercise. If I understood you correctly, your question was can we make a difference in IP rights about their quality; and if that is your message, I doubt whether it is legally defendable, because we have in the Treaty of Rome and in many constitutions of the member states the absolute protection of property, which also means intellectual property; and we have this highly sophisticated system developed by the Court of Justice that you cannot interfere with a right as such but only with its exercise. I just wanted to make sure whether we are still within this concept, or whether we are now turning the wheel, so to speak, and are going to interfere with the right as such.

STEPHEN KON

What I'm saying is that in order to determine whether, to use your terminology, the exercise of an intellectual property right may infringe EU or national competition rules, it is necessary to look at the nature of the right and the manner in which it was granted, as well as its pure exercise. I do not believe that is an infringement of any Community provision protecting property rights, I believe it's simply saying that in undertaking the investigation as regards how a right is exercised, you've got to look at that right, and you've got to put into the factual matrix and economic matrix of that exercise the nature of that right, how it was granted, and the circumstances giving rise to that grant. Now if you want to put the badge on it of that being the exercise of the right, that's fine; but I don't think you're considering an IPR any differently than you are any other property right that may be impacted by the Community rules or the exercise of any other contractual right. I believe simply that what you're saying is that you have to look at the circumstances.

I mean, let us take the example of the Walker case in the United States; there a patent was granted fraudulently, and the evidence was that it was then sought to be enforced. Now do you say that what you're attacking in that situation is the existence of the property right, or the exercise of that particular right? It seems to me that what you're doing is simply undertaking an investigation into the circumstances in which exclusionary conduct is taking place, and it seems to me entirely appropriate for that purpose that you have to look at the right and the circumstances giving rise to it.

JOHN FRANK

There can certainly be cases where the exercise is a problem, but I think there's a danger of going so far and saying that it's all up in the air. I also think there's a slightly anti-democratic aspect to say that even though there's been legislation adopted by democratic processes, we're going to reshuffle the deck, so to speak, at every opportunity, it's all ad hoc.

STEPHEN KON

I don't think one's been shuffling the deck; I think that in looking at the circumstances under which competition law will intervene, you have to look at all the facts and circumstances giving rise to that intervention, it's nothing more than that. And when one's looking at an IPR, one should be entitled to look at the circumstances under which that right came into being. I did say it was controversial.

AMELIA FLETCHER

I think I might just say one thing on this issue, something that Doug mentioned as well, which is that actually, patents in particular by many other IP rights, you can't necessarily rely on the right being valid until it's been held valid and infringed by a court. Now in the UK, to my knowledge and as far as I'm aware, less than 50 per cent of all patents that are litigated before our courts are held valid and infringed. So when you talk about the sacrosanct nature of the existence of an IP right, I think it would be a mistake to assume, simply because it's been examined and granted, that it's necessarily an IP right that when all the circumstances are taken into consideration, whether it be by a national court or by a competition authority, depending on circumstances, it will necessarily be held to justify the degree of protection that's given to it.

NIGEL PARR

You've certainly succeeded in being controversial, Stephen, so congratulations on that. I'm struggling slightly, because being a lawyer one does try to grasp for some sort of guidelines or principles; but are you saying, and would each of the panel agree, that let's assume for example a company spent some money, not a huge amount but a reasonable amount, on innovation and comes up with a good mousetrap, a better mousetrap and gets a patent and it's not litigated. Everybody goes out to buy it, they think that it's a very good mousetrap, it actually works, whenever I've set a mousetrap I've never caught anything, so perhaps this one would work; and they make what Amelia might call super-normal profits and they've got that for twenty years. Now lots of other people decide that this is actually rather a nice thing to do, I'd quite like to have a slice of the action, I'd like to have a licence. The proprietor says no, I'm quite happy calling in all the profits for myself. Now that's clearly on one side of the paradigm; I assume you're saying there are no circumstances there in which you would see an anti-trust authority intervening. So if that is on one side of the paradigm, and I would say clearly on the other side of the paradigm, very consistent with what Pat was saying, that if patents aren't actually valid and granted, they will be litigated, they will be held invalid.

Are we saying that an anti-trust authority could actually sit in judgment on the grant of the right? And clearly as you say, if something's obtained by fraud you shouldn't be able to enforce it. So if one sort of chips away at those issues, an improperly granted patent, some right obtained by fraud, what principles are you suggesting should guide the anti-trust regulator?

STEPHEN KON

I think I made it clear that I was considering in particular where the intellectual property right was exercised for exclusionary purposes; and what I'm saying is that in circumstances where the intellectual property right is exercised for exclusionary purposes, one should be entitled to consider the legitimacy of that right and the nature of that right etc. as part of any anti-trust investigation. I don't think the situation you've described is any different from—and indeed, one's got to look at the other essentials of the market, such as the existence of dominant position or at least breachable restriction of competition. I don't think it's any different, the situation you've described, from saying that one can have discount policies, one can have all sorts of commercial activities that normally and invariably will not infringe the competition rules. There may be circumstances that arise where there is doubt as regards the manner in which that doubt is being exercised, where it's legitimate to look at the circumstances behind that. I don't think I'm saying any more than that within the intellectual property context; I'm merely saying don't treat the intellectual property right as in some sense immune from investigation as part of your overall anti-trust investigation.

THE HON JUDGE NICHOLAS FORWOOD

Val—perhaps we could have a word for posterity.

VALENTINE KORAH

Thank you very much. I'm interested that Stephen thinks that we should have everything relevant in deciding competition rules. Insofar as we're looking at N11, the onus is going to be on the plaintiff. As you were saying, half the patents litigated turn out not to be valid and infringed; isn't this going to end up as *per se* legality? I'm also very much minded of the *Metropole* judgment of the CFI last September, where ancillary restraints were very narrowly defined—you know, you shan't have a rule of reason, you shan't balance except under 81.3. Under 81.3, of course, the onus of proof is on the other side, so the difference will still matter even after national courts can consider 81.3. And all the civil lawyers I meet are minded to say that the national courts can't cope, and that is how one should understand the *Metropole* judgment—that the rule of reason is altogether too difficult for lawyers, something that economists may understand, but civilian, I mean civil law judges, will find very difficult. We're used to reading American cases, we're used to the open texture of English law, and to applying policy issues, and not merely following words. I don't know whether you want to respond—I hope you do.

JOHN FRANK

Stephen, the concern I've got, just analytically I think, is that every exercise of an intellectual property right is by its nature exclusionary.

JOHN FRANK

Yes, but you were saying you'd only do it if the exercise were exclusionary.

STEPHEN KON

Yes, and if it satisfies the other requirements of Articles 81 or 82. That doesn't mean that every time you exercise an intellectual property right—but what I'm saying is, if questions arise as regards the matter in which that exclusionary right is exercised, and gives rise to an inquiry under the competition rules, it is at that point that you should be entitled to look at—well, I won't go through it again.

HELEN JENKINS

Helen Jenkins, Oxera. I can put an economist's point of view on this debate so far—I think that most economists would think that we're talking here about innovation incentives and dynamic efficiency, but you can imagine scenarios where you are trading off some sort of public welfare, consumer welfare, which was mentioned I think by Pat and Amelia. And you can imagine scenarios where the exercise of a property right does indeed harm consumer welfare in some sense, and economists might make those judgments. But then, the point that Ali was also making was you have this letter effect, which you might think of as regulatory risk, which then affects the perception, the forward-looking perception of innovation; and even though you could think of only one example of the balance tipping one way or another, it's certainly a relevant public policy question, whether you want to enhance the possibility of regulatory risk, which then influences all sorts of other investment decisions by innovating companies. But I think that it's an interesting question to ask—it's not an irrelevant question, and it's obviously difficult to think then, who is the requisite body that can make that sort of trade-off in any one case, particularly if they have very broad implications.

THE HON JUDGE NICHOLAS FORWOOD

Amelia, if you'd like to answer that—but I'd like to leave some interesting questions open for next year's conference.

AMELIA FLETCHER

I wasn't going to answer it, I was just going to raise another question, which is, I think that sometimes in discussion we seem to be verging towards saying exclusion tends to be anti-static competition and pro-dynamic competition. If you can exclude potential licensees, then you can stop competition today and that will help competition over the longer term. What I actually think may have not been looked at enough is where exclusion stops innovation; that is, where by exploiting your patent, not only do you stop competition today but you stop competition and innovation tomorrow, and I think that's a very important area.

CHAPTER SEVEN

Public Enforcement—Papers and Discussion from the Second Annual Competition Conference

1. Problems of Criminalisation

Mark Clough, QC*

I'm going to make comments in three areas. The first—let me stress the seriousness of the UK Enterprise Bill, which Margaret Bloom's paper has very concisely set out for you, and I recommend that you read that if you want to see an overview of the current proposals, especially in the context of criminalisation. It's a very serious matter, and I wonder how many of us here today are actually qualified to discuss the criminalisation of competition law—how many competition experts here have ever visited a criminal in a cell. It's a serious subject, which merits our debate, but I'm sad to say that it is not receiving sufficient debate outside this room, because of the nature of the change in English law that should be debated, if the Government is correct, in the homes of every English family.

Now having said that rather sardonic comment, which is a change from my approach to this conference last year, let me turn first to the current public enforcement situation that we've heard described. I think it's fair to say that the US leads the world in anti-trust enforcement, and I'm surprised that we haven't heard from anyone yet that in the US that system marries the civil system and the public enforcement system very well, and that the strength of public enforcement encourages the private enforcement through the courts and damages claims. I think we can certainly acknowledge that.

Europe seems to be, as I've said many times before, on a strange path hell-bent on decentralisation of its competition enforcement; Ireland and the UK enjoy strong leadership as indeed does Italy, which is also represented at this conference, and are doing their best to operate efficient, politically correct regimes based on criminalisation. At the international level, the European Community leads the discussions in the WTO; discussions that are embryonic and intended to deal with the international trade aspects of competition law in the globalised market that we hear so much about.

Well, against that background, let me ask my question, which is the second point: will criminalisation of competition law assist in international public enforcement of competition? Now all of us here who believe that competition law enforcement has a public welfare benefit will agree that this objective is sensible, and that the objective of taking steps to improve international enforcement through co-operation and indeed even encouraging moves

* Ashurst Morris Crisp, London. Speech given at the Second Annual Conference on International and Comparative Competition Law, BIICL, May 2002.

towards uniformity in the rules of substance and remedies is to be encouraged. But let us look at the main jurisdictions again. The US is the home of cartels; shipping and aviation through the support of IATA are strongly supported by the US government, and have been historically. These cause great costs to the industry involved in international trade. The trends that I perceive from looking at the statistics of US cartel cases indicate, for whatever reason, that foreign companies tend to be fined more than US companies, and their foreign employees tend to be sent to prison more frequently. There may be a good reason for that, but that is what the statistics show. Europe still allows block exemptions for cartels in the same way as does the US, and so does the UK through its parallel exemption procedure.

Now you may ask is that hypocrisy, or will it change, like the telecommunications industry and the energy sector are changing? European decentralisation—the decentralisation of fifteen competition authorities in the general sense could hardly be said to contribute to the international co-operation in the field. And in particular, Europe's policy of disintegration of competition enforcement while maintaining centralised cartel enforcement will clearly be jeopardised by the UK Enterprise Bill. The rules on criminalisation and custodial sentences must conflict with the uniform application of EU law. What's going to be the position for an individual who is alleged to be party to a cartel investigated by the EC Commission in Brussels and investigated in the UK? Are they going to be allowed, for example, to rely on the criminal level of privilege against self-incrimination in Brussels because they're likely to be sent to prison in the UK, because the UK also has jurisdiction? And finally on this point, why do we have no proposals for criminalisation at EU level? Is there a good reason for it? I just raise these questions because this is meant to be a forum for discussion, and we have some of the world's leading regulators here who will be able to answer those questions I'm sure.

So, moving on to my third point, which I call the mechanisms—if you like, some general questions on the way the Enterprise Bill was intended to work, and the implications that the existence of an administrative procedure under the Competition Act, of a criminal procedure under the Enterprise Bill, changes, and civil claims for damages in the courts under the Competition Act or for infringement of EC Competition Law.

First of all, if the UK criminalisation policy is correct, why does it not apply to the use of dominance? For example, it should be possible to prove that a chief executive has dishonest intentions in certain abuse cases. I believe that abuse is not covered by the Irish law, either. Secondly, is there any need for criminalisation of competition law in the UK, when the offence of conspiracy to defraud is already being used in a serious fraud investigation into an alleged cartel in the generic pharmaceutical industry in the UK? This has been widely publicised, and those of you who read Private Eye may have read a rather amusing article about this investigation. And thirdly, will criminalisation have the opposite effect to that which is intended? We've heard John Fingleton say that in Ireland he's had a lot of difficulties, and his slides amply demonstrate them. Will it even bring competition law into disrepute, not only in this country but in the rest of Europe, if the criminalisation doesn't work, because juries have not yet been educated to consider cartels to be the equivalent of theft, and I quote Margaret on that use of the word 'theft'.

Now what about the right of defence in self-incrimination? This is not the time for me to go into a laborious attempt to distinguish between those rights under the administrative procedure and the Competition Act, and the criminal procedure in Article 6.1 of the Convention of Human Rights, but it strikes me that the conflict between what you might call full rights under the *Saunders* case law, or even slightly modified rights under *Brown* and the green environment case, which David Warne who was involved in it can perhaps tell us about later, is likely to be far broader than that allowed under the *Mannesmannröhren-Werke* line of cases in an administrative context both at EC and UK level. I think it's going to be a minefield, and I don't really see how it's going to work. And finally, I see the same problem arising in the context of leniency. Let's look at leniency for a second—how's it going to work? What will a whistle-blower have to deal with? He'll have to deal with EC administrative law fines and the EC Commission context; he'll have to deal with the OFT regarding Competition Act fines on his company, and he'll have to deal with the OFT regarding his immunity from prosecution in this country. But he knows all the time that his company could also face a damages action in the UK, especially in the competition appeal tribunal, under the proposals in the Enterprise Bill. As John Fingleton said, Ireland has experienced major practical difficulties in adapting competition law to criminal court procedures. Is the UK likely to do any better? Thank you.

2. Criminal Enforcement—the Irish Experience

Dr John Fingleton*

Well, I'm the outlier—I don't know if you remember when Bill Kolasky's slide was up showing the downward line, that Ireland was up there with the 7 per cent growth rate and very low regulations. So my task here today is to tell you that if you do what we do, you'll all have 7 per cent growth rates over a ten-year period; that's called imperialism—Irish style!

I think the biggest challenge for a small economy like Ireland is actually in the design of good law. We don't have the critical mass that you have in Europe, the UK and the US, and so we've made several attempts in the last ten years to get it right. I'd like to acknowledge the fact that Margaret Bloom, Jim Griffin and many other people here from the Commission have been very helpful to us in designing our law—I'll mention the Treasury as well, as Paul Boateng came and gave a very nice speech on criminal law enforcement last year, which was very helpful. We introduced competition law in 1991, Article 81 and 82 equivalents based on a system of private enforcement, which didn't work; after 5 years *Master Foods* was the great product of that five-year period, yet again continuing our contribution to EC jurisprudence or EU jurisprudence, *Magill* being another one, and then we introduced the Competition Act in 1996. And because we, like America, cannot impose administrative fines or fines with a civil standard of proof, it was decided that we needed to criminalise all of competition law, 81 and 82, the whole lot, because of this competition problem. And so we got company fines, personal fines and prison sentences—and there's a slide in my presentation that gives the numbers.

It also established the post of Director of Competition Enforcement, who carries out investigations and makes recommendations to the authority. And it gave the authority public enforcement powers for the first time, because previously as I said there was only private enforcement. This works in a very interesting way, because we can bring a civil case ourselves, and we can bring a summary criminal proceeding for which the maximum fine was I£1,500; but for the serious criminal stuff, the trials on indictment before juries, the case went to our Director of Public Prosecutions, which is like the UK Crown Prosecution Service. A similar system applies in Canada, but in the US, of course, it's integrated into the Department of Justice; and this is actually, without wishing to be undiplomatic, one of the greatest

* Chairman, Irish Competition Authority. Speech given at the Second Annual Conference on International and Comparative Competition Law, BIICL, May 2002.

difficulties in implementing our criminal provisions—I'll come back and explain why. That's just the numbers—I'll pass over that.

The experience of the first five years of criminalisation in Ireland. Well first of all, the authority said that it wasn't going to try and criminalise 82 and most of 81; we're going to focus on hard-core cartels for criminal sanctions. The government increased the staff of the authority, although it didn't resource it properly, but the authority developed considerable expertise, in fact I would say it devoted almost all its energy in the first three or four years to criminal investigations. It dealt with a large number of complaints each year; it used all its powers very fully, and two very large files were sent to our Director of Public Prosecutions, one in 1998 and one in 1999.

Now it needs to be emphasised that a criminal investigation (and Jim has alluded to this and I think Margaret will say as well) is hugely resource-intensive because of the forensic fact-finding nature. You don't need a lot of sophisticated IO economists to tell you whether or not the price-fixing agreement damages consumers; but you do need a lot of other skills in that process, and the authority I think did a very good job on those files—there's been no disagreement with the Director of Public Prosecutions as to the quality or the decision of the authority that the file needed to be sent over. Peter settled a lot of cases as well during the period. The authority brought civil proceedings against publicans and others; it used injunctive proceedings under the civil process very successfully, largely against trade associations who tried to block trade in order to get what they wanted. And it brought one summary criminal prosecution, which was instituted before I arrived but followed through by me; it was a resale price maintenance agreement and there was a lot of other stuff in the background, but two criminal fines of £500 were imposed.

It was largely a test case to see if we could get it through the District Court without a constitutional challenge, which we did. But there were some serious problems. First of all, they sort of gave the authority one hand and tied the other hand behind its back; we had a search power, but we had to be invited in to search. We didn't tell people this, and largely, they let us in; but in fact we also had to take copies, so we had to invest in a lot of portable photocopiers, which usually don't work very well. And of course the criminal courts require originals as best evidence! So we had this huge problem in some of our cases if we took them forward, in persuading the courts to accept the photocopies as best evidence, given that that's what the statute stated. So there were these minute legal problems; a lot of these have now been addressed, but the authorities did the investigation rather well considering the powers.

There was a huge staffing crisis, because the place wasn't properly resourced; people were put on three-year contracts and were not told until the day before the end of the three-year contract that the government had not got around to renewing their contract, so they all left of course. So I presided over a 75 per cent staff turnover in 2000, which happily has been mostly ameliorated. But the biggest problem has been the delay in the files going to the Director of Public Prosecutions, and that's something that I think—it's not a problem that the DPP has taken a different view from us on the cases, but that his office, I gather, has about 17 people dealing with 7,000 criminal cases. It's not like your Serious Fraud Office, which as Margaret will say only deals with fraud; it deals with murder, rape and other issues. Our file creeps up to the top of the pile and then unfortunately somebody gets murdered and it pushes our files quite far down again. This is a very unsatisfactory situation, and so one of the things we're now considering is whether we actually need to engage in public advocacy for more resources for the DPP's office earmarked to deal with what I call white-collar criminal enforcement; because the government is putting so much resources and changing the law on not just competition law but company law and other regulatory law enforcement, but it hasn't given the DPP's office the resources to carry it through, and that's now the critical bottleneck.

Anyhow, we've just introduced a new law—and policemen are added to the staff in the office, we now have several of those working with us, doing the forensic cartels. The new act was passed, and focuses on hard-core cartels; we've removed the prison sentences on individuals for the 82 and part of the 81 violations (I've given the figures there). We've improved search and arrest powers—we can search homes and we can break and enter, well, use reasonable force to enter. We've just appointed a former member of the Federal Trade Commission to be the member of the authority directing cartel investigations—Terry Calvani, he's probably known to many people here. We have a leniency—an immunity programme, we call it for legal reasons at home, which is very similar to the US one. And I think that probably the most interesting thing that we've done is, we have this difficulty with hard-core cartels. As I've said, you want a very clear rule—we wanted a US *per se* rule, we could apply a US *per se* rule to our US domestic equivalent of 81, and basically disapply 81.3 in national law, but we couldn't do that to 81.3, and we need to have symmetry between our equivalent to 81 and Article 81.

So what the UK has done is very clever, and it was my preferred solution, which is to create a separate dishonesty offence; but that didn't run in Ireland, for whatever reason. So what we've done is voted for presumptions on 81.3; so in our statute it says that an agreement at fixed prices, and it defines hard-core cartel in terms of fixing prices by the producers of substitutes, not by competitors, because if they're fixing prices they may defined legally as not being competitors—it got very messy in the statute. But where that happens, it will be presumed that its object is to restrict competition; it's a rebuttable presumption, but it basically means that it's up to them to do the proof on 81.3, not us. The idea is that this will reduce economic evidence before juries. As I said, I probably favour the slightly clearer UK approach, because I much prefer a clearer ability to do this at EU level as the best solution; but we're going to see if it works. So what's interesting is, we have the US model, we're now going to see how we work this through the Irish courts, and the UK is going to have a third model, which Margaret's going to talk about. I think now is a very exciting time to be looking at criminal enforcement in Europe, and how different countries are trying different things.

Finally, I just say that there are three things I think you really need. Legal clarity—as I said, one of these three rules; resources, including access to police and their investigative skills, which are very important because otherwise you have to write endless law giving us equivalent power to the police; and either a direct ability to prosecute, like the US has, or a very good relationship and a good mechanism with adequate resources in the prosecutions office.

Finally, I just say, I think that this is going to become a big issue for Europe—other countries have had provisions for some time, often for collusion in government contracts, but they haven't been very successful—Austria's just rescinded its one, and I think one Scandinavian country has backed away from its one. I think that some countries in Europe, by experimenting this way, are going to succeed in running for these criminal investigations and prosecutions properly, and that's going to put a lot of pressure on other EC/EU countries and on the Commission itself to think about criminalisation at the broader level, because it's going to become difficult, if UK and Irish-based cartels are subject to prison sentences but the very large EU cartels are not unless they happen to span the US market and get caught in the US as well; so I think we're seeing the germination of a long-term debate in Europe about criminalisation, and what Ireland, the UK and other countries are doing is very interesting. Thank you.

3. Key Challenges in Public Enforcement

Margaret Bloom*

There are many challenges in public enforcement. Which ones are most interesting to this audience? I have selected those faced by the Office of Fair Trading over the last year in enforcing the hugely significant Competition Act 1998. This year, the equally significant Enterprise Bill will introduce criminal enforcement for hard core cartels—alongside many other important provisions. Hence, I have also selected the challenges—and opportunities—of criminal enforcement.

I. KEY CHALLENGES OVER THE LAST YEAR: COMPETITION ACT

Many of the key challenges of the last year were concerned with securing effective enforcement of the Competition Act. The second anniversary of commencement of the Act was on 1 March 2002. Effective enforcement requires sufficient, expert staff; active uncovering of anti-competitive behaviour; good build up of quality cases; wise selection of priorities; and wide business awareness of the Act. How well did we meet these challenges?

A. Recruitment and training

In order to implement the new Act effectively we have recruited nearly 90 lawyers, economists, investigation officers and others to join the existing expert staff at the OFT. HM Treasury responded most constructively to our need for additional resources. Without that it would not have been possible to run an effective enforcement regime. In terms of professional expertise, our nearly 60 principal case officers are approximately one third lawyers, one third economists and one third investigation officers or generalist competition experts. There is a broadly similar pattern among the equivalent number of case officers. These staff are supported by other lawyers and economists in specialist legal and economic branches. The Legal Division leads, in particular, where our decisions are appealed to the Competition Commission Appeal Tribunal (CCAT). The specialist economic branch is headed by our Chief Economist.

* Director of Competition Enforcement, OFT. Paper given at the Second Annual Conference on International and Comparative Competition Law, BIICL, May 2002. The views expressed are personal.

We have also invested significantly in training our staff. Around 140 of them—together with others from the sector regulators with concurrent Competition Act powers—have completed or are studying for the Certificate of Competition Policy. Management Development Partnership and Nottingham Trent University developed this training for the Competition Act for us. Other training is also being provided.

Have we achieved sufficient, expert staff to enforce the Competition Act? We are well on the way to doing this. But we are still recruiting as we strengthen and deepen our teams. In terms of expertise, our staff compare very well with those employed by the parties whom we are investigating. However, some of these parties have remarkably deep pockets when pursuing challenges against us.

B. Uncovering anti-competitive behaviour

Complaints are the main way in which we uncover anti-competitive behaviour. Complaints in the last year were around 70 per cent higher than under the old legislation at some 1,300 cases. Some of these involved multiple complaints. While the increase in numbers was a most gratifying response to our campaign 'Complain; don't notify', the quality was much less so. Only around 5 per cent of the cases are ones where, following preliminary investigation, we have reasonable grounds for suspecting an infringement of one or both of the prohibitions in the Act. That is, section 25 of the Act is satisfied and our formal powers of investigation can be used. Hence, 95 per cent of complaint cases do not satisfy this fairly low threshold. Around ten per cent of complaints from large firms meet this threshold. While only 1 per cent of those from individuals do so. Clearly we need to do more to increase the quality of complaints through guidance and our programme for business awareness. It is, of course, often difficult for complainants to identify anti-competitive behaviour. To give an obvious example, identical prices for a product or service from a number of firms could indicate either a competitive market or collusion.

For cartels, informants are key. Some of these are applicants for leniency. By the end of April we had agreed leniency—with at least one of the parties—in 14 cases (some of which involve resale price maintenance). So far one of these cases has concluded with an infringement decision (Arriva plc and FirstGroup plc).[1] In three others we decided the evidence is not sufficient to warrant the commitment of further resources to proceed to an infringement decision. In over half of the 14 cases we knew nothing about

[1] See Competition Act 1998 Public Register on the OFT website for decisions under the Act <http://www.oft.gov.uk/Business/Competition+Act/Decisions/index.htm>.

the cartel (or resale price maintenance) before the leniency application. Even when leniency applicants come in after we have started an investigation, they can deliver real value. For example, in one case the information provided cut the investigation time by about a half.

Typical complaints, that may satisfy section 25, are refusal to supply, resale price maintenance, price discrimination, predation and exploitation. For some of these, the complaints are self-enforcing—a most effective form of enforcement. While we are investigating a refusal to supply, for example, the complainant may subsequently inform us that the complainee has started to supply because he has informed them of our investigation. Normally, we take no further action as a matter of administrative priority. Some complainants try to secure as much publicity as possible from the media in the hope of pressurising the complainee—and also the OFT. Such publicity has no effect on our priorities. A surprising number of complaints concern resale price maintenance in branded goods. These may come in as refusal to supply a discounter. Typical complaints of predation involve local bus or local newspaper markets. We are also receiving a variety of complaints concerning activities by public sector bodies including allegations of cross-subsidy of commercial activities from statutory functions. The reach of the Competition Act is significantly wider than its predecessor statutes given the interpretation of 'undertaking' as in Community law as a result of section 60.

In the last year we normally had over 40 cases where section 25 was satisfied. We used our powers to obtain written information over 1000 times. In some cases these notices have required a substantial amount of information. But we are conscious of the burden on business and are careful to focus questions on the information that is necessary to investigate the potential infringement. The responses from the law firms vary from those carefully targeted on our questions to those who may hope that voluminous material will overwhelm us. Our case officers are not readily overwhelmed (but are sometimes underwhelmed).

Between October 2000 and April 2002 we carried out 21 on site investigations. These involved either or both section 27, where we enter premises and require production of documents and/or information, and section 28, where we enter and search premises. For the latter, we obtained 43 warrants to search premises. All applications for warrants to either the High Court in London or the Court of Session in Edinburgh were successful. Some of the section 27 visits were conducted with prior notice and two cases involved private homes.

Have the raids worked well? Yes, but it will be very useful to be able to take non-OFT IT experts with us on searches conducted under a warrant when the necessary provisions in the Enterprise Bill are passed. The minimal extent to which these raids were picked up by the media was also a success. We do not announce them, but some one else may alert the media.

C. The build up of quality cases

How successfully have these over 40 cases developed? How has our build up of cases progressed? First, some statistics. Experience so far is that around half of the section 25 cases under investigation are likely to run through to a final infringement decision. These are put on our 'cases in the pipeline' list. Cases involving raids almost invariably will be on this list. As will notification cases. We have—I am pleased to report—only had 16 notifications in total: 10 cases for decision under the Act, 4 for guidance and 2 airline alliances under EC law.[2] Seven of these cases are current. The work involved in notifications should not be underestimated. The notification for the British Airways/American Airlines Alliance, for example, required a substantial team of economists and lawyers for months before the Alliance was abandoned. A city lawyer commented that the £13,000 fee for a notification for decision 'is a bargain'. He is right. The fee is intended to cover the full cost of the work. Given the complexity of most of the notifications, I fear it is a significant underestimate.

When a case moves to 'cases in the pipeline' a project plan is produced. Its key points of fact, law and economic logic will also have been summarised in a skeleton argument that is discussed with John Vickers who is closely involved in all the key cases. Project planning is a considerable challenge. In order to maintain momentum it is important to have challenging plans. On the other hand, this means that any delays hit the forecast decision date. We are introducing better systems and training for case officers in project planning.

Our time planning on cases needs to improve—and we need to complete them faster. Partly this depends upon more resources as mentioned earlier—and on experience. However, it is now clear that it is not possible to complete all the procedures involved in an infringement case in less than nine months from satisfying the section 25 threshold. Even in a straightforward case this would be a very challenging target. Our procedures are broadly modelled on those of the European Commission with some simplifications. They are encapsulated in a substantial Procedures Manual. When

[2] See Competition Act 1998 Public Register on the OFT website for notifications under the Act <http://www.oft.gov.uk/Business/Competition+Act/Notifications/index.htm>. See EC Arts 84 and 85 Enforcement Regulations Public Register on the OFT website for the airline alliance notifications. <http://www.oft.gov.uk/Business/Legal+Powers/Enforcement+Regulations.htm>.

that has settled down we plan to issue a much simplified public version. But that is for the future.

Our public target is to complete 75 per cent of investigations of suspected anti-competitive practices (but not cartels) within six months from section 25. For cartels, the target is to complete 75 per cent of cases within twelve months from the start of an investigation. These targets include all those cases that are dismissed—ie the majority of cases. Arguably, they are far from ideal targets if the key cases fall into the 25 per cent that take more than 6 or 12 months. I believe our cases are handled at least as rapidly as those by other authorities, but we are keen to improve. Self evidently, speed must not be at the expense of quality.

In the year to end March 2002 we issued nine published decisions.[3] Three were infringement decisions with fines, 2 exemptions and 4 non-infringement decisions. We issued three unpublished section 47 decisions explaining why we would not vary or withdraw an existing published decision. Three section 35 notices on proposed interim measures were issued. One was resolved by informal assurances and one by agreement between the parties. No interim measure directions were made. We have also handled four appeals to the CCAT.[4] An important measure of the quality of our decisions will, over time, be through the judgments of the CCAT. Their judgment upholding our infringement decision in *Napp Pharmaceuticals Holdings Limited and Subsidiaries* (although with a somewhat reduced fine) was a key one in this regard. Although the judgments in *Institute of Independent Insurance Brokers* and *Aberdeen Journals Limited* set aside our decisions, they provided important clarification of how the new Act should be applied. In the last year we also won our final case under the old regime of the now repealed Resale Prices Act 1976. This case ended the last remaining exemption—for branded over-the-counter medicines—from the general ban on resale price maintenance. Major retailers cut prices sharply and rapidly.

So far, I estimate that around half of the cases in 'cases in the pipeline' will result in an infringement decision. This is approaching a quarter of the cases that cross the section 25 threshold plus the notifications. In addition there will be a number of non-infringement decisions.[5]

[3] Anove n 2.

[4] See CCAT website for appeals <http://www.competition-commission.org.uk/appeals/current.htm#cases01>.

[5] We published a non-infringement decision (The North and West Belfast Health and Social Services Trust) on 30 Apr 2002 following the CCAT preliminary judgment in *BetterCare Group Limited*. The CCAT concluded that we had made a decision in our correspondence with BetterCare.

D. Selection of priorities

How can we ensure that we use our resources to produce the maximum benefit from the new regime? How should we prioritise our work? These are key questions. We have made it clear that we wish to concentrate on cartels and other serious infringements in order to deliver maximum value from the new regime. In addition there are the notifications and the large number of complaints that do not concern anti-competitive behaviour. Careful selection of cases for 'cases in the pipeline' is one answer. These are the cases where our resources are primarily targeted. Apart from the notifications they are the cases involving potentially the most significant infringements and/or precedent value. The work necessary to identify and then dismiss complaints that do not involve anti-competitive behaviour is now well tuned and kept to the minimum. But we need to be careful not to 'throw the baby out with the bathwater'. Even where a complaint may possibly involve anti-competitive behaviour we may decline to pursue it if it is of low administrative priority, for example, a possible minor infringement in a small market with little value as a precedent.

Apart from the above, there are two other areas where we spend significant resources. The first involves confidential 'informal guidance' to business on individual agreements or practices. This is to assist business certainty—particularly given the newness of the regime—beyond our published guidance material on the Act. We have given such guidance (in written or oral form) in around 120 cases in total. We consider this is an important service to business. It is clearly appreciated by those who receive this (free!) guidance. In addition, it helps to reduce the number of notifications.

The second area concerns those cases where potentially there is a significant infringement but after fairly extensive investigation the file is closed. This may be after we have issued a Rule 14 notice (broadly equivalent to the EC statement of objections) setting out the case against the party or parties and received written and oral representations. Some of these cases have involved raids and/or leniency. However, we must always keep an open mind on cases and be willing to dismiss those where the evidence is not sufficiently strong to warrant the commitment of further resources to proceed to an infringement decision. We expect to publish more cases where our investigation leads to action by the party or parties that removes a potential infringement.

We publish those cases where we consider we have reached a non-infringement decision. Following the *BetterCare* judgment, it is likely that the OFT will adopt a larger number of non-infringement decisions. These will probably be less detailed in their reasoning than those to date. They may well be cases where reasonable grounds to suspect an infringement were not established at any stage. They are likely to include some cases where the investigation is not public knowledge.

E. Increasing business awareness

Increasing awareness is important both so that those businesses suffering from anti-competitive behaviour can bring complaints to us and to deter anti-competitive behaviour. Our target was to increase the level of awareness of the Act by small and medium sized enterprises to 60 per cent by March 2002. This compares with 23 per cent in 1999. Surveys conducted for the OFT record awareness in 2000 and 2001 at 43 and 53 per cent respectively. The figure for this March was 52 per cent. An active programme of talks throughout the UK, regional visits, business advice open days, a video and guidance material have all contributed to this improvement in awareness since 1999. Awareness will also be significantly increased as we issue more prohibition decisions with significant fines.

One of the conclusions of a survey conducted for the DTI of over 100 competition experts from around the world was that 'Only 10 per cent of British respondents thought that competition policy was important to the UK public. This compared with 83 per cent in the USA.'[6] The British figure needs to get far closer to the US one. Our enforcement of the Competition Act will play a major part in achieving this through demonstrating its benefits to business and consumers. John Vickers described some of the benefits achieved so far in a recent speech *Competition is for consumers*.[7]

F. The challenges of the Competition Act

How well are we doing? My conclusion is that we have achieved much in the last year in meeting the enforcement challenges of the Act. But it is still early days and this assessment is one that others outside the OFT need to make.

II. CRIMINAL ENFORCEMENT FOR HARD CORE CARTELS

I now turn to the challenge of criminal enforcement. The Enterprise Bill[8] introduces a new criminal offence for cartels. This is a free-standing offence

[6] *Peer review of the UK Competition Policy regime*, published Apr 2001, available on the DTI website: <http://www.dti.gov.uk>.

[7] <http://www.oft.gov.uk/News/Speeches/2002/Competition+is+for+consumers.htm>.

[8] <http://www.publications.parliament.uk/pa/cm200102/cmbills/115/2002115.htm>.

based on 'dishonesty'[9] involving price-fixing, market sharing, limitation of supply or production and bid-rigging. These are the most serious forms of anti-competitive activity. Examples of evidence which would point to dishonesty would be likely to include attempts to disguise or hide activity (eg holding secret meetings and the absences or destruction of records) either alone or in combination with a failure to seek legal advice, when it is normal practice to do so.

The offence will apply to natural persons—and only apply in respect of horizontal agreements. We will continue to use our civil Competition Act powers to fine undertakings involved in those cartels where we use the criminal powers against individuals. There will be a maximum custodial sentence of 5 years, with fines as an alternative or addition. The Serious Fraud Office (SFO) will be the lead prosecutor in England, Wales and Northern Ireland. The OFT will have prosecution powers as well. The Bill provides for 'no-action' letters that can be issued to those in England, Wales and Northern Ireland to whom the OFT grants leniency. We will issue guidance on the terms of the leniency programme, including *pro forma* 'no-action' letters. Applications for 'no-action' letters can be made by individuals independently of their employers, or on behalf of employees or directors by undertakings that are also seeking leniency in respect of civil penalties. In Scotland, the decision to prosecute rests with the Lord Advocate who will take into account a report from the OFT.

The new criminal offence will be an extraditable offence. Extradition requests by the US will not be automatic, as the criminal offences are not identical. The UK courts would need to review any requests.

The Bill makes provision for criminal investigations by the OFT if there are reasonable grounds for suspecting that the criminal offence has been committed. Such grounds might include records of secret meetings, statements from employees or a complaint. The powers of investigation can only be used in relation to the criminal offence. They are modelled broadly on those available to the SFO under section 2 of the Criminal Justice Act 1987. The OFT may require, in writing, persons to answer questions or provide information or documents. The OFT may also apply for a warrant to search premises and be assisted by others, for example, IT experts.

The Bill has safeguards in relation to respecting legal professional privilege and restricting the use in criminal proceedings of statements made under

[9] The 'Ghosh' test for dishonesty is well established in case law. Juries are asked to consider (i) whether what was done was dishonest according to the standards of reasonable people, and (ii) whether the defendant realised that this was the view of reasonable people. Only if the answer to both questions is 'yes'—beyond any reasonable doubt—can dishonesty be proven.

compulsion, whether pursuant to the powers of investigation in the Bill or the Competition Act 1998. Even where the OFT seeks voluntary statements from those under criminal investigation, the safeguards of the Police and Criminal Evidence Act 984 (PACE) will be applied—such as the right to silence, the right against self-incrimination, the right to legal representation and the right to breaks, embassy access and religious needs. Suspects will be cautioned before statements are taken.

The Bill grants the OFT access to intrusive surveillance powers through amending the Regulation of Investigatory Powers Act 2000 (RIPA). The Chairman of the OFT[10] may issue an authorisation for the planting of surveillance devices. One of the criteria for which an authorisation may be granted under RIPA is for 'the purpose of preventing or detecting serious crime'. Surveillance must be necessary and proportionate. All applications for authorisation are subject to the scrutiny and approval of the surveillance commissioners. The OFT intends to outsource the technical deployment of intrusive surveillance to either HM Customs & Excise or the National Crime Squad. Memoranda of Understanding have been drawn up for this. The OFT has applied separately to the Home Office for an Order to grant authorised officers access to directed surveillance (essentially monitoring the movement of people and vehicles) and covert human intelligence sources (essentially the use of informants). The OFT has also applied to the Home Office for an Order to grant authorised officers access to communication data (primarily postal and telephone records). Both of these applications are under RIPA. The Orders will require affirmative resolution by Parliament.

A number of questions have been raised by others over these powers, including:

- Will the OFT be able to handle these new powers effectively?
- How will civil and criminal investigations be carried out successfully on the same cartel?
- How will the UK regime work alongside the EC civil regime, including the different leniency policies?
- Are these new powers necessary? Will they be used?

These are addressed below.

10 The Bill abolishes the office of the Director General of Fair Trading. The OFT is to be a body corporate with a Chairman and at least four other members of the board.

A. Will the OFT be able to handle these new powers effectively?

Yes. Much preparation has already been done by the OFT and the SFO including planning arrangements for the handling of cases, developing a Memorandum of Understanding covering these arrangements and planning necessary training in criminal investigation proceedings and the appropriate provisions of PACE. This work was started alongside the Hammond/Penrose report that was commissioned and published by the OFT last autumn on *The proposed criminalisation of cartels in the UK*.[11]

The OFT will undertake the initial investigation and will inform the SFO as soon as a case appears likely to lead to a criminal prosecution. A decision may be taken at that point to hand over the case to the SFO for prosecution or the OFT may continue the investigation for a period in close co-operation with the SFO (so called 'extended vetting') before a decision is taken. Once the SFO has taken over a case, it will appoint a 'case controller' to oversee the joint SFO/OFT team which will take it forward. In this way the expertise of the OFT in handling cartel investigations and of the SFO in criminal prosecutions will be used to maximum benefit. Further work will continue as the Enterprise Bill is debated in Parliament. As soon as possible more of this planning work will be made public. The OFT is clear that these are very important new powers for which we need to be very well prepared.

B. How will civil and criminal investigations be carried out successfully on the same cartel?

This was one of the issues addressed by the Hammond/Penrose report.

> We believe that it should be possible to operate a criminal investigation and prosecution regime applicable to individuals in cartels in parallel with a civil investigation and prosecution regime applicable to undertakings engaged in cartel activity; although to do so will not be without certain difficulties.

At an early stage an assessment will be made of whether a cartel is likely to be sufficiently serious to justify criminal enforcement. All those cases where criminal enforcement is a possibility will be pursued to criminal standards of evidence gathering from the start. In the early stages of each case, the criminal investigation against the individuals will proceed in parallel with the civil one against the undertakings, under their appropriate powers of investigation. The civil case may well be able to go as far as the Rule 14 notice and the written and oral representations as all of this is confidential. But the final civil decision will need to await the conclusion of the criminal trial in order to avoid any risk of prejudicing the outcome of the trial. The

[11] <http://www.oft.gov.uk/News/Publications/Leaflet+Ordering.htm>.

considerable benefit of increased deterrence is well worth the delay in issuing these decisions.

C. How will the UK regime work alongside the EC civil regime, including the different leniency policies?

We have worked closely with the European Commission to ensure that the interface between Community and national law is carefully worked out. This has included discussions with the Commission on leniency policies. An undertaking should apply for leniency to both the OFT and the Commission where the cartel involves more Member States than the UK. The first undertaking to apply in a cartel should be eligible under the EU civil leniency policy and the UK civil leniency policy for full leniency unless they were the instigator of the cartel, compelled others to take part or played the leading role. Their directors and staff should also be eligible to apply for 'no-action' letters in relation to criminal prosecution. These will be issued by the OFT where guilt is admitted, there is a real risk of prosecution and certain other conditions are satisfied. These other conditions are likely to be similar to those which apply for full immunity under the civil leniency policy ie must not be the lead cartel member, must cease involvement in the cartel, must co-operate fully with the investigation and must make a full disclosure. In this way we have ensured the compatible working of the EU and UK regimes. The OFT will discuss with the Commission the handling of individual EC cartel cases where the UK may wish to mount a criminal prosecution. These will be considered case by case.

D. Are these new powers necessary? Will they be used?

The short answer to both questions is 'Yes'. We are uncovering around one cartel a month. We are now uncovering more serious ones. This activity is equivalent to theft. It has no redeeming features. Effective deterrence is very important. However, we will select carefully the cartels for criminal prosecutions, concentrating on the serious ones. We expect that there will be a relatively small number of prosecutions—but they will have a significant deterrent effect. The first prosecutions will reach the courts in a few years.

4. Key Challenges in Public Enforcement Against International Cartels

James M Griffin*

I. INTRODUCTION

I am delighted to be here today to share with you some of our experiences in the United States in the criminal investigation and prosecution of cartels—experiences that convince us that fighting cartels must be a priority of all competition law enforcement agencies around the world. I can assure you that enforcement of our criminal antitrust laws against cartels—be they domestic or international—that prey on American businesses and consumers is one of the highest priorities of the Antitrust Division. Cartels cannot and will not be permitted to act with impunity at the expense of American businesses and consumers. I know that Margaret Bloom and John Fingleton are equally determined to protect British and Irish businesses and consumers from the harm that can be inflicted by cartels and to aggressively investigate and prosecute those that are found to be operating in England and Ireland.

Today I want to talk first about what I see as the major challenge facing us as competition law enforcers, particularly as we investigate and prosecute international cartels in criminal regimes. Second, I will mention what I believe to be the most significant recent accomplishment in the fight against international cartels. Finally, I will outline some of the reasons we believe that individual penalties, particularly prison sentences, provide the optimal deterrent to cartel conduct.

II. MAJOR CHALLENGE IN INVESTIGATING AND PROSECUTING INTERNATIONAL CARTELS

Let me begin with a word about the significance of international anti-cartel enforcement. None of us need government statistics to convince us that the Irish, UK, and US economies are becoming increasingly globalized. The manifestations of increased export and import trade are observable everywhere in our daily lives. While this increased trade has many benefits, the openness in trade also creates more opportunities for international cartels to flourish at the expense of our businesses and consumers. Faced with this

* Deputy Assistant Attorney General for Criminal Enforcement, Antitrust Division, US Department of Justice. Paper given at the Second Annual Conference on International and Comparative Competition Law, BIICL, May 2002.

growing challenge, the Division in 1993 stepped up its own enforcement efforts to ensure that international cartels are not free to prey on Americans with impunity. A few of our enforcement statistics demonstrate just how global our trade and commerce, the cartels that prey upon that trade and commerce, and our efforts to detect and deter those cartels have become.

A comparison of the Division's criminal docket last year with those of previous years demonstrates its continued emphasis on cracking international cartels that target U.S. businesses and consumers. While ten years ago, the Antitrust Division only opened a few investigations of suspected international cartel activity, today there are over 30 grand juries around the country investigating suspected international cartel activity. Similarly, ten years ago, the Division filed only two cases against foreign-based companies, both involving domestic conspiracies, and did not bring a single case against a foreign individual defendant. Moreover, in the four preceding years, the Division did not bring a single case against either a foreign firm or a foreign national. By comparison, nearly *70 per cent* of the companies charged by the Division last year were foreign-based firms, and roughly *33 per cent* of the individual defendants were foreign nationals. The Division has convicted foreign executives from Germany, Belgium, The Netherlands, England, France, Switzerland, Italy, Sweden, Canada, Mexico, Japan, and South Korea for violating U.S. antitrust laws. Moreover, executives from Canada, France, Germany, Switzerland, and Sweden have submitted to US jurisdiction and served prison sentences in the United States for antitrust crimes.

While these results certainly are gratifying, much remains to be done. And what we have learned over the past several years is that the greatest challenge to the continued successful investigation and prosecution of international cartels—particularly in a criminal regime—is obtaining sufficient evidence to charge and to convict those individuals and firms that engage in international cartels. In the first place, cartels are secret conspiracies. Cartel members simply do not broadcast to the world that they have met and agreed to limit output and raise prices. On the contrary, cartel members go to great lengths to avoid detection of their fraudulent conduct. More often than not, even the customers of the cartel members are unaware that they are being victimized. These characteristics of a cartel make it one of the most difficult white collar crimes to investigate and prosecute. In addition, evidence of an international cartel may be located in several different jurisdictions throughout the world and sufficient evidence to successfully prosecute the cartel may not be found in any one jurisdiction. With all these hurdles to overcome, I think it is clear why I say that obtaining sufficient evidence to charge and to convict those individuals and firms that engage in international cartels is the public enforcement authority's greatest challenge.

Even so, it is evident from the statistics quoted above that we have found some ways to obtain evidence of a cartel, even though that evidence is located outside the reach of our own search warrants and grand jury subpoenas. Among the methods available to us are Mutual Legal Assistance Treaties, government-to-government requests for assistance through the exercise of domestic compulsory process to obtain foreign located evidence, Letters Rogatory, border watches, and informal cooperation between enforcement officials. Of all the tools available to us, perhaps the most significant source of foreign-located evidence is the Division's Corporate Leniency Policy. The Division's Corporate Leniency Programme—which provides for a complete pass from prosecution for companies and their executives who are the first to come forward, cooperate, and meet the programme's other requirements—has played a major role in cracking the majority of the international cartels that the Division has prosecuted. Indeed, many now view the Leniency Policy not so much as absolution for the guilty, but rather as the anti-cartel enforcers' most potent weapon. The extraordinary success of this programme has generated widespread interest around the world. As a result, we have consulted with a number of foreign governments in drafting and implementing effective leniency programs in their jurisdictions.

The adoption of effective leniency programmes by foreign antitrust enforcers has a direct impact on the Division's efforts to prosecute international cartels, because the existence of an effective leniency policy in another jurisdiction may influence whether an organization comes forward under the leniency programme in the United States. In some cases, companies which have exposure in multiple jurisdictions for their cartel conduct may want simultaneously to seek immunity in the jurisdictions where they are at risk. If differences exist in the respective leniency programmes such that a company believes that it can not be assured of immunity in the jurisdiction where it faces the greatest, or even just significant, exposure, then it may decide against reporting its conduct anywhere, thus depriving all enforcement authorities ready access to evidence perhaps scattered around the world. Nowhere is the need for convergence in leniency programmes more important than between the US and the European Commission ('EC') leniency programmes. Until recently, there have been significant differences in the application of our respective leniency programmes. Fortunately, these differences, and the concerns that they have raised, are ending.

III. MOST SIGNIFICANT RECENT ACCOMPLISHMENT IN FIGHT AGAINST CARTELS

In discussing what I believe to be the most significant recent advancement in the fight against international cartels, you might think that I would point to some of the Division's FY01 prosecution highlights as the most significant accomplishments of the year. You probably expect me to list the fact that the Division obtained more than $280 million in criminal fines, the second highest fine total in the Division's history, with the average corporate fine topping $18 million; or the fact that the average jail sentence last year increased to 15 months as the most significant accomplishment of last year. While the high fines and rising jail sentences in Division cases garner much of the recent public attention surrounding anti-cartel enforcement, it is the recent actions of antitrust authorities abroad—one in particular—which will have the biggest impact on how international cartels are investigated, prosecuted, and defended in the United States and around the world. Because I believe that our most daunting challenge is gathering sufficient evidence, regardless of where it is located, to prosecute international cartels, it follows that a significant advancement in our ability to obtain such evidence would be viewed by me as a major step forward in anti-cartel enforcement. Early this year the EC took such a step.

On 13 February 2002, the EC adopted a new leniency policy to replace its 1996 Notice on the Non-Imposition or Reduction of Fines in Cartel Cases ('1996 Notice'). The revised programme establishes a far more transparent and predictable policy than its predecessor and brings the EC's programme closely in line with the Division's Corporate Leniency Policy. In fact, in greatly reducing the amount of discretion involved in assessing amnesty applications and in creating the opportunity for companies to qualify for full immunity after an investigation has begun, the blockbuster revisions are similar to the ones made by the Division when we expanded our programme in August 1993. Let me mention just a few of the important provisions of the new EC leniency programme.

- Complete immunity from fines goes to the first member of a cartel to inform the EC of an undetected cartel by providing sufficient information to allow the EC to launch an inspection on the premises of the suspected companies.
- Even after the EC begins an investigation, full immunity may still be available if the company provides sufficient evidence to enable the EC to establish an infringement.
- The previous band or sliding scale reduction in fines for the first company to report cartel conduct was abandoned in favor of an automatic, full 100 per cent immunity grant.
- The new policy provides for prompt written notification to a leniency applicant as to whether it conditionally qualifies for full immunity.
- The revised programme does not exclude from full immunity those cartel

members that played an instigating or determining role, rather it simply requires that the leniency applicant not have taken steps 'to coerce other undertakings to participate in the infringement.'

The EC's new programme provides increased transparency, predictability, certainty, and a bigger prize (100 per cent immunity from fines) to the first company to qualify under the leniency programme. These attributes will serve as a powerful new inducement to create a race to Brussels every time the EC reveals one of its investigations with the execution of dawn raids or corporate counsel discovers an infringement through a corporate compliance programme.

In addition, with a flurry of cases announced at the end of last year, the EC set the stage for its new leniency programme by demonstrating a clear commitment to rewarding companies who are the first to come forward and report cartel activity, while at the same time imposing heavy fines on those who engage in cartel activity and do not provide timely cooperation. Until November 2001, the EC had never granted full 100 per cent immunity to a company that came forward and cooperated pursuant to its 1996 Leniency Notice. The EC then did it twice within a month, and it did so in two of the biggest cartel matters ever prosecuted by the EC.

The first 100 per cent leniency grant was awarded in the EC's investigation of the worldwide vitamin cartel.[1] The French corporation, Aventis S.A., was granted full immunity in regard to its participation in the vitamin A and E cartels after being the first company to cooperate with the EC in these matters. On November 21, 2001, the EC fined eight companies a total of more than 850 million euro for participating in cartels affecting vitamin products, including fines of 462 million euro against F. Hoffmann-La Roche AG ('HLR') and 296 million euro against BASF AG.[2] Aventis, which has previously announced its acceptance into the Division's leniency programme, likely avoided hundreds of millions of dollars in fines in the US and Europe as a result of its decision to come forward and seek leniency. In addition, unlike both HLR and BASF, which had three of their high-level European executives serve time in US prisons, the officers, directors and employees of Aventis received non-prosecution protection in exchange for their cooperation with the Division.

[1] Press Release, European Commission, Commission Imposes Fines on Vitamin Cartels 4 (21 Nov 2001). Commission press releases are available at <http://europa.eu.int/rapid/start/cgi/guesten.ksh>.

[2] The Division's prior prosecution of the vitamin cartel has resulted, to date, in the conviction of ten corporations and twelve individuals, the imposition of nearly $900 million in fines, and the incarceration of eleven vitamin executives.

Shortly after the vitamin immunity decision was announced, the EC announced its second-ever grant of full immunity to Sappi Limited (South Africa) after the company came forward and supplied information on a price-fixing cartel in the European carbonless paper market.[3] While Sappi, which was identified by the EC as one of the three largest companies in the cartel, paid nothing in fines, the EU imposed fines against ten other companies totaling over 310 million euro, including a 184 million euro fine against Arjo Wiggins Appleton, the alleged leader of the cartel.

The EC's timing in announcing these cases on the eve of the introduction of its revised leniency programme could not be more telling of its commitment to the transparency and predictability embodied in its new leniency programme. While the new programme on paper is a tremendous improvement in terms of the level of transparency that it provides to potential leniency applicants, the real test is how it is implemented, which is why these recent cases are so important. They demonstrate that the EC is committed to fairly rewarding leniency applicants who are the first to report cartel activity with full immunity. This signal was clearly sent even before the new policy went into effect.

I have no doubt that the EC's message, together with the revised leniency programme, will lead to a substantial increase in the number of firms reporting international cartel activity to both authorities. The cooperation provided by leniency applicants will result in both authorities obtaining evidence of cartels, regardless of the location of that evidence, which neither authority on its own easily could have obtained. The EC's new leniency programme is a significant new addition to the international cartel prosecutor's arsenal of weapons, and I believe it will prove to be the most significant achievement in the fight against international cartels in the past several years.

IV. MOST EFFECTIVE SANCTIONS

In light of the bold initiative by the UK government in introducing criminal penalties for individuals engaged in hard core cartel conduct, I would be remiss if I did not say a few words to this audience about what we in the US believe to be the most effective sanction against cartel conduct. I will begin with the obvious. You will not be surprised at what I have to say.

First, one cannot talk about the most effective sanction without a clear understanding of the effect one intends to achieve by the imposition of the sanction. The goals of sanctions—particularly incarceration—generally are said to be retribution, societal protection, rehabilitation, specific deterrence,

[3] Press Release, European Commission, Commission Fines Ten Companies for Carbonless Paper Cartel 4 (20 Dec 2001).

and general deterrence. It is generally agreed that, in most cases, the only relevant goals of sanctions against cartels are retribution and general deterrence and, between those, general deterrence is by far the most important. So, I begin with the proposition that the goal of sanctioning cartel conduct is general deterrence, ie, to deter others from engaging in the offending conduct.

In the 1980s a number of scholarly articles were written addressing the adequacy, or lack of adequacy, of corporate fines as a deterrent to cartel conduct.[4] The beginning hypothesis was that in order to achieve optimal deterrent effect, corporate fines would have to be more than the anticipated gain from engaging in the cartel divided by the risk of detection. The risk of detection in the United States (at the time by far the most active anticartel enforcement jurisdiction in the world) was estimated to be between 13 per cent and 17 per cent. The estimated increase in price resulting from cartel conduct was 10 per cent (a figure we now generally regard as low), which was estimated to result in a 5 per cent increase in corporate profit resulting from the cartel. Finally, the average length of a cartel was determined to be six years (a figure we also now consider to be low). The optimal fine was then calculated to be 187 per cent of the commerce affected by the cartel. Such a fine would have bankrupted over 60 per cent of the firms convicted of cartel conduct in the US during the period. The actual fines imposed were found to be less than 1 per cent of the level necessary to deter cartel conduct. While fines have increased significantly since these studies were conducted—both in dollar amounts and as a percentage of affected commerce—they are not now and never will be anywhere near the optimal fine level established by those studies. Not surprisingly, these studies and articles reached the conclusion that the imposition of corporate fines alone is not a sufficient deterrent to cartel conduct, a conclusion with which we wholeheartedly agree.

In considering, what penalty would be most effective in achieving the goal of deterring others from engaging in the offending conduct, we should keep in mind that the conduct we want to deter is the deliberate, rationale conduct of individuals acting in pursuit of corporate gain and their own advancement in knowing and intentional disregard of the law. That being so, it seems intuitive that corporate fines alone would not be the most effective deterrent to cartel conduct. Even individual fines coupled with corporate fines would not seem to be sufficient. In most instances, a corporation

[4] A number of those articles are mentioned and nicely summarized in a recent paper authored by Wouter PJ Wils, 'Does The Effective Enforcement of Articles 81 And 82 EC Require Not Only Fines On Undertakings But Also Individual Penalties, In Particular Imprisonment?' (Address before 2001 EU Competition Law & Policy Workshop/Proceedings, Robert Schuman Centre For Advanced Studies, European University Institute, available at <http://www.iue.it/RSC/competition2001/Wils.pdf>).

could simply reimburse the individual executive for the fine imposed, thereby rendering the individual penalty little more than an increase in the corporate penalty. Therefore, the two together would need to be at least the size of the optimal fine, ie, 187 per cent of effected commerce, and that is not going to happen anytime soon.

The nature of the conduct also suggests that it maybe uniquely deterrable. That is, because the infringement results from the deliberate, rationale conduct of individuals motivated not 'by desperation or need, but by arrogance and greed,' the introduction of an extremely distasteful variable outside the familiar parameters of cost-benefit analysis may well cause executives to forego opportunities to 'swindle the unsuspecting public.'[5] While there are no studies of which I am aware that have attempted to quantify the general deterrence value of prison sentences in cartel cases, it is generally accepted that such sentences do, in fact, deter. While it is not possible to quantify the undetected, ie, cartel behavior that does not occur because deterred by the perceived risk of incarceration, it seems clear that when the risk of jail is introduce into the equation, the conventional businessman's risk/reward analysis breaks down, and that it is that break down which is critical to the effective deterrence of antitrust crime.

I will close with two brief anecdotes that I think nicely illustrate this point. Donald Baker, a former Assistant Attorney General in charge of the Antitrust Division, now a prominent member of the antitrust bar in the United States, tells the following story about a senior executive of one of his clients. This senior executive was committed to adherence to the antitrust laws and to the success of the company's antitrust compliance programme. He also was in favor of criminal penalties for those who engage in cartels because he believed that the threat of jail was the only penalty that would clearly focus the full attention of the individual on the potential consequences of his actions. As he explained to Baker:

> So long as you are only talking about money, the company can at the end of the day take care of me—but once you begin talking about taking away my liberty, there is nothing that the company can do for me.

Finally, I can tell you, from my own 25 years experience in prosecuting individuals engaged in cartels, that I have listened to many lawyers tell me that their individual clients would gladly pay a much higher fine than we were going to recommend the court impose if only we would drop our recommendation that the court sentence the client to jail. On the other hand, I have never heard one lawyer tell me that his or her client would

[5] George B Daniels, US District Court Judge, Sentencing Hearing—22 Apr 2002, *US v Taubman* (SDNY).

spend a few extra days in jail if we would lower our fine recommendation. It may not be proof positive, but it's enough for me, at least, to conclude that relatively short, but fairly certain, jail sentences have the potential to deter hard core cartel conduct in a way that no corporate or individual fine—regardless of amount—ever can.

Discussion from the Second Annual Competition Law Conference—Public Enforcement

PETER FREEMAN

I congratulate Margaret on her presentation—it was very clear, very crisp as always. I thought it had a bit of ambiguity in it, in that at the end you said there were going to be very few prosecutions; I'm always a bit uncomfortable about the arguments for criminalisation, which include the idea that actually there'll be very few cases, and I was wondering, without being too much of a debater, whether the office had correctly forecast the number of cases it would need to bring and the resources that would need to be made available under the Competition Act, or whether you feel confident that you had correctly predicted the number of prosecutions that would need to be brought under the Enterprise Act?

MARGARET BLOOM

Thank you, Peter. First of all, just to say, I think I actually said relatively few—I was very careful—rather than very, but never mind. On your point on resources, given that Alex is sitting in the audience, perhaps he could rush back to Treasury and write out a bigger cheque! But more seriously, the reason why I said relatively few is, we have looked at the cartel cases that we've had to date and we're now uncovering something like one a month, they're getting more serious. Of the ones that we have had so far, we've judged as to which ones of those we would use the criminal powers against. Some of them we are not going to, because it just doesn't merit using the criminal powers; and we think from those that we've uncovered, and at the rate we're uncovering, relatively few a year is actually the number of cases. It may turn out that there are even more, in which case we'll be back to Alex for more resources.

I'm not sure whether you're asking that the fact that there aren't going to be vast numbers of cartel prosecutions means that we don't need the powers; I can't remember the number they have in the States, which is a much larger economy. They do have clearly a fair number, but it's not vast numbers. I think that this is probably something for Jim to comment on—the fact that a number of executives are actually convicted of hard-core cartel and sent to prison, that I think will have a very significant impact in terms of deterrents, and I'm aware, when we talk to in-house counsel who act for firms that have staff both in Europe and in the US, their approach is very different. It's very clear also from the companies we're dealing with, which have international parents, how the US end takes it really seriously; but perhaps that's something for Jim to talk about.

JIM GRIFFIN

Yes—I would just add that we believe in the US, and I think as Margaret says particularly in-house counsel believe, or a number of them believe, that the criminal penalties focus the mind of the individual on the consequences of his or her action, unlike any corporate fine can do. And recently, we've prosecuted cases in the US where I have been told by counsel for European and other foreign executives that their clients, in carrying out the cartel conduct, never anticipated anything other than a corporate fine and believed that therefore it was the corporations' call as to whether they engaged in that conduct or not.

JOHN FINGLETON

I think in Ireland, one of the things that has happened is that boardroom decisions have added competition to the checklist—you know, tax compliance, compliance with other law and so on. Probably that has begun to happen for the first time, and that's a welcome development—I believe that's because of the personal liability of company directors. I would add as well that with the level of fines needed to act as proper economic deterrents, there's a low probability of detection, and given that we're dealing with the criminal burden of proof, a low probability of prosecution when you do detect something that you may believe yourself is a violation. But when you multiply that low probability by the value of the extra profit from a cartel violation, you can get into a situation where it's quite profitable to continue in cartels if the only sanction is a fine on the company.

I think that the alternative, if we really want to deter cartels, is fines that are just so high that they risk putting companies out of business and actually diminishing competition, an argument that's well made in the US; that a proper balance between personal liability and corporate liability is more appropriate. In fact corporate fines, which may ultimately hurt consumers or transfer money from group within society to another, may not be that productive from a public enforcement point of view; whereas we need to come up with effective sanctions. There are some countries in Asia that use things like public apology and so on as well, but sanctions that actually affect the individual making the decision as opposed to things that transfer money from one group within society to another.

MARK CLOUGH

I just wanted to say something from the practising lawyer's point of view. In our firm, we have some concern that the OFT hasn't really appreciated that the Competition Act has had a major effect in this country, and that business is seeking to comply with competition law to a very large extent. It can't be denied, and if you're running the risk of being sent to prison, you'll no doubt focus even more on the subject; but the question is twofold, one of proportionality but secondly of the premature introduction of criminal sanctions in this country, so soon after the Competition Act has come into force. I think I could summarise that viewpoint by saying, shouldn't the industry be given a little more time to comply with the act? Because generally they seem to be wanting to

CLAUS DIETER EHLERMANN

Claus Dieter Ehlermann. Last year in Florence, at our annual competition workshop, we discussed after private enforcement in a special session, the question of fining versus criminal defences. And Jeremy Lever will remember that our American participants, but also I think their European counterparts said, that chief executive offices consider indeed going to prison to be qualitatively substantially different, and one of the participants observed that in spite of highly increased fines in Europe, you never see any effect on share prices. So companies seem not to care; and I don't want to make publicity for one of the books outside, however there is a book by Walter Wills that incorporates an extremely interesting article about how high fines have to be in order to be deterrent if you take into account the chances of not being detected. If you want to cream off, at least cream off the benefits—the companies go bankrupt, and therefore the fines will probably never be high enough to have that deterrent effect.

MARGARET BLOOM

I'd just like to say I totally agree.

MARK CLOUGH

I don't think anyone can deny that—in fact, in Jim's paper he set out the figures, if you don't want to buy the book—sorry Claus. I said before, I don't think you can deny, as I said before, that criminal sanctions really heighten the interest, but the question is whether it's really proportionate, and in this country, whether it's even politically, let alone morally, correct to bring in criminal sanctions only two years after the Competition Act.

MARGARET BLOOM

Perhaps you should have brought in the Competition Act earlier, but never mind.

JEREMY LEVER

It isn't true that we haven't experienced criminalisation in this country. By the time that the Restrictive Trade Practices Act was repealed, a very large number of companies were subject to orders of the Restrictive Practices Court. Breach of those orders was contempt of court, and the directors were liable to be personally fined or sent to prison. They weren't ever, but we have experience of it, and it's quite interesting to ask oneself what was the effect of the widespread but rather erratic and irrational spread of potential criminal liability?

JIM GRIFFIN

It's my understanding that criminal liability attaches to repeat offenders. We've been prosecuting criminal cases in the United States for over 100 years, and I'm not aware of very many repeat offenders—once caught, the conduct stops and is not repeated for some time, generations perhaps. So I don't think that a criminal penalty for a repeat offender in cartel case is really much of a deterrent, because I don't think it was viewed as a realistic possibility.

MARGARET BLOOM

I think Jeremy was actually asking a rather different question—the fact that under old legislation, if you breached the orders that was potentially a criminal offence, as contempt of court in a sense. Maybe the best answer to that is to look—apart from Ireland, there are other states that do have criminal sanctions in the area of cartels. They don't use them very much, and so I think the difference is, if you have the criminal powers in your jurisdiction, is the authority going to use them? I think that's the critical question—I wasn't familiar with what it was like under the Restrictive Trade Practices Act, but I assume that those companies that had an order made against them didn't fear that they were likely to end up with some of their executives facing criminal prosecutions.

ADAM ALDRED

Adam Aldred, Addleshaw Booth & Co. I envisage a practical difficulty if a director of a company for whom my firm acts, and others similarly, comes to them and says I've got a confession to make, I've been involved in this cartel. We don't actually act specifically for that director—we act for the company. I then have a situation where potentially, that person ought to take separate legal advice if the criminal sanctions come in, but I'm also faced with the dilemma: how do I deal with the company's predicament? Do I rush off and ask for leniency, and then, how will that actually impact upon this director, potentially? And I've got a question for Margaret: What steps are there in place to protect or make clear for us that if we go to Europe for leniency, will that have an effect as far as the criminalisation is concerned? And I was also interested in the American experience—how do you deal with those conflicts, and how do the parties get their (drowned out)?

MARGARET BLOOM

Very quickly—on the leniency, going to Europe will not do anything for the UK. What you need to do is go in as soon as you can to Europe, come in to us—the first company in can get civil leniency, their directors and executives can also benefit from criminal provided you're the first one in. Under the criminal one you can also, individuals may be able to get in. We'll be putting out guidance and pro forma no-action letters.

DAVID CORDER

My name is David Corder. The only point I want to make was whether at the end of the contempt proceedings, having done one in the *Readymix Concrete* case, where I think fines were imposed on every company for doing it again as it were (they'd already done it once), to have the order against them. I suspect, I think that most of the companies ended up being fined, and I think the main sanction was having to spend four weeks or something with lawyers, having to give evidence. I think that was probably the most effective system.

And it has happened here; the judge made it quite clear that in any future instances he would consider imprisonment. It was rather unfortunate I think that no publicity was given at all, but he made it abundantly clear that contempt would end up in future cases in imprisonment. I'm not sure that there were any subsequent contempt cases—maybe the experience was too much for everyone in that case.

ENQUIRER

I haven't read the new Irish Act that's just come out, but do the Irish and the British competition authorities envisage that the criminal sanctions can be sought against a participant within obviously your respective jurisdictions, in a pan-European cartel? And if yes, are you concerned about the marked discrepancy between the treatment of individual participants in that cartel between different member states? And if you're not going to use it that way, is there a danger, a concern that small cartels will attract criminal sanctions but the really big ones, stretching across Europe, will not unless they're so big that they stretch into the United States, in which case Jim Griffin can go after them?

MARGARET BLOOM

That's an extremely good question—the answer is yes, we do intend, because it would clearly be invidious if it was just the small UK cartels, it is far more difficult obviously if it's a pan-European cartel, not least because the question about if there's already been a decision, a civil decision made in Brussels, are we then able to bring a criminal case here in terms of rights of defence and so forth? We've had quite a bit of discussion with Brussels on that; we need to consider each case and how it's best handled in terms of who goes first, but it is a very important point; and on your point Peter about whether it's fair to the other members of the big pan-European cartel, we're already in an unfairness position vis-à-vis the US and the non-US. It will only become fair when theft is treated similarly in all jurisdictions.

JOHN FINGLETON

In Ireland, in the design of our law, it is very clear that whether or not there's an effect on trade between member states is immaterial, and that was very deliberate. We could have had a narrow per se rule in the US style for our domestic law, as I said, but we were concerned that we should not be treating the small regional cartels that might exist very harshly and allowing ones that happen to go across borders to go kind of free. I think this is going to be a big issue in the context of modernisation, this is where we discussed this, as to how cases get allocated; and Claus Dieter Ehlermann hosted the conference in Florence where this came up, and the question of case allocation is potentially going to be a very tricky subject in modernisation. That's something that I think we're still grappling with the solution to.

SECOND ENQUIRER

What I'm going to start with is an observation related to the previous discussion, and then a question. The observation is related to the Restrictive

Trade Practices Act—I happen to be the OFT lawyer responsible for the Readymix Concrete case. One of the things that was striking about that case was that the directors who had been made the subject of orders in the 1970s, or directed the company that was made the subject of those orders in the 1970s, carried on participating in cartels almost without a break, and when those orders were given to those companies it clearly hadn't been very effective.

The question I have is in a rather different area; it seems to me that one of the practical problems that criminalisation is going to bring about is that the OFT is likely to find it more difficult to get co-operation from companies, in the context particularly of dawn raids. And the question, or whoever asked the question earlier, made this point to some extent—if you're in a situation where directors are having to get separate advice, and the advice to them is often going to be that they will have to get separate advice once a dawn raid starts, it is actually going to be quite difficult then to get them to cooperate in many of the ways that are essential if a dawn raid is going to be effectively done. Because in practice, most dawn raids rely to a great extent in practice on the co-operation of the companies, and that means the cooperation of the individuals within those companies; and it may be much more difficult to get it.

MARGARET BLOOM

Very briefly—on your point about difficulty in getting cooperation with the companies, actually a number of in-house counsel have already told us that they think when we have the criminal powers, it will enable them to get their staff to cooperate with us better. I don't know what makes you think, George, that at the minute some individuals in companies necessarily co-operate to the extent they should; so I think the position may be rather different.

JOHN FINGLETON

We've had no problem with getting companies to co-operate with us. They've even let us in, as I said.

RHODRI THOMPSON

Yes—Rhodri Thompson of Matrix. There's a future of this change that I don't know has been spelt out, but it is that there is in fact quite a lot of experience in the English courts in recent years of the reverse process, in which criminalised activities, such as VAT fraud or importation of immigrants into the

United Kingdom, are becoming subject to a civil relief. The question's being raised about whether or not the procedural protections that have always been available in the criminal regime should also now be available in the civil regime, which is effectively a quasi-criminal sanction, especially where the sanctions are very severe on the civil side. Has the Office of Fair Trading borne in mind the significant risk that once there is criminalisation and individuals are subject to criminal sanctions, that the procedures, which have always been somewhat under scrutiny in any event for the purpose of imposition of Article 6 of the Human Rights Convention, will become more under scrutiny; so not only will there be the severity of fines, there will also be a crossover problem between the civil and criminal regimes? I think it's inevitable that there will be further pressure brought to bear, not only in the UK but also in Europe.

MARGARET BLOOM

I can be very brief. A good question—yes, we have borne that in mind and it's an issue that we're very conscious of. Thank you.

DEREK MORRIS

We're virtually at an end, but I did promise John Fingleton he would just very briefly respond to two points that Mark Clough raised in his presentation—so John.

JOHN FINGLETON

Mark made the point that criminalisation might be bad for business—I mean, businesses are frequently the buyers in these markets that are cartelised. In Ireland, we've actually had very positive support, for the most part, from business in favour of criminalisation.

The other point he raised, the point about why abusive dominance shouldn't be criminalised, and this is something we gave a great deal of thought to in Ireland, I think that for us there's a big difference between people meeting secretly, usually in hotel rooms, and fixing prices in the style of our competitor is the friend, our customer is the enemy, and people sitting down in board rooms and thinking how do we get a higher share in this market, what I would describe as Microsoft or Intel style. If you were in the business of criminalising people for what are strategic decisions that depend very much on the market facts, I think then I would agree that you have gone too far; but we're not talking about doing that here in the UK, as I understand it, and certainly not in Ireland. I don't think there's any reasonable basis for arguing that criminalisation should extend that way; or to misinterpret what's happening in criminalisation and move in that direction.

DEREK MORRIS

Okay, I'm going to issue the first stop-now order to myself; in fact I think we're three or four minutes over and we should draw matters to a close. Could I just say that I think it's a great credit to BIICL that they have been able to bring together first of all three such key regulatory figures in the enforcement area, and one very distinguished advocate for one of their customers. Do not be fooled by how pleasant and charming they all appear (laughter), they are very much at the very sharp end of this very difficult area, and I do hope you'll agree with me that today has been extraordinarily helpful, bringing them all together; the number of questions is I think strong evidence of that. It's been very helpful and very interesting, and on your behalf I would like to thank them all very much.

CHAPTER EIGHT

Private Enforcement—Papers and Discussion from the Second Annual Competition Law Conference

1. Eurotort with a Europrocedure?

Diana Good*

I. THE IMPACT AND RELEVANCE OF THE ENTERPRISE BILL 2002[1]

For all European competition lawyers, it has been frustrating that notwithstanding the fact that Articles 81 and 82 of the Treaty of Rome have been part of our laws for decades and that there have been many interlocutory decisions and settlements, there is still no body of substantive case law and no awards in damages for breach of these Articles in the English courts and no greater progress in other EU Member States.[2] US lawyers continue to find it hard to credit the absence of a body of case law such as has been developed in the US.

The European Commission is, of course, keen to decentralise and encourage actions before national courts and many legal systems have been trying to help create a Eurotort. The UK (perhaps later in the day than others) is working hard at introducing legislation which will facilitate the private enforcement of competition law. But will it work? Even if it works in the UK, how can it work across Europe? I propose to explore at least some of the issues which arise. And there are many of them—particularly in the kind of cross-border litigation which ensues following the finding by the European Commission of European-wide or even global cartels.

The Competition Act 1998, with its introduction of Chapter I and Chapter II infringements along the lines of Articles 81 and 82, provided an indication of the determination of the Government to bring competition law up to date in the UK. No sooner have these new powers started to be used than on 26 March this year the Government introduces the Enterprise Bill and states its determination to create a world class competition regime in the UK.

The Enterprise Bill represents a huge opportunity for the development of case law in this field which would remove many of the current uncertainties. The drafting of the Bill in relation to private enforcement is a vast improvement on the consultation paper but there is a real risk that the House of

* Linklaters & Associates, London. Paper given at the Second Annual Conference on International and Comparative Competition Law, BIICL, May 2002.

[1] Bill No. 115, introduced in the House of Commons on 26 Mar 2002.

[2] In *Donovan v Electricity Supply Board* [1994] 2 IR 305, the Irish High Court held that the claimants were entitled to damages in respect of an abuse of a dominant position. While damages were not awarded by the court at trial, the court held that it would hear submissions on quantum if no settlement could be reached between the parties.

Commons reading is going to be too superficial in the time available and that a number of important unresolved questions still need attention.

I am going to look at some of the benefits of the Enterprise Bill but also identify a number of problems which have yet to be resolved. For any competition litigators currently involved in competition litigation proceedings, it is fascinating to try to work out what difference this legislation will make and where this might lead in terms of creating a precedent for the creation of a harmonised procedural environment in which the Eurotort might flourish.

II. THE BINDING NATURE OF FINDINGS OF INFRINGEMENT

It is clearly intended that it should be much easier to bring and pursue proceedings in the UK and I believe that the proposals will achieve this at least to a significant extent. The most important aspect of this is probably the proposal that previous findings of infringement should be binding in all courts.

Section 18 will insert a new Section 58A[3] into the 1998 Act by which in any proceedings before the court for damages in respect of Chapter I, Chapter II, Article 81 and Article 82 infringements, the court will be bound by a prior finding of infringement by the OFT.

[3] Section 58A: Findings of the infringements

(1) In any proceedings before the court for damages in respect of an infringement of –

(a) the Chapter I prohibition;

(b) the Chapter II prohibition;

(c) the prohibition in Article 81(1) of the Treaty;

(d) the prohibition in Article 82 of the Treaty;

the court is bound by a decision mentioned in subsection (2) in respect of the infringement.

(2) The decisions are–

(a) a decision of the OFT that the Chapter I prohibition or the Chapter II prohibition has been infringed;

(b) a decision of the OFT that the prohibition in Article 81(1) or Article 82 of the Treaty has been infringed;

(c) a decision of the Tribunal that the Chapter I prohibition or the Chapter II prohibition has been infringed, or that the prohibition in Article 81(1) or Article (82) of the Treaty has been infringed.

(3) Subsection (1) does not have effect in respect of a decision–

(a) before the end of the period during which an appeal may be made under section 46 or section 47, or under the EC Competition Law (Articles 84 and 85) Enforcement Regulations 2001 (S.I. 2001/2916), with respect to a decision of the OFT;

(b) before the end of the period during which an appeal may be made under section 49 or under those Regulations with respect to a decision of the Tribunal (whether a decision falling within subsection 2(c) or a decision on an appeal mentioned in paragraph (a));

(c) before the end of the period during which an appeal may be made to the House of Lords;

(d) and in each case, if any such appeal is made, before the appeal is determined.

It is, of course, already a matter of common law that European Commission decisions are binding (see both *Iberian*[4]and *Masterfoods*[5]) but now the proposals in the Bill put it beyond question that findings by the regulators must be followed by the courts. This will potentially save years of interlocutory argument and mean that proceedings can concentrate on the difficult questions of causation and loss rather than there being any question that the claimant has to re-prove liability.

However, there are still some areas of uncertainty:

(a) What happens if the OFT or the European Commission only find an infringement over a shorter period of time than the total life of, say, the price fixing activity? In those circumstances, will the claimants have to re-prove the existence of a cartel? Indeed, Section 16 (which introduces a new Section 47A[6] into the 1998 Act) indicates that the Competition Appeal

[4] *Iberian UK Ltd v BPB Industries and British Gypsum Ltd* [1996] 2 CMLR 601.

[5] *Masterfoods Ltd (t/a Mars Ireland) v HB Ice Cream Ltd* (C344/98) [2001] All ER (EC) 130.

[6] 47A: Award of damages by the Tribunal

(1) A claim for damages may be made to the Tribunal in respect of an infringement of -

(a) the Chapter I prohibition;

(b) the Chapter II prohibition;

(c) the prohibition in Article 81(1) of the Treaty;

(d) the prohibition in Article 82 of the Treaty;

(e) the prohibition in Article 65(1) of the Treaty establishing the European Coal and Steel Community;

(f) the prohibition in Article 66(7) of that Treaty.

(2) Damages may be awarded in respect of an infringement only if -

(a) the OFT has made a decision that the Chapter I prohibition or the Chapter II prohibition has been infringed;

(b) the OFT has made a decision that the prohibition in Article 81(1) or Article 82 of the Treaty has been infringed;

(c) the Tribunal has made a decision that the Chapter I prohibition or the Chapter II prohibition has been infringed, or that the prohibition in Article 81(1) or Article 82 of the Treaty has been infringed;

(d) the European Commission has made a decision that the prohibition in Article 81(1) or Article 82 of the Treaty has been infringed; or

(e) the European Commission has made a decision that the prohibition in Article 65(1) of the Treaty establishing the European Coal and Steel Community has been infringed, or has made a finding under Article 66(7) of that Treaty.

(3) In awarding damages the Tribunal is to apply the same principles as would be applied by a court in awarding damages for a claim in tort or, in Scotland, delict.

(4) Otherwise than with the permission of the Tribunal, where subsection (2)(a), (b) or (c) applies, no claim under this section may be made -

(a) before the end of the period during which an appeal may be made under section 46 or section 47, or under the EC Competition Law (Articles 84 and 85) Enforcement Regulations 2001 (S.I. 2001/2916), with respect to a decision of the OFT;

(b) before the end of the period during which a further appeal may be made under section 49 or under those Regulations with respect to a decision of the Tribunal (whether a decision falling within subsection (2)(c) or a decision on an appeal mentioned in paragraph (a));

(c) before the end of the period during which an appeal may be made to the House of Lords;

Tribunal may only award damages if a decision as to infringement has been made by any of the OFT, the Tribunal or the European Commission. This would seem to indicate that in circumstances where the claimants wish to claim outside the period of infringement found in the relevant decision, the claimants will have to bring proceedings in the High Court which would not be so bound. Of course, there is a considerable deterrent for claimants wishing to prove the existence of a cartel without the benefit of a regulatory finding of infringement. The cost and difficulty of bringing such a claim may well be prohibitive.

(b) Another point of detail is that under the new Section 58A(2)[7], it would appear to be the case that the OFT first has to reach a decision that there has been an infringement of either Article 81 or Article 82 and the fact of a finding to this effect by the European Commission will not be sufficient to bind the courts.

(c) Finally, the drafting of the provision makes it clear that the new Section 58A[8] will only operate to make findings of infringement binding on UK courts. There is no similar provision requiring the Competition Appeal Tribunal to follow such findings when hearing claims for damages under the proposed Section 47A.[9]

II. A BODY OF EXPERT JUDGES

It will be of significant benefit that there will now be scope for developing a body of judges with genuine expertise in this area. Section 13[10] of the Bill provides that the Competition Appeal Tribunal will consist in any given case of a Chairman with two lay members who might well be an economist and an accountant. It will, of course, take time for a body of judges who

(d) and in each case, if any such appeal is made, before the appeal is determined.

(5) Where subsection (2)(d) or (e) applies, no claim under this section may be made -

(a) before the end of the period during which proceedings against the decision or finding of the European Commission may be instituted in the European Court;

(b) if any such proceedings are instituted, before those proceedings are determined.

(6) This section does not affect any right a person may have to commence civil proceedings in respect of an infringement mentioned in subsection (1).'

[7] See n 3. [8] See n 3. [9] See n 6.

[10] Section 13: Constitution of Tribunal for particular proceedings and its decisions

(1) For the purposes of any proceedings before it the Tribunal shall consist of a chairman and two other members.

(2) The chairman must be the President or a member of the panel of chairmen.

(3) The other members may be chosen from either the panel of chairmen or the panel of ordinary members.

(4) If the members of the Tribunal as constituted in accordance with this section are unable to agree on any decision, the decision is to be taken by majority vote.

(5) Part 1 of Schedule 3 (which makes further provision about the decisions of the Tribunal and their enforcement) has effect.

are truly familiar with competition litigation to be developed but, as and when there is such a body of judges, this will make a huge difference to the development of this area. The fact that the Competition Appeal Tribunal will be the only genuinely UK court capable of resolving disputes emanating from each of England, Wales, Scotland and Northern Ireland will also be of considerable benefit.

III. BUT MULTIPLE POINTS OF ENTRY

However, it is to be noted that the High Court will still have jurisdiction and that there are a number of cases where proceedings will still, necessarily, be commenced in the High Court such as those where the competition rules are used as a shield rather than as a sword. A huge number of Euro issues arise in the context of Euro defences as opposed to Euro claims. Further, although an action may be founded on an infringement of competition law, it is often the case that alternative causes of action (and remedies) will be pursued with respect to the same set of facts. As presently formulated, there is no scope for such actions to be determined by the Competition Appeal Tribunal. The Enterprise Bill does provide for the potential transfer of proceedings between the High Court and the Competition Appeal Tribunal but this variety of points of entry to the courts and the Competition Appeal Tribunal (and the inability of the Tribunal to deal with alternate causes of action) may create difficulties and the potential for inconsistencies between the two developing bodies of case law.

IV. CAUSATION AND LOSS

Once previous findings of infringement are binding on the courts, the real area for dispute resolution will be causation and loss. The Enterprise Bill is more or less silent on this question although it does make clear that 'in awarding damages the Tribunal is to apply the same principles as would be applied by a court in awarding damages for a claim in tort' (see new Section 47A(3)[11]). This appears to be a curiously unnecessary and limiting constraint on the Competition Appeal Tribunal's discretion to resolve many of the questions which remain open in competition litigation. Does this mean that the CAT will not be able to award any other remedies such as restitution or an account of profits? It is a standard part of the weaponry of claimants in cases of breach of Article 81 to claim restitution. There are various reasons for claiming restitution, one of which is the potential for

[11] See n 6.

avoiding what might otherwise be raised as US style pass-through defences.[12] Is it really the case that the Government intends to prevent restitutionary claims in proceedings before the CAT? Whilst one can understand the Government's reluctance to seek to codify rules in relation to loss and causation, it must be the case that the Government intends to give the CAT discretion in this area so that it can develop the law. This is one of the areas which the House of Lords will have to look at, if not the House of Commons.

The fact that the Enterprise Bill does not seek to codify principles in any way leaves it up to the courts and the CAT to develop case law in relation to the complex issues of causation and loss which arise in competition law cases. One indication of the Government's determination that the CAT should develop this area of law are the rules which deal with the withdrawal of proceedings and which are set out in Schedule 3, Part 2 to the Bill at Section 20. This section provides that the Tribunal's rules may make provision preventing a party who has instituted proceedings from withdrawing them without the permission of the Tribunal and further enabling the Tribunal to publish any decision which it would have made in any proceedings, had the proceedings not been withdrawn.

[12] These defences are based on the argument that loss suffered by a direct purchaser may be passed down by them to an indirect purchaser so that the result is that the direct purchaser suffers no (or only some) loss and the remaining loss is suffered by the indirect purchaser. The approach taken in the US varies from State to State. At Federal level, the policy is demonstrated in *Hanover Shoe Inc v United Shop Machinery Corp.* 392 US 481 (1968) and *Illinois Brick Co. v Illinois* 431 US 720 (1977). In *Hanover Shoe*, the Supreme Court held that a passing on defence cannot be argued in order to escape liability for an unlawful over-charge once the direct purchaser has proved injury and the amount of damages. In *Illinois Brick* the Supreme Court held that the plaintiffs who purchased goods indirectly from an antitrust violator could not recover damages for overcharges passed on to them through a chain of distribution. The court held that as a matter of law, only those who purchase directly are 'injured in their business or property' within the meaning of s.4 of the Clayton Act. However, this decision has been strictly limited to actions by indirect purchasers under the Clayton Act, and the Supreme Court in *California v ARC American Corp* 490 US 93 (1989) rejected the argument in *Illinois Brick* that State statutes permitting indirect purchasers to sue for overcharges violated the policy of *Illinois Brick*. The court concluded here that *Illinois Brick* did not pre-empt States from adopting statutes that permit indirect purchasers to recover damages for overcharges paid as a result of violations of State antitrust laws. In *FTC v Mylan Labs, Inc*, 62 F. Supp 2d 25, 37 (DDC 1999), the District Court for the District of Columbia held that the Federal Trade Commission may seek equitable remedies such as disgorgement in a competition case under s 13(b) of the FTC Act. In another ruling in that case (99 F Supp 2d 1) the court held that States with statutes that prompt courts to consider decisions interpreting section 5(a)(1) of the FTC Act (which prohibits unfair or deceptive acts or practices) rather than the Clayton Act would be entitled to seek restitution on behalf of indirect purchasers.

A. Potential for delay

One very real question is whether the development of an adequate body of case law is not going to be hampered by continuing delay. There are two particular areas which indicate that there may still be considerable delays notwithstanding the binding nature of earlier findings of infringement.

The new Section 47A(4)[13] states that no claim may be made 'otherwise than with the permission of the Tribunal' pending an appeal against a decision of the OFT or the Tribunal.

This appears to give the Tribunal the discretion to allow proceedings to be commenced notwithstanding the fact of an appeal in these circumstances and begs the question how far the Tribunal will be willing to go to order the steps prior to substantive trial to be completed.

Of more concern is the provision in Section 47A(5)[14] which indicates that where an appeal is pending against a European Commission decision, no claim may be made until, ultimately, those proceedings are determined. As we all know, appeals first to the Court of First Instance and then to the European Court of Justice can take years. If no proceedings can even be commenced before the Tribunal pending the final resolution of those appeals, there may be very real problems such as the expiry of the limitation periods and/or the very practical problem that witnesses may retire or die or simply fail to recall events which took place many years before.

B. Criminal investigation/prosecution

Another significant cause of potential delay is the fact that the Enterprise Bill also introduces the criminalisation of serious cartels for participating individuals. The fact that there are going to be concurrent civil and criminal regimes may also lead to delay or even prejudice claimants' chances. Although the Bill is silent on the point, the normal course would be for criminal proceedings to be resolved first because of what would otherwise be the risk of prejudice to those criminal proceedings. Indeed, the OFT may not be able to decide in relation to infringement until the criminal investigation and proceedings have been resolved.

The OFT has indicated that it intends only to pursue very few criminal cases but it has to be recognised that the more significant the cartel, the greater likelihood that criminal proceedings may be brought. It is in those significant cartels that claimants may have suffered most loss and therefore are most in need of being given a remedy in damages. It may be that there is

[13] See n 6. [14] See n 6.

even greater prejudice caused to civil claimants than mere delay. What if the criminal prosecution fails? Does this mean that there will be no finding of an infringement by the OFT? If this is correct, in precisely those cases where the claimants may have suffered most loss, the criminal regime may prejudice the recovery of financial compensation.

V. RESOURCES

There are also very real questions as to the resources available to the CAT. It is bound to become very stretched. The Tribunal may find itself dealing with any number of both cross-border international claims and the consumer actions which are introduced by the new Section 47B[15] (inserted in the 1998 Act by Section 17 of the Bill). In circumstances where conditional fee agreements are increasingly popular in group litigation and the Government's proposals include provision for claims to be brought on behalf of consumers, the number of claims brought before the Tribunal may start to swamp it. With the availability of procedural weaponry (such as disclosure) which is not available in civil law jurisdictions, the CAT may

[15] 47B: Claims brought on behalf of consumers

(1) A claim may be made under section 47A by a specified body on behalf of two or more individuals who have claims under that section as consumers and in respect of the same infringement.

(2) A claim may be made on behalf of an individual only with his consent.

(3) If two or more individuals have made a claim as consumers under section 47A in respect of the same infringement, a specified body may with the consent of each individual continue the claim on their behalf.

(4) In deciding any claim made or continued under section 47A by virtue of this section, the Tribunal may award damages to an individual on whose behalf a claim is made or continued.

(5) An individual claims as a consumer if the claim is in respect of an infringement affecting (whether directly or indirectly) goods or services to which subsection (6) applies.

(6) This subsection applies to goods or services which–

(a) the individual received, or sought to receive, otherwise than in the course of a business carried on by him (notwithstanding that he received or sought to receive them with a view to carrying on a business); and

(b) were, or would have been, supplied to the individual (in the case of goods whether by way of sale or otherwise) in the course of a business carried on by the person who supplied or would have supplied them.

(7) A business includes–

(a) a professional practice;

(b) any other undertaking carried on for gain or reward;

(c) any undertaking in the course of which goods or services are supplied otherwise than free of charge.

(8) 'Specified' means specified in an order made by the Secretary of State, in accordance with criteria to be published by the Secretary of State for the purposes of this section.

(9) An application by a body in an order under this section is to be made in a form approved by the Secretary of State for the purpose.

(10) The power to make an order under this section is exercisable by statutory instrument subject to annulment in pursuance of a resolution of either House of Parliament.'

rapidly become a victim of its own success if cross-border claims are brought in before the Tribunal as well.

VI. PROCEDURE: SCOPE FOR HARMONISATION?

As to procedure, provisions are made in the Tribunal's rules for the kind of procedural protection that one would expect to see such as costs, disclosure, witness statements and injunctions but the rules certainly do not seem to provide for any wholesale incorporation of the Civil Procedure Rules. Much of the weaponry introduced by the CPR (such as Part 36 Offers)[16] do not appear to be incorporated in the Tribunal rules. Similarly, the provision for injunctions is cursory. I would urge that real care be taken to incorporate the best of the CPR.

In passing, I observe that Section 16(2)[17] of the Tribunal rules set out in Schedule 3 makes it a criminal offence for a party, without reasonable excuse, to fail to comply with requirements in relation to disclosure or attendance before the Tribunal to give evidence to produce documents. On any basis, this is bound to concentrate the minds of those participating in such proceedings!

There remains a huge job to be done in terms of harmonising the procedural environment. We have a Euro tort but we have no truly harmonised procedural environment in which that Euro tort can flourish.

The Brussels Convention[18] has recently been overhauled by means of the Council Regulation 44/2001 of 22 December 2000[19] but it remains a very imperfect instrument. Even what is meant by the commencement of proceedings (for the purposes of establishing which court is first seized) means something very different from one jurisdiction to another.

The European Commission has repeatedly stated that it wishes to both encourage private enforcement of EU competition law and to decentralise

[16] A Part 36 offer is an offer (made in accordance with the Civil Procedure Rules) to settle a claim made by either party in writing, which may relate to the whole claim or part of it. The Court will take the Offer into account when making any order to costs. The making of a Part 36 Offer will have other consequences on the proceedings as set out in the CPR Part 36.

[17] Schedule 3, s. 16(2): A person who without reasonable excuse fails to comply with -

(a) any requirement imposed by virtue of sub-paragraph (1)(c); or

(b) any requirement with respect to the disclosure, production, recovery or inspection of documents which is imposed by virtue or sub-paragraph (1)(g),

is guilty of an offence and liable on summary conviction to a fine not exceeding level 3 on the standard scale.

[18] The Brussels Convention (1968) on jurisdiction and the enforcement of judgments in civil and commercial matters.

[19] Council Regulation (EC) No 44/2001 of 22 Dec 2000 on jurisdiction and the recognition and enforcement of judgments in civil and commercial matters.

that application of competition law in general. In September 2000, the Commission put forward a proposal for a new Council Regulation which, amongst other things, will give national courts the power to directly apply the exemptions contained in Article 81(3). The proposed Council Regulation specifically acknowledges that private enforcement of competition law before national courts is both desirable and under utilised. The proposed Regulation was generally approved by the European Parliament in September 2001 and is presently being finalised by the Commission. Even if the Competition Appeal Tribunal and the development of a serious body of case law by experienced judges in London is all a huge success, the system is still crying out for real harmonisation on a European-wide basis. The proposed Council Regulation will not address the differences of practice and procedure between the national courts applying EU competition law. The US experience demonstrates how critical it is for claimants to be able to require discovery and compel the attendance of witnesses. In the UK, we have the ability to compel both discovery and witness evidence. The Netherlands has recently introduced some discovery weaponry. But until parties are able to compel such evidence in all jurisdictions, we are unlikely to see the decentralisation which the European Commission wishes to see. Surely the Community should introduce a directive for minimum procedural rules before all national competition courts?

2. Damages in EC Competition Law

David Vaughan, CBE, QC*

I. INTRODUCTION

In any developed legal system there must be a mechanism whereby losses caused by actions contrary to the law may be recovered in an action brought by an individual. Thus Article 10 of the EC Treaty makes it the duty of national courts to ensure the legal protection of rights which individuals derive from Community law. According to Advocate-General Jacobs in Joined Cases C-430/93 and C-431/93 *Van Schijndel v SPF* [1995] ECR I-4705, the underlying assumption of the Treaty is that Community law rights can be protected by national remedies enforced through national courts in accordance with national procedural rules.

In this context, the Court of Justice has developed two important principles: the principles of non-discrimination and the principle of effective protection. By virtue of these principles, the national rules applicable to Community law cases cannot be less favourable than those relating to similar actions of a domestic nature, so that in so far as a Member States allows a damages action for infringement of its domestic competition law, it could be argued on this basis that damages must also be available where the Community Competition laws are infringed. Furthermore, the national rules must not render the enforcement of Community rights impossible or excessively difficult. This latter principle was elegantly articulated by Lord Bingham CJ in *R v Secretary of State for the Home Department, ex p Gallagher*, where he stated that:

> It is a cardinal principle of Community law that the laws of Member States should provide effective and adequate redress for violations of Community law by Member States where these result in infringement of specific individual rights conferred by the law of the Community.

II. DAMAGES IN EC COMPETITION LAW

It has long been recognised that damages were available for breach of Article 82. This has not been seriously disputed since *Garden Cottage Foods Ltd v Milk Marketing Board* in 1983. Although the issue was not decided definitively in that case, Lord Diplock, with whom three other Law

* Brick Court Chambers. Paper given at the Second Annual Conference on International and Comparative Competition Law, BIICL, May 2002. The author gratefully acknowledges assistance received in the preparation of this paper from John O'Flaherty.

Lords agreed (Lord Wilberforce dissenting), refused interlocutory relief on the grounds that damages would be an adequate remedy when the matter came on for final trial. Subsequent cases adopted the approach of the majority in this case however. For example, in *An Bord Bainne Co-operative v Milk Marketing Board* [1984] 1 CMLR 519 at para 24, Neill J stated that although the House in *Garden Cottage Foods* had not decided definitively that a breach of Article 82 gives rise to a cause of action in English law,

> the speeches provide compelling support for the proposition that contraventions of EEC regulations which have 'direct effects' create rights in private law which the national courts must protect.[1]

Similar conclusions were reached in *Bourgoin v MAFF*[2] where Parker LJ considered that *Garden Cottage Foods* was "clear authority that a private law action for breach of Article 86 against an undertaking sounds in damages".

It has also been widely accepted that third parties who have suffered as a result of an agreement in breach of the competition laws can sue the co-contractors for damages: *Plessey v GE* [1990] ECC 384. This proposition was regarded as self-evident by the Court of Appeal in *MTV Europe v BMG Records* [1997] EuLR 100, where Lord Bingham MR stated:

> It is not an issue between the parties that these UK proceedings are legitimate in principle. Articles 85 and 86 have direct effect in this country, and damages for breach by a party claiming to be injured cannot be awarded by the Commission. For that purpose, an action in the national courts is the appropriate means of seeking recompense.

Similarly, on the Community level, in *HJ Banks v British Coal Corporation* Case C-128/92 [1994] ECR I-1209, Advocate-General Van Gerven was of the opinion that

> as a result of its obligation to ensure that Community law is fully effective and to protect the rights thereby conferred on individuals, the national court is under an obligation to award damages for loss sustained by an undertaking as a result of the breach by another undertaking of a directly effective provision of Community Competition law.

III. DAMAGES FOR PARTIES TO AN AGREEMENT CONTRARY TO ARTICLE 81(1)

What was not clear, and indeed was considered unarguable by many, was

[1] This case was disposed of before trial upon acceptance by the claimant of a multi-million pound sum which had been paid into court by the defendant.

[2] [1986] 1 QB 716 at 787D.

whether one party to a contract could sue another party to that contract for damages suffered as a result of the contract being unlawful in breach of Article 81.

In *Gibbs Mew plc v Gemmell* [1998] EuLR 588, a case where the defendant had entered into tied house arrangements with the plaintiffs, the Court of Appeal had held that the defendant had no counterclaim either for damages for breach of Article 81(1) or for restitution for two principal reasons:

1. Article 81(1) was designed to protect competitors of the parties to the agreements; the parties to a beer tie offending Article 81(1) are the cause, not the victims, of the restriction of competition. IN the case of a vertical distribution agreement, the competition which Article 81 protects is competition between third parties and the parties to the agreement, and it is only third party competitors who can recover damages for breach of Article 81.

2. Article 81 not only makes an agreement automatically void, but contains a prohibition and is a penal provision and thus a breach is an illegality. Applying English law principles as laid down in *Boissevain v Weil*[3] and *Tinsley v Miligan*,[4] a party to an illegal agreement cannot claim damages for loss caused to him by being a party to the illegal agreement. The exception to the principle of *in pari delicto* had no application because all parties to the agreement are subject to the prohibition, and in any event Article 81(1) is not concerned with inequality of bargaining power but rather with the effect of the agreement on competition. Further the exception had no application to a claim under an illegal contract.

In *Trent Tavern v Sykes*[5] a differently constituted Court of Appeal followed the decision in Gibbs Mew and declined to make a reference to the Court of Justice. Both Courts (as well as many first instance decisions) contended the contrary view to be unarguable. In both *Langdon* and *Passmore v Morland* the House of Lords refused leave to appeal, without giving reasons (in line with the practice of the House).

IV. *COURAGE* v *CREHAN*[6]

The issues came before the Court of Appeal once again in *Courage Ltd v Crehan* [1999] EuLR 834, one of five tied house cases which came before the Court together. In *Crehan*, the tenant, Mr Crehan, concluded two leases with Inntrepreneur Estates Ltd, jointly owned by Courage Ltd and Grand Metropolitan plc. Under the lease, the tenant was bound to purchase a fixed minimum quantity of beers exclusively from Courage at the "list price"

[3] [1950] AC 327. [4] [1994] 1 AC 340. [5] [1998] EuLR 571.

[6] The author acts for Mr Crehan in the ongoing litigation in this case.

specified in the agreement. The problem arose when the market price for beer at which the tenant's competitors were able to buy from the same brewer became far lower than the list price at which the tenant was bound to purchase. Inevitably, this made the tenant uncompetitive and in this particular case the tenant was forced out of business. Courage brought an action for the recovery from Mr Crehan of £15,000 for unpaid deliveries of beer. Mr Crehan claimed that the beer tie was void as being contrary to Article 81(1). On this occasion the Court concluded that, because the points arose in many cases and were of the greatest importance, it should refer to the Court of Justice a number of questions:

1. May a party to a prohibited tied house agreement rely upon Article 81(1) to seek relief from the courts from the other contracting party?

2. Is the party claiming relief entitled to recover damages alleged to arise as a result of his adherence to the clause in the agreement which is prohibited under Article 81?

3. Should a national law which provides that courts should not allow a person to rely on his own illegal actions as a necessary step to recovery of damages be allowed as consistent with Community law?

4. If the answer to question 3 is that in some circumstances such a rule may be inconsistent with Community law, what circumstances should a national court take into consideration?

The Court of Justice answered these questions as follows:

1. An individual can rely on a breach of Article 81 before a national court even where he is a party to a restrictive contract:

- (a) Article 81 is a fundamental provision which is essential for the functioning of the internal market;
- (b) The absolute nullity provided by Article 81(2) can be relied on by anyone;
- (c) Article 81 is of direct effect which includes granting rights to individuals.

2. A party claiming relied is entitled to recover damages alleged to arise as a result of his adherence to the prohibited clause:

- (a) An absolute bar would be contrary to the principle of effective protection. If a co-contractor has a right not to be subject to a restrictive agreement, declaratory relief would not in all circumstances provide effective protection;
- (b) The existence of such a right to claim damages would positively

strengthen the enforcement of Community competition rules by discouraging unlawful agreements. This is a public policy argument and has wider implications than merely affording a remedy to a co-contractor.

3. Article 81 precludes a rule of national law which bars absolutely a claim for damages simply because the Claimant is a party to the unlawful contract. Such a rule should be disregarded because:

(a) It is contrary to the principle of effective protection;

(b) It would not act to discourage breaches of the competition rules.

4. A Claimant can sue his fellow co-contractor for breach of Article 81 unless the Claimant is significantly responsible for the distortion of competition.

Thus, following the ruling in *Crehan*, a party to a restrictive agreement can rely on a breach of Article 81 of the Treaty to claim damages from the other contracting party, except where that party bears significant responsibility for the distortion of competition.

In determining when a party bears significant responsibility for the distortion of competition, the Court set out two main considerations which must be taken into account:

1. The degree of the Claimant's participation in the unlawful agreement. Relevant considerations here are the extent to which the Claimant actively initiated and formulated the unlawful agreement or encouraged its operation. In this context however, an eagerness to enter into the agreement should not necessarily be equated with a willingness to be bound by terms which act to the Claimant's detriment.

2. The economic position of the Claimant and the respective bargaining power of the parties. The Court referred here to whether the Claimant "found himself in a markedly weaker position than the other party, such as seriously to compromise or even eliminate his freedom to negotiate the terms of the contract and his capacity to avoid the loss or reduce its extent".

V. CONSEQUENCES OF *CREHAN*

In practice, the decision in *Crehan* will mean that companies involved in vertical[7] arrangements will need to take into account when negotiating

[7] Advocate-General Mischo expressly stated in his opinion that the right to damages should not apply to horizontal agreements, and it is difficult to imagine one party to a typical horizontal agreement, such as a price-fixing or market-sharing agreement, being in a markedly weaker position as required under the ECJ's test.

contracts, the risk of a successful claim for damages against them. Companies with significant market power will need to be particularly careful as they may not benefit from the Block Exemption on Vertical Agreements. In particular, the firm will need to guard against using negotiating strategies which may make or appear to make weaker the bargaining position of the other contracting party.

Furthermore, the Court of Justice in *Crehan* was almost certainly significantly influenced by the decision of the US Supreme Court in *Perma Mufflers, Inc v International Parts Corp* (1968) 392 US 134. This raises the possibility of a general move towards a more US-influenced system for the enforcement of competition law.

The *Crehan* decision will also have a significant effect upon the availability of damages in cases in the UK under the Competition Act 1998, by virtue of section 60 of that Act.

Finally, the decision at least raises the possibility of action being taken for damages under Article 81 in what would previously have been considered to be classic abuse of dominance cases, where such a case might not have been taken under Article 82 because of difficulties in proving dominance. For example a margin squeeze perpetrated on a contractual basis which might not have been pursued under Article 82 because the abusive firm, while having significant market power may not have reached the threshold for dominance, might now be pursued under Article 81.

VI. UNCERTAINTIES FOLLOWING *CREHAN*

The decision in Crehan leaves a number of important questions unanswered, including:

1. The ECJ did not expressly set out a precise and positive test to which a contracting party's right to claim damages would be subject. The only clear statement provided was that:

   (a) The right is protected in principle under Community law;

   (b) It may only be excluded where the Claimant bears significant responsibility for the distortion of competition.

2. It is unclear whether a passing on defence will be allowed under Community law or whether the Court of Justice will follow the American approach in not allowing such a defence. This defence arises where for example, the up-stream supplier who is part of a price fixing cartel charges its purchaser an artificially high price which that purchaser then passes on to its own end customers rather than absorbing. In such a case, a passing

on defence w would involved the Defendant saying that the Claimant has in fact suffered zero loss as it has passed all of the increased price on to its customers. The only possible loss then would be lost sales, which may be zero, and will in any event be extremely difficult to quantify.

3. In assessing damages, it is unclear to what extent a Claimant who does not bear significant responsibility for the distortion of should have to give credit for the benefits it enjoyed from the restrictions contained in the agreement.

4. As regards causation, will the "direct causal link" required in State liability cases be applied or will it be sufficient if the Claimant "materially contributed" to the Defendant's injury?

5. What will be the effect of previous Commission or Court of Justice decisions in (a) the same case or (b) analogous cases in actions for damages under Article 81 in the national courts?

6. What will be the standard of proof required by a national court where a plaintiff brings a claim under Article 81? In *Shearson Lehman Hutton Inc v Watson Co Ltd* [1989] 3 *CMLR* 429 at 570, Webster J was of the view that as an infringement of Article 81 carries with it a liability to penalties, he should apply a higher standard of proof than in normal civil proceedings but lower than in a criminal case. On the other hand, in the Irish case of *Masterfoods Ltd v HB Ice Cream Ltd* [1992] 3 *CMLR* 830 at 873, Keane J applied the normal civil standard, namely proof on the balance of probabilities.

VI. CONCLUSION

There is nothing to suggest that the English courts are not more than capable of dealing with cases involving claims for damages for breach of Community (and domestic) competition law. Indeed, I would suggest that the only reason that there has not yet been a successful claim is that the cases taken have either failed to make out one or more elements of the claim, or the evidence simply did not support the claims being made. In any event, the decisions in *Arkin v Borchard Lines* (which is currently before Colman J) and in *Crehan*, in which the substantive claim for damages will be tried in February 2003, will give a much clearer picture of how the English courts are likely to approach this issue.

Annex 1
Recent UK Competition/State Aid Cases as reported in the European Law Reports

EuLR Reference	Name	Type of case	Damages claimed?[1]
[1997] 1	*Iberian UK Ltd v BPB Industries*	Abuse of dominance	Yes
[1997] 27	*Oakdale (Richmond) Ltd v National Westminster Bank*	Anti-competitive agreement and abuse of dominance	No
[1997] 100	*MTV Europe v BMG Records Ltd*	Abuse of dominance	Yes
[1997] 265	*Wilander v Tobin*	Restraint of trade	No
[1997] 277	*Richard Cound Ltd v BMW*	Restraint of trade, block exemption, Art. 85(1)	Yes
[1997] 313	*Wagamama v City Centre Restaurants*	Trade mark infringement	No
[1997] 334	*Benford Ltd v Cameron Equipment*	Distribution agreement contrary to Art. 85(1)	No
[1997] 407	*R v Secretary of State ex p Getty Trust*	State Aid	No
[1997] 435	*Potato Marketing Board v Hampden-Smith*	Abuse of dominance; Art. 37	No
[1997] 535	*Clover Leaf Cars Ltd v BMW*	Art. 85(1); block exemption	No
[1997] 577	*Yorkshire Water Services Ltd v Jarmain & Son Ltd*	Abuse of dominance	No
[1997] 597	*HJ Banks & Co Ltd v BCC*	Breaches of Article 4, 60, 65 and 66 of ECSC; Arts. 85 and 86 EC Treaty	Yes
[1997] 712	*First County Garages Ltd v Fiat Auto (UK) Ltd*	Art. 85(1), (2)	Yes
[1998] 98	*Heathrow Airport Ltd v Forte (UK) Ltd and others*	Abuse of dominance	No
[1998] 116	*Hinde Livestock v Pandoro Ltd*	Arts. 34 and 86	No
[1998] 223	*Intergraph Corporation v Solid Systems*	Copyright infringement; Arts. 85 and 86	Yes
[1998] 253	*R v MAFF ex p The Dairy Trade Federation*	Arts. 5 and 86	No
[1998] 266	*Norbain SD Ltd v Dedicated Micros Ltd*	Abuse of dominance	No
[1998] 327	*Fulton Motors Ltd v Toyota (GB) Ltd*	Dealership agreement; Article 85; block exemption	No
[1998] 350	*Easyjet Airline Co Ltd v British Airways plc*	Cross-subsidy contrary to Art. 86	No (strike out application)
[1998] 438	*R v Customs and Excise ex p Lunn Poly*	State aid; infringement of principles of non-discrimination and proportionality	No

EuLR Reference	Name	Type of case	Damages claimed?[1]
[1998] 483	*Inntrepreneur Estates (CPC) Ltd v Bayliss*	Public house tied lease; Art 85	No
[1998] 493	*Harrison v Mathew Brown plc*	Public house tied lease; Art 85	No
[1998] 507	*Greenalls Management Ltd v Canavan*	Public house tied lease; Art 85; block exemption	No
[1998] 516	*Roberts v Greene King plc*	Public house tied lease; Art 85; block exemption	No
[1998] 530	*Mathew Brown plc v Campbell*	Public house tied lease; Art 85; block exemption; misrepresentation	No
[1998] 540	*Greenalls Management Ltd v Philbin*	Public house tied lease; Art 85	No
[1998] 550	*Parkes v Esso Petroleum Co Ltd*	Agreement contrary to Article 85; misrepresentation; breach of warranty; commercial agency	Yes
[1998] 571	*Trent Taverns Ltd v Sykes*	Public house tied lease; Art 85	Yes
[1998] 580	*Passmore v Morland*	Public house tied lease; Art 85	No
[1998] 588	*Gibbs Mew v Gemmell*	Public house tied lease; Art 85; block exemption	Yes
[1998] 666	*Philips Electronics v Ingman Ltd*	Patent enforcement; Art. 86	Yes
[1998] 699	*Application by Peninsula Securities Ltd for JR*	State aid	No
[1999] 97	*Application by Anley Maritime Agencies Ltd for Judicial Review*	Abuse of dominance	No
[1999] 195	*Williams and Cardiff RFC v Welsh Rugby Union and others*	Arts 85 and 86	No
[1999] 409	*Inntrepreneur Beer Supply Co v Crehan*	Public house tied lease; Art 85	Yes
[1999] 492	*Trent Taverns Ltd v Sykes*	Public house tied lease; Art 85	Yes
[1999] 501	*Passmore v Morland*	Public house tied lease; Art 85	Yes
[1999] 653	*R v Commissioners of Customs and Excise ex p Lunn Poly*	State aid	No
[1999] 755	*Sandvik Aktiebolag v KR Pfiffner (UK) Ltd*	Patent infringement	Yes
[1999] 834	*Crehan v Courage Ltd*	Public house tied lease; Art 85; block exemption	Yes
[2000] 25	*Parks v Esso Petroleum Co Ltd*	Commercial agency; exclusive purchasing agreement contrary to Art 81	Yes
[2000] 232	*Arkin v Borchard Lines*	Abuse of dominance	No

Table (*continued*)

EuLR Reference	Name	Type of case	Damages claimed?[1]
[2000] 276	*Sockel GmbH v The Body Shop*	Refusal to supply contrary to Art 82	No
[2000] 493	*Glaxo Group Ltd v Dowelhurst Ltd*	Concerted practice contrary to Art 81	No
[2001] 80	*HMSO and another v AA*	Abuse of dominance; breach of copyright	No
[2001] 150	*Whitbread plc v Falla*	Beer supply agreement; Art 81	No
[2001] 325	*R v Secretary of State for Trade and Industry ex p BT3G and One to One*	State aid	Yes
[2001] 401	*GIL Insurance Ltd v Commissioners of Cusoms and Excise*	State aid	No
[2001] 770	*Hendry and others v WPBSA*	Abuse of dominance; restraint of trade; Art 81; Competition Act 1998 ss2, 18	No
[2001] 822	*R v SSTI ex p BT3G Ltd and One 2 One*	State aid	Yes

Notes: [1]Many of the cases noted are hearings relating to preliminary issues or claims for interlocutory relief and an indication that damages were not sought does not necessarily mean that damages were not sought in the main action.

Source: European Law Review

Annex 2
References from the UK Courts to the ECJ in Competition/State Aid Cases, 1974–2002

Case No.	Name	Alleged Infringement	Damages claimed?
C-51/75	*EMI Records Ltd v CBS UK Ltd*	Trademark infringement	No
C-238/87	*Volvo (AB) v Erik Veng (UK) Ltd*	Refusal to supply intellectual property rights	No
C-128/92	*HJ Banks & Co Ltd v BCC*	Breaches of Article 4, 60, 65 and 66 of ECSC	Yes
C-18/94	*Hopkins v National Power*	Discrimination contrary to Article 86 and ECSC Articles 4 and 63	Yes
C-453/99	*Courage Ltd v Crehan*	Breach of Article 81	Yes

Sources:(1) The Alec Stone Sweet and Thomas L Brunell Data Set on Preliminary References in EC Law; (2) ECJ

3. The Role of Mediation

Adam Aldred*

Competition litigation is set to increase as claimants become more aware of their rights. Indeed, that pace will quicken as further competition law reforms take effect and individuals who are harmed have more effective rights of redress.

I. WHY MEDIATE

My experiences[1] lead me to conclude that mediation offers an excellent forum for resolving these complex and what would otherwise be very expensive claims. Such claims can thereby be resolved in private whilst preserving confidentiality. It is thus possible to avoid what the defendant may regard as unwanted scrutiny by the press or the competition regulators. Mediation can also preserve ongoing commercial relationships whereas litigation often damages them.

If the dispute were to be left to the civil courts to decide, the outcome can often be difficult to predict as most High Court judges are on unfamiliar ground when dealing with competition cases. On the other hand, mediation leaves the parties in control of the process, and the outcome.

II. WHEN TO MEDIATE

If there is a dispute, it is as important in a competition case as any other to identify the client's commercial objectives. Once identified it is necessary to come up with a strategy to manage the dispute. That strategy will vary depending on whether the claimant is an innocent victim or is also implicated in the anti-competitive behaviour. It will also vary depending on whether the defendant has already been the subject of adverse decisions of competition regulators or courts. For the purposes of this paper, I have approached the question of mediation from the perspective of a dispute involving innocent claimants where there has not been any relevant adverse decision by a competition regulator or court affecting the defendant.

If the client's objective (or a principal objective) is to resolve the dispute,

* Partner, Addleshaw Booth & Co, London. Paper given at the Second Annual Conference on International and Comparative Competition Law, BIICL, May 2002.

[1] Adam Aldred acted for Dillons the Bookstore and then Asda in the High Court litigation that effectively forced UK publishers to abandon the agreement whereby they imposed minimum resale prices on books (ie the Net Book Agreement). In 2001, Adam acted for over 20 claimants alleging, *inter alia*, abuse of a dominant position by a well-known household name.

then negotiation and mediation should be placed at the heart of the strategy from the outset. Failure to do so will mean that the opportunity to negotiate or mediate the dispute to a satisfactory resolution may be lost. This is simply because of the importance of secrecy to defendants in these types of cases: from a defendant's perspective, much of the damage has been done as soon as the allegation has become public and settling the claim with unseemly haste may damage its reputation further. Often, given the PR and regulatory consequences, defendants have little alternative than to fight on. Accordingly, mediations are most effective before the dispute has been made public, court proceeding have been instituted or complaints lodged with regulators.

III. HOW TO MEDIATE

I have compiled the following checklists for the benefit of (1) claimants, (2) defendants and (3) both claimants and defendants.[2]

1. *Checklist for claimants*

- For small and medium sized businesses, taking on a large company and asserting breaches of competition law is both time consuming and costly. Accordingly, if there are others who have suffered similarly, they should band together and speak with a united voice.
- Establish a negotiating committee that comprises an odd number, preferably no more than three. Ensure that it has full authority to seek advice and to represent the entire group.
- Put together a fighting fund and share the financial burden.
- Some claimants may be in an ongoing commercial relationship with the defendant. Those who have ceased trading or have even gone into liquidation as a result of the anti-competitive practices should be invited into the group, as this adds to the group's critical mass and provides tangible evidence of the effect of the anti-competitive behaviour. Also, those who have ceased trading can benefit from any goodwill the defendant may have towards those who still have commercial relationships with it. That goodwill and association may provide them with an invitation to the negotiating table when they would stand no chance by themselves.
- Work through a fully thought out strategy. Depending on the type of case, prepare in final draft form:

[2] Competition litigation involves complex factual and legal issues. Professional advice should always be taken on the application of the law, and the tactics to be adopted, in any particular case.

(1) a complaint to the European Commission and/or Office of Fair Trading;

(2) a Statement of Case fully particularising the claim;

(3) letters to local MPs and MEPs; and

(4) press releases for use as the campaign unfolds (use a good public relations company or a law firm with that capability).

- The best approach then is to let the defendant know that you have all the bullets ready to fire, but not to pull the trigger until you have the opportunity to sit down and negotiate, whether directly or, preferably, through mediation.
- The defendant will want to keep all the bullets in the gun, no matter how 'confident' it might be that the claim is unfounded.
- The simple fact is that if there is any substance to the allegations and the regulators take up the complaint, the potential fines which can be levied by the European Commission or the Office of Fair Trading can make the value of the claimants' claims appear modest.
- The defendant will be more inclined to settle, and settle quickly, the more organised and efficient the claimants appear to be, and depending on the extent to which the defendant wants to continue to trade with the claimants.
- It is vital that the value of the claimants' claims is realistic and will withstand close scrutiny. Engage a forensic accountant to audit the figures, comment on the claim and play devil's advocate, even if the claimants have put together their quantum figures using in-house accountants.
- Consider using econometric analysts to assist in defining the relevant product and geographic markets.
- Ensure that there is clear agreement between the claimants as to how the proceeds of any settlement are to be divided, before a settlement is achieved. This will help avoid the possibility of any disputes between the claimants after the event. Also, the process of distributing any funds to claimants must be transparent and should be properly audited.

2. *Checklist for Defendants*

- Take allegations of anti-competitive practices seriously and undertake an audit to access the risk. External legal advisors should do this task, so as to preserve legal professional privilege in so far as possible.

- A defendant should not underestimate the ability of small businesses to unite behind a common cause.
- Probe, test and challenge any weaknesses in the claimants' case. Obvious areas include the definition of the relevant product and geographic markets, the quality of evidence supporting the allegation of anti-competitive conduct and quantum of loss.
- Make sure the commercial people with the ongoing commercial relationships remain involved and do not abrogate all responsibility to the legal team.

3. *Checklist for both Claimants and Defendants*

- Choose an experienced mediator who has the requisite skills and experience of this type of case or similar complex cases. If the mediator is not familiar with competition law, he or she should be assisted by a pupil mediator who is.
- Be thoroughly prepared.
- Be creative as to possible solutions and be realistic as to the outcome.
- If not already present, claimants should consider introducing, if possible, a non-competition law based claim as an escape route for the defendant. Few people would look twice at a settlement resolving a breach of contract claim or agency dispute.
- If there are confidentiality provisions, such as in a mediation agreement or a settlement agreement, where there are multiple claimants and defendants, each should individually sign a notice specifically confirming and recording their understanding of the confidentiality provisions.
- Finally, a note of caution—any settlement agreement must be competition law compliant. If not, all the parties to it might be susceptible to scrutiny by the competition regulators and exposed to potential fines. This is one reason why the mediator ought to be familiar with competition law or have support from someone who is.[3]

[3] Extracts may be copied with prior permission and provided authorship is acknowledged.

4. Private Enforcement of Competition Rules and its Limits

Professor Denis Waelbroeck*

Contrary to the situation that prevails in the United States, for example, private enforcement of EC competition rules before national courts (through actions for injunctive relief or for damages or otherwise) has remained so far very uncommon in Europe.

The Commission itself, in its White Paper on 'modernisation', arrives thus at the somewhat disenchanting conclusion that—more than forty years after the entry into force of the EC Treaty–

complainants remain reluctant to apply to the national courts (. . .) when they consider they have been harmed by an infringement of Community law', a situation which it attributes to the fact that 'undertakings involved in national proceedings are still able to notify their restrictive practices to the Commission in order to thwart the actions of the body to which the matter has been referred.[1]

Indeed, according to the Commission, the fact that national courts have not the power to exempt agreements under EC Article 81(3) seriously 'hampers application of the Community competition rules by the Courts (. . .) of the Member States'.[2] The Commission hopes however to remedy this situation by reforming the system and more specifically by abolishing the notification procedure and making EC Article 81(3) directly applicable.

How far this reform will remedy the situation has however—rightly in our view—been questioned by several authors.[3] In strict legal terms, it is indeed

* Avocat at the Brussels Bar; Professor in EC Competition Law at the Free University Brussels and the College of Europe, Bruges. Paper given at the Second Annual Conference on International and Comparative Competition Law, BIICL, May 2002.

[1] See White Paper on Modernisation of the rules implementing Arts 81 (ex 85) and 82 (ex 86) of the Treaty, COM(1999) 101 final/2 (12 May 1999), at para 39. The view is thus very often expressed by Commission civil servants that the notification system makes it 'possible to bring court proceedings in practice to a halt by lodging a notification within the Commission' (see eg W Wils, 'The modernization of the enforcement of Arts 81 and 82 EC', Fordham Corporate Institute 2000, p 352). See also eg Schaub ('Modernisation and EC competition law' in Fordham Corporate Law Institute 2001, p 144) who finds it 'untenable that the Commission's exemption monopoly continues to block the appropriate participation of national (. . .) courts in the enforcement of Article 81'.

[2] See recital 3 of the Proposal for a Council Regulation on the implementation of the rules on competition laid down in Articles 81 and 82 of the Treaty, [2000] *OJ* No. C 365 E/284.

[3] See eg S Kon, 'The Commission's White Paper on Modernisation', in Fordham International Antitrust & Policy, 1999, p 239 : 'even to the most optimistic supporter of decentralized enforcement, it is doubtful whether such lack of enthusiasm for domestic enforcement can be attributed solely to the problems occasioned by exclusive jurisdiction of the Commission in applying Article 81(3)'.

difficult to see how the notification procedure and the absence of direct applicability of Article 81(3) can have had any impact *at all* on private enforcement.

Contrary to what the Commission claims, there is clearly no way how a notification could 'thwart' national proceedings.[4] Under Article 9(3) of Regulation 17, the Commission may currently only deprive 'the authorities of the Member States', and not 'the courts of the Member States' of their competence in applying Articles 81 and 82.[5] It can moreover do so only once it has 'initiated a procedure' (a mere notification by the parties does not have this effect; it is necessary for the Commission to take a formal decision to open the procedure[6]). Therefore, the widely held and often repeated Commission view that the notification system has 'thwarted' private enforcement is in my view clearly based—at least legally—on an erroneous reading of the current rules.[7]

Obviously, this is not to say that one should be against the new possibility which shall be given to national courts to apply EC Article 81(3).[8] The new system, in so far as it allows national courts to exempt themselves restrictive agreements has indeed the advantage of logic and simplicity. National courts will no longer have to declare void an agreement which deserves in principle an exemption. In practice however, it seems to me that it is unlikely that this new power will change much because courts would—as past experience shows—always find ways to avoid such an iniquitous result. For my part, at least, I am not aware of any case in the past where an agreement deserving exemption was annulled by a court, simply because the court had not the power itself to exempt it under EC Article 81(3).

So while the 'modernization' project clearly involves some progress as regards private enforcement, in terms of both logic and simplicity, it is also most unlikely that the mere removal of the Commission's exemption

[4] Similarly, a notification does not mean that 'the competition authorities automatically lose their jurisdiction (Article 9(3))' as the White Paper seems to imply at para 39; only the 'initiation of a procedure' by the Commission has this effect.

[5] See ECJ, Case 127/73, *BRT/SABAM*, 30 Jan 1974, [1974] ECR 51.

[6] See ECJ, Case 48/72, 6 Feb 1973, *Brasserie de Haecht II*, [1973[ECR 77, paras 16–8: 'Article 9, when referring to the initiation of a procedure under Articles 2, 3 or 6 obviously concerns an authoritative act of the Commission, evidencing its intention of taking a decision under the said Articles (. . .) the simple acknowledgement of receipt of a request for a negative clearance or of a notification for the purposes of obtaining exemption under Article 85(3) of the Treaty cannot be considered as initiating a procedure under Articles 2, 3 or 6 of Regulation 17'.

[7] See further for my vies, in *Cahiers de droit européen*, 2001, 'La modernization des règles de concurrence', 203 et seq.

[8] Art 6 of the draft new regulation states that 'National courts before which the prohibition in Article 81(1) of the Treaty is invoked shall also have jurisdiction to apply Article 81(3)'.

monopoly will suddenly—through some sort of magic stroke—open the floodgates of private enforcement. Or in other words :

> just as undue optimism was expressed by the Commission that domestic enforcement would be encouraged significantly by its Co-operation Notice, so similar optimism is misplaced if, as appears to be the case, the Commission sees the repeal of Article 9(3) of Regulation 17 and the movement towards directly applicable exemption system as revitalizing domestic enforcement before national courts.[9]

So how can the overall lack of success in effective enforcement of Articles 81 and 82 before national courts really be explained? What does account for the fact that in the EC, competition law is developed quasi-exclusively by a centralized antitrust agency, the EC Commission, under the control of the Court, while in the US the law is almost entirely made by the courts?

Is this due—as is sometimes invoked—to the allegedly excessive readiness of competition authorities to accept complaints and the fact that lawyers prefer as a result the 'easy route' to 'let the Commission do the work' rather than starting actions in court which are more costly and time-consuming?

In my view, and beyond the fact that I am not convinced that competition authorities too readily accept complaints, if private enforcement was a true possibility, it would have been used long ago. Judicial actions before courts are in fact in many ways more attractive for private parties than public enforcement. Indeed :

- in order not to be accused of 'denial of justice', national courts are obliged to apply the competition rules fully, and so to protect the individuals while a competition authority only acts when it finds a public interest in so doing;
- national courts can be quicker than public authorities and can in particular grant interim relief (while interim relief before the Commission remains seldom and takes on average two years to be ordered);
- national courts must give effective remedies, which may include damages, while a public competition authority has more limited powers;
- a national court can also handle in parallel competition law arguments and other arguments, which a competition authority cannot.

[9] S Kon, op cit, loc cit. According to the Commission's new proposal of regulation replacing Regulation 17, the removal of the Commission's monopoly under Art 81(3) is designed to take away workload from the Commission which could be taken over by national courts. According to recital 7 of this proposal : 'National courts have an essential part to play in applying the Community competition rules. When deciding disputes between private individuals, they protect the subjective rights under Community law, for example by awarding damages to the victims of infringements. The role of national courts here complements that of the competition authorities of the Member States. They must therefore be allowed to apply Articles 81 and 82 of the Treaty in full.'

The fact that private enforcement has not been used, despite these numerous advantages, shows in my opinion that the problem lies elsewhere than in mere 'convenience' for the lawyers to let the competition authority do the work.

Nor can the reluctance to use judicial proceedings in Europe in my view be attributed to a 'cultural difference' between Europe and the United States (consisting essentially in a greater level of litigeousness and a stronger competition culture in the United States than in Europe). In my experience, there is indeed at least one thing lawyers can be trusted for, that is to start actions when those are available (from the lawyer's perspective, a court action is undeniably more lucrative than a mere administrative complaint before the Commission).

At the core of the difficulties of private enforcement in Europe are therefore not so much the inapplicability of Article 81(3) by national courts, nor any supposed 'laziness' of lawyers, nor cultural differences, but in my view mainly three reasons, ie (1) evidentiary difficulties, (2) ailing judicial systems and (3) costs.

I. EVIDENTIARY DIFFICULTIES

When looking at decisions of national courts applying EC Articles 81 and 82, it is striking that the only cases reported almost always concern vertical agreements (distribution, agency, franchise, licensing, . . .). In most of these cases, it is one party that is claiming the illegality of a clause in an agreement signed by itself.[10] These actions moreover often fail for, as stated by M van der Woude,[11] courts are rarely 'charmed with a competition law argument raised by the party which itself contributed to or initiated the restrictive practice'.

[10] This was so also in the recent *Courage/Creehan Case* (Case C-453/1999; judgment of 20 Sep 2001) in which the Court of Justice established the conditions for liability for anti-competitive behaviour. The whole problem in that case was precisely to know whether the signatory of a contract could rely on a breach of Art 81(1) of the Treaty before a national court to claim damages from the other party to the contract which—being in a stronger position—had forced on it anti-competitive clauses. The Court of Justice found that 'it is for the national court to ascertain whether the party who claims to have suffered loss through concluding a contract that is liable to restrict or distort competition found himself in a markedly weaker position than the other party, such as seriously to compromise or even eliminate his freedom to negotiate the terms of the contract and his capacity to avoid the loss or reduce its extent, in particular by availing himself in good time of all the legal remedies available to him' (point 33). In *Garden Cottage Foods Ltd.* (House of Lords, [1984] 133), which is one of the very few other cases where damages were granted in the absence of a prior decision of the Commission, the plaintiffs could also rely on a contract which had been unduly terminated in a discriminatory way.

[11] M van der Woude, 'National Courts and the draft Regulation on the application of Articles 81 and 82 EC', in 'Modernisation of the Application and Enforcement of European Competition Law', Leuven, Centre for a Common Law of Europe.

Thus, a rapid check of the 157 cases under EC Articles 81–2 brought before national courts which were reported in the *Cahiers de droit européen* for the years 1967–97 indicates that two thirds (104) of these related to vertical agreements where one party claimed the illegality of clauses in an agreement signed by itself. 15 of the horizontal cases related also to one party in an agreement claiming its illegality (eg excessive conditions imposed by a trade association; unfair conditions imposed by a copyright collection association, etc). The other cases were either a follow-up of a Commission decision, or actions against alleged abuses of dominant position (eg use of an intellectual property right to prevent parallel imports; illegal termination of a contract, . . .), where there was a straightforward abuse which was easy to establish.

Thus the cases were almost exclusively of a *contractual nature.*

The main problems in competition law however arise in relation with horizontal cartels, or certain types of exclusionary abuses of dominant position (such as predatory pricing, discriminatory pricing, excessive pricing, etc), ie the more serious infringements, where the victim is not a *contracting party* who wants to be relieved from his contractual obligations (and to that effect relies on the nullity of the agreement under Article 81(2)), but a *third party* or at least a party who does not have access to confidential information (such as costs) to know whether there is excessive pricing or predatory pricing. In those cases, injury will always result from a—normally secret—anticompetitive practice. In such a case, that third party will in practice face a very troublesome task in trying to prove that there has been an infringement.

Indeed, while it is normally always the applicant who bears the burden of proof, in most of our legal systems—at least the continental ones—*the problem lies first and foremost in the fact that there is no equivalent to the anglo-saxon pre-trial disclosure/discovery procedure*, that is to say there is no right for a party to a procedure to require the opposing party to disclose all 'relevant documents' in its possession. In Belgium for instance, an application may only be made for a Court order to request another party to produce a specific, *identified* document, but never to obtain all documents that may possibly be useful for the case.

A fortiori, in most continental systems there is not only no discovery procedure but also no 'third party discovery' (ie no discovery ordered against a party who is not actually a party to the proceedings).

There is no procedure either to obtain orders for answering *interrogatories*, as they exist in the United Kingdom and in Ireland (in the US, this latter procedure is widely used).

Moreover, the protection of *business secrets* makes it—rightly—very difficult to obtain sensitive documents relating to a competitor, supplier, or customer.

In those circumstances, it is not surprising that—unless the competent public law authorities have already established the restrictive behaviour by a formal decision—plaintiffs stand in practice little chance to clarify the situation in court.

This may explain why—when we look for instance at the above-mentioned reports of the *Cahiers de droit européen*—they do not mention one single case where this has been the case. Similarly (and unless I am mistaken), all references for preliminary rulings made so far to the Court of Justice in competition cases also related either to mere contractual disputes or to straightforward abuses of dominant position (which required no major evidentiary issues). Horizontal issues were very seldom discussed (the only examples that come to my mind are *Zuechner*, *Gøttrup-Klim*, *Bagnasco* and *Vlaamse Reisbureaus*) (see in Annex a table on preliminary rulings by the Court of Justice in competition cases which gives a fair picture of the issues raised).

Also, if I look at my own practice, it seems to me that the only case where I succeeded in establishing a secret cartel was after starting a procedure before a US Court, which ordered discovery (so as to establish whether it had jurisdiction or not). Ultimately, although the US Court found that it had no jurisdiction, the documents thus obtained proved decisive in establishing in Europe the existence of the cartel.[12]

It follows that except in such peculiar circumstances (or possibly also except in the United Kingdom and Ireland which are to my knowledge the only European countries where a disclosure/discovery system exists), it is unlikely that Articles 81 and 82 will ever receive—under the present procedural rules—any meaningful application in Europe outside of mere contractual disputes.[13]

Secondly, beyond the absence of a discovery system, it seems to me that another significant difficulty—which is common to all continental judicial systems—lies in the absence of a *cross-examination* system. Where the procedure—as on the Continent—is not adversarial, it will indeed mostly be very difficult to obtain any meaningful statement from witnesses.

Thirdly, another hurdle (at least in many judicial systems in Europe) lies in

[12] The case having decided by on arbitration court, it remains unfortunately unpublished.

[13] See European Competition Lawyers Forum's Report on the EU Commission's White Paper on Modernisation of the Rules implementing Articles 81 and 82 of the Treaty, 26 Jul 2000, General report by Philippe Chappatte.

the difficulties also to obtain the *appointment of experts*.[14] For instance, in Italy, Article 61 of the Code of Civil Procedure provides that an expert can be appointed only if the judge requires the answering of specific technical questions set out in an order of the Court. Experts play however a crucial role in competition cases both to explain the technical aspects of the case and to address economic issues, such as market definition, possibilities of leveraging, of predatory practices, etc.

For all these reasons, it is clear to me that most non-contractual actions under EC Articles 81 and 82 will generally already fail because of basic evidentiary difficulties.

Fourthly, a further difficulty in the case of *injunction proceedings*, which are generally quoted as one of the main advantages of a procedure for private enforcement, lies in the fact that in the vast majority of cases, national courts will normally dismiss the application as being too complex, and thus going beyond the traditional scope of such proceedings.[15]

Finally, as to *damages*, which are generally quoted as the second main advantage of a procedure for private enforcement, they will normally be excluded in mere contractual disputes where one of the parties claims injury as a result of a contractual provision it has itself signed (which as stated above are and will remain the main cases of private enforcement). Indeed, it will be hard to show causality between the illegal behaviour and the damage as the applicant normally accepted the restrictive clause in signing the disputed contract. Circumstances similar to the *Courage Case* will remain exceptional.

II. AILING JUDICIAL SYSTEMS

A second but no smaller hurdle in the application of competition rules lies in my view in the complexity of issues normally raised by these cases (eg market definition, weighing advantages against restrictions, . . .).[16] This makes it in practice generally a daunting task for national courts who are neither prepared nor equipped for such a challenge. Indeed, even though it is true that the numerous new notices and guidelines surrounding EC

[14] See A-J Braakman, 'The application of Articles 81 and 82 of the EC Treaty by National courts in the Member States' (European Commission, 1997); see <http://europa.eu.int/comm/dg04/law/enten/natintro/eu/maintoc.html>).

[15] See A-J Braakman, 'The application of the modernized rules implementing Articles 81 and 82 EC Treaty in injunction proceedings : problems and possible solutions', Fordham Corporate Law Institute 2001, 161.

[16] In *Delimitis* (Case C-234/1999, judgment of 28 Feb 1991, [1991] ECR I-935), the ECJ has recognized that even for the Commission, this is a complex task, eg to determine whether an agreement forms part of a cumulative network of similar agreements.

competition rules will provide some orientation to national judges,[17] the problem remains that the cases are complicated and time consuming and that national courts can only apply competition law effectively if they have the necessary resources. The reality unfortunately is however that in most of our judicial systems, at least on the Continent, courts suffer from:

> shortages of staff, poor facilities, low salaries, no administrative support, archaic working methods and an endemic lack of funds.[18]

Moreover, the greater emphasis put in the new rules on economic analysis rather than automatic application of a legal rule will not facilitate the courts' task to apply competition law.

All these shortcomings will make it in my experience extremely delicate in many cases to argue competition law before national courts.

Finally, it is unlikely in my opinion that this situation will be greatly remedied by the possibility in Article 15(1) of the proposed new regulation for the national courts to call upon the expertise of the Commission and assist them in the application of the competition rules.[19] This possibility—although in a slightly less elaborated form—has existed for many years,[20] but has never been very successful, at least to my knowledge. Indeed, judges remain in my experience generally reluctant to use this possibility and when the Commission intervenes *ex officio*, this is generally perceived with mixed feelings by the judge (as well as the party against whom the Commission takes position). Moreover, again in my experience, these Commission opin-

[17] See White Paper, at paras 70, 71, and 78.

[18] M van der Woude, op cit, loc cit.

[19] Art 15 of the proposed Regulation reads as follows:
1. In proceedings for the application of Article 81 or Article 82 of the Treaty, courts of the Member States may ask the Commission for information in its possession or for its opinion on questions concerning the application of the Community competition rules.
2. Courts of the Member States shall send the Commission copies of any judgments applying Article 81 or Article 82 of the Treaty within one month of the date on which the judgment is delivered.
3. For reasons of the Community public interest, the Commission may, on its own initiative, submit written or oral observations to courts of the Member States on the subject of proceedings in which questions concerning the application of Article 81 or Article 82 of the Treaty arise. It may have itself represented by competition authorities of the Member States. Acting on their own initiative, competition authorities of Member States may likewise submit written or oral observations to the national courts of their Member State.
To this end, the Commission and the competition authorities of the Member States may request the national courts to transmit to them any documents necessary.'
According to recital 18 of the draft Regulation, the main purpose of these arrangements is to allow for 'consistency in the application of the competition rules'.

[20] See Commission Notice on Cooperation Between National Courts and the Commission in Applying Articles 85 and 86 of the EEC Treaty, [1993] *OJ* C 39, p 5; see also ECJ, *Delimitis*, C-234/89, [1991] ECR I-992 and *van der Wal*, C-174/98 P and C-189/98 P, [2000] ECR I-47.

ions are often drafted by junior staff, without having heard the parties beforehand so that the Commission, after discussion with the parties, may finally come to a conclusion exactly opposite to the one given—a bit too hastily—to the national court.

If national courts have difficulties in the interpretation of the law, they should therefore in my view rather continue to use the preliminary ruling proceeding contained in EC Article 234, where both parties are heard before the ECJ gives its ruling, rather than relying on the Commission to provide them with a correct legal answer.

The procedure in Article 15 of the draft regulation should therefore in my view essentially be useful to obtain factual or technical information (eg are there parallel cases pending before the Commission or elsewhere?). This is also apparently what the ECJ had in mind in its *Delimitis* judgment when it opened the possibility for national courts to request opinions from the Commission.[21]

III. COSTS

A third difficulty, particularly in countries such as the United Kingdom, where the above evidentiary difficulties are not as acute, and where the judicial system is less 'ailing' lies in costs which may act as a significant disincentive in the application of EC Articles 81 and 82.

The rule that the litigant who loses has to pay the legal costs of the litigant who wins clearly discourages claimants given the uncertainties of what they will be able to establish. Moreover, the unavailability of class actions, contingency fee arrangements and treble damages are further reasons that differentiate Europe from the United States and render private enforcement both more costly and less attractive.

[21] See *Delimitis* judgment, quoted above, at para 53:
'53. It should be noted in this context that it is always open to a national court, within the limits of the applicable national procedural rules and subject to Article 214 of the Treaty, to seek information from the Commission on the *state of any procedure* which the Commission may have set in motion and as to the *likelihood of its giving an official ruling* on the agreement in issue pursuant to Regulation No. 17. Under the same conditions, the national court may contact the Commission where the concrete application of Article 85(1) or of Article 86 raises particular difficulties, in order to obtain the *economic and legal information* which that institution can supply to it. Under Article 5 of the Treaty, the Commission is bound by a duty of sincere cooperation with the judicial authorities of the Member State, who are responsible for ensuring that Community law is applied and respected in the national legal system (Order of 13 July 1990 in Case C-2/88, *Zwartveld* [1990] ECR I-3365, para 18).' (emphasis added)

IV. CONCLUSION

In view of the above shortcomings, it seems to me that the Community should indeed not 'expect crowds of lawyers to flock in front of the court buildings in order to file lawsuits on the day the new Council Regulation enters into force'.[22] The Community should realise that if it is serious in its desire for private enforcement, this can only be done by going significantly further in its current decentralization process and envisaging the introduction of harmonized procedural rules allowing for the efficient application of competition rules by national—specialized (?)—courts (these rules should allow discovery proceedings, cross-examination, expert economic evidence, and possibly treble damages, contingent fees, etc).[23] The sad reality is however that this is probably an extremely ambitious task which—knowing at least the shortcomings of the Belgian judicial system—appears slightly unrealistic.

Therefore, before pushing for mere private enforcement, it seems to me that it would be worthwhile seriously considering the respective merits of a system of private enforcement, as it currently exists before US courts, and the current system of public law enforcement applied in the EU. The US system—ie a system exclusively based on judge made law—is indeed not without shortcomings, as courts (and particularly 'grand juries') are not always best trained to judge on such matters, and as moreover discovery procedures may in practice prove to be excessively costly and burdensome.[24] It would therefore in my view be interesting to start a thorough comparison of the restrictive merits of the two systems before embarking in any major reform.

In any event, and whatever the shortcomings of the current EU system may be, it is important that the Commission—and national competition authorities—should realize the limits and difficulties of private enforcement. Public enforcement being currently often the only real alternative open for the victims of the most serious restrictive behaviours, complaints should generally receive serious consideration by public authorities. Interestingly, the CFI recognized in this respect that even where the Commission has no

[22] M Monti, 'Effective Private Enforcement of EC Antitrust Law', Sixth EU Competition Law Workshop, Florence, 1–2 Jun 2001.

[23] See in favour of a harmonization of procedural rules S Kon, op cit, loc cit. In general, the issue is probably much wider than antitrust. One may indeed wonder whether, to get an efficient court system, discovery, cross-examination, etc may not also be a requirement for many more reasons than private enforcement of antitrust law.

[24] 'The unsatisfactory track record of the American courts in antitrust' is for instance discussed by Th. Arthur in 'Application and enforcement of federal antitrust statutes by Courts in the United States', in Modernisation of the Application and Enforcement of European Competition Law, Leuven, Centre for a Common Law of Europe, 2001.

exclusive competence, as for the application of EC Articles 81(1) and 82 (where this competence is shared by the Commission with national courts), the Commission should not ignore the limits to the rights of judicial protection which the national judge is able to grant.[25]

[25] See CFI, *Second Automec Case* (T-24/90), 18 Sep 1992, para 89, [1992] ECR II-2223; CFI, *Riviera Auto Case* (T-185/96 et al), 21 Jan 1999, para 52, [1999] ECR II-93; see also HG Schermers and D Waelbroeck, Judicial Protection in the EU, 6th Edition, Kluwer, 2001, at para 959.

ARTICLE 81 (VERTICAL ISSUES)	ART. 81 (HORIZONTAL ISSUES)	INTELLECTUAL PROPERTY	DOMINANT POSITION (ART. 82)	UNDERTAKINGS ART. 86
LTM v MBU (Exclusive Distribution)	Zuechner v Bayerische Vereinsbank (Concerted Pratice)	Parke, Davis v Centrafarm (Patent Rights)	Greenwich v SACEM (Copyright 82)	Muller (Article 86 (2))
De Haecht v Wilkin I (Exclusive Purchase)	Gettrup-Klim v DLG (Buying Group)	Sirena v Eda (Trade Marks)	Télémarketing v CLT (Tying 82)	Sacchi (Public Monopoly)
Cadillon v H˜ss (Exclusive Distribution)	Carlo Bagnasco (Inter Bank agreement)	Deutsche Grammophon v Metro (Copyright)	Basset v SACEM (Copyright 82)	Debauve (Monopoly)
Béguelin v GL (Exclusive Distribution)		BRT v SABAM II (Copyright)	Bodson v Pompes Funébres (Articles 86 and 82)	Inter-Huiles (Article 90)
Dassonville (Exclusive Distribution)		Van Zuylen v Hag (Trade Marks)	Volvo v Veng (Patent Rights 82)	Roussel v Netherlands (Pricing Legislation)
Van Vliet v Dalle Crode (Exclusive Distribution)		Centrafarm & De Pijper v Sterling Drug (Patent Rights)	Alsatel v Novosam (Article 82)	Van der Haar v Kaveka (Pricing Legislation)
De Norre v Concordia (Exclusive Purchasing)		Centrafarm v Winthrop (Trade Marks)	Maxicar v Renault (Patent Rights 82)	Bond van Adverteerders (Monopoly)
Lancôme v Etos (Selective Distribution)		EMI-CBS (Trade Mark Rights)	Ministére Public v Tournier (Excessive Pricing 82)	Bodson v Pompes Funébres (Art. 86 & 82)
L'Oréal v De Nieuwe AMCK (Selective Distribution)		Terrapin v Termova (Trade Mark Rights)	Lucazeau v SACEM (Excessive Pricing 82)	Höfner v Macrotron (Article 86)
Salonia v Poidomani & Baglieri (Selective Distribution)		Hoffmann-La Roche v Centrafarm (Trade Mark Rights)	Dieglo Call (Article 82)	ERT v DEP (Article 86)
Ciments et Bétons v Kerpen (Resale Prohibition)		Centrafarm v AHP (Trade Mark Rights)	GT-Link v DSB (Article 82)	Mereci v Siderurgica (Article 86)
BNIC v Clair (Price-Fixing)		Coditel v Ciné-Vog (Copyright)	Oscar Bronner (Essential Facilities)	RTT v GB-Inno (Article 86)
AMP v Binon (Selective Distribution)		Membran/K-Tel v Gema (Copyright)	Van der Woude (Scope of Articles 81,82 & 86)	Poucet (Concept of Undertaking)
Pronuptia v Schillgalis (Franchising)		Dansk Supermarked v Imerco		Corbeau (Article 86)
DOMINANT POSITION (ART. 82) (Copyright & Trade Mark)	UNDERTAKINGS ART. 86	RTICLE 81 (VERTICAL ISSUES)	ART. 81(HORIZONTAL ISSUES)	INTELLECTUAL PROPERTY

ARTICLE 81 (VERTICAL ISSUES)	ART. 81 (HORIZONTAL ISSUES)	INTELLECTUAL PROPERTY	DOMINANT POSITION (ART. 82)	UNDERTAKINGS ART. 86
Ahmed Saeed v Zentrale (Price-fixing)		Merck & Co v Stephar (Patent Rights)		Phil Collins (Article 86)
Delimitis v Henninger Bräu Exclusive Purchasing)		Pfizer v Eurim-Pharm (Trade Mark Rights)		Lagauche (Article 86)
Metro v Cartier (Selective Distribution)		Polydor v Harlequin Record Shops (Copyright)		Decoster (Article 86)
Almelo v Ysselmij (Exclusive Purchasing)		IDG v Beele (Counterfeit)		Taillander (Article 86)
Volkswagen (Regulation 123/85)		Keurkoop v Nancy Kean Gifts (Design Rights)		SAT v Eurocontrol (Concept of Undertaking)
BMW (Regulation 123/85)		Coditel v Ciné-Vog (Copyright)		Banco de Credito v Velncia (Article 86)
Van Schijndel (Application of Article 85 by National Court)		Prantl (Design Rights)		Corsica Ferries (Article 86)
Grand Garage Albigeois (Regulation 123/85)		Kohl v Ringelhahn (Logo)		La Crespelle (Article 86)
Nissan France (Regulation 123/85)		Pharmon v Hoechst (Patent Rights)		Saddik (Exclusive Rights)
Fontaine (Selective Distribution) Undertaking)		Cinéthèque (Copyright)		French Insurance (Concept of Undertaking)
VAG v SYD-Consult (Selective Distribution)		Allen & Hanburys v Generics (Licence of Right)		Banchero (Exclusive Rights)
Cabour v Arnor (Selective Distribution)		Warner Brothers v Christiaensen (Copyright)		Job Centre (Exclusive Rights)
Neste (Exclusive Purchasing		Thetford Corp. v Flamma (Patent Rights)		Raso (Exclusive agreement)
		Bayer v Süllhöfer (Patent Licence)		Becu (Article 86 (ex 90))
		EMI v Patricia (Copyright)		Albany (Article 86 (ex 90))
		CNL-Sucal v Hag (Trade Marks)		Brentjens (Article 86 (ex 90))

ARTICLE 81 (VERTICAL ISSUES)	ART. 81 (HORIZONTAL ISSUES)	INTELLECTUAL PROPERTY	DOMINANT POSITION (ART. 82)	UNDERTAKINGS ART. 86
		Cholay (Copyright)		Drijvende Blokken (Article 86 (ex 90))
		Generics v Smith Kline (Licence of Right)		Deutsche Post (Article 86 (ex 90))
		Deutsche Renault v Audi (Trade Marks)		Pavlov (Article 86 (ex 90))
		IHT v Ideal-Standard (Trade Marks)		Van der Woude (Scope of Articles 81,82 & 86)
		Bristol-Myers Squibb (Trade Marks)		TNT/Traco (Article 86 (ex 90)
		PMA Pharma (Trade Marks)		
		Eurim-Pharma (Trade Marks)		
		Graffione (Trade Marks)		
		Merck II (Patents)		
		Phyteron (Trade Marks)		
		Dior v Evora (Trademarks)		
		Sabel v Pume (Trademarks)		
		Loenders-loot (Trademarks)		
		Silhouette International Schmied (Trade Mark)		
		Foreningen af Danske Videogramdistributör (Copyright)		

Discussion from the Second Annual Competition Law Conference—Private Enforcement

SIR CHRISTOPHER BELLAMY

Well, there's a question at the end—how far do we want to develop private enforcement in any event, and where should the balance be between public enforcement and private action? Now, with the benefit of those short presentations, are there any questions from the floor on this issue? Yes, Nicholas?

NICHOLAS KHAN

Nicholas Khan, Blackstone Chambers. First of all, to begin with, a comment rather than a question—I agree with Diana Good's comment about the rather eccentric patchwork of procedural permutations that seems likely to result from the Enterprise Bill. One area that I think has not been touched by the Enterprise Bill, and my knowledge of it is imperfect, is that of interlocutory relief. It's true, as Diana's paper says, that in many cases where High Court action is sought, competition will be used as a shield rather than as a sword, but my understanding is that it will have to be used in particular as a rapier when one wants to seek an injunction, as will often be the case, in connection with a Chapter 2 infringement action. I wonder what the members of the panel think about making use of the expertise of the Competition Appeals Tribunal for interlocutory relief rather than, as seems to envisaged, only for damages cases?

The other question I had relates to the possible developments resulting from *Courage v Crehan*; insofar as the Court explained what it meant about the exclusion of the right of the co-contractor to sue where he bore significant responsibility for the distortion of competition, the Court referred to the question of whether the co-contractor had availed himself in good time of the remedies open to him. The Court seems to be suggesting that this goes not merely to mitigation of damages, but to the very existence of a right to bring an action, and I wonder what members of the panel think about the complications that result in the ensuing litigation, like the final act of *Courage v Crehan*, in the light of that qualification of the Court's judgment. I don't recollect that this question was a live issue in the case before the Court, when it was in fact argued, and seems to have come out in Court of its own volition. Thank you.

SIR CHRISTOPHER BELLAMY

Thank you very much, Nicholas—I'll ask the panel to have a go at those. Could I just say that insofar as there are any questions that concern the Competition Appeals Tribunal, the tribunal itself is indifferent to what happens, that is to say, indifferent in the sense that a referee is indifferent, or doesn't mind what happens—our only interest, if we have an interest at all, is to see that the UK system as a whole is a workable system. I wouldn't want anyone to feel inhibited in any way about commenting on the way in which we should go, from our point of view—we've got quite enough to do as it is. Diana, would you?

DIANA GOOD

Well, there is provision in the schedule to the act, which sets out the tribunal's procedures for interim orders to be made on your injunctions question, and it says that the tribunal can make any order on an interim basis granting any remedy that the tribunal would have had power to grant in its final decision. But I would agree with you, it falls a long way short from the entire injunction panoply that's available under the CPR, and one of the things I've said in my paper is, I would urge the tribunal to take advantage of the best of the CPR. That doesn't necessarily mean taking it on lock, stock and barrel, but certainly the best of it; and I mean, you're absolutely right, in any Article 82.2 consideration, one of the first things you're likely to want to consider is whether or not you need to try to get an injunction.

Of course, a great deal of the case law that we have at interlocutory level has been borne out of that consideration, whether damages are an adequate remedy or whether an injunction is necessary. I think that if the tribunal is to be as successful as I hope it will be, it's going to need to instil in the claimants the confidence that it has the full range of powers available to it and will be able to use them in the same way in which the High Court does.

DAVID VAUGHAN

Thank you—if I can, on the *Courage* point. I think that type of argument was present in the *Factortame* case; I think in the judgment in *Factortame*, the court intimated that people had to move quickly in order to protect themselves. But certainly in *Courage*, it hasn't been an issue up to now—everything is sort of open for issues, I suspect, and we'll just have to wait and see. Of course it would be quite difficult if all the cases had been rejected up to then; it's been unarguable to complain about somebody who didn't start it, and up to then an arguable case—but that may be part of the pleadings rather than the answer to your point.

I think the only other point I'd like to make of course is that the OFT themselves do obviously have powers to take interim measures, and the court itself has power to deal with the interim measures granted by the OFT. One of the problems is, of course, on interlocutory relief in the High Court, which is purely a personal position; and usually the reason for granting an injunction would be the public interest rather than the private interest of an individual. The courts would be reluctant to order someone to do something on an interlocutory basis, or to stop doing something on an interlocutory basis if they were going to try and defend it. *Garden Cottage* was not a great example of how open courts are going to be to grant interlocutory relief, when Lord Diplock said well, they didn't really deserve protection because they were just a small company.

SIR CHRISTOPHER BELLAMY

I've got a question down here—I'm just going to make one comment on David's comment. One thing that exercises my mind from time to time in this area is that when it's a private court of action and you're going for interlocutory relief, then under normal rules you have to give a cross-undertaking of damages. When it's a public enforcement, public interim remedies taken against a firm to stop it abusing its position, it is not normally the case that you ask for a cross-undertaking of damages from the public authority. That's a crucial difference as to who you can get to take the case—but that's just a passing comment.

JOHN FINGLETON

John Fingleton. In Ireland, in fact, they almost do ask for a cross-undertaking from access to damages. We haven't escaped that lightly. (SIR CHRISTOPHER BELLAMY: And do you give it?) Usually the judge has been very nice to us, but we're not exempt. We can ask for it, but it is not yet ordered against us—not yet, but there's no reason in principle why it shouldn't be. In general, our Council have argued very well, but there's no objection in principle.

SIR CHRISTOPHER BELLAMY

Because you're performing a public duty?

JOHN FINGLETON

Yes—because we're acting on behalf of the competitive process and consumers. that's the argument. Just again, on the question of public versus private that Denis raised—the discovery is, even in the civil jurisdiction, and in the jurisdiction we have in Ireland and England it's very limited in a number of respects. First of all, it's very time-consuming, secondly, judges can be extremely cautious in the orders they give for discovery, and thirdly, it's not very useful for dealing with cartel-type cases. So it is very limited, and I think it raises a very serious question at European level about how well-funded our public agencies are—that's going to become critical with modernisation and you know, it really matters if your case goes to an agency that's not well-funded. When I looked at the huge resources afforded to telecommunication regulation across Europe, and at how poorly the competition authorities did, I think there's a public policy gap there.

But I wanted to ask two questions. The first one was in response to Diana Good's comment on Illinois Brick and so on. I've formed the view that it will be very difficult for private parties ever to get damages in Ireland, because of the type of problem you have to pass through defence, and I'm wondering would you recommend in the UK that the Enterprise Bill should actually have a clear rule as to standing in damages in the statute. The second question that comes up is the question of the interaction or co-operation between public and private, and there's a number of issues. We've often gone to court looking for interlocutory relief, and private parties have gone on the same day to the same court at the same time; and that has been very successful.

Secondly, we are constantly asked whether we would file amicus briefs, and we're now finding that reports and other documents we've produced are being called as testimony in courts. Members of the authority and myself have been subpoenaed to give evidence in private litigation; and do you envisage a situation where Margaret Bloom is going to be hauled down to give evidence in private litigation because the OFT has said something in the context of, say, an advocacy report in the past on that market?

SIR CHRISTOPHER BELLAMY

Thank you very much—Diana.

DIANA GOOD

In terms of pass-through, and I'd be interested to hear what Margaret has to say on this, I think that some consideration was perhaps given to codifying an award of damages approach. It doesn't surprise me at all that the act doesn't attempt to do that—it would have been interesting if it had attempted, but it doesn't surprise me. I think that it is still very much open to the Courts and the tribunal, if it gives itself that discretion, to determine this question—I think that it is at large. Clearly in the States there is an extra driving feature, which is a public policy approach in terms of deterrents, but I think we're witnessing exactly that thrust and determination in terms of public policy approach here in the UK. So I think it's entirely up for grabs—clearly it would put it beyond doubt if it were to be legislated for in one way or the other, but as we know, in the States many states have come out with different legislation, dealing with the point themselves. So there is no obvious answer.

SIR CHRISTOPHER BELLAMY

Thank you. Margaret, I don't know whether you want to comment at some point on whether you wish to see any future scope for a kind of informal co-operation between private parties and the OFT, one emphasising civil action and the other as a sort of public authority supporting what the civil plaintiffs are trying to do. Or perhaps we've not got as far ahead in our thinking as that?

MARGARET BLOOM

Well, it was more the case that there's a choice—you can either go through the private process or the public process. I know that one is addressing redress and the other is deterrents, but what we would strongly urge, and in fact the approach we take, is that parties are not using both at the same time, because that is not a good use of resources. So it's really a question of which one is the better one to go to, and that's something that they then get legal advice on; they come to us and if there is a case, there's been very little experience but there's one case that was in the court and was stayed and we continued, and so it's a slightly different point—it's just a question of not using the limited resources to address the different aspects of the same issue at the same time. On your point about cross-undertaking, yes, I agree with everything you said, Christopher—it's an interesting difference between the approach as to if somebody comes to us for an interim measures as to if somebody goes to the Court for protection.

SIR CHRISTOPHER BELLAMY

I suppose one ought, strictly speaking, to say that the question of whether the OFT or the Director of the OFT as it's become, should give a cross-undertaking interim measures proceeding. It's not yet actually been argued before the appeal tribunal, so that's not a question on which there's yet been any decision. And I think that one should also say that the appeal tribunal obviously has to be resolutely open-minded about *Illinois Brick* and all those cases, which are not, as I understand it, uniformly followed in all states in the US—our American friends will comment on that. Until we've had it argued, we're not able to take any position at all on whether there's a passing-through defence or not. So with those comments, are there any other questions? Yes—Peter, and then I think after that there's a lady at the back.

PETER ROTH QC

Just a little footnote to what's been said. First of all, as I understand the US position, there's quite a divergence between federal anti-trust laws and state anti-trust laws. I think it's *ARC America* where it's been upheld the divergence by the Supreme Court, which is how the class actions continue in the state. So the position over there is slightly more complicated. And secondly, I think that one of the difficulties about legislating more clearly in this area, in the way Diana was just raising, is that we are seeking to follow European jurisprudence, and these issues of course haven't been decided in Luxembourg. In some of these damages issues, arguably this one as well, just as *Courage v Crehan*, we would really await or might ourselves have to initiate by reference developments at the level of Luxembourg.

SIR CHRISTOPHER BELLAMY

Well, that again is another very important philosophical point, at which point you move over from the national system to the Community system; or is it a point of law? I think there was a questioner just behind you.

NIAMH MCCARTHY

Thank you. Niamh McCarthy—I just wanted to add a footnote on the *Courage v Crehan* case as well, which is, I spend a lot of my time practising in Paris, and the French Supreme Court, the Cour de Cassation, in its commercial division, has just handed down a judgment in February of this year, so that's post-*Crehan* judgment. The court has found the complete opposite, in that a co-contractor cannot sue for damages under Article 81.1, so I don't know how we're going to go in Europe where there could be such divergence, not only from the procedure point of view but in terms of substance.

SIR CHRISTOPHER BELLAMY

Was that before *Courage v Crehan*, or after?

NIAMH MCCARTHY

Post. I don't know—I wasn't involved in the case, so I don't know if *Crehan* was argued in that case, but the French Supreme Court judgment was handed down about five months after *Crehan*.

SIR CHRISTOPHER BELLAMY

Well, we'll have to see if there's a *demande de réouverture de la procédure oral* or something, I don't know. Yes, I mean, it's the sort of—speaking personally, one is not surprised either at the view that you've just mentioned from the Cour de Cassation, or the view that the Court of Appeal originally took, it's a very traditional view, really, that the judges are inclined to take in that situation. No doubt we'll have to work with *Courage v Crehan*, and it will open up—how far it opens up, of course, is another matter still to be litigated. Any other questions or comments? Yes—Denis.

DENIS WAELBROECK

Yes, I would like to take up two or three points that have been raised. First, on the amicus briefs, I think that one should be cautious there, again, I'm speaking from my own experience with the *de limitis* type of letters issued by the Commission in procedures. I had one case, it was a complex selective distribution agreement that I had notified to the Commission among a number of notification cases, and then there was a procedure about the legality of the selective distribution system. I got a letter of three lines sent by the Commission to the Court that it was a system that would never be exempt as it was so manifestly illegal. I was very surprised, I lost the case before the French court, and three years thereafter I got an exemption from them, partly even negative clearance from the Commission, without having made any modification to the system as notified.

I had two other cases where the judges were so upset by the Commission's sending a letter intervening in the procedure that they interrupted me immediately and said no, we don't want to see this letter. So I think that *amicus curie* briefs may be useful if you give some economic background that the Commission may have on a given market; but the Commission is not well placed on a national competition authority to decide a case on behalf of a national judge. The national judge will hear the arguments of both parties, the Commission can act as a *deus ex machina* and it can be a very junior civil servant who has written the letter, and without any control just decide issues that are often very complicated. So I would ask that you be cautious there.

The other issue is the pass-through issue. I never fully understood the pass-through issue, but it seems to me, and I always regret that the Court of Justice never made the full step as proposed by Advocate-General Maccini and then by Advocate-General Tizzano in the *Comtec* case; either the price is passed on to the customer, but then because you are more expensive, you lost market and also you suffer damage, as in the *Crehan* case. So however you look at it, you lose; you lose either because you will use your margin, or because you lose in terms of market share, so I have difficulties with the very concept of pass-through defence. I don't think that following the suggestion that was made, there is anything in Community law that would prevent the United Kingdom to exclude this sort of defence in the Community law system. Simply, in *Hans Just* and all the other judgments, there is nothing that prevents national systems from having a pass-through defence, but you could exclude it I think.

DAVID VAUGHAN

My reaction on Mike's speech or the question of the Commission is exactly the same as Denis's. The only time I've known any judge being asked to do so was in one of the early beer cases, Mr Justice Morritt in a case called *Bayliss*, and he had no doubt that he could make up his own mind about this matter and that nobody wherever, whether in the OFT or wherever, was going to help him any more than the evidence he'd heard. And I think that I would be very cautious about doing; if the Commission supports you, you rather wonder what is their objective in supporting you if you're against them, and then it may be quite a good thing.

So it just depends—I suspect the judge should deal with the case himself without outside intervention. I very much agree with Denis' point on the pass-through defence; it seems to me that if competition law is to be a deterrent, as the Court of Justice has said, then putting obstacles in the course of the deterrent would be counter to the spirit if not the words of the judgment in *Crehan*. But anyhow, that may be a partisan view, and no doubt that issue, I suspect, will be in the *Crehan* case of not the *Arkin* case at the moment.

SIR CHRISTOPHER BELLAMY

It's worth just mentioning that, I think it's Article 15 of the Commission's modernisation proposals, at least in an earlier draft and I think in the current draft, still gives the Commission the right to turn up in a national court as an amicus and make submissions. That drafting is being stoutly resisted by a number of member states—not all, but a number—and if there are those here who feel that it really is the wrong road to be going down, the sooner those views are put again to the United Kingdom government, the better. Something needs to be done about it—the negotiations are now at a very advanced stage. Yes—any other questions?

DAVID VAUGHAN

Sorry—one other thing—you were talking about cross-undertakings. There was a case that didn't end in a decision, but where the OFT were taking interim measures against a company, where the company was effectively pursuing a complaint by a complainant about a particular conduct, and we argued (I was for the potential defendant) that the complainant should have to give a cross-undertaking for damages. The argued reason for that was that in community law, in cases like *Camera Car* and *NCC*, the coal case that Christopher and I did years ago, there was a requirement that the complainant should give a cross-undertaking. We said that this would be the only way that was consistent with the human rights protection of the company, and that you have to have a cross-undertaking from somebody, and effectively, in that type of case, the public/private sort of case, the complainant should give the cross-undertaking. It didn't revolve in the decision, but if it had, you'd have had the point.

MARGARET BLOOM

One last thought, on the question of discovery. I mean, I'd agree obviously that US discovery is much, much more effective than any discovery that we know; on the other hand, our discovery is very effective. The Netherlands have just introduced discovery rules, in January this year as I understand it, so things may change there. But just one question I have in my mind is, where litigation is pursued for years in this case, pursuing all the discovery opportunities in this case, in relation to the operation of a worldwide cartel, and discoveries are obtained from worldwide cartelists, and then later there is investigation and then litigation in Europe, I have to say that I think there must be a case for the undertakings of confidentiality, which prevent the parties and lawyers in the proceedings in the US. There must be a case for those being lifted so that European proceedings can take advantage of the discovery that's been obtained in the US.

DAVID VAUGHAN

Thank you, if I can say it that would obviously be extremely worrying. Certainly the rules in the United Kingdom, or in England and Wales anyhow, are that you are not entitled to make use of discovery for any other purpose.

MARGARET BLOOM

Absolutely, and I realise that what I'm saying is provocative, but on the other hand, if one's talking about the same cartelists, who have been operating the same cartel, it does seem rather bizarre that one has to go back to square one and with less powerful procedures.

DAVID VAUGHAN

Well, I jumped at the provocative remark.

SIR CHRISTOPHER BELLAMY

If you add in the criminal dimension, all kinds of potential complications arise. I'm rather alarmed by the various comments that have been made in the hall today, and Denis rather demonstrates what I've been trying to say for the last three years, that there are major problems with decentralisation. In the context of this panel, it's in the context of civil enforcement, but I think those people from the Commission here should actually pay some attention to this, and perhaps to go back to what Diana said at the outset, which Denis has reinforced, there must be a need for the co-ordination of procedures and remedies in the European Union if there's going to be decentralisation, and I wonder what you'll think about that.

And finally, I wonder what the panel thinks is going to happen in your court when EC law pushes aside UK competition law; which of course is what is going to happen if there is decentralisation, where there's an effect on trade between member states.

ANOTHER SPEAKER

Well, presumably Christopher will apply Section 60 of the act and apply Community law in that position, as he's bound to do, and lead to disapplication of national law if there's a conflict. I don't see that being a legal problem—there may be all sorts of other problems, but I don't see that it's necessarily a legal problem. Yes.

HARRY WHEAL

Harry Wheal—Section 60, if you read it closely, is a masterpiece of ambiguous drafting (laughter), but no doubt we shall have to cross all these bridges when we get to them. There was an interesting discussion going on in Treviso yesterday, about how Italy is going to handle the modernisation proposals, and certain of the thought was that there should be some system for trying to channel or funnel litigation arising from the modernisation proposals into two or three specific court centres, I think one in Milan, one in Rome and probably one in Naples, so that rather than trying to train the entire judiciary in this rather arcane subject matter, you would at least have some centres where there were designated courts capable of dealing with this litigation, and a small cadre of judges with experience of doing it. I suspect that some solution like that is likely to be necessary in most member states—to start off with, anyhow.

DAVID VAUGHAN

I think that would be very helpful, but I think it's also the case that you have a lot of cases where it's the euro-defence that's coming forward, and so to come back to Nicholas Khan's point about injunctions, it's often the defendants that are actually raising the competition defence. I remember being opposite Jeremy on six or seven different occasions during the Net Book Agreement litigation; we were just being injuncted left, right and centre and we were continuing to say look, we've got a competition defence, and of course you end up before whichever judge to which that plaintiff wants to bring his contractual claim. When you're trying to argue that point. ultimately it may be a question of removing that to an appropriate competition forum.

SIR CHRISTOPHER BELLAMY

Thank you. Well, ladies and gentlemen, I think that does complete our session before lunch. Could I just ask the panellists in the next session, that is after lunch, to be sure to meet before lunch in order to discuss what they're going to say (laughter). I haven't forgotten—you thought I had, but I hadn't. I'm sure you'd like to thank all our panellists for their contribution this morning. Thank you very much.

CHAPTER 9

Analysis of Market Power—Discussion from the First Annual Competition Law Conference, May 2001

JOHN VICKERS

It seems to me that the discussion has raised some extremely interesting and important broad issues about the role of economic evidence and analysis in a legal framework, and has illustrated that very sharply by cases that Derek and others have mentioned. I think we owe it to the next session to finish in about five minutes, so now, questions: I don't want to put anyone on the spot, but this conference was organised by the Institute of International and Comparative Law, these broad issues and the illustrations of them have a long history in US anti-trust, and I thought any perspectives from the jet-lagged would be very interesting. But that's not meant to confine things.

JEREMY LEVER

It used to be said that one of the great benefits of competition was that the intra-marginal purchaser or customer got the benefit of the marginal price; and so, I entirely agree with what Derek Ridyard said this morning, but you do sometimes get monopolists who segment the market by reference to elasticity of demand, and they end up making monopoly profits. That doesn't seem to me to be compatible with consumer welfare, and we should be concerned about that; but is that just a rather special case?

DEREK RIDYARD

I don't disagree with that, and I think that when you're looking at price discrimination, what you're talking about is situations where the intra-marginal consumers don't get the benefit of the marginal precisely, because that's the whole point of price discrimination. I think that the tricky question, when it comes to Mike Walker's comments too, is that. given the comments that Carne has made, which I think are absolutely right in principle, that competition isn't just about productive efficiency, it's about rivalry and the benefits that flow from it: how do you achieve that kind of solution through the application of a prohibition-based law like Article 82? And I think that the difficulty is that it's fine to sit down and take some kind of global optimal, saying that we could try and make this market work better and wouldn't it be nice if we did, but Article 82 doesn't say that, it says that it's illegal to be in a dominant position. And if you're going to do that by encouraging entry that is in some sense inefficient, has higher costs than the incumbent, then you're necessarily putting a lot of obligation on the incumbent firm, the dominant firm, to do things to encourage a common entry even though it's against its private interests to do that. Now of course, competition law is about imposing that kind of judgment, but I think the difficulty is, it's very hard to find a very consistent set of principles that allow you to get to a better world through the application of Article 82 in this format.

JEAN-FRANÇOIS BELLIS

It is concerning the comparative perspective: I think it's very important indeed to look at what is being put on view, and in the area of discounts especially, I think it's clear, and Barry could confirm this, that there is no equivalent in US law to what we have in European law. And there is a good illustration of this strong dissimilarity of practice, which is given by the British Airways case. Last year, Virgin sued British Airways before a New York court, basically alleging anti-trust violations similar to those that were condemned by the Commission in the decision of last year. The case never went to trial—it was dismissed by the judge as being totally devoid of legal merit. So here, we have one area of European competition law in which the new focus on economic analysis is totally absent; in fact what we have are basically rules of business chivalry that are imposed on companies that have the misfortune of having convinced too many consumers that their product is superior. And you know I represented Michelin in that case, and the client one day asked a Commission official: why are you imposing on me obligations that you are not imposing on my competitors? And the answer, I think, summarised very well the spirit in which these rules are developed; the official said well, you are so big, so in your case it's *noblesse oblige* (laughter).

DEBRA VALENTINE

I guess from the US perspective, this concept of things being *per se* forbidden or *per se* allowed really is very odd, it's very strange. The one thing that I do find interesting, and unfortunately I just can't give you enough information about this, is that my sense is that the DOJ's predatory pricing case against American airlines was largely based on a con theory, which does make some sense—I mean, it's quite interesting to ask whether your prices are covering your avoidable costs, but whether they're made in preference to some, or that those actions have been taken in preference to some more profitable alternative. That case was thrown out and since I haven't had a chance to really look at anything the court's done there, I can't give you the answer as to whether the courts have totally dismissed the con perspective, but I think it'll be interesting. I don't think this is an area that we'll see developed in the next administration.

BARRY HAWK

I think the panel has been really kind to US anti-trust law. I mean, there's predatory pricing, and then there's price discrimination. I say too that for price discrimination, we have in the US a separate statute prohibiting price discrimination, the Robinson-Patman Act, which politicians love and will not get rid of—it's clearly intended to protect small boutiques. Enforcers by and large don't like it, economists hate it, so there isn't that much enforcement, but a special statute on price discrimination. There's no good counterpart—well, the Article 82 counterpart is Section 2, monopolisation, and there it's true that most price discriminations as an abuse of dominant position almost invariably lose. So in that sense, you are Salisbury Tower; so it's very tolerant, but it has this special statute that people are embarrassed to talk about, but it's there.

CHAPTER 10

E-Commerce—Discussion from the First Annual Competition Law Conference, May 2001

LORD JUSTICE MUMMERY

My role is strictly non-speaking; I shall attempt to play the part of a silent and sagacious judge, and follow the advice given by Bernard Levin in an article in *The Times*, when the Lord Chancellor announced that he was relaxing the rules and would now allow judges to speak in public. Bernard Levin's comment was that anybody who wanted to listen to a judge speaking in public needed to have his head examined; and in his view, judges should only be allowed to say three things in public. One was 'dismissed with costs'; two was 'usher, will you please open the window'; and three was to thank kindly members of the public who helped a judge across the road. So I shall keep to that role; I shall ask the speakers to keep well within the limits, so that we finish by one o'clock and don't run over into the lunch break, and I shall ask the speakers to follow the example set by all good advocates, which is not to make speeches but to make points. With that advice I'll start with Susan Bright, who wrote the paper, and who's going to highlight some of the issues for discussion by other panel members and, if there's time, by members of the audience. Susan.

SUSAN BRIGHT

Thank you. I thought we might start with the basics—what is e-commerce? What we're going to be talking about today are transactions over the Internet, so that means sales of products and services, either to businesses or to consumers. And those goods or services can be delivered either over the Internet itself, for example information, music, reading the *Wall Street Journal*, or physically—they may still have to be delivered to you by post, or whatever. Generally, when looking at transactions over the Internet, they've been divided into what are called B2B, business-to-business transactions, and then B2C, business to consumers.

What we're talking about is on-line sales, but in relation particularly to B2Bs, they've also developed exchanges, or what might be called e-marketplaces, which bring together a number of suppliers and buyers. The importance of the Internet for transactions is vast; the estimates of how much business is transacted over the Internet already vary enormously, as do the productions for the future, even the next year or two. But what is clear is that business-to-business transactions account for a lot more than business-to-consumers at this stage, probably 90% or more of all transactions are actually business-to-business. The reason for that is because consumers and small businesses are worried about using the Internet, they're worried about safe payment, who they're dealing with, how can they get comeback if they don't like the product that they buy, how are they actually going to get these products delivered to them, and what's going to happen with their personal data. But what is clear is that despite the burst of the dot-com bubble, e-commerce is certainly here to stay. I think the question is more: how quickly will it grow?

So looking at the competition authorities, in many areas the legal and regulatory framework is trying to catch up, and so for example in the European Union we have directives on e-commerce and also on electronic signatures. But in the competition field, the key tools we already have, and they're Articles 81 and 82 of the EC Merger Regulation, and then also national rules of member states in relevant cases. To set the scene, my view is that e-commerce generally should be regarded as pro-competitive; it should lead to integration of geographic market places, it should lead to efficiency, increased transparency, and ultimately downward pressure on prices, hopefully to the benefit of consumers. The authorities have started to take decisions; we've had a number of decisions now both under the EC merger regulation and also Article 81, comfort letters in various cases, and I think we'll see more and more of that, and I know the Commission are looking at a number of cases now. And also, there's been a lot of talking about e-commerce, policy development last year, the US, the Federal Trade Commission has an open forum, there's been an OECD round table on e-commerce and competition, the OFT has commissioned a number of discussion papers.

So now turning to the key issues—I mean, there are many issues in this area, but for today I've listed six, which will be looked at by various members of the panel. The first one is market definition: what will the impact of e-commerce be on market definition? Is e-commerce and on-line selling going to lead to the definition of new markets, or is on-line selling simply a new channel to market? And of course the answer to that may well vary; but taking books as an example, if you want to buy a book you can go into a shop in the High Street, you can buy a book by mail order, and now you can buy a book on line. Are they all different ways of buying books, or are they all separate markets?

Secondly, the geographic market—I think generally one would expect, if anything, that the Internet will expand geographic markets, but that may not always be the case. For example, where products have to be delivered, it's going to be constrained to national markets still. The second issue is market integration. One of the purposes of competition policy in the EU is market integration and breaking down barriers to trade between member states. Clearly the Internet has a tendency to break down geographic barriers too, given the location of the buyer and the seller is becoming much less important. But suppliers may wish to limit the use of the Internet by their distributors and to stop parallel trade—things don't necessarily change, and I suspect that this area may raise some interesting questions.

The third issue is network dominance—turning to exchanges and e-marketplaces, will these have a tendency to network effects, where the value to an individual user of a particular market place will increase as more and more people join it, to the extent that the market may eventually tip so that this particular exchange may dominate, raising serious barriers to entry for other competing exchanges? Is this going to be an area where that's going to be the case? And secondly, structure: looking at a market place, who owns it and who controls it? Many market places are being set up by key industry participants. If they have a successful exchange, will they be prepared to be involved in a competing exchange? Will they want to try to tie in users by requiring exclusivity, exclusive use of the exchange—and does this raise any issues?

Exchange of information is obviously a feature of electronic e-marketplaces, but they bring together competitors, and so there's a concern that this may lead to collusion, and that these market places, or at least the chat rooms that are often associated with them, may well become the smoke-filled rooms of the future. I think all this can be dealt with both by technology to prevent competitors from getting access to sensitive information on each other, and also by various Chinese walls that are put in place in appropriate cases; and indeed the Commission has already started to look at this with its comfort letter on the bollbrocker.com case, which was an electronic brokerage involving six major banks.

Next, access—if an exchange is important and people need to participate in it, will it be necessary to have rules on membership? If an exchange is controlled by a number of key competitors in the market place, will they want to stop people from being involved in that? Will there have to be membership rules? What about discriminatory terms—maybe the owners of the exchange will want to have better terms than others. What sort of issues does this raise?

And finally, joint purchasing and selling—well clearly, issues relating to joint purchasing and selling are not too new, but the Internet I think, given that it makes it much easier to search for products, may certainly tend to make it easier for people to get together to buy things together. Will this be an issue? Well clearly, that depends on what their combined market power is likely to be, and also, whether they are getting together to buy things, for example office supplies, or whether they're getting together to buy things that they're then going to sell on to others. So, what is their market power on the purchasing market, and then what is their market power on the onward selling market? Those are the issues that I would raise. Thank you.

DAVID WOOD

Thank and good morning, ladies and gentlemen. I'm going to pick up on a couple of the practical issues raised in Susan's presentation, which are questions that relate to the applicability of Article 81.1, and these are market integration and marketplace regulation. I should first say that unlike the Commissioner, the comments I'm about to make are my personal views and not those of the Commission. The internal market is more than a customs union; it's an area where states are not allowed to hinder the free movement of goods, services, capital and people. We have competition rules that underpin that single market, and these are intended to prevent private undertakings from taking measures that could amount to private barriers to trade. We could say that competition policy in the EU has the overt purpose of integrating national markets into a unified market. E-commerce fits into this quite well; businesses are of course free to choose whether they trade on the Internet or not, but I think we would say that they're not at liberty to impede other people from trading on the Internet, since this can be a valuable means of breaking down internal borders.

Therefore, while certain conditions can be imposed in the context of selective distribution agreements, I think we will say that limitations on the use of the Internet will amount to hard-core restrictions, and will almost certainly prevent the application of group exemption rules. We can go further and say that conditions restricting the ultimate destination of the goods should not be allowed, and there have been cases in the past such as *Ford/Volkswagen*, and I think Internet sellers should fall into the same category. It may be that those decisions, that jurisprudence will have to be reassessed in the light of the ADALAC judgment and the appeal against that judgment; but in principle the Commission is still committed to using the competition rules against manufacturers that wish to restrict parallel trade. And we saw just recently the press release about the Glaxo dual pricing system.

Secondly, national regulations may be put in place to allow businesses to limit competition between themselves, provided there's no effect on trade between member states. One recent example of this is an Austrian law that allows book publishers to fix book prices, which specifically excludes the cross-border internet book trade. I use this example because laws allowing book price fixing tend to encourage the use of the Internet; first of all they encourage circumvention by booksellers, but they also encourage book buyers to try and find a cheaper place to buy books, and that is now the Internet. So far we've said that if national systems are put in place that allow price fixing measures such as for books, if they are also applied to nationals in other member states, that will probably bring that national law into conflict with community law. There will be an effect on trade between member states.

The third issue there is to say that intellectual property rights may also hamper the development of certain Internet e-commerce services, and now we've got the US case of the Amazon one-click; but that's not really the topic of market integration, so I'll move on to my next topic, which is the regulations put into place to govern B2B exchanges. So far, the Commission has examined four general types of B2B exchange: buyer-managed exchanges, supplier-managed exchanges, market-maker exchanges and content aggregators. The third and fourth of those tend to be not run for the benefit of the owners—the owners tend not to be users of the service. But where the owners do use the service, they are likely to have an incentive to ensure that the market place has rules that favour them. There's certainly an incentive for that; and we would say that market regulations, at first sight, could often be pro-competitive because they provide security and stability and increase the number of people wanting to do business on a particular exchange. So therefore, those kinds of regulation will fall outside Article 81.1. But we also have exclusionary rules, not simply inclusionary rules—rules that might have discriminatory pricing or might refuse access, and the question that has arisen is can we apply Article 81.1 to those kinds of rule, where the exchange is not dominant and where the owners are also users.

So there's no unilateral management and there's no dominance. Under German law, professional associations are obliged to allow businesses to become members if a denial would constitute a competitive disadvantage for the business; but that's an express provision, and there's no such express provision in Community law. So therefore, should we imply such a condition, and apply it to B2B exchanges? That would be akin to treating a B2B exchanges as a trade association, rather than a joint venture; and I think we could say that although the jurisprudence of the courts in Luxembourg is ambiguous, they're the Florimex cases, there's something counter-intuitive about trying to apply old jurisprudence about trade associations to something as modern as a B2B exchange. And I'd say the Commission's case law on commodity exchanges is not particularly helpful either, because it doesn't really analyse what the Article 81.1 issue is.

So what could there be that would bring a B2B exchange into Article 81.1? Again, I'm ignoring collusion and information exchange issues here. Article 81.1.d talks about unjustified discrimination and the application of dissimilar conditions; and so an example of that would be if smaller users were charged more or if there were different entry prices to the exchange. But unlike in the US, in the Robinson Patman Act, we have I think never applied Article 81.1.d to control price discrimination by a single non-dominant undertaking. I suppose that might be looked at again if the customers of the business that wanted access to the exchange were suffering some kind of competitive harm; so on a B2B exchange we're looking at the customer end down at the lower level. But if there were no harm there, it would be difficult to see why you would be worried about a restriction on access to the B2B exchange.

A second possible restriction of competition arises from express or applied agreements to funnel liquidity into an exchange. Well, that's tantamount to an agreement not to do business elsewhere, or to put less of your businesses elsewhere. So you don't need to have overt restrictions, such as: you're not allowed to invest in another exchange, or you're not allowed to do business on another exchange, but equally, that amounts to a restriction of competition.

Very briefly, conclusions: market integration. Clearly if we want to preserve and increase the use of the Internet in the single market, we have to avoid businesses using blocking parallel trade. So I think that is an important issue for us. As for market place regulation, there doesn't seem to be a lot of point at the moment to seek to apply Article 81 to B2B exchange rules unless and until issues of dominance arise. Thank you.

Tim Cowen

I'm just going to make five points and one consequence, or one potential conclusion. I'd like if I may, I cleared this just earlier with Margaret, if everybody would think for the course of these points that they're sitting in the shoes or the position of Margaret Bloom or any competition authority official that is faced with problems in e-commerce or a potential competition complaint in e-commerce or any of the associated high-tech industries. And then at the end, I'd like you to change position and think of it from somebody like me who has to advise companies in this industry about what to do and what the rules are.

My first point is that when you're dealing with market power, the starting point for analysis is frequently the historic information that existed in last year's markets, about what your volumes hit or what your revenues are. In many high-tech industries, they simply didn't exist; so the accusation that you have market power can either be proven by lack of information, it depends what the presumption is and I note with great interest what David Vaughan was saying earlier on, that we need to have some serious focus on, and be brave in that procedure and I think in that context, burden of proof.

So my first point is that historical information, which is the starting point for market analysis, is often absent in many of the cases that are alleged to be competition problems. The second point, and an illustration of this is the *MCI/Wellcome* merger, is that speed of change may exacerbate a competition problem or take it away. You know the market is moving extremely quickly, but you don't know whether that's going to reinforce an existing dominant position or completely obliterate it so it's no longer a problem. And given the fact that you haven't got much information to go on, this does cause some problems from an analytical point of view.

You then have to take account of my third point, which is technology shifts; as a consumer, you are often faced as you go into the High Street, Dixons or wherever, with a bewildering array of products that do more or less the same thing, or tell you that they're doing very similar things. If you're interested in things like palm, you're looking at e-mail, can you use a mobile phone for e-mail, is that going to be a substitute for a little hand-held device? And then you find that there's a press release in the newspaper that you're reading, that someone's invented something that can do all of these things and it's going to be out very shortly. The problem really can be referred to the consumer difficulty faced by CDs and LPs; from an analytical point of view, you might say that they look different, they've got different prices, but from the demand side analysis, you'd say that they're in different markets. But if you don't take account of the system of the CD and the CD player, you fail to understand that the two are actually systems competitive with each other rather than product competitors. I guess the essence of the point about technology shifts is that things may look different, they may have different price characteristics or quality characteristics from a demand side analysis, but they may do more or less the same thing, so they may actually be substitutes. Imagine you're sitting there in a competition authority's shoes trying to work out what the market is.

Fourthly, we have network effects, which you can go into in enormous detail, but suffice it to say that it has either the virtue of taking away monopoly power, or reinforcing it; and you probably don't know which is going to be the outcome, given the information you've got. And then finally, my point is about intent; if you look at predatory pricing, typically looking through the case law, you find that intent is important, in fact critical, looking at cases like *AKCO*. How can you know whether somebody has set out to predate when you don't know what the market is going to look like? It means that you can interpret internal documents, whatever documentation, either as an intent to compete or as an intent to predate—I think it's a difficult, nay almost impossible, moving target to hit. So what's my conclusion, or the consequence—my sixth point? It's that faced with all these things, jurisdiction becomes particularly important, because the competition authority not only is faced with all of these difficulties of analysis, but also they are, as a consequence of the proposals for decentralisation of competition law, faced with not even knowing whether they've got the jurisdiction to deal with it. And then you turn round and you look at things, if you would, from my perspective: is there an issue, faced with all these difficult analytical questions? Perhaps you can see your way through that, but in future it will be even more difficult to work out which jurisdiction would be responsible for giving you an answer.

That's all I'd like to say; I think that as a postscript, I wouldn't give up. I think the analytical tools are there; there's been a debate about whether or not as a consequence of these issues many people are coalescing around, understanding that these are very serious issues, that there really isn't much point in trying to apply competition law in these high-tech markets. I don't think that's the case; I think that some of the procedures and some of the ways in which we analyse these things, and certainly jurisdiction and being clear about who has which jurisdiction, need to be cleaned up and clarified. But I certainly wouldn't give up. Thank you.

STEPHEN WEATHERILL

Thank you. I'd like to add to this portrayal of e-commerce regulations by inviting a widening of the discussion beyond competition law, which we could classify as rules preventing e-traders from doing particular things, most obviously pursuing anti-competitive practices; and also to touch on intervention in the market by public authorities, which requires e-traders to do particular things, most obviously to provide information, for example in the name of consumer protection.

Now the fact that laws of market regulation vary state by state in the European Union may impede inter-state business, including e-business, by forcing traders to adopt different strategies for differently constituted national markets; of course those local rules may be challengeable under the Court's free movement case law, but nevertheless that case law does not establish an absolute rule of mutual recognition, and gives space to the enforcement of local rules. Moreover, a litigation-based strategy for building a reliable internal market for any sector is *ad hoc*, it's *expo facto*, it's insufficient on its own. So in building a stable internal market, there's a supplementary contribution needed from the European Community legislature; that's the terrain of harmonisation, that's common rules for the common market, and in the e-commerce sector it's Directive 31 of 2000.

Now, the e-commerce directive establishes a package of harmonised regulatory requirements, which are imposed on European e-traders via national implementing legislation, which must be introduced by 17 January 2002. These requirements cover, for example, requirements for the e-trader to provide information allowing him or her to be readily identified; and they cover, among other things, restriction on unsolicited commercial communications. Now the essence of the e-commerce directive under Article 3 is to establish a principal home state control—a country of origin principle, the essential point being that the e-trader's home state carries a responsibility to ensure that the e-trader plays by the rules, and then the state at which the e-trade is targeted is disabled from intervening to regulate in a manner that would impede integration. So in the pursuit of the European market, there's been a redistribution of regulatory competencies between states under European community legislation. What that means, as Recital 22 of the Directive makes perfectly plain, is that the home state provides regulatory protection, 'not only for the citizens of its own country, but for all community citizens'.

And we might there contrast competition policy under Regulation 17/62, where the Commission as a European body enforces on behalf of all community citizens, whereas under the e-commerce directive and a great many directives of harmonisation, the state acts for all community citizens. Now I find that already intriguing, consumers outside the e-trader's home state have no stake in that state's political process, yet the e-trader's state authorities are fixed with the responsibility to act on their behalf. That seems to reflect the building of a European market without an accompanying European regulatory structure equipped with general competence; instead, state regulatory structures have to be reshaped by European Community law to accommodate extra state interests affected by market building. So specifically, State X enforces the law for the benefit of State Y citizens. But on that model, there's a pretty strong incentive for an e-trader's home state public authorities to avoid rigorous supervision of their traders, especially where any harm consequent on lax enforcement will be inflicted on citizens of another member state; and I might as a footnote there raise the anxiety that this might be exactly a concern that would be sharpened in the field of competition policy, where we can move into a post-Regulation 1762 world. But assuming that there are incentives for home states to under-enforce the rules, a heavy emphasis is therefore placed on the means for policing non-compliance by home states.

One important development is in the management of the internal market generally, and in relation to e-commerce in particular, is an attempt to develop systems of administrative co-operation in the European Community. That means administrative co-operation that is both horizontal—horizontal in the sense of administrative authorities in different member states working together, and vertical in the sense of member state authorities working more intensively with the Commission to secure an oversight of what's actually happening in the management of the market under European community secondary legislation. And the e-commerce directive reflects that in Article 19, by insisting on the provision of information between relative administrative authorities, thereby to reduce the chances of home state authorities concealing unlawful practices and under-enforcement. It's on that point that I conclude by making an explicit connection back to the lead paper, particularly to the final sentence of it, and to some of the discussion earlier. E-traders are globalised regulators are not, but regulators are increasingly building co-operative networks that reflect their need to map the explosion of transnational commercial activity. That's true of competition law, it's also true of agencies charged with the function of enforcing laws of consumer protection, investor protection and so on. I suppose it's a species of globalisation of regulation, it is what political scientists helpfully label multilevel governance, with overlapping and mutually supporting systems of rule-making and enforcing that transcend the state, as the market already has, but do not simply stick to reconfigure the state at European or at global level. It's a much more subtle process, and to me a much more appealing process. Thank you.

JOSÉ RIVAS

Thank you very much, Mr Chairman. Let me start by saying that I feel myself in quite an awkward position, because you have told us that we have to be very conscious with the time, and my time is already up before I start. And in addition, being the last in the panel also has its disadvantages, which is that some of the sexy points have already gone, and in fact part of my point has already been dealt with. Let me see where I can combine both—finish very quickly and add a little bit to what has already been said on the point, in fact, by David Wood. Basically, what I wanted to talk about is access to an exchange; and to bring matters to the limit, whether those that operate an exchange can refuse access to other parties. We have already been told by Susan and by David that this will depend on the nature of the exchange; and probably it's an issue that will come more often than not in situations where the group of players in the market own that exchange and operate it. I think that I have read too often that from the competition law point of view, access to an e-market shall be open to everyone; and my point is a little bit to try to defend to the contrary.

First of all, it will depend on case by case, and second, there may be more freedom to refuse access than perhaps it is believed. I was relieved to hear David Wood, and if I understood correctly what you said, basically you say that the limit in general is Article 82 rather than Article 81. There may be situations under 81, but rather exceptional, such as the application of discrimination, and that would fall under a paragraph of letter D of Article 81, but so far that has not been applied. So what I'm trying to say here is that I fully agree with that, and that was the conclusion I wanted to reach. I base this in fact, because I think the starting point is freedom of contract; and I would like to recall paragraph 56 of the opinion of Advocate-General Jacobs in the *Oscar Bonner* Case, where he said: 'It is apparent that the right to choose one's trading partners and freely to dispose of one's property are generally recognised principles in the laws of the member states, in some cases with constitutional status. Incursions on those rights require careful justification'. So with this starting point, I think it is as simple as if we create something and we should be able to keep it for ourselves. I'm not denying the fact there have been, or there may be, limits to that position; but that could be, indeed should be, a starting point.

So competition laws should only interfere in a situation with very good reason. I have tried to find commission decisions that could illustrate this point, and I have had to go to the off-line word to try to illustrate it, and I found a relatively new Commission decision dated 10 May 2000 in the *Eurovision* Case. Basically, this case was about a group of broadcasters that complained they had not been admitted to this group of broadcasters the Eurovision or EBU, and they complained that those rules that excluded them were contrary to Article 81.1. The paragraph of the Commission in this decision, I think it is interesting—because the Commission says clearly, 'the Commission considers that the membership rules of a professional association, of broadcasters in this case, cannot in themselves restrict competition within the meaning of Article 81.1. There can be no obligation on such associations under Article 81.1 to accept members against their will. And now two interesting sentences: this is particularly true for associations like the EBU, with a market position that does not allow them to eliminate competition (very important), and third parties wishing to create similar associations are free to do so. There was no difficulty after the analysis of the Commission in creating parallel systems. So it would relate these to B2B, I think they are two extremes.

The first extreme is where Article 81.1 does not create a problem, so there should be no difficulties; the parties should be capable of restricting access to other members; for example, when they are other alternative ways to achieve similar efficiencies, where there are a number of similar market places that they could join. What is the other extreme? The other extreme is Article 82, we have heard: situations where B2B becomes close to an essential facility. And the question that I raise myself is: has this really happened, so far? Are there that many cases—I don't that this is what has happened so far in administrative practice, so even this situation seems quite unlikely to happen. So to conclude, Mr Chairman, in respect of what you have told us, I was glad to hear from the representative of the Commission that Article 82 is most of the time to limit more freedom of the players to decide who can participate and who cannot participate. And to me that is the right application of Article 81 in that respect. Thank you very much.

SUYONG KIM

Suyong Kim from Denton Wilde Sapte. I've got a question that is really a follow-up point to José Rivas's point about access, and also a comment, or a question really, to David Wood. It follows up on the question on access because it's in relation to David's point about discrimination. When you are dealing with an exchange where you have owners of the exchange also participate, and they grant themselves favourable prices, discriminatory prices in one sense or different prices, how can you attack them under Article 81 or under Community law? I mean, obviously you could attack them under Article 82 if they were dominant or if it was an essential facility—but under Article 81, can you elaborate how you would find a case against them?

DAVID WOOD

Well, I hope I was saying that it would be very unusual to try to do so. So far, I haven't seen any logical argument for doing it, unless there's an effect on the downstream consumers; so I would say that I think that we wouldn't try to do that.

VIVIAN ROSE

Vivian Rose, Government Legal Service. You said that it was very unlikely that there would be action under Article 81, and I wonder whether the panel would like to comment on this suggestion; that the development of e-commerce and the new markets, and the question of whether they are new product markets or parts of the old product markets, really highlights perhaps a gap in the EC competition law regime, of the inability to control the unfair creation of a dominant position, that you have to wait, it seems, until the essential facilities have become essential or until the exchange has acquired a dominant position without being able to control the methods in which that market position is acquired. Do you think that there is this loophole? Do you see it as a loophole, and would the e-commerce developments really suggest ways in which one could try and deal with that aspect of competition policy? Maybe David Wood could deal with that.

DAVID WOOD

Thank you. Well, I think this is the problem of tippy markets—you may leave it too long and then find you have got a dominant exchange, but the discussion of Article 81 was to see whether there was anything you could do in the meantime, and I don't really think there is. I think there's an even bigger problem, which is if you have a very volatile market, exchange might become an essential trading partner overnight if liquidity dried up elsewhere. It might be the case with financial services markets, less with, I suppose, other markets.

STEPHEN WEATHERILL

It sounds like a severe risk of over-regulation of essential facilities, which as a doctrine was severely criticised for creating disincentives to invest; if we're going to have a doctrine that says we're going to stop you even getting the essential facilities in the first place, there might be a very serious disincentive to invest, so I'd be very worried about going down that route, I think.

SUSAN BRIGHT

Yes, I was just going to say that if that position of market dominance is created by a merger, then we have the ECMR to deal with that, which can deal with it at that stage; but otherwise I agree, let's wait until somebody gets the dominant position, and then it's still not a problem—let's see if they abuse it.

PROFESSOR SIRAGUSA

Couldn't the panel certainly recognise there may be cases in which even before reaching a dominant position, if you have a very important exchange already in place, even if there are some alternatives; if a supplier is excluded from having access to that exchange, so he cannot use that exchange to offer his products, this must be a situation, could be a situation in which

Article 81 may be applicable. He is in fact excluded from a substantial part of the market on the basis of an agreement between all the members of that exchange, which does not admit him as a supplier. I don't think we need to reach the point of essential facilities or a dominant position to conceive that in cases like that, 81 might apply.

TIM COWEN

Can I just make a comment—I think that both the previous question and this one are potentially quite dangerous. I think that the idea—I mean, what we're actually talking about is some of the most chaotic markets in the world. If you think about the Internet markets, this is the most notoriously chaotic inventive, innovative thing that's happened in the last I don't know how long. If you look at it in that way, and then say well theoretically, there might be a problem about a bunch of people coming together and we need to intervene and regulate other people's access to a treading platform or something, I think you need to tread extremely warily. I think you should stand back at 10,000 feet and say: well, is there really likely to be a competition issue here, given the nature of what's happening in the underlying economics?

CHAPTER 11

National Competition Authorities: Discussion from the Second Annual Competition Law Conference, May 2002

Enrique Gonzalez Diaz

We have two categories of cases; in the first the parties are not concerned about their timing, and consequently they don't resort to the mechanisms that are available to them under the rules of procedure of the court to expedite the treatment of the case. And then we have a second category of cases in which the parties to a transaction are actually interested in preserving the effectiveness of their transaction, and in those cases I think that we have two avenues that I have mentioned before. We have the avenue of interim measures, in which you can seek the debunking of the suspension obligation attached to the prohibition decision; and we have some precedents in which this procedure has been used, *Kali und Saltz* being one of them. And we have the other category of cases, where the parties are more interested in a speedy solution of the case on the merits, and then they resort to the accelerated procedure; we have two pending cases, which are *Schneider/LeGrand* and *Tetra Laval/Sidel*, and as I said before, we will see a judgment in these two cases before the end of the year. So I honestly do not believe that the mechanisms are not there to preserve the effectiveness and speediness of the treatment of cases in court.

Having said that, another set of criticisms has been levelled about the handling of procedures at the administrative level; that is to say, before the actual Commission decision is allotted. And I think that there we have to reflect very seriously before we seek to modify substantially the system that we have now in place; because we can all try to imagine, to play around with the system, try to introduce new guarantees and so on, but I think that we also have to try to preserve the efficiency of the system, the ability of the Commission to come to the right result by having the time to investigate and to clarify the rather complicated issues of law and fact and economics, and consequently, and without saying that we are closed to any potential improvement of the process—and we are more than happy to think about it, as you know we have launched in our green paper this debate, and we are in the process of examining the comments that we have received—we will carefully scrutinise these comments, and we will analyse anything that we could do to improve the system as far as the administrative part of the review process is concerned.

But I think that the guiding principle should be that we should preserve the effectiveness and efficiency of the process, taking into account that at the end of the process there is the possibility, and in my view totally justified, of bringing the case to court and to have a speedy resolution of the case if we use the right mechanisms that are on offer here. I was a bit long, Chairman, but I wanted to clarify this point.

BILL KOLASKY

We have a corporate counsel forum in Washington, twenty counsel from twenty American companies that had been through the merger review process in Europe and in the United States. In April we went over to Brussels, met with members of the Private Competition Bar in Brussels, then members of the European Business community; and then in April we had another corporate counsel forum with senior in-house counsel from some twenty major European companies with US subsidiaries, all of whom had been through the process both in Europe and in the United States. And the concerns that are reflected in this question were very much on their mind; this was something that all of them felt very passionately. They had criticisms for our system for being too costly and too burdensome, for taking too long and not being transparent enough, but what they kept coming back to, and wanting to say over and over again, was this problem and concern about lacks of checks and balances. . . .

When Enrique says that time and delay are not major problems, I must say that this is not what we're hearing from the business community and from practitioners. With respect to the role of judicial review, those practitioners and business community representatives very much stress the slowness of the review process and the fact that even with fast track, by the time you get a judicial decision, your deal is more likely than not dead. Prior to joining the Justice Department last September, I practised extensively in the merger area both in Brussels and in Washington, and I was very pleased that three of the transactions I handled in Brussels, the largest three, we were able to get the transaction cleared during the second phase without a statement of objections. And the reason why we viewed that as critical is that we recognise, and our clients recognise, that had we gotten a statement of objections, it would probably have been extremely unlikely that we would have had the deal cleared.

I was a little surprised at Enrique's statistics, because we went over the reports of the European Commission on merger reviews for the last seven years, and what we found was that in fact, as a percentage of notifications, the number of challenges went up from about 6 per cent in 1996 to roughly 15 per cent in 2000, and came down slightly on 2001 to about 10 per cent or 11 per cent, so that may be the number that he's using.

With respect to the types of checks and balances, as all of you know, in the United States we have as our principal check the fact that we cannot block a merger ourselves. If we don't like a merger, and the parties are not willing to abandon it, we have to file a complaint with the federal court and get an injunction from a federal judge. We usually win those cases, but we occasionally lose; the fact that we know we're going to have to persuade an independent decision-maker that we're right imposes an incredibly effective check on our discretion and our decision-making.

Now that's not to say that this is the best system for you here in Europe; there are obviously other ways to have checks and balances. I've seen some of the comments that have been filed on the green paper, and there are a number of very good suggestions there. One is expanding the role of the hearing officer, so that you have a hearing officer who actually makes a substantive recommendation; another is having the hearing becoming an evidentiary hearing rather than what is more of a legislative-style hearing. Another possibility is expanding the role of the advisory committee, perhaps by designating a lead country, a national competition authority who would be the lead in developing a recommendation as to whether or not to support the staff.

Another suggestion that was made, I think by John Davies at Freshfields, was that perhaps the hearing should be held before the statement of objections, that is, before the staff writes a complaint, in effect. And then the final possibility, which I don't think I've seen in any of the comments, but I think is potentially very valuable, is something that we do in the United States, both at the Federal Trade Commission and at the Justice Department; and that is, we have an independent staff of professional economists, PhD industrial organisation economists—we have fifty of them on the staff. Although they work very closely with lawyers who are investigating the merger, they prepare their own independent recommendation, so that we senior decision-makers have a recommendation from the lawyers and a recommendation from the economists. I can tell you, those recommendations do not always match.

So there are a number of ways to have checks and balances built into the system, other than our system of forcing the Commission to go to court to get an injunction. I'm not saying, because obviously I represent a sister agency now, I'm not commenting on the merits of what we've heard from the business community, but I am saying that there seems to be real concern out there.

JOHN FINGLETON

The Irish Competition Authority has made a submission, and echoes many of the particular points that Bill just mentioned. I think the first thing to say, though, is that this process whereby the Commission holds itself up for public scrutiny is extremely welcome, and it's not appropriate that we should use it as a stick to beat the Commission for what it's doing. I think it's a hugely welcome development, and something that in our own member states we actually need to do more, and to copy the Commission's good example in this regard. From our point of view, I think, in answer to the questions asked, we took the view that the current system works well, and focused on what I would describe as minor modifications in the current system; and they focused on greater use of the advisory committee, making more use of economics, and perhaps employing economists as economists, rather than necessarily just as case officers within the Commission.

Thirdly, on strengthening the role of the hearing officer, I think these are points that have been echoed from other national competition authorities and private players as well. There's one other point I think we made on this, which was that we thought that something should be done about the appeals process and speeding it up; but that's not a marginal change, it might require quite substantial change—I'm not a lawyer, so I can't think whether the treaty needs to be revised. But certainly a special chamber of the Court of First Instance that would hear cases quickly, is something we would see as important, not just for private parties—I think it's very unsatisfactory for the Commission itself if it has to wait three years to get a decision in a case like *Airtours*. It doesn't do much good for investment and for business generally if there's that legal uncertainly hanging over merger policy for a long period of time. So I think that speeding up the appeals process would actually be in the interest of both the private parties and the Commission, and maybe something that we should, although it's a big hurdle, all be working towards.

MARGARET BLOOM

Thank you—just briefly to say that the UK also very much endorses and welcomes the fact that the Commission put this up for discussion. The official UK response, which is up on the DTI web site, is jointly from DTI and OFT and is also based on extensive consultation with business and other who are interested, has very similar themes to the points that both Bill and John have been mentioning. They've put forward as 'suggestions for the debate' the two areas that are put forward as the most desirable ones in terms of considering, which are the possibility of dividing the merger task force into two parts, so that cases will be in one part in phase one and if they move into phase two they will be looked at by a completely different team; and the second one in the pair that we are most interested in is the peer review, from appointing a chief economist with other staff working with them, then the idea of strengthening the role of hearing officer and also the advisory committee with member states; they're ideas that are put up as 'should be considered'. And lastly, reflecting comments that have been made earlier, the idea of reforming the judicial appeal is a much more difficult one, and all that the UK has done is said that this is an area that needs more thought.

JORGEN HOLGERSSON

Thank you. Being Dutch myself, and having read my Montesquieu, I think that I have understanding for what has been said about the separation of functions within the Union. On the other hand, they have it in my country, Sweden, where the competition authority has to go to court in the first instance to have a merger forbidden; and it's a very cumbersome procedure both for business and for the competition authority. So from the business community, they say that we don't care about the legal certainty that you're talking about, and we will have first the procedure and not have this court procedure. So there we are, and I think that you can see some other solutions; one we heard about during the Swedish negotiations of membership in the EEA, where one of the biggest countries within the Union had a contact with us and asked us to ask for a separate body and for merger control. We said that we are demanders in this case, and so we can't put it on the table. Now I have seen a report from a think-tank here in Britain, which proposes something like this separate; so of course you can have other solutions, but it's a lot of work to see how you will manage such a thing. Thank you.

WALTER STOFFEL

Just one remark that I would like to make, and not as a Swiss, but as a continental lawyer. I think there's really something of a cultural difference that comes into play here, and this has to do with the importance of a court system in a society. In order to have such a system work, courts must be used, must be rapid in handing out injunctions; and then go on, confirming a dream for a minute, if we look at how the United States court dealt with Hewlett Packard Compaq case, the challenge brought by Walter Hewlett—I found that really admirable, it was very rapid and in one month or six weeks the whole deal was cleared, the question was there and everything could go on. This would be much more difficult I think before a European, and certainly a continental court, and it has to do with something with them. I had an experience before I was on the Competition Authority—I was in the appeals commission and we had only one case, a merger case, that has been appealed before the Appeals Commission. It was extremely difficult to tell to this body that we cannot allow twenty days of time to prepare briefs for a party, that there must be shorter periods, that we must have a ruling within two months; and they went crazy, how can you do that? Everybody must have the right to explain himself, and so on; it was not two months, it was not half a year, but it was very difficult, and there is quite an English cultural problem, I think.

CLAUS-DIETER EHLERMANN

Thank you very much, Walter. Questions from the audience—I may abuse my role and ask one question, I think. I remember this debate vividly with respect to the Commission's action under 81 and 82; is it really possible to confine the debate to mergers? Isn't it a question of separation of functions much more urgent, to a certain extent, with respect to fining hard-core cartels? Right, I saw an arm raised over there—yes?

JOANNA MCDWYER

Joanna McDwyer, from FIPRA. I'd like to ask Enrique Gonzalez Diaz if he could comment please on the inter-service consultation procedure for mergers, because we've talked quite a lot in the course of this discussion about the internal checks and balances within the process, and I would quite like to hear your views about how these actually work when, for example, the merger task force consults the other parts of the Commission, for example, the parts of the Commission dealing with industry, DG Enterprise, Economics and DG Economic and Financial Affairs, And specifically, would you ever envisage an enhanced role, perhaps for the economists, in the Economic and Financial Services, who are in a sense detached—they are in a different part of the European Commission from the merger task force, where you have your lawyers and legal team and economists advising you? Within DG Economic and Financial Affairs there is a team of economists; and I wonder if there are circumstances in which we might envisage an enhanced role for those economists? At the moment, their role is purely advisory; and they tend to become involved when we are looking at phase two cases.

ENRIQUE GONZALEZ DIAZ

If you don't mind, I will make some comments on the comments of the other panellists and in particular on the comments made by Bill Kolasky. I read that there are complaints actually on both sides of the Atlantic; European companies also complained bitterly about the procedure in the United States, they have characterised the procedure as a 'black box', because they are unable to know exactly what is going on until the moment when they are disclosed the bad news that we are going to take you to court unless a settlement is put to us. I know that this is a very unfair characterisation of the way things are done in the United States, because I know that is not the way in which they are done in practice, but we hear these complaints too, and we know that you are reviewing those procedures too. By the same token, I would like to stress that we are more than open to considering any improvements, manageable improvements to our system that would make our system better. However, the only claim that I am not willing to accept at this stage is that we don't have an effective judicial review. When I look at the United States and the so-called 'fast' delivery of judgments, we are always referring to the delivery of a judgment on interim measures and on injunctive relief; yes, there you can get a judgment relatively quickly, but if you want to appeal that judgment and want a judgment on the merits of the case, that takes much longer.

Now if we look at the situation in Europe, we have also a system of injunctive relief; if the Commission takes a decision prohibiting a deal, which essentially means that you cannot carry out a transaction, this transaction can be challenged in court, and the operative part of the decision whereby you cannot carry on with a transaction can be suspended by the court. I remind you of the facts of *IMS*; in *IMS*, the Commission takes a decision ordering to do something, and the court within a very short period of time suspends the decision, despite the serious implications of the suspension on the viability of one of the complainants. The complaint put to the President of the Court in that case is, if you suspend this decision, this company is going to go out of business. Despite the huge implications of that particular decision, the President of the Court, after looking at the facts, came to the conclusion that all in all, the balance of interest was not in favour of maintaining that Commission decision, and he ordered the suspension of that decision.

I see no reason in law or in fact that would prevent the President of the Court of First Instance from taking exactly the same approach in a merger case; and if anything, historically, the *Kali und Salz* order of the court confirms that the President of the Court is more than willing to suspend a Commission decision when he feels that the Commission decision may be tainted by illegality. I see them out, the *Kali und Salz* decision was quashed by the Court of Justice thereafter.

So we have this aspect of injunctive relief that is there, is available and can be used; whether or not companies or their legal advisers are familiar with this type of procedure is a separate issue, but the rules are there, and anyone can read them and seek to apply them. Then in addition, and I stress this point, if the injunctive relief is not sufficient for a company, they can resort to the accelerated procedure; and these two companies have recently done so, and we hope to show by the end of the year that the system actually works. That doesn't mean that the Court of First Instance couldn't do with more staff and more judges, as all these things obviously need further consideration; and the Commission would be more than happy to support the court in any initiative to strengthen their staff and resources to deliver a better service in the field of not only merger control but many other aspects of European law.

Then, I think I could tackle one of the points raised, which is essentially the separation raised between the legal advice and the economic advice in competition matters; it is true, I think that Bill Kolasky's totally right in saying that we don't have a clear-cut separation of the opinion of the economists and the opinion of the lawyers in the case, because we have joint teams of lawyers and economists. However, we should bear in mind, and that links up to the question on inter-house consultation, that a number of services within the Commission and within DG competition are involved in the decision-making process within the Commission. For example, our decisions and our preparatory acts leading to a final decision are reviewed within DG competition by the sectorial unit, which normally monitors the industry, and also by the directorate in charge of the co-ordination of cases, which is headed by a PhD in microeconomics, you heard him speaking yesterday, Mr Mehta.

So we have some internal checks and balances within DG competition to get the analysis right. In addition to that, and that again connects to the question that you raised, the Director-General in charge of financial affairs has a unit composed of PhD economists that follows very closely the Commission decisions, not only in second-phase cases but also in first-phase cases. They analyse the economic point of view as well, and they report (and this is important) independently to the Commission, they don't report to the Competition Commissioner. They can report, they can give their advice on the economics of the case to the Commission as a whole. And maybe, to clarify your point, I think it should be stressed that they are involved at every step in the procedure; they have access to all the documents that they wish to see in order to phone their view, they attend the hearing, they attend the Advisory Committee, and consequently they're heavily involved. Does that mean that the system couldn't be improved? No, I think that we are currently reflecting on the possibility of maybe emulating other competition authorities, and we are thinking about the possibility of maybe having a separate set of economists, who have more time to reflect on policy issues and at the same time to look into cases more carefully. That is a possibility to which we're not hostile; we don't think that it is going to necessarily change the quality or the motivation of our decisions, because whenever we have considered that there was an additional need for economic analysis, the Commission has either resorted to its own resources within the Commission or to outside economic advice. But having said that, if that is the way to improve the day-to-day working of the machine, that is something that no doubt Commissioner Monti will take into account in reviewing the several possibilities to improve the system.

BILL KOLASKY

I want to say, as Margaret and John did, that I very much commend the European Commission DG comp for its green paper and for opening up this to discussion; this is exactly the way we competition authorities should behave and I think the open-minded way in which the Commission is doing that is very important. The only point I was making, Enrique, with respect to judicial review, was the Rochemon point, that there seems to be a difference of view between you and many of the people who feel that their mergers, who feel that they did not really have an effective and timely judicial review. What I really wanted to do was just address one of the points that Enrique made on the facts as to our practice; it is not true that our courts do not issue decisions on the merits in merger cases in a short period of time.

It is true that the Federal Trade Commission, if they announce that they're challenging a merger and the parties refuse to abandon it, has to go to court to get a preliminary injunction and if that is granted, the deal cannot go forward and then it is subject, theoretically, to an administrative hearing at the FTC, although the parties almost never do that, so the PI hearing really is on the merits for all practical purposes. At the Justice Department, our practice is to consolidate the trial on the preliminary injunction and the permanent injunction, so that we get a final decision on the merits from the court. In one case that we brought last fall, involving a merger of two companies in the computer disaster recovery area, we had a final decision on the merits within three weeks of filing our complaint. That was record time, but it is not at all uncommon to have a final decision on the merits within three months; so the process really does work under our system. Three months is about the average—the longest is six months, on the merits. But I very much respect the point that Walter was making, which is that the system would only work if you have a set of courts that are accustomed to being able to move that quickly.

CLAUS-DIETER EHLERMANN

Right, thank you very much—we now move to the third question, which still is merger control. It is picking up one of the points that were made this morning: should there be an efficiency defence for mergers? Margaret?

MARGARET BLOOM

I can be quite brief on this—the answer is yes, in fact the Enterprise Bill allows for this, but in terms of relevant customer benefits. It's narrowly defined, and it won't be used very often; but it is an efficiency defence, but in terms of an entirely consumer welfare standard.

WALTER STOFFEL

All the Swiss statutory laws allow for it, but we are rarely confronted with a pure efficiency defence case. Generally, the problem that we have is that the merger has international clear benefits if you state it this way, and it causes a problem within the small internal market. This is a way of an efficiency, and this explicitly allows, is a ground that is stated by the course being taken into account by the authority in deciding whether it should let a merger go on.

JOHN FINGLETON

I think the short answer is yes, but there are a lot of qualifications. The first one is that where a merger is to increase its market power, we know from economics that market power removes the largest incentive for cost reduction, and so consequently the Williamson model, which shows a simultaneous increase in market power and a reduction in cost, is a static model that's not based on what I would describe as a reasonable dynamic process. So we have to be very sceptical that cost efficiencies can be realised in cases where we have unilateral market power of the sort of monopoly type. That means, or may mean, that there's a set of cases in between what you would call monopoly mergers and that still restrict competition, where an efficiency defence would be useful. And I think that one of the reasons why we've been proposing this substantial lessening of competition tests at the European level, is that we believe the efficiency tests may be more useful in that interval of cases.

Now of course I think that Enrique would probably argue, and I won't disagree, that it may be possible to do that within the existing dominance test; I think that's one of the things that we're going to spend a lot of time discussing in the next while in Europe. One other qualification is, I think we're going to have to be very careful not to use efficiency as an offence in place of a defence, and that is the case where a merger that makes two firms more efficient will necessarily harm rivals, who may very well say oh, I'm harmed, I may well be eliminated from this market, and a reduction in the number of competitors in the longer term will reduce competition and should be stopped. This is referred to earlier as the 'paramutual'—I haven't heard that, weighing the saddles of the more efficient horse. I think we have to be careful to avoid that; I think perception is the word, rather than actuality, because I think that perception can be created, and that's a question I think of how we reason decisions, and I'm not sure that efficiencies ever are used, certainly in our own jurisdiction we haven't used, efficiencies as an offence in that way. Thank you.

BILL KOLASKY

I have just one quick comment on efficiencies, and I think the debate is really not over whether, but how; I think there is one important point I wanted to make, which is that it really is a misnomer to think in terms of an efficiency defence. As soon as you say that, you're thinking of failing company defences, for example, where you're putting a very heavy burden on the parties because you've already concluded that the merger is going to substantially lessen competition or create a dominant position. What we have done is instead to integrate efficiencies into our competitive merger analysis, so in deciding whether a merger is likely substantially to lessen competition, we take the efficiencies into account basically to rebut the *prima facie* case that otherwise might arise from an increase in market concentration.

The second point is that—well, there are two more points, very quickly. One is that if you do have an efficiency as a 'defence', it is very important that you apply something of a sliding scale; that is, the greater the feared increase in market power, the more evidence the parties have to show of real efficiencies and the larger those efficiencies have to be. Two more—I'm sorry, I'm going to make two more quick points (laughter)—one a response to John, which is, I wouldn't agree that if prices are going to rise in the near term, you won't still get the benefit of the efficiencies, because just as you have dynamic effects of increases in market power, you also have dynamic effects of efficiencies. The final point is merger specificity, which is really the key point—that is, how much of a showing needs to be made for the parties to achieve the same efficiencies or comparable efficiencies but for the merger? There, over time, we've come to apply a likelihood standard; in other words, the burden is simply to show that the efficiencies would not likely be achieved but for the merger, and that brings into play not only the technical feasibility of the efficiencies, of alternative means of achieving the efficiencies, but also the cost of doing so, including the transaction cost associated with it. So that's all a very important part of the analysis.

CLAUS-DIETER EHLERMANN

Thank you, Bill—Enrique?

ENRIQUE GONZALEZ DIAZ

Well, I have very little to add other than that I consider that taking efficiencies into account is part of our mandate under Article 2 of the merger regulation. I agree with Bill Kolasky that indeed there is a question of sliding scales in the sense that the more anti-competitive the merger is, the less room for efficiencies to be taken into account; I also agree that the guiding principles in dealing with efficiencies should be first of all that they should be quantified and identified, that they should be merger-specific, that is to say there shouldn't be a less respectable time in which to achieve the efficiencies, and obviously there the important question is what test.

There is a test of likelihood, strong probability that is obviously something to be discussed; and obviously and very importantly because in Europe we have a consumer welfare test, these efficiencies need to be passed on to the consumers at least in as much as is necessary to compensate for the detrimental effect on competition from the merger. And I think that on the basis of these very general guiding principles, the Commission considers that efficiencies could and should be taken into account in merger cases, but always making the proviso that it is up to the parties to develop these arguments and to substantiate their claims on efficiencies.

RORY CHISHOLM

Rory Chisholm, FIPRA UK. Sorry, I hesitated because it's not the world's most important question, perhaps, but no-one's actually defined, with the exception of Margaret Bloom, who related it to consumers specifically, what efficiencies mean. And it occurs to me that you may all be talking about different types of things.

MARGARET BLOOM

In the interests of trying to be brief, I didn't go into all the details that are set out in the Enterprise Bill—this is actually in the explanatory notes, explaining it—but it talks about benefit. This is a merger where it might—

there's a problem in terms of substantially lessened competition, so the question is, are you then going to allow it? Under exceptional circumstances, it might be allowed if it satisfies a relevant customer benefit. Those benefits have got to be to customers who are actually affected by the merger, and it gives examples in the explanatory notes of efficiencies that produce so-called network benefits (there's a long paragraph on that), one on large economies of scale (there's an explanation of that), and then another example of more innovations through research and development benefits. No doubt there are other examples set out in the merger guidelines in the US, but there's quite a bit—if you want to look on the explanatory notes to the Enterprise Bill, there's quite a lot there for the UK test.

CLAUS-DIETER EHLERMANN

Thank you, Margaret—I find it remarkable that the legislation endeavours to define, because that's one of the most intriguing questions for me.

MARGARET BLOOM

Sorry, I should be clear—they are just explanatory notes.

BILL KOLASKY

I'll answer your question very briefly and then refer you to an article. Our view is that efficiencies should be defined very broadly—there are at least four different broad categories that economists think about. Production efficiencies/cost savings are one, and efficiencies through synergies combining complementary skills, that's all productive efficiencies. Allocative efficiencies are very important, that is, moving prices that are currently above marginal cost closer to marginal cost. Third is dynamic efficiencies, that is innovation, and investment of the type Margaret spoke of; and finally transactions cost savings. If you think about some of our cases under Section 1, under your Article 81 in the vertical area, transactions cost savings of vertical integrations are one of the key reasons we allow firms to integrate vertically, either through internal growth or through merger.

So all four of those are very important types of efficiencies; I don't think you should necessarily require parties to quantify them, it's very hard to quantify allocative or transactional efficiencies, and we generally do not quantify market power effects to the extent they could be quantified—they could be, but you shouldn't expect it in every case. I'm publishing an article in about a month that will include as an appendix a taxonomy of these four types of efficiencies, prepared by one of our smartest young economists, and I commend that to you.

MARGARET BLOOM

Could I just very quickly say, in view of Claus' saying that he was surprised that this was set down in the legislation? Not only is it only in the explanatory notes, but it does say that these examples are illustrative only, so do not assume those are the only ones.

JEREMY LEVER

Can one not worry that the more anti-competitive the merger, the greater the immediate cost savings are likely to be, because of the duplication that exists between competing organisations? In that sense, competition is very inefficient, we've got two longs, three longs going the same way and the more anti-competitive you are.

CLAUS-DIETER EHLERMANN

Thank you—that's very much linked to John's point about the raising of barriers of entry with efficiency, so that efficiency becomes an argument against the merger. Enrique.

ENRIQUE GONZALEZ DIAZ

Very quickly, I think that most of the efficiencies that are claimed in merger cases have been alluded to today; but just one point on quantification or identification of efficiencies. I think this is going to be one of the difficult points of debate in the future with regard to efficiencies. I venture the following idea; I think that insofar as market power and the detrimental effect on prices can be measured, then I think that the notifying parties must also make an effort to measure and to counter the quantification of the market power by the competition authority. On the other hand, when this quantification of market power cannot be done directly but is done qualitatively, then I understand that if the efficiencies or the synergies cannot be quantified precisely, then we have to resort to a more qualitative analysis, which will make the overall analysis of the transaction a little bit more, I think, subjective.

But I think we have to face the fact that some of the efficiencies indeed can be quantified; for example, efficiencies in terms of reductions in marginal costs following the rationalisation of plants and things like that, they can be quantified. Other synergies or efficiencies may be more difficult to quantify, and consequently they will have to wait against the competitive effect; and again, as Bill Kolasky mentioned before, the stronger the likely anti-competitive effect, the weaker weight will be attributed I think to efficiencies.

CLAUS-DIETER EHLERMANN

One area where the US and the EU have traditionally taken different approaches relates to monopoly leveraging; that is, using a dominant position in a market to gain a competitive advantage in a neighbouring market. Are there sound reasons for differences in approach, or should we seek greater convergence in this area? You remember, it was one of the points that Bill Kolasky had in his impressive list of divergences, mainly of the notion of abuses of dominant positions. So where do we start? Why don't we start in the inverse order? Jorgen.

JORGEN HOLGERSSON

Yes—very briefly, I think that my answer is yes, and I can say so because I have had in my office a case where we have handled it in that case. But having said this, I'm quite aware of the problems that it can cause, so my answer is yes.

WALTER STOFFEL

Thank you. Well, we certainly never have applied it otherwise than when the industry was regulated and the monopoly power came about in a field that was regulated, and therefore spread out in non-regulated fields, I think that there the case is clear. Otherwise, the question is really whether there should be differences or not; I think as a principle in this field I would not fear differences. I would see some need of harmonisation in the merger area, but in this field we can also competition on competition theories and competition outcomes, and of course I think it's useful to discuss it, but I don't think there's an immediate need to harmonise them.

And in this sense, in the really excellent talk from Bill this morning, there is one sentence that I really dislike a little bit, and it says 'competition law protects competition and not competitors'. It's not that I think this is wrong, but I think it's very close to an empty formula. Certainly competition law should not protect an inefficient operator, that's obvious, as competition will drive out inefficient operators of business. But competition law may well protect an operator who is willing to compete, and who is hindered to compete because of anti-competitive conduct by other competitors; and this is very much about decentralised enforcement of competition, and so one takes some kind of a modern formula of the invisible hand. So I think the formula is right and wrong at the same time, and this is something that makes it quite close to an empty formula; I have just encountered it recently in the decision *Baustahl*, and I would rather prefer you to strike out this sentence, it's certainly true, but say what you mean.

JOHN FINGLETON

I'm not sure that the differences are always as great as they're made out to be—if you look at the *Kodak* decision in the United States and the *Hugin* case here, we've both decided that leverage into other markets where you have after-markets for spare parts, a similar standard has been applied. Maybe Bill would characterise *Kodak* as a decision that more properly belongs in Europe, I'm not sure, but the divergence is not great always as great and I think you can pick, it's like looking at the Bible for examples of things. You can always pick on cases that are going to maximise the differences, and you can pick on cases that will minimise them. I think there's a much broader political point here, and that is that anti-trust is not as we see it now, particularly in the United States, there to control firms from getting very large in a way that threatens democracy as opposed to raising market power. We could deal with this issue in the context of media mergers and newspaper mergers, and we took the view there that even if one firm had 80 per cent or 90 per cent of a newspaper or a broadcasting market, that although it might do that and be the most efficient operator, there was a wider public interest concerned with size in terms of democracy and it was reasonable to apply a separate standard, not a competition standard, to control that if you like for a democratic purpose.

And so what we have is an asymmetric competition test, whereby we decide (and this is in the context of mergers, but it could apply more generally) whether or not there's an effect on competition, and if we decide that there's no effect on competition, the minister can then apply a public interest test. But if we decide there is an effect on competition, the minister has no role and the public interest test does not arise. Now admittedly it's in the context of mergers, but it does take account of the political reality that there are sometimes concerns that go beyond the narrow anti-trust concerns, and these are best illustrated in the United States with the New York Times coverage of the *Microsoft* case, which I don't think was really a question about how the court should interpret the anti-trust standard, but a much wider debate about you know, if one company is more efficient, say we get into the area of photographic libraries or making modems and so on, at what stage does this conglomerate merger stop? I think that outside of the anti-trust community, this is a huge question, and we shouldn't be too blinkered in at least being aware that it's a big question, because parliaments enact laws, not anti-trust specialists, as I discovered with the process in Ireland.

MARGARET BLOOM

I was going to take a rather similar line to John Fingleton in saying that the differences had perhaps been over-emphasised; in fact, at least one of the cases in Europe, which is *BPB Industries* and *British Gypsum*, which was very similar to the basis that Bill put in his speech, as understood in the US, it would be against the law if you are using your competitive advantage in a neighbouring market in order to maintain your existing monopoly in the market in which you're already a monopolist. *BPB Industries* was exactly on this basis, and this is a situation in which it was partly through I think establishing their reputation that they would be aggressive in seeing off other potential competitors, and also in the associate market, it could enable somebody to get a foothold in getting into the main one.

So I'm not sure the difference is as big, but there is one thought as to why possibly there might be arguments; certainly in the UK we're noticing that with the new Competition Act, we have a surprising number of cases where public bodies who are enjoined to be competitive and enter into wider markets, they're clearly dominant and the question is are they undertaking, but assuming they're undertakings, they're dominant in one market and then they are providing commercial services in another one, maybe it depends how you define the market. None of those cases have got far enough to reach conclusions, but we have a fair number of complaints; that might be a reason for being different, I don't know, we need to come back next year and see.

BILL KOLASKY

I'll be very brief, because I did speak on this subject this morning. I don't want to over-emphasise the degree of difference between the United States and Europe on monopoly leveraging, I honestly don't know how great the difference is, in part because the leading EU cases on this tend to be somewhat old, and I think that this is an area that will benefit from discussion on similarities and dissimilarities between our approaches. I very much liked Walter's point about rivalry among competition regimes, and I thoroughly agree that we ought not to see convergence for its own sake, but that we ought to talk about these issues nevertheless. On John's point, I just can't resist—'competition not competitors being an empty formula' is just too big a topic to get into in the time I have, but it's a provocative statement. On John's point, I think the *Kodak* case is a good illustration of where our law has sometimes strayed into this area, and it's certainly true in the old tying law generally, but *Kodak* is one of those Supreme Court decisions that has been very narrowly construed by our lower courts.

ENRIQUE GONZALEZ DIAZ

I'll be brief—I think, again I agree with some of the comments made before.

I don't see the differences as being so significant; I can see that in some individual cases we may have come to different conclusions in using the foreclosure theories in the merger field. Just to quote a few examples; we agreed with the DOJ in *Allied Signal Honeywell*, we disagreed in *Boeing/Hughes* where we cleared a transaction without conditions and the Fair Trade Commission on a vertical foreclosure case came to the conclusion that there were competition concerns that needed to be addressed by way of undertakings. So we disagreed there; and we also disagreed in *GE/Honeywell*, where we felt that remedies were required and the US came to a different conclusion.

Now the question is: when we go back to the principles and to sources that we're using to evaluate these cases, are we applying different tools, are we relying on different economic literature? I don't think so; I think that we are looking at the same sources, but that as it happens, when we come to applying these sources, which stem from the body of economic thinking that was mentioned this morning by Bill Kolasky but obviously did not stop with the Chicago School but continued with other thinkers in the field of industrial economics with the same manuals and the same papers, and we tried to apply them correctly to the facts of the case, sometimes we disagree on the assessment of the cases, but honestly I don't think there is a gulf between us and the United States in thinking about these problems.

CLAUS-DIETER EHLERMANN

Thank you, Enrique. It has been a great privilege to have the opportunity this afternoon to introduce first Jeremy Lever as usual, and to preside over this most prestigious panel. I would like to thank you all for sacrificing the larger part of a Friday afternoon, and I understand that in London a Friday afternoon is something very peculiar, and we should express our usual way of thanking the panel for a splendid presentation [applause].

I would like to thank you also for your brave endurance, for staying after a day and a half almost for the rest of the day; the organisers have asked me to draw your attention to this additional leaflet. You have had in your pack of documents lots of announcements of future conferences, one more valuable than the other; however, this is an announcement for next year's third annual competition conference, and it might very well be that it is preceded or followed by a similar conference on international trade and WTO matters, that will be seen, as perhaps they will run even in parallel. And then, on the other side of that sheet, you have the annual meeting of the British Institute of International and Comparative Law, which of course takes place this year in June.

Now that I have done that on behalf of the organisers, but on behalf of all of you and myself, I would congratulate Mads Andenas and his colleagues for, well, I had the privilege of attending the conference on Wednesday, for three extraordinary days for you, two very rich and stimulating days of presentations and discussions. I think the fact that this is the second time indicates that there is a series, there is a tradition, and I would like to encourage on behalf of all of you the British Institute to maintain that position and perhaps even enlarge it. But London is, as Bill has said, a wonderful place to do that; we need European counterparts to follow, competition is an intellectually enriching debate as much as selling products and services. And with that I leave this place and give over to the organiser.

MICHAEL HUTCHINGS

Thank you very much, Dr Ehlermann—I'm not going to detain you for very long. I'm very appreciative on behalf of Mads Andenas and the Institute for your very kind words. One further parish notice, just before I conclude; there is a reception afterwards hosted by Monckton Chambers. Can you also leave your badges behind, because FIPRA would like to be able to reuse them, I'm afraid they do cost money. The other parish notice is, we have urged you before and I would sincerely urge you again if you are not already members, please join—it's very cheap, it costs £85 per year but the benefits are enormous, and you will save that in one go by applying for next year's conference.

Just drawing the conference together, it's impossible to summarise the wealth of topics that have been raised and the debate that has been generated; I take three point from the conference, one legal, one cultural and one logistical. The legal point is that in his opening remarks, Mr Mehta referred to the development of a common enforcement culture; well, my comments on that are twofold. As Denis Waelbroeck said, he explained the difficulties of bringing a damages action in a Belgian court; do we have a common enforcement culture? And then we heard someone from the floor saying that the French *Cour de Cassation* had come to a completely different decision on the ability of a party to a contract to sue the other party for damages, compared with the English court decision in *Courage v Crehan*; do we have a common enforcement culture? I think that illustrates the need for continuing conferences of this type, to debate our differences and see where convergence can come from.

My cultural point comes from last night; for those of you who were at the dinner, Giuseppe Tesauro described the difference between bringing complaints, making and bringing cases before the courts, and bringing complaints to national competition authorities. Bringing complaints to national competition authorities he described as bringing love letters—that is something I will remember from this conference, and I will remind John Vickers of that the next time it has to happen.

And the final, logistical point is that Frederic Jenny is the most severe of chairmen, and I think those of us in the audience appreciated his chairmanship and the fact that he started off the conference with very precise chairmanship. I know he trod on a lot of speakers' toes, for which we apologise but we don't apologise very much, because I'm on the side of the people sitting in the audience. But the point I was going to make was that when he started, he told the speakers that they only had time for their conclusions. Simon Holmes said he had ten points—Frederic Jenny said you don't have time for ten points in six minutes. Simon Holmes did his ten points in six minutes, so it proves it can be done, and that's a model for the future.

And finally, thanking our speakers, I do want to make one point. This institute is here partly to contribute to the public policy debate—that's part of its function. It is in a slightly strange position, bridging the gap between the judiciary, the public bodies and the private practising profession, and it goes without saying, the academic profession as well; and it is very much part of the aim of the Institute to be part of the public policy debate. With that in mind we are enormously grateful to those of you who are here, and those who have already departed, particularly Enrique and Bill, and Margaret Bloom who has helped us in developing this conference, and her colleagues. We are really grateful to you for participating—it has proved that there is scope for debate and discussion, and I think, development of new ideas. So we are very appreciative. A conference of this type, though, only succeeds if the audience participate, and we do, finally, hugely appreciate the contribution made by the audience throughout the conference, and we very much hope you will be here next year. Thank you very much. [Applause].